W9-CNP-481

Rick Steves'

SWITZERLAND

Rick Steves'

SWITZERLAND

AVALON
TRAVEL

CONTENTS

Top Destinations in Switzerland

ZÜRICH • APPENZELL

BERN & MURTEN •

LUZERN & CENTRAL SWITZ.

GIMMELWALD & THE BERNER OBERLAND •

LAKE GENEVA & FRENCH SWITZ. •

PONTRESINA, SAMEDAN & ST. MORITZ

❹

❶

ZERMATT & THE MATTERHORN •

❷

❸

LUGANO •

BUS

Scenic Rail Journeys:
❶ Golden Pass
❷ William Tell Express
❸ Bernina Express
❹ Glacier Express

INTRODUCTION

Little, mountainous, efficient Switzerland is one of Europe's most appealing destinations. Wedged neatly between Germany, Austria, France, and Italy, Switzerland melds the best of all worlds—and adds a healthy dose of chocolate, cowbells, and cable cars. Fiercely independent and decidedly high-tech, the Swiss stubbornly hold on to their quaint traditions, too. Join the cheese-makers high atop an alp, try to call the shepherds on an alphorn,

and hike through some of the world's most stunning mountain scenery.

This book breaks Switzerland into its top big-city, small-town, and rural attractions. It gives you all the information and suggestions necessary to wring the maximum value out of your limited time and money. If you plan three weeks or less in Switzerland, this lean and mean little book has all the information you need...unless you're a skier. This is a fair-weather book—it focuses on the highlights of summertime fun (but for basic info for a winter visit, see the Switzerland in Winter chapter).

Experiencing Europe's culture, people, and natural wonders economically and hassle-free has been my goal throughout three decades of traveling, tour guiding, and writing. With this guide-book, I pass on to you the lessons I've learned.

Rick Steves' Switzerland is a tour guide in your pocket. The book includes a balance of cities and villages, mountaintop hikes and lake cruises, thought-provoking museums and sky-high gondola rides. It covers the predictable biggies while mixing in a healthy dose of Back Door intimacy. Along with Luzern, the Matterhorn, and the Glacier Express, you'll experience windswept Roman ruins and ramble through traffic-free alpine towns. I've been selective, including only the top destinations. For example, the country is dotted with alpine villages—but Gimmelwald is a cut above.

The best is, of course, only my opinion. But after spending a third of my adult life exploring and researching Europe, I've developed a sixth sense for what travelers enjoy. Just thinking about the places featured in this book makes me want to yodel.

About This Book

This book is organized by destinations, each one a mini-vacation on its own, filled with exciting sights and homey, affordable places to stay. It's updated regularly, but things change. For the latest, visit www.ricksteves.com/update, and for reports and experiences—good and bad—from fellow travelers, check www.ricksteves.com/feedback.

In the following chapters, you'll find these sections:

Planning Your Time offers ideas on how best to use your limited time.

Orientation includes specifics on public transportation, helpful hints, local tour options, easy-to-read maps, and tourist information (abbreviated **TI** in this book).

Self-Guided Walks take you through interesting neighborhoods, with a personal tour guide in hand.

Sights, described in detail, are rated:

▲▲▲—Don't miss.

▲▲—Try hard to see.

▲—Worthwhile if you can make it.

No rating—Worth knowing about.

Sleeping describes my favorite hotels, from good-value deals to cushy splurges.

Eating serves up a range of options, from inexpensive *Stübli* to fancy restaurants.

Connections outlines your options for reaching nearby destinations by train and bus. I've also included route tips for drivers in car-friendly regions.

Switzerland in Winter provides tips for enjoying the Alps in snow, and describes some uniquely Swiss holiday traditions.

Switzerland: Past and Present gives you a quick overview of Swiss history and its notable citizens.

Map Legend

⅃	Viewpoint	✈	Airport	———	Pedestrian Zone
↑	Entry Point	Ⓣ	Taxi Stand	o++++++o	Funicular
🛈	Tourist Info	Ⓜ	Metro Stop	------	Railway
🆆🅲	Restroom	🅃	Tram Stop	⊢——⊣	Tram Line
🏰	Castle	Ⓑ	Bus Stop	ⅢⅢⅢⅢ	Stairs
🏯	Church	🛥	Boat Stop	------	Trail
🕌	Mosque	🅿	Parking	)⚊⚊(	Tunnel

Use this legend to help you navigate the maps in this book.

INTRODUCTION

The **appendix** is a traveler's tool kit, with telephone tips, useful phone numbers, transportation basics (on trains, buses, boats, car rentals, driving, and flying), recommended books and films, a festival list, climate chart, handy packing checklist, a hotel reservation form, and survival phrases in German, French, and Italian.

Browse through this book and choose your favorite sights. Then have a great trip! Traveling like a temporary local and taking advantage of the information here, you'll enjoy the absolute most of every mile, minute, and franc. As you travel the route I know and love, I'm happy you'll be meeting some of my favorite Swiss people.

Planning

This section will help you get started on planning your trip—with advice on trip costs, when to go, and what you should know before you take off.

Travel Smart

Your trip to Switzerland is like a complex play—easier to follow and really appreciate on a second viewing. While no one does the same trip twice to gain that advantage, reading this book's chapters on your intended destinations before your trip accomplishes much the same thing.

Design an itinerary that enables you to visit sights at the best possible times. Note holidays, festivals, and days when sights are closed. Sundays have the same pros and cons as they do for travelers in the US (special events, limited hours, banks and many shops closed, limited public transportation, no rush hour). Saturdays are virtually weekdays, with earlier closing hours and no rush hour. Popular places are even more popular on weekends—especially sunny weekends. Many sights are closed on Monday (head for the hills).

Budget Tips

Switzerland is pricey, but there are ways to stretch your dollars. For example, you can cut down on restaurant costs by having scenic picnics or seeking out self-service cafeterias (often attached to department or grocery stores), which offer delicious food at a fraction of the cost of dining out.

Many expensive alpine lifts offer discounted "early bird" tickets for the first trip of the day. Train trips get cheaper when you choose the right railpass (see all the deals on page 357); the Swiss Pass is a swinging deal for most travelers.

Save on Sightseeing with the Swiss Pass

The Swiss Pass railpass—offering consecutive-day or flexi-day coverage of Switzerland's trains, boats, and buses, and a 50 percent discount on lifts—also covers admission to more than 400 Swiss museums.

The Swiss Pass doubles as a Swiss Museum Pass (which otherwise costs about 150 SF) to cover the museum admissions, but only during its validity period—for a consecutive-day pass, that means from the day you activate your pass (i.e., use it for the first time) until the last day it's valid for travel. If you have a flexipass, visiting a museum can use up a day of your pass. To get the most out of a flexipass, use it to visit a museum either on the same day you arrive at that destination or on the day you depart. Unlike flexipasses for most other countries, the validity of a Swiss flexipass ends with your last used-up travel day—for

Be sure to mix intense and relaxed periods in your itinerary. To maximize rootedness, minimize one-night stands (and, where possible, opt for three-night stands). It's worth a long drive or a train ride after dinner to be settled into a town for at least two nights. People renting private rooms are also more likely to give a good price to someone staying more than one night. Every trip—and every traveler—needs at least a few slack days (for picnics, laundry, people-watching, and so on). Pace yourself. Assume you will return.

Perhaps more than anywhere else in Europe, weather plays a huge factor in your sightseeing in Switzerland. The mountains are stunning—when it's not raining. But bad weather needn't ruin a trip. Switzerland has plenty of rainy-weather options. And it's so small and has such a slick train network that you can easily double-back later to visit the mountaintop hideaway that was clouded over your first time through.

Be flexible. For maximum spontaneity, consider traveling without room reservations (realizing that this comes with some risk). For example, you might plan on three days split between more information, see "Transportation" in the appendix.

The following sights, which are described in this book, are free with the Swiss Pass (for a full list of museums covered by the Swiss Pass as well as the Swiss Museum Pass, see www.museums pass.ch):

Zürich—Swiss National Museum and Rietberg Museum.

Luzern—Rosengart Collection, Depot History Museum, Bourbaki Panorama, Glacier Garden, Richard Wagner Museum, Museum of Art Luzern, and the Museum of Natural History, plus Fortress Fürigen Museum nearby in Stansstad. (The Swiss Transport Museum is 50 percent off with the pass.)

Bern—Museum of Fine Arts, Paul Klee Center, and Einstein Museum.

Near Murten—Roman Museum in Avenches.

Near Interlaken—Ballenberg Open-Air Folk Museum in Brienz.

Zermatt—Matterhorn Museum.

Appenzell Region—Appenzell Museum and Appenzell's two modern art museums, and folk museums in Stein and Urnäsch.

Lausanne—Collection de l'Art Brut, Olympic Museum, and City History Museum.

Lake Geneva Region—Château de Chillon.

French Swiss Countryside— Gruyères' Castle, H. R. Giger Museum, and Tibet Museum.

the city of Bern and the mountainous Berner Oberland region. If it's raining as you approach the area, head for Bern. If it's sunny, make a beeline for the mountains, then hit Bern on your way out of the area. To help you decide, tune into TV stations and websites that show the weather in various parts of the country. Many high-altitude observation decks have 24-hour cameras that pan slowly back and forth, showing you exactly what you'll see when you get up top (for example, www.swisspanorama.com for the Berner Oberland, www.zermatt.ch for Zermatt).

Reread this book as you travel, and visit local TIs. Upon arrival in a new town, lay the groundwork for a smooth departure; write down (or print out from an online source) the schedule for the train, bus, or boat you'll take when you depart. Drivers can plan (with the help of the TI, if needed) the best route to their next destination.

While traveling, take advantage of the Internet and phones to make your trip run smoothly. By going online at Internet cafés or your hotel and using the phone (buy a phone card or carry a mobile phone), you can get tourist information, learn the latest on sights (special events, tour schedules, etc.), book tickets and tours, make reservations, reconfirm hotels, research transportation connections, and keep in touch with loved ones.

Connect with the culture. Enjoy the hospitality of the Swiss people. Slow down and be open to unexpected experiences. Ask questions—most locals are eager to point you toward their idea of the right direction. Keep a notepad in your pocket for organizing your thoughts. Wear your money belt, and familiarize yourself with the currency. Those who expect to travel smart, do.

Trip Costs

Five components make up your trip cost: airfare, surface transportation, room and board, sightseeing and entertainment, and shopping and miscellany.

Airfare: A basic round-trip US-to-Zürich flight costs $700–1,400, depending on where you fly from and when. If your trip extends beyond Switzerland, consider saving time and money by flying "open jaw" (into one city and out of another; for example, into Zürich and out of Paris).

Surface Transportation: For the two-week whirlwind trip described on page 10, allow $600 per person for public transportation (second-class, 15-consecutive-day Swiss Saverpass, plus high-mountain trains and lifts, and reservation fees for scenic trains) or $500 per person for a car rental (based on two people sharing a two-week rental, including parking fees, gas, and insurance). Car rental is usually cheapest if arranged from the US (see "Renting a Car" on page 363). You can purchase a Swiss railpass before you leave home, or wait until you arrive in Switzerland—most of the passes are sold at Swiss train stations. These passes come in such a wide selection that many travelers save money with a railpass, even for short visits (see "Transportation" on page 355).

Room and Board: You can easily manage in Switzerland on an average of $110 a day per person for room and board. A $110-a-day budget per person allows an average of $15 for lunch, $25 for dinner, $5 for snacks, and $65 for lodging (based on two people splitting the cost of a $130 double room that includes breakfast). That's doable. Students and tightwads eat and sleep on $50 a day ($25 per hostel bed, $25 for groceries).

Sightseeing and Entertainment: In big cities, figure $5–15 per sight, and about $50 for each major alpine lift. Though hiking is free, lifts to some of the best high-altitude trails aren't. An overall average of $25 a day works for most. Don't skimp here. After all, this category is the driving force behind your trip—you came to sightsee, enjoy, and experience Switzerland.

Shopping and Miscellany: Figure $3 per coffee, beer, and ice-cream cone. Shopping can vary in cost from nearly nothing to a small fortune. Good budget travelers find that this category has

Major Holidays and Weekends

Popular places are even busier on weekends, and holidays can bring many businesses to a grinding halt. Plan ahead and reserve your accommodations and transportation well in advance. Mark these dates in red on your travel calendar: Easter (April 4 in 2010, April 24 in 2011), Ascension Day (May 13 in 2010, June 2 in 2011), Whitsunday and Whitmonday (May 23-24 in 2010, June 12-13 in 2011), Corpus Christi (June 3 in 2010, June 23 in 2011), Assumption of Mary (Aug 15), All Saints' Day (Nov 1), Christmas, December 26, and New Year's Day. Also check the list of holidays and festivals on page 371 of the appendix.

little to do with assembling a trip full of lifelong and wonderful memories.

When to Go

The "tourist season" runs roughly from May through September. Summer (July–Aug) has its advantages: the best weather, snow-free alpine trails, very long days (light until after 21:00), and the busiest schedule of tourist fun. In late May, June, September, and early October, travelers enjoy fewer crowds, milder weather, and the ability to grab a room almost whenever and wherever they like.

During the *Zwischenzeit* ("between time"—that is, between summer and ski seasons, roughly April, early May, late Oct, and Nov), the cities are pleasantly uncrowded, but the weather can be iffy, and resort towns such as Zermatt and Mürren are completely dead (with most hotels and restaurants closed).

During ski season (Dec–March), mountain resorts are crowded and expensive, while cities are quieter (some accommodations and sights are either closed or run on a limited schedule). The weather can be cold and dreary, and nighttime will draw the shades on your sightseeing before dinner. But Christmastime traditions (such as colorful markets and special Christmas foods) can warm up your trip at a chilly time of year.

Pack warm clothing for the Alps, no matter when you go—the weather can change suddenly.

Know Before You Go

Your trip is more likely to go smoothly if you plan ahead. Check this list of things to arrange while you're still at home.

You need a **passport**—but no visa or shots—to travel in Switzerland. You may be denied entry into certain European countries if your passport is due to expire within three to six months of your ticketed date of return. Get it renewed if you'll be cutting it

Switzerland at a Glance

▲▲**Zürich** Bustling cosmopolitan city—Switzerland's largest by far—with upscale shops and a charming riverside old-town quarter full of pointy church spires and pealing bells.

▲▲**Luzern** Touristy yet worthwhile town of historic wooden bridges, picturesque streets, and vintage steamships that ply lovely Alp-ringed Lake Luzern.

▲▲▲**Bern** Cozy capital of Switzerland tucked in a sharp river bend, with arcaded shopping promenades, medieval clock towers, and museums devoted to Albert Einstein and artist Paul Klee.

▲**Murten** Quaint, small walled town sitting right on the German/French linguistic fault line, with nearby Roman ruins and museum in Avenches.

▲▲▲**Gimmelwald and the Berner Oberland** Rustic village spectacularly perched on a cliff in this mountainous region—popular for its alpine towns and scenic hikes, lifts, and train rides—with touristy Interlaken as the gateway.

▲**Zermatt** Glitzy ski resort still sporting some traditional old-fashioned touches, in a valley at the foot of the famous Matterhorn.

▲▲**Appenzell** The most traditional Swiss region, known for pastoral scenery, small towns, cows, folk museums, and, just a cable-car ride away, the rustic retreat at the cliffs of Ebenalp.

▲▲**Lake Geneva and French Switzerland** Small-but-sophisticated lakeside city of Lausanne (with excellent l'Art Brut and Olympic museums), Switzerland's best castle experience at Château de Chillon, the cute cheesemaking center of Gruyères, and pleasant scenery of the surrounding countryside.

▲**Lugano** Leading city of Italian-speaking Switzerland, with a tidy if dull urban core, scenic boat trips on Lake Lugano, and mountain lifts to lakeside peaks.

▲**Pontresina, Samedan, and St. Moritz** Romansh-speaking mountain resort region, anchored by three towns: touristy Pontresina, humble Samedan, and swanky St. Moritz.

▲▲**Scenic Rail Journeys** Four famous train rides, each offering panoramic views and crisscrossing the country.

close. It can take up to six weeks to get or renew a passport (for more on passports, see www.travel.state.gov). Pack a photocopy of your passport in your luggage in case the original is lost or stolen.

Book your rooms in advance if you'll be traveling during peak season (July and August) and any major **holidays** and festivals (see sidebar on page 371).

Call your **debit- and credit-card companies** to let them know the countries you'll be visiting so that they won't deny your international charges. Confirm your daily withdrawal limit; consider asking to have it raised so you can take out more cash at each ATM stop. Ask about international transaction fees.

If you're interested in **travel insurance,** do your homework before you buy. Compare the cost of the insurance to the likelihood of your using it and your potential loss if something goes wrong. For details on the many kinds of travel insurance, see www.rick steves.com/plan/tips/insurance.htm.

To **rent a car** in Switzerland, you'll need to bring along your US driver's license.

If you'll be traveling by train, consider getting a **railpass** (a particularly good idea in Switzerland) and research your options (see page 357 and www.ricksteves.com/rail for all the specifics).

To take one of the popular **scenic trains** during high season (July–Aug), you may want to reserve ahead. See page 299 for details and advice.

Because **airline carry-on restrictions** are always changing, visit the Transportation Security Administration's website (www .tsa.gov/travelers) for an up-to-date list of what you can bring on the plane with you, and what you have to check. Remember to arrive with plenty of time to get through security.

Sightseeing Priorities

Depending on the length of your trip, here are my recommended priorities. Assuming you're traveling by train, I've taken geographical proximity and transportation connections into account.

3 days:	Berner Oberland
5 days, add:	Luzern
7 days, add:	Bern and Lausanne, connecting with Golden Pass scenic rail journey
10 days, add:	Zermatt and Appenzell, linking with Glacier Express train
14 days, add:	Lugano and Pontresina area, connecting with Bernina Express and William Tell Express train rides
16 days, add:	Zürich and Murten
21 days, add:	More day trips (central Switzerland, French Swiss countryside), more hikes, and time to slow down

Switzerland's Best
Two-Week Trip by Train

Day	Plan	Sleep in
1	Arrive Zürich Airport, head to Appenzell	Appenzell or Ebenalp
2	All day for Appenzell and Ebenalp	Appenzell or Ebenalp
3	Leave early for Luzern	Luzern
4	Luzern	Luzern
5	William Tell Express to Lugano	Lugano
6	Bernina Express to Pontresina area	Pontresina
7	Pontresina area (St. Moritz, Samedan, lifts and hikes)	Pontresina
8	Take Glacier Express; if good weather, head for Zermatt; if bad weather, consider going straight to Lausanne (see below)	Zermatt
9	Zermatt, Matterhorn-view lifts	Zermatt and hikes
10	If good weather, spend more time in Zermatt, go late to Lausanne; if bad weather, leave early for Lausanne	Lausanne
11	Take the Golden Pass to the Berner Oberland. If good weather, go early; if bad weather, linger in Lausanne/Lake Geneva area and leave late	Berner Oberland (Gimmelwald or Mürren)
12	All day for lifts and hikes in the Berner Oberland	Gimmelwald or Mürren
13	More time in the Berner Oberland	Gimmelwald or Mürren
14	Early to Bern, then on to Zürich	Zürich
15	More time in Zürich, or fly home	

Notes

Zermatt isn't worth the trip in bad weather. If your reservations are flexible, consider skipping that leg and going straight to Lausanne (take the Glacier Express only to Visp, then change for Lausanne). If you have extra time in Switzerland, I'd suggest spending it in (listed in order of priority): Murten and Bern, Zürich, Lausanne and the Lake Geneva area, Lugano (relaxing) or the Luzern area (day trips). For a short trip of a week or so, I'd just focus on the Berner Oberland, Luzern, and Bern. (If you're trying to decide between focusing on the Berner Oberland or the more famous Zermatt/Matterhorn region, see the sidebar on page 191.)

Railpass: The best railpass for this itinerary is a Swiss Pass, specifically the 15-consecutive-day Swiss Saverpass ($365 second class, $550 first class, prices are per person for 2 or more traveling together, solo travelers 26 or older pay about 15 percent more, confirm latest prices at www.ricksteves.com/rail; figure an additional $120 total in reservation fees for all the scenic rail journeys). This pass doesn't cover mountain lifts, but it does earn you a 50 percent discount on most of them.

By Car: Although this itinerary is designed for public transportation, it can be done by car with a few modifications. Obviously, you won't take the scenic rail trips. Instead, drive from Appenzell straight to the Pontresina area, then continue through Tirano and on to Lugano (via Lake Como in Italy). From Lugano, drive to Zermatt (crossing again through Italy) and resume the above itinerary, visiting Luzern at the very end before returning to Zürich. The French Swiss countryside and the area around Murten merit more time if you have a car.

Beyond Switzerland: Switzerland, right in the middle of Western Europe, splices neatly into a multicountry trip by car or train. For instance, the Appenzell region is a likely gateway to Germany's Bavaria or Austria's Tirol. Italy's Lake Como is a stone's throw from Lugano or Ticino (in fact, the Bernina Express bus drives right alongside it)—and Milan is not much farther. If you're in Lausanne, you're literally looking at France (across Lake Geneva)—a handy train ride whisks you to Lyon or Chamonix. And big Swiss cities are efficiently connected by night trains and fast day trains to destinations in all of these countries and beyond.

Where Do I Find Information On...?

Credit-Card Theft	See page 15.
Packing Light	See the packing list on page 375.
Phoning	See "Telephones" on page 349.
Language	See page 348.
Making Hotel Reservations	See page 24.
Tipping	See page 16.
Tourist Information Offices	See page 347.
Updates to This Book	See www.ricksteves.com /update.

The map on page 11 and the two-week itinerary on the previous two pages include everything listed here (except Murten), plus modifications for a longer or shorter trip.

Practicalities

Emergency Telephone Numbers: In Switzerland, dial 112 for medical or other emergencies. For police, dial 117.

Borders: While Switzerland isn't in the European Union, it recently joined the Schengen Zone, which means border controls are now a wave-through. Even so, remember that when you change countries, you must also change phone cards, stamps, and *Unterhosen*.

Time: In Switzerland—and in this book—you'll use the 24-hour clock. It's the same through 12:00 noon, then keep going—13:00, 14:00, and so on. For anything after 12, subtract 12 and add p.m. (14:00 is 2:00 p.m.)

Switzerland is generally six/nine hours ahead of the East/West Coasts of the US. The exceptions are the beginning and end of Daylight Saving Time: Europe "springs forward" the last Sunday in March (two weeks after most of North America) and "falls back" the last Sunday in October (one week before North America). For a handy online time converter, try www.timeanddate.com/worldclock.

Business Hours: Swiss shops are generally open Monday through Friday 9:00–18:30, Saturday 8:00–16:00, and closed Sunday. They are often open later on Thursdays; smaller shops often close at lunchtime.

Medical Help: If you get sick, do as the locals do and go to a pharmacist. They can help you with almost any ailment. If you need in-depth attention, ask your hotelier for the nearest hospital.

Watt's Up? Europe's electrical system is different from North

America's in two ways: the shape of the plug (two round prongs) and the voltage of the current (220 volts instead of 110 volts). For your North American plug to work in Europe, you'll need an adapter, sold inexpensively at travel stores in the US. As for the voltage, most newer electronics or travel appliances (such as hair dryers, laptops, and battery chargers) automatically convert the voltage—if you see a range of voltages printed on the item or its plug (such as "110–220"), it'll work in Europe. Otherwise, you can buy a converter separately in the US (about $20).

Discounts: Although discounts are generally not listed in this book, youths (under 18) and students (with International Student Identity Cards) often get discounts—but only by asking. To get a teacher or student ID card, visit www.statravel.com or www.isic.org.

News: Americans keep in touch in Europe with the *International Herald Tribune,* published almost daily throughout Europe and online at www.iht.com. Other newsy websites include http://news.bbc.co.uk and www.europeantimes.com. Every Tuesday, the European editions of *Time* and *Newsweek* hit the stands with articles of particular interest to travelers in Europe. Sports addicts can get their fix from *USA Today.* Many hotels have CNN or BBC television channels.

Money

This section offers advice on getting cash, using credit and debit cards, dealing with lost or stolen cards, and tipping.

Cash from ATMs

Throughout Europe, cash machines (ATMs) are the standard way for travelers to get local currency. Bring plastic—credit and debit cards. It's smart to bring two cards, in case one gets demagnetized or eaten by a temperamental machine. As an emergency backup, bring several hundred dollars in hard cash (in $20 bills rather than hard-to-exchange $100 bills). Don't use traveler's checks—they're a waste of time (long waits at slow banks) and a waste of money (in fees).

You'll find ATMs all over Switzerland, always open and providing quick transactions. To withdraw money, you'll need a debit card—ideally with a Visa or MasterCard logo for maximum usability—plus a PIN (Personal Identification Number). Know your PIN code in numbers; there are only numbers—no letters—on European keypads.

Before you go, confirm with your bank that your card will work overseas, and alert them that you'll be making withdrawals in Europe; otherwise, the bank may not approve transactions if it perceives unusual spending patterns. (Your credit-card company

Exchange Rates

I've priced things throughout this book in the local currency. Switzerland, which isn't a member of the European Union, has retained its traditional currency, the Swiss franc. The international abbreviation for the Swiss franc is "CHF," but in Switzerland you might also see it abbreviated "SF" or "SFr." For simplicity, I use "SF" in this book.

1 Swiss franc (SF) = about $1.

One Swiss franc is broken down into 100 rappen (or "centimes," in French Switzerland). There are coins for one, two, and five francs, plus several coins for very small denominations of rappen. The small coin with real value is the 50-rappen (marked with "1/2" rather than "50"). It looks like a tiny dime, but is equivalent to a half-dollar. In a handful of change, it's easy to identify as the only one with ridges.

---

may do the same thing—let them know about your travel plans, too.) Also ask about international transaction fees; see "Credit and Debit Cards," on the next page, for more.

The German word for "cash machine" is *Bankomat* or *Geldautomat;* the French name is *distributeur automatique.* If the machine refuses your request, try again and select a smaller amount (some cash machines limit the amount you can withdraw—don't take it personally). If that doesn't work, try a different machine. Note that many cash machines don't issue receipts for your transactions.

Bank machines often dispense high-denomination bills, which can be difficult to break (especially at odd hours). My strategy: Request an odd amount of money from the ATM (such as 280 SF instead of 300 SF); or, if that doesn't work, go as soon as possible to a bank or a large store (such as a supermarket) to break the big bills.

In case you need a bank in Switzerland, they're generally open Monday through Friday from 8:00 to 17:00. Post offices (business hours) and train stations (long hours) usually change money as well.

To keep your cash safe, use a money belt—a pouch with a strap that you buckle around your waist like a belt and wear under your clothes. Thieves target tourists, even in safe Switzerland. A money belt provides peace of mind, allowing you to carry lots of cash safely. Don't waste time every few days tracking down a cash machine—withdraw a week's worth of money, stuff it in your money belt, and travel!

Credit and Debit Cards

For purchases, Visa and MasterCard are more commonly accepted than American Express. Just like at home, credit or debit cards work easily at larger hotels, restaurants, and shops, but smaller businesses prefer payment in local currency (in small bills—break big bills at a larger store or a bank). If receipts show your credit-card number, don't toss these thoughtlessly.

Fees: Whether used for purchases or ATM withdrawals, credit- and debit-card transactions often charge additional, tacked-on "international transaction" fees of up to 3 percent plus $5 per transaction. Note that if you use a credit card for ATM transactions, it's technically a "cash advance" rather than a "withdrawal"—and subject to an additional cash-advance fee.

To avoid unpleasant surprises, call your bank or credit-card company before your trip to ask about these fees. Ask your bank if it has agreements with any Swiss banks for lower withdrawal fees. If the fees are too high, consider getting a card just for your trip: Capital One (www.capitalone.com) and most credit unions have low-to-no international transaction fees.

If merchants offer to convert your purchase price into dollars (called dynamic currency conversion, or "DCC"), refuse this "service." You'll pay even more in fees for the expensive convenience of seeing your charge in dollars.

Dealing with "Chip and PIN": Some parts of Europe (including Switzerland, but more noticeably in France, Great Britain, Ireland, Scandinavia, and the Netherlands) are adopting a "chip and PIN" system for their credit and debit cards. These "smartcards" come with an embedded microchip, and cardholders enter a PIN code instead of signing a receipt. In most cases, you can still use your credit or debit card at the cashier and sign the receipt the old-fashioned way. A few merchants might insist on the PIN code, making it helpful for you to know the PIN code for your credit card (ask your credit-card company); in a pinch, use cash or your debit card and PIN code instead.

US credit or debit cards don't work at many automated machines (such as ticket machines in a train station, or a pay-at-the-pump gas station). But in most of these situations, there's usually a cashier nearby who can take your card and make it work.

Damage Control for Lost Cards

If you lose your credit, debit, or ATM card, you can stop people from using it by reporting the loss immediately to the respective global customer-assistance centers. Call these 24-hour US numbers collect: Visa (410/581-9994), MasterCard (636/722-7111), and American Express (623/492-8427).

At a minimum, you'll need to know the name of the financial

Why No Swiss Euros?

You can't help but wonder why the efficient Swiss are stubbornly hanging on to their old franc while surrounded by countries basking in the ease and convenience of the euro. The answer is simple: It's too expensive for the Swiss to change. The Swiss enjoy lower mortgage interest rates and a more stable currency than the rest of Europe. But even more importantly, a huge part of the Swiss economy is based on providing a safe and secret place for wealthy people from around the world to stash their money. When bank fees are figured in, people who "save" in Swiss banks actually earn negative interest—they *pay* the Swiss to keep their money. Compliance with European Union regulations in order to join the euro zone would mean the end of Switzerland's secret banking industry. The Swiss are not inclined to deal such a devastating blow to their economy.

But even though Switzerland hasn't officially adopted the euro, the majority of Swiss hotels, restaurants, and shops (especially in touristy areas) accept smaller euro bills. Most businesses will not take euro coins or larger bills, and you'll usually get bad rates (and your change in Swiss francs). Many coin-operated phone booths even accept euros (marked with a big yellow €). But unless this is your last chance to use up leftover euros, spend francs in Switzerland instead—you'll save money, and they're prettier.

institution that issued you the card, along with the type of card (classic, platinum, or whatever). Providing the following information will allow for a quicker cancellation of your missing card: full card number, whether you are the primary or secondary cardholder, the cardholder's name exactly as printed on the card, billing address, home phone number, circumstances of the loss or theft, and identification verification (your birth date, your mother's maiden name, or your Social Security number—memorize this, don't carry a copy). If you are the secondary cardholder, you'll also need to provide the primary cardholder's identification-verification details. You can generally receive a temporary card within two or three business days in Europe.

If you promptly report your card lost or stolen, you typically won't be responsible for any unauthorized transactions on your account, although many banks charge a liability fee of $50.

Tipping

Tipping in Europe isn't as automatic and generous as it is in the US—but for special service, tips are appreciated, if not expected. As in the US, the proper amount depends on your resources, tipping philosophy, and the circumstance, but some general guidelines apply.

Restaurants: Tipping is an issue only at restaurants that have table service. If you order your food at a counter, don't tip.

At restaurants that have a waitstaff, service is included, although it's common to round up the bill after a good meal (usually 5–10 percent; so for an 18.50-SF meal, pay 20 SF). Give the tip directly to your server. Rather than leaving coins on the table, the Swiss usually pay with paper, saying how much they'd like the bill to be (for example, for an 8.10-SF meal, give a 20-SF bill and say *"Neun Franken"*—"Nine francs"—to get 11 SF change).

Taxis: To tip the cabbie, round up. For a typical ride, round up to the next franc or two on the fare (to pay a 13-SF fare, give 15 SF); for a long ride, round up to the nearest 10 (for a 75-SF fare, give 80 SF). If the cabbie hauls your bags and zips you to the airport to help you catch your flight, you might want to toss in a little more, but not more than 10 SF. If you feel like you're being driven in circles or otherwise ripped off, skip the tip.

Special Services: At hotels, porters expect a franc for each bag they carry (another reason to pack light). Leaving the maid a franc or two per overnight at the end of your stay is a nice touch. In general, if someone in the service industry does a super job for you, a small tip (1–2 SF) is appropriate...but not required.

When in doubt, ask. If you're not sure whether (or how much) to tip for a service, ask your hotelier or the TI; they'll fill you in on how it's done on their turf.

VAT Refunds for Shoppers

Wrapped into the purchase price of your Swiss souvenirs is a Value-Added Tax (VAT) of 7.6 percent (one of the lowest in Europe). If you make a purchase of more than 300 SF at a store that participates in the VAT-refund scheme, you're entitled to get most of that tax back.

Getting your refund is usually straightforward and, if you buy a substantial amount of souvenirs, well worth the hassle. If you're lucky, the merchant will subtract the tax when you make your purchase. (This is more likely to occur if the store ships the goods to your home.) Otherwise, you'll need to:

Get the paperwork. Have the merchant completely fill out the necessary refund document, called a "cheque." You might be asked for your passport at the store.

Get your stamp at the border or airport. Process your cheque(s) at your last stop in Switzerland by the customs agent who deals with VAT refunds. It's best to keep your purchases in your carry-on for viewing, but if they're too large or dangerous to carry on (such as knives), track down the proper customs agent to inspect them before you check your bag. You're not supposed to use your purchased goods before you leave. If you show up at customs wearing your new Swiss watch, officials might look the other way—or deny you a refund.

Collect your refund. You'll need to return your stamped document to the retailer or its representative. Many merchants work with a service that has offices at major airports, ports, and border crossings, such as Global Refund (www.globalrefund.com) or Premier Tax Free (www.premiertaxfree.com). These services, which extract a 4 percent fee, can usually refund your money immediately in your currency of choice, or on credit your card (within two billing cycles). If the retailer handles VAT refunds directly, it's up to you to contact the merchant for your refund. You can mail the documents from home or, quicker, from your point of departure (using a stamped, self-addressed envelope or one that's been provided by the merchant). You'll then have to wait—it could take months.

Customs for American Shoppers

You are allowed to take home $800 worth of items per person duty-free, once every 30 days. The next $1,000 is taxed at a flat 3 percent. After that, you pay the individual item's duty rate. You can also bring home duty-free a liter of alcohol (slightly more than a standard-size bottle of wine; you must be at least 21), 200 cigarettes, and up to 100 non-Cuban cigars. You may take home vacuum-packed cheeses; dried herbs, spices, or mushrooms; and canned fruits or vegetables, including jams and vegetable spreads. Baked goods, candy, chocolate, oil, vinegar, mustard, and honey are OK. Fresh fruits or vegetables are not. Meats, even if canned, are generally not allowed. Remember that you'll need to carefully pack any bottles of wine and other liquid-containing items in your checked luggage, due to the three-ounce limit on liquids in carry-on baggage. To check customs rules and duty rates before you go, visit www.cbp.gov, and click on "Travel," then "Know Before You Go."

Sightseeing

Sightseeing can be hard work. If you're spending time in urban Switzerland, use these tips to make your museum visits meaningful, fun, efficient, and painless.

Plan Ahead

Set up an itinerary that allows you to fit in all your must-see sights. If you have your heart set on particular sights, it's always smart to confirm the latest hours by checking their websites or asking at the local TI.

Don't put off visiting a must-see sight—you never know when a place will close unexpectedly for a holiday, strike, or restoration. If you'll be visiting during a holiday, find out whether a particular sight will be open by phoning ahead or visiting its website. Keep in mind, too, that opening times can change without warning.

When possible, visit key sights first thing (when your energy is best) and save other activities for the afternoon. Hit the highlights first, then go back to other things if you have the stamina and time.

Study up. To get the most out of the self-guided walks and sight descriptions in this book, read them before your visit.

At Sights

Here's what you can typically expect:

At churches—which often offer interesting art (usually free) and a welcome seat—a modest dress code (no bare shoulders or shorts) is encouraged.

Major museums and sights may require you to check daypacks and coats, usually for free (though many museum lockers require a 2-SF coin deposit—take your coin from the back of the locker door before leaving). The checkrooms are generally safe, but if you have something you can't bear to part with, stash it in a pocket or purse. To avoid checking a small backpack, carry it under your arm like a purse as you enter. From a guard's point of view, a backpack is generally a problem, whereas a purse is not.

Photography is sometimes banned at major sights. Look for signs or ask. If cameras are allowed, flashes or tripods usually are not. Flashes damage oil paintings and distract others in the room. Even without a flash, a handheld camera will take a decent picture (or buy postcards or posters at the museum bookstore). If photos are permitted, video cameras usually are, too.

Many sights rent audioguides, which generally offer excellent recorded descriptions in English. If you bring along your own pair of headphones and a Y-jack, you can can sometimes share one audioguide with a companion and save money.

Expect changes—pieces can be on tour, on loan, out sick, or shifted at the whim of the curator. To adapt, pick up any available free floor plans as you enter, and ask museum staff if you can't find a particular item.

Major sights often have an on-site café or cafeteria (usually a good place to rest and have a snack or light meal). The WCs at many sights are free and clean. Many places sell postcards that highlight their attractions. Before you leave, scan the postcards and thumb through the biggest guidebook (or skim its index) to be sure you haven't overlooked something that you'd like to see.

Most sights stop admitting people 30–60 minutes before

closing time, and some rooms may close early (often 45 minutes before the official closing time). Guards usher people out, so don't save the best for last.

Every sight offers more than what is covered in this book. Use the information in this book as an introduction—not the final word.

Sleeping

I favor accommodations (and restaurants) handy to your sightseeing activities. Hotels are expensive in Switzerland, so I've scoured the options and presented you with the best values, from $25 bunk beds to fancy-for-my-book $250 doubles.

Accommodations in Switzerland are normally comfortable and come with a cold buffet breakfast. Plan on spending $100–150 for a double room in a hotel or $60–100 for a double (with the bathroom down the hall) in a small guest house or a private home.

A triple is much cheaper than a double and a single. While hotel singles are expensive, rooms in private homes *(Privatzimmer)* often have a flat per-person rate. Hostels and dorms always charge per person. Especially in private homes, where the boss changes the sheets, people staying several nights are most desirable. One-night stays are sometimes charged extra.

I look for places that are friendly; clean; a good value; small; family-run; located in a central, safe, quiet neighborhood; English-speaking; and not mentioned in other guidebooks. I'm more impressed by a handy location and a fun-loving philosophy than by hair dryers and shoeshine machines.

I also like local character and simple facilities that don't cater to American "needs." Obviously, a place meeting every criterion is rare, and all of my recommendations fall short of perfection— sometimes miserably. But I've listed the best values for each price category, given the above criteria. I've also thrown in a few hostels, private rooms, and other cheap options for budget travelers. The very best values are family-run places with showers down the hall and no elevator.

During these times of economic uncertainty, many hotels will likely be discounting deeply to snare what customers they can. Try to avoid paying "rack rates" (the highest rates a hotel charges). I'd recommend emailing several places and asking for their best prices; you'll find that some are eager to discount. This can save you big bucks, with prices potentially far below those listed in this guidebook.

When the economy bounces back, you'll find prices more firm, though they can soften off-season, for stays of two nights or longer, or for payment in cash (rather than by credit card).

INTRODUCTION

Sleep Code

To help you sort easily through the listings, I've divided the rooms into three categories based on the price for a standard double room with bath:

$$$ Higher Priced
$$ Moderately Priced
$ Lower Priced

To give you maximum information in a minimum of space, I use the following code to describe the accommodations. Prices listed are per room, not per person. Unless otherwise noted, English is spoken and cold breakfast is included. You can assume a hotel takes credit cards unless you see "cash only" in the listing (private accommodations rarely take plastic).

When a price range is given for a type of room, that means the prices fluctuate with the season, room size, or length of stay.

S = Single room.
D = Double or twin. Double beds are usually big enough for non-romantic couples.
T = Triple (often a double bed with a single bed moved in).
Q = Quad (usually two double beds).
b = Private bathroom with toilet and shower or tub.
s = Private shower or tub only (the toilet is down the hall).

According to this code, a couple staying at a "Db-150 SF" hotel would pay a total of 150 Swiss francs (about $150) for a double room with a private bathroom and an included breakfast.

If I mention "Internet access" in a hotel listing, there's a public terminal in the lobby for guests to use. If I specify "Wi-Fi," you can generally access it in your room (usually for free), but only if you have your own laptop.

Always mention when you reserve a room that you found the place through this book; some of the hotels listed offer special deals to my readers (while many places ask you to show this book in person to get a discount, don't wait till you get there to request the Rick Steves price—do so while making your reservation). Before accepting, confirm your understanding of the complete price.

Smoking is prohibited in many Swiss hotels, some by law (depending on the region) and some by choice. If it's important to you to have a non-smoking room, ask for one.

Any room without a bathroom has access to one in the

corridor. Most hotel rooms have a sink. For environmental reasons, towels are often replaced in hotels only when you leave them on the floor. In cheaper places, they aren't replaced at all, so hang them up to dry and reuse.

Pay your bill the evening before you leave to avoid the time-wasting crowd at the reception desk in the morning, especially if you need to rush off to catch your train. And, as always, I appreciate feedback on your experiences.

Pensions

Compared to hotels, pensions (small guest houses) and rooms in private homes give you double the cultural intimacy for half the price. While you may lose some of the conveniences of a hotel—such as lounges, in-room phones, daily bed-sheet changes, and credit-card payments—I happily make the trade-off for the lower rates and personal touches.

Small guest houses go by several inexact German names: *Pension, Gasthaus, Gästezimmer,* even "B&B" (in French, it's also *pension*). In many parts of Switzerland, people rent out rooms *(Zimmer)* in their homes to travelers. Look for *Zimmer Frei, Zimmer mit Frühstück,* or *Privatzimmer* signs in German-speaking areas and *chambres d'hôte* in French Switzerland. Booking direct saves both you and your host the cut the TI takes.

You'll get your own key to a private room that's clean, comfortable, and simple, though usually homey. Some pensions are like mini-hotels, with a separate entrance and several rooms, each with a private bath. Others are family homes with spare bedrooms (the rooms sometimes lack sinks, but you have free access to the bathroom and shower in the home). Most include a hearty continental breakfast.

Don't confuse *Privatzimmer* with the *Ferienwohnung,* which is a self-catering apartment rented out by the week or fortnight.

Hosteling

If you're traveling alone, hosteling is the best way to conquer hotel loneliness. Hostels are also a tremendous source of local and budget travel information.

Switzerland has a wonderful network of youth hostels (*Jugendherberge* in German, *auberge de jeunesse* in French), all either independently operated, or belonging to the Hostelling International (HI) network.

All Swiss hostels are open to members of all ages. Hostel bunks usually cost $25–35 per night (plus $3–4 sheet rental if you don't have your own). While many hostels have a few doubles or family rooms available upon request for a little extra money, plan on gender-segregated dorms with 4 to 20 beds per room. Many hostels serve good, cheap meals and/or provide kitchen facilities.

If you plan to stay mainly in hostels, bring your own sheet (or pay extra at each place to rent one). Though hostel clerks might tell you over the phone that they're fully booked, most hold a few beds for people who drop in, or they can direct you to budget accommodations nearby.

Established, "official" HI hostels are marked with either a triangular logo or a logo showing a tree next to a house. They tend to have a family atmosphere and attract student groups. These hostels require membership ($28 per year, sold at hostels in most US cities or online at www.hihostels.com, US tel. 202/783-6161). Those without cards simply buy one-night guest memberships for 6 SF.

Choose your hostel selectively. Hostels can be cozy mountain chalets, serene lakeside villas—or antiseptic spaces overrun by noisy school groups (most common on summer weekends and school-year weekdays). Though HI hostels are clean and predictable, they can also have an institutional feel. The independent hostels, sometimes called "backpackers," tend to be smaller than HI hostels, with fewer regulations, no school groups, and no membership fees. I prefer these informal private hostels, which are usually more fun and more intimate-feeling than the HI variety—perfect for getting to know fellow travelers and hostel owners. Some of the hostels are even geared for special-interest guests, such as bicyclists or families traveling together. For a list of some independent hostels, see www.swissbackpackers.ch.

Camping and Other Budget Beds

Campers can manage with *Let's Go* listings (see "Other Guidebooks" on page 367) and help from the local TI (ask for a regional camping listing). Your hometown travel bookstore should also have guidebooks on camping in Europe. You'll find campgrounds just about everywhere you need them. Look for *Campingplatz* signs. You'll meet lots of Europeans—camping is a popular, middle-class-family way to go. Campgrounds are cheap ($10 per person), friendly, safe, more central and convenient than rustic, and rarely full.

A fluffy straw bed awaits you at a number of farms that have opened their haylofts to sleepy tourists. It's a fun hostel alternative and more comfortable than you'd think (see www.abenteuer-stroh .ch/en for details).

Many hotels, restaurants, and campsites provide dormitory-style accommodations. Look for the word *lager,* which indicates cheap dorm beds—often a loft lined with mattresses. These slumber mills may be less charming than cozy hostels, but they're cheap and convenient.

For serious hikers and climbers, mountain huts are an essential alpine experience. Don't expect ski-lodge comfort: These practical, adventurous places are simple, offering a warm place to sleep and (usually) breakfast and dinner. Most mountain-hut guests are long-distance hikers, connecting one hut to another along an extended hiking trail. You'll pay about $30 a night for your bunk, and a little more for grub (see www.sac-cas.ch for more information).

Making Reservations

Given the quality of the places I've found for this book, I'd recommend calling for rooms in advance (especially for mountain resorts during summer weekends). Book several weeks ahead, or as soon as you've pinned down your travel dates. Note that some holidays jam things up and merit your making reservations far in advance (see "Major Holidays and Weekends" sidebar on page 7). Just like at home, holidays that fall on a Monday, Thursday, or Friday can turn the weekend into a long holiday, so book the entire weekend well in advance.

Requesting a Reservation: To make a reservation further in advance, contact hotels directly by email, phone, or fax. Email is the clearest and most economical way to make a reservation. Or you can go straight to the hotel website; many have secure online reservation forms and can instantly inform you of availability and any special deals. But be sure you use the hotel's official site and not a booking agency's site for my recommended hotels—otherwise you may pay higher rates than you should. If phoning from the US, be mindful of time zones (see page 12). Most recommended hoteliers are accustomed to guests who speak only English.

The hotelier wants to know these key pieces of information (also included in the sample request form on page 376):

- number and type of rooms
- number of nights
- date of arrival
- date of departure
- any special needs (e.g., bathroom in the room or down the hall, twin beds vs. double bed, air-conditioning, quiet, view, ground floor, etc.)

When you request a room, use the European style for writing dates: day/month/year. Hoteliers need to know your arrival and departure dates. For example, for a two-night stay in July, I would request: "2 nights, arrive 16/07/11, depart 18/07/11." (Consider in advance how long you'll stay; don't just assume you can extend your reservation for extra days once you arrive.)

If you don't get a reply to your email or fax, it usually means the place is already fully booked (but you can try sending the message again, or call to follow up).

Confirming a Reservation: If the hotel's response includes its room availability and rates, it's not a confirmation. You must tell them that you want that room at the given rate. Many hoteliers will request your credit-card number for a one-night deposit to hold the room. While you can email your credit-card information (I do), it's safer to share that personal info by phone call, fax, two successive emails, or secure online reservation form (if the hotel has one on its website).

Canceling a Reservation: If you must cancel your reservation, it's courteous to do so with as much advance notice as possible—at least three days. Simply make a quick phone call or send an email. Family-run hotels and B&Bs lose money if they turn away customers while holding a room for someone who doesn't show up. Understandably, many hotels bill no-shows for one night.

Hotels in larger cities sometimes have strict cancellation policies. For example, you might lose a deposit if you cancel within two weeks of your reserved stay, or you might be billed for the entire visit if you leave early. Ask about cancellation policies before you book.

If canceling by email, request confirmation that your cancellation was received to avoid being accidentally billed.

Reconfirm Your Reservation: Always call to reconfirm your room reservation a day or two in advance. Smaller hotels and B&B owners appreciate knowing your time of arrival. If you'll be arriving after 17:00, be sure to let your hotelier know. On the small chance that a hotel loses track of your reservation, bring along a hard copy of your emailed or faxed confirmation. Don't have the TI reconfirm rooms for you; they'll take a commission.

Reserving Rooms as You Travel: You can reserve while on the road, giving yourself the flexibility to modify your itinerary to adapt to the weather (spending rainy days in cities and sunny days in the mountains). You could call hotels a few days to a week before your stay. If you want to travel without any reservations at all, you'll have greater success snaring rooms if you arrive at your destination early in the day. When you anticipate crowds (weekends are worst), call hotels at about 9:00 on the day you plan to arrive, when the hotel clerk knows who'll be checking out and which rooms will be available.

Eating

The Swiss eat when we do and enjoy a straightforward, no-nonsense cuisine. Specialties include delicious fondue, rich chocolates, a melted cheese dish called raclette, *Rösti* (hash browns), fresh dairy products (try *Birchermüesli* for breakfast), 100 varieties of cheese, and Fendant—a good, crisp, local white wine.

Restaurants and Budget Options

When restaurant-hunting, choose a spot filled with locals, not the place with the big neon signs boasting, "We Speak English and Accept Credit Cards." Venturing even a block or two off the main drag leads to local, higher-quality food for less than half the price of the tourist-oriented places. Locals eat better at lower-rent locales.

Different kinds of restaurants offer different experiences. Hotels often serve fine food. A *Gaststätte* is a simple, less expensive restaurant. A *Weinstübli* (wine bar) or *Bierstübli* (tavern) usually serves food. Mountain huts—called *Hütte*—generally have hot chocolate and hearty meat-and-potato meals. Smoking is gradually being phased out in Switzerland's eateries, but the laws vary by city and canton, not by type of restaurant (a fine restaurant in *über*-traditional Appenzell is more likely to allow smoking than a bar in modern Zürich).

If you're not too hungry, order from the *kleine Hunger* (small hunger) section of the menu. Many restaurants offer half-portions, which is a great relief on your budget (although two people save even more by sharing one full portion).

Most restaurants tack a menu onto their door for browsers and have an English menu inside. If you ask for the *Menü* (or *menu* in French), you won't get a list of dishes; you'll get a fixed-price meal of several courses. If you simply want a list of what's cooking, ask for *die Speisekarte* (dee SHPIE-seh-kar-teh; *la carte* in French).

Only a rude waiter will rush you. Good service is relaxed (slow to an American). To wish others "Happy eating!" offer a cheery *"En Guete!"* When you want the bill, request the *"Rechnung, bitte."* (See the "Survival Phrases" in the appendix for more tips.)

Swiss restaurants are expensive, but there are several excellent budget alternatives. The Co-op and Migros grocery stores are the hungry hiker's best budget bet; groceries, while about 50 percent more than US prices, are a huge savings over any restaurant. These supermarkets often come with cheap non-smoking self-service cafeterias, with good food at much lower prices than restaurants with table service. In most big cities, you'll find Manor department stores, which usually feature wonderful self-service eateries called "Manora"—with lush salad bars, tasty entrées, and fresh-squeezed juices (I've listed several specific Manora locations in this book). Bakeries are another great place for a snack or affordable light meal.

Swiss Cuisine

Here at a crossroads of Europe, the food has a wonderful diversity: heavy *Wurst*-and-kraut Germanic fare; delicate, subtle French cuisine; and pasta dishes *all'Italiana*.

Aside from clocks and banks, Switzerland is known for its cheese. Gruyère cheese is hard, with a strong flavor; Emmentaler is also hard, but milder (and looks like what we call "Swiss cheese"). Appenzeller is the incredibly pungent cheese from the northeast of Switzerland, with a smell that verges on nauseating...until you

taste it. Two of Switzerland's best-known specialties are cheese-based. *Käsefondue* is usually Emmentaler and Gruyère cheese melted with white wine, garlic, nutmeg, and other seasonings. You eat it with a long fork, dipping cubes of bread into it. Raclette is cheese slowly melted on a special dish; as it softens, scrape a mound off and eat it with potatoes, pickled onions, and gherkins. (In restaurants, raclette often comes as little slices of cheese already melted.)

Another must-try dish, most typical in the mountains of the German-speaking areas, is *Rösti:* traditional hash browns with alpine cheese, often served with a bit of bacon or ham, or with an egg cracked over it...yum.

Despite all the cheese and potatoes, the Swiss tend to be health-conscious; after all, they invented muesli. While the dry muesli served at every breakfast buffet is unremarkable, *Birchermüesli*—a yummy mixture of fresh yogurt, fresh fruit, and juice-soaked oats—is worth seeking out in supermarket delis and on café menus. Menus often feature a *Fitnessteller* ("fitness plate")—usually a large mixed salad that comes with a steak, chicken, or fish. *Bio* means organically grown (a *Biolädeli* is a store that sells organic products).

Of course, each region has its own specialties. In French-speaking Switzerland, white wine and heavy cream are used in many dishes, and horsemeat (formerly imported from Eastern Europe, now imported from the US, New Zealand, and Australia) is common. The cuisine in eastern Switzerland (Pontresina, St. Moritz) uses chestnuts in many forms, wild mushrooms, and air-dried beef. Southwestern Switzerland (Zermatt area) specializes in all kinds of cheese, and their favorite white wine is Fendant.

Swiss wine is good, but expensive because of high production costs and mostly small vineyards. The Swiss certainly have plenty of wine-making experience—they've been growing grapes since Roman times. Since Swiss wine is not well-known outside of the country, and very little is exported, this is your chance to try the local *Wein/vin/vino*. About two-thirds of the production is white, and much of that is made from the Chasselas (a.k.a. Fendant) grape. The dry, white Fendant is great with cheese dishes. Fruity St. Saphorin wines from the slopes above Lake Geneva rank among the best Swiss whites. If you're in Murten, sample the local Vully wine (both red and white) from sunny lakeshore vineyards. Dôle, a light-bodied red wine made from the Pinot Noir grape, is popular for sipping.

Menus list drink size by the deciliter (dl, tenth of a liter). In German-speaking areas, order wine by the *Glas* (glass) or *Viertel* (quarter liter, or 8 oz.). Order it *süss* (sweet), *halb trocken* (medium), or *trocken* (dry); *weiss* (white), or *rot* (red). You can say, "*Ein Viertel Weisswein* (white wine), *bitte* (please)." For fun, try ordering the same thing in colloquial Swiss German: "*Ä Viertel Wiisewyy, bitte*" (ih FEER-tehl VEE-seh-vee, BIT-teh).

In French Switzerland, wine comes either by *le verre* (a glass, 1–2 dl), *la carafe* (3 dl or 5 dl), or *la bouteille* (bottle). Order by requesting "*Un verre de vin blanc, s'il vous plaît*" (or "*vin rouge*" if you prefer red). In the Ticino region, *un boccalino* is a small, decorated eight-ounce ceramic jug filled with the local red wine.

Swiss beer is surprisingly good and inexpensive. Most of the beer is light, golden-colored lager, but you'll also find other types, such as *Hefeweizen* and *Dunkel* (dark) beers. Each pub has one brand of a local beer on tap, with others available in bottles. Feldschlössen is the largest brewery in the country, and you'll see its red-castle logo all over. But the Swiss are loyal to their local brews; for example, in the Appenzell region, the local Appenzeller is the beer of choice. The standard size, measured in centiliters (cl), is a *Stange* (33 cl); the smaller size is called a *Herrgöttli* (20 cl). Beer mixed with lemon-flavored pop is called a *Panaché*. In summer, this lightly sweet, sudsy drink is more refreshing than straight beer.

Instead of Coke, try a local favorite: Rivella, a carbonated, vitamin-rich soft drink made with 35 percent milk serum. Its unusual (but not unpleasant) taste doesn't resemble milk at all; it's more like chewable vitamins. It comes in four colors: red is regular; blue is low-calorie; green is mixed with green tea; and the newest variety, yellow, is soy-based. Tap water, which many waiters aren't eager to bring you, is *Leitungswasser* (*l'eau du robinet* in French). Ask for it by name, or you'll receive—and be charged for—*Mineralwasser* (*mit/ohne Gas*, with/without carbonation).

How Was Your Trip?

Were your travels fun, smooth, and meaningful? If you'd like to share your tips, concerns, and discoveries, please fill out the survey at www.ricksteves.com/feedback. I value your feedback. Thanks in advance—it helps a lot.

As an alternative to hot chocolate, try Ovomaltine. The Swiss have a fondness for this hot drink—a malt-derived vitamin supplement, flavored with chocolate so kids will drink it. (In the US, our Ovaltine is an Asian variation on this drink—considered by the Swiss to be a cheap copy.)

And, of course, there's chocolate. The Swiss changed the world in 1875 with their invention of milk chocolate. Nestlé, Suchard, and Lindt are the major producers. Stroll the chocolate aisle of a grocery store and take your pick.

Traveling as a Temporary Local

We travel all the way to Europe to enjoy differences—to become temporary locals. You'll experience frustrations. Certain truths that we find "God-given" or "self-evident," such as cold beer, ice in drinks, bottomless cups of coffee, hot showers, and bigger being better, are suddenly not so true. One of the benefits of travel is the eye-opening realization that there are logical, civil, and even better alternatives.

Americans are enjoying a surge in popularity in Europe these days. But if there is a negative aspect to the image Europeans have of Americans, it's that we are big, loud, aggressive, impolite, rich, superficially friendly, and a bit naive.

My Swiss friends (and Europeans in general) place a high value on speaking quietly in restaurants and on trains. Listen while on the bus or in a restaurant—the place can be packed, but the decibel level is low. Try to adjust your volume accordingly to show respect for their culture.

While Europeans look bemusedly at some of our Yankee excesses—and worriedly at others—they nearly always afford us individual travelers all the warmth we deserve. Judging from all the happy feedback I receive from travelers who have used this book, it's safe to assume you'll enjoy a great, affordable vacation—with the finesse of an independent, experienced traveler.

Thanks, and happy travels—*gute Reise!*

Back Door Travel Philosophy
From *Rick Steves' Europe Through the Back Door*

Travel is intensified living—maximum thrills per minute and one of the last great sources of legal adventure. Travel is freedom. It's recess, and we need it.

Experiencing the real Europe requires catching it by surprise, going casual..."Through the Back Door."

Affording travel is a matter of priorities. (Make do with the old car.) You can eat and sleep—simply, safely, and comfortably—anywhere in Europe for $120 a day plus transportation costs. In many ways, spending more money only builds a thicker wall between you and what you've traveled so far to see. Europe is a cultural carnival, and time after time, you'll find that its best acts are free and the best seats are the cheap ones.

A tight budget forces you to travel close to the ground, meeting and communicating with the people. Never sacrifice sleep, nutrition, safety, or cleanliness to save money. Simply enjoy the local-style alternatives to expensive hotels and restaurants.

Connecting with people carbonates your experience. Extroverts have more fun. If your trip is low on magic moments, kick yourself and make things happen. If you don't enjoy a place, maybe you don't know enough about it. Seek the truth. Recognize tourist traps. Give a culture the benefit of your open mind. See things as different but not better or worse. Any culture has plenty to share.

Of course, travel, like the world, is a series of hills and valleys. Be fanatically positive and militantly optimistic. If something's not to your liking, change your liking.

Travel can make you a happier American, as well as a citizen of the world. Our Earth is home to six and a half billion equally precious people. It's humbling to travel and find that other people don't have the "American Dream"—they have their own dreams. Europeans like us, but, with all due respect, they wouldn't trade passports.

Thoughtful travel engages you with the world. In tough economic times, it reminds us what is truly important. By broadening perspectives, travel teaches new ways to measure quality of life.

Globetrotting destroys ethnocentricity, helping us understand and appreciate other cultures. Rather than fear the diversity on this planet, celebrate it. Among your most prized souvenirs will be the strands of different cultures you choose to knit into your own character. The world is a cultural yarn shop, and Back Door travelers are weaving the ultimate tapestry. Join in!

SWITZERLAND

Switzerland is one of Europe's richest, best organized, most expensive countries. Like the Boy Scouts, the Swiss count cleanliness, neatness, punctuality, tolerance, independence, thrift, and hard work as virtues...and they love pocketknives. The country is an enjoyable mix of bucolic peace and daring adventure. Around every alpine turn, you feel you could get a glimpse of Heidi milking a cow or James Bond schussing past on skis.

Nearly half of Switzerland—Europe's most mountainous country—consists of uninhabitable rocks and rugged Alps. It seems that any flat land (and quite a bit of hilly land) is cultivated into tidy little farms. While landlocked, Switzerland has more than its share of clear rivers and big, beautiful lakes with a striking mountain backdrop (such as Lake Geneva, Lake Murten, Lake Luzern, and Lake Lugano—all covered in this book).

Despite the country's small size, Switzerland is unusually diverse. Its wild geography has kept people apart historically, helping its many regions maintain their distinct cultural differences. Switzerland is at a linguistic crossroads of Europe, with four official languages: German, French, Italian, and Romansh (an obscure Latin dialect).

And yet, regardless of which language is spoken, the entire country is unmistakably Swiss. Everyday things like the post office, train station, or familiar products have the same logos, but in different

The abbreviation for Swiss Federal Railways—in German, French, and Italian

SWITZERLAND

Switzerland: Western Europe's Linguistic Crossroads

You'd be forgiven for thinking of Switzerland as a "German" country. The heart of Switzerland, with about three-fifths of the population and most of the famous cities and sights, is linguistically (as well as culturally) Germanic. But even here, Germans and Austrians don't feel quite at home. As if keeping alive an archaic code for insiders, the Swiss speak to each other in the lilting, fun-to-listen-to "Swiss German," or *Schwyzertütsch*, then switch seamlessly to standard German (or English) when interacting with outsiders.

German | Italian
French | Romansh

Surrounding the German-speaking core is a more colorful Romance language–speaking fringe—French (to the west), Italian (to the south), and Romansh (tucked in the southeastern mountains). Switzerland's biggest canton, officially trilingual, is its linguistic melting pot: the southeastern region called Graubünden (in German), Grigioni (in Italian), and Grischun (in Romansh).

Subtle differences in cuisine, climate, and landscape seem to match the linguistic boundaries. German-speaking Switzerland enjoys a vigorous efficiency reminiscent of Germany's. The pace in genteel French-speaking Switzerland is a bit mellower, the cuisine and lifestyle more refined, resembling France's. And the relatively balmy Italian-speaking canton of Ticino comes with a touch of chaos and lust for life that's not far removed from Italy proper (which surrounds it on three sides). You can spend a week in Switzerland and feel almost as if you've traveled from Paris to Munich to Rome... without ever crossing a border.

languages. And everywhere you go, you'll notice a dedication to orderliness and organization that distinguishes Swiss culture. It's refreshing to visit a predictable place where, once you've got the gist of things in one city, you generally know what to expect in the next.

That sort of orderliness doesn't happen by itself. The Swiss jealously guard their way of life. If you accidentally drop a scrap of paper on the ground, someone might cross the street to be sure you pick it up. As if belonging to an exclusive club that's careful about admitting new members, the Swiss strike some visitors as a bit stand-offish—polite but not gregarious, welcoming but perhaps a bit suspicious. If you find the Swiss to be a little buttoned-down, remember that the payoff is a beautiful place where the trains run on time, the streets are clean, and every flower petal is perfectly in place.

While it's one of Europe's most progressive "big-government" countries—with high taxation, ample social services, and liberal drug policies—Switzerland's devotion to order and predictability also give it a sometimes surprising conservative streak. Traditional mindsets persist in the remote mountain hamlets—shockingly, women weren't guaranteed the right to vote in federal elections until 1971.

Historically, Switzerland is one of Europe's oldest democracies. Born when three states (cantons) united in 1291, the Swiss Confederation grew to the 26 cantons of today. The "CH" decal on cars doesn't stand for chocolate...but for "Confoederatio Helvetica," the country's official title (using the Latin name avoids linguistic controversy). The country is named for the Celtic Helvetii tribe that lived here back in Roman times. The Confederation government is decentralized, and cantonal loyalty is very strong.

Similar to the US, each of the 26 Swiss cantons is semi-independent. Just as we might debate "states' rights" in the US, the Swiss wrangle with just how much autonomy to allow each of their cantons. Considering that each canton comes with not only its own political concerns, but also its own language and cultural heritage, cantonal independence is particularly important and delicate.

With the exception of the Protestant Reformation (see the sidebar on page 48), Swiss history has been pretty quiet...and that's just how the Swiss like it. They're happy to be high and dry in the mountains, watching from above the fray as the tides of history swirl around them (for an overview, see the Switzerland: Past and Present chapter). Stubbornly independent, or maybe just smart, Switzerland loves its neutrality and stayed out of both World Wars. But it's far from lax when it comes to national defense—on the contrary, the Swiss are legendary for their military readiness. A vast reserve army and a countryside

Switzerland Almanac

Official Name: The Confoederatio Helvetica, or Switzerland, has a different name in each of its four official languages: Schweizerische Eidgenossenschaft (German), Confédération Suisse (French), Confederazione Svizzera (Italian), and Confederaziun Svizra (Romansh). Locals shorten those to "die Schweiz," "la Suisse," "la Svizzera," and "la Svizra."

Population: Switzerland has 7.5 million people (similar to the population of Virginia). 60 percent of them speak German as their main language, 20 percent speak French, 7 percent speak Italian, and about 0.5 percent speak Romansh. About 23 percent of Swiss residents come from other countries—ranging from EU businesspeople to immigrant workers. The populace is 42 percent Catholic, 35 percent Protestant, 2 percent Orthodox, 4 percent Muslim, and 17 percent other or unspecified.

Latitude and Longitude: 47°N and 8°E, similar latitude to Washington State or Quebec, Canada.

Area: 16,000 square miles; twice the size of New Jersey, or half the size of South Carolina.

Geography: Switzerland sits at the crossroads between northern and southern Europe. The Alps are Europe's high point and continental divide, from which the major rivers flow—Rhine, Rhône, Danube, and Po. Switzerland's highest point is the 15,200-foot Monte Rosa (specifically, the summit called Dufourspitze), along the Italian border. Though Switzerland is mostly mountainous, the center of the country consists of rolling hills and large lakes.

Biggest Cities: One in seven Swiss lives in or near Zürich (pop. 370,000 in the city; 1 million in the metropolitan area). Geneva has 186,000 people, and Basel has 167,000. The capital is Bern (pop. 123,000).

Economy: Like a fine watch, Switzerland's economy just keeps on ticking. The Gross Domestic Product is $315 billion, similar to Washington State. Its per-capita GDP of $43,000 is

embedded with hidden fortresses have earned Switzerland its unique ability to preserve its right to self-determination well into the 21st century, even though it's surrounded by bigger, stronger nations. Through the tumult of the 20th century, no foreign invaders dared to try cracking this nut.

Even so, for more than a century and a half, a different kind of invasion—of tourists—has descended on Switzerland each summer (for hiking season, all summer long but busiest July–Aug) and each winter (for ski season, roughly Christmas through Easter). You'll share the trails and lifts with a deluge of international visitors—from Europe, the US, and the rest of the world. Because several Bollywood movies have used the Swiss Alps as a stand-in among Europe's highest (but still 9 percent less than the US). The franc is strong, workers are highly skilled, and unemployment is half the European Union average. Blessed with hydropower and using nuclear technology, Switzerland generates 99 percent of its electricity with virtually no oil.

Currency: 1 Swiss franc (SF) = 100 Rappen/centimes = about $1.

Government: Founded in 1291 as a confederation of cantons, the country is still a model of federalism, balancing the needs of its different linguistic/ethnic groups. No single political party (or two or even three parties) dominates the political landscape. The president, chosen by the legislature, serves for just one calendar year. The two-house Federal Assembly consists of the 46-seat Council of States and the 200-seat National Council, elected for four-year terms.

Flag: Switzerland's white cross on a distinctively square red background may have been the inspiration for the red-on-white symbol of the International Red Cross.

The Average Swiss: He or she has 1.43 children and will live to be 80. A typical Swiss man serves at least 260 days of compulsory service in the military. The average woman spends two hours a day on housework. He or she travels about 1,300 miles a year on a train, the equivalent of crossing the country six times. Sixteen percent of the average Swiss income goes to taxes, and 20 percent of the household budget is spent buying insurance. Every month, the average Swiss drinks a quart of alcohol and eats two pounds of chocolate.

for Kashmir, Switzerland is popular with tourists from India. And Middle Eastern visitors flock here to escape the heat. Locals report that there's a spike in Muslim Middle Eastern tourists in the weeks leading up to the sacred, month-long observance of Ramadan... when their numbers drop to virtually zero, as Muslims go back home to spend time with their families.

Though not a European Union member—that neutrality thing again—Switzerland conforms to EU standards to stay competitive. Major Swiss money-makers include banking (especially secret, private accounts from around the world), insurance, watches (from top-of-the-line pieces to inexpensive Swatches), chemicals and pharmaceuticals, chocolate (Nestlé is the biggest producer), tourism, and precision instruments. Swiss-made equipment helps make everything from clothing to ballpoint-pen tips to parts for the Mars Exploration Rover. Swiss ingenuity is nowhere more apparent than in the famous Swiss Army knives, which come in sizes big and small, with as many—or as few—tools as any armchair MacGyver could need. Some newer models even come with USB flash drives and LED lights.

Perhaps owing to its economic might, Switzerland has earned a reputation for being one of Europe's most expensive countries. A night on the town can be a major splurge. More and more locals call sitting on the pavement around a bottle of wine "going out." Hotels with double rooms for less than $100 are rare. Even dormitory beds are expensive. If your budget is tight, be sure to chase down hostels (many have private rooms for couples and families) and keep your eyes peeled for *Matratzenlagers* ("mattress dorms"). Hiking is free, though major alpine lifts run around $50.

Switzerland has more than its share of cosmopolitan cities. My favorites—Zürich, Luzern, Bern, Lausanne, and Lugano—are covered in this book. Each one offers an enticing, I-could-live-here glimpse of the appealing and uniquely Swiss urban quality of life: efficient trams and buses gliding around town, manicured pedestrian zones teeming with locals enjoying their cit-

ies, crystal-clear rivers and lakes made accessible by scenic cruise boats, eclectic restaurants offering a tasty range of both Swiss and international cuisine, and low-key but generally compelling museums. While Switzerland lacks a world-class metropolis on par with Paris or Rome, all of its cities are surprisingly engaging—especially if bad weather keeps you from heading for the hills.

But let's face it: Travelers don't flock to Switzerland for its cities. Spend most of your time getting high in the Alps. You can climb onto a train in one of Switzerland's most bustling stations and, within an hour or two, step off into an idyllic time-warp world where traditional culture still thrives. Alpine villages (such as Gimmelwald) and towns (such as Appenzell) give you a taste of rural Switzerland, and are the perfect base for pastoral countryside hikes or riding lifts to dramatic cut-glass alpine panoramas.

If you're in the countryside on a Sunday, you'll most likely enjoy traditional music, clothing, and culture. At the end of a day of hiking, you can retreat to a village enclave preserving a colorful, rustic, rural way of life. Because the Swiss government values the

traditional lifestyles, it subsidizes families to raise cows and make cheese the old-fashioned way. In the spring and again in the fall, you might be lucky enough to see a parade of cows on their way up to or back down from the high-mountain pastures. For the whole story, see "Swiss Cow Culture" on page 158.

The cows have also had a big impact on Swiss cuisine—especially cheese. Two of the most revered Swiss cheeses are the smooth Gruyère cheese (from the town of Gruyères) and the stinky Appenzeller cheese (from the region of Appenzell). In these areas, you can watch the cheese being made—just as it has been for centuries...or at modern facilities that use new technology to carry out the same age-old processes (including robots that tenderly rub and flip each aging wheel of cheese). Cheese shops (*Käserei* in German) sell a fragrant festival of mold, perfect for picnicking or for making two famous Swiss culinary specialties: fondue (a pot of cheese melted into wine) or raclette (cheese melted over potatoes and other vegetables). But after a few days of cheese plates for breakfast, cheese sandwiches for lunch, and cheese specialties for dinner, even the biggest cheese-lovers might find they need a dairy detox. For more on Swiss cuisine, see page 26.

Switzerland's public transportation system is tops, whether you want to go across the country or straight up into the mountains. The country is crisscrossed with fine autobahns and arguably Europe's most efficient rail system. Boats ply the tranquil waters of the country's many lakes, and PostBuses (operated by the post office) pick you up in the rare situations where trains let you down. You can even go *through* the mountains, thanks to long tunnels (but you'll miss the views). Try the variety of fun cogwheel trains, funiculars, and cable cars that deliver you—no matter the season—from sunny valleys up to dizzying heights and snowy vistas. For a rundown of your options—from cable cars to gondolas to funiculars—see "Lift Lingo" on page 359.

Switzerland's best attraction might just be hiding between the cities and the villages: In this land of dramatic mountains

SWITZERLAND

Understanding the Alps

Switzerland's snowy, rugged mountains are its claim to fame—and most likely the main reason for your visit. Fortunately, you don't have to be a mountain climber to see the Alps up close, as the Swiss transportation system is as remarkable as its mountains—its cog railways, gondolas, and cable cars whisk you up into the type of scenery that's only accessible in some countries by ropes, pitons, and crampons.

The Alps were formed by the collision of two continents. About 100 million years ago, the African plate began pushing north against the stable plates of Europe and Asia. In the process, the sediments of the ancient Tethys Ocean (which occupied the general real estate of the modern Mediterranean) became smooshed between the landmasses. Shoving all this material together made the rocks and sediments fold, shatter, and pile on top of each other; over millennia this growing jumble built itself up into today's Alps. As you travel through the mountains, look for folds and faults in the rocks that hint at this immense compression, which is still happening today—the Alps continue to rise by at least a millimeter each year (which is basically balanced out by erosion).

The current shape of the mountains and valleys is the handiwork of at least five ice ages over the last two million years. Glaciers flowed down the mountain valleys, scooped out Switzerland's beautiful lakes, and carried rocks far away from where they had formed. The Alps were the first mountains extensively studied by geologists, and many of the geological terms that describe mountains originated here. Once you learn how to recognize a few of the landforms shaped by glaciers, you can easily spot these features when you visit other alpine areas. Study glacier exhibits in museums and visitor centers to train your eye to recognize what you're seeing.

Glaciers are big and blunt, so they make simple, large-scale marks on the landscape. If a valley is U-shaped (with steep sides and a rounded base), it likely was scoured out by a glacier. Switzerland's Lauterbrunnen Valley, as well as Yosemite Valley in the US, are classic examples.

A **cirque** (French for "circus") is the amphitheater-like depression carved out at the upper part of a valley by a glacier. If two adjacent cirques erode close to each other, a sharp steep-sided ridge forms, called an **arête** (French for "fishbone"). Cirques and arêtes are common in mountains with glaciers. More rarely, when three or more cirques erode toward one another, a pyramidal peak is created, called a **horn.** The Matterhorn is the world's most famous example. Glaciers flowed down all sides of this mountain, scooping material away and creating the distinctive sharp peak.

A common feature left behind by retreating glaciers is a **moraine,** a pile of dirt and rocks carried along on the glacier as it advanced, then dumped as the glacier melted. The Lindenhof in Zürich, a hilltop square once crowned with forts to defend the town, perches on a moraine.

Alpine glaciers can only originate above the snowline, so if you see any of these landforms (U-shaped valleys, cirques, horns, or moraines) in lower elevations, you know that the climate there used to be colder. The effects of a warming climate have profoundly hit the glaciers of Switzerland, which have lost at least a third of their volume since the 1950s. Some studies project that at that rate most glaciers in Switzerland could virtually disappear by the end of the century, affecting water storage and hydroelectric power generation.

In higher elevations, mountainsides have become less stable due to the melting of permafrost. A heat wave in 2003 caused several rockfalls on the Matterhorn, resulting in trail closures and the evacuation of dozens of climbers trapped on the summit. The ski resort of Pontresina built a dam in 2002 to protect the town from a potential landslide from its nearby mountain.

Another consequence of the warming climate is that winter weather no longer reliably produces snow at altitudes that it did in the past—which is bad news for Switzerland's huge ski industry. Seeing a future of ever-warmer winters, the Swiss are putting their ingenuity to the test. In many resorts, that means not just putting snow machines on ski slopes, but also investing hugely in new spas, convention centers, and other attractions that don't require snow.

With their acute awareness of their alpine climate's fragility, the Swiss are especially keen to explore green technology— even high up in the Alps. In 2009, for example, the new Monte Rosa mountain refuge opened in the Alps near Zermatt. Unlike the rustic chalets that dot other mountain areas, this one isn't a stone hut but a futuristic-looking, high-tech building that gets 90 percent of its energy from solar power. Its inauguration received a fair amount of press, as the hut is considered an example of how Switzerland's technological innovation can help keep its mountains white and its valleys green.

and picture-perfect farms, perhaps more than anywhere else in
Europe, the journey is the destination. The Swiss Railway markets several scenic journeys that
run along the country's prettiest
routes, many with special panoramic trains designed to maximize views (for all the details, see
the Scenic Rail Journeys chapter).

But don't let the tourist hype give you tunnel vision. A sunny day
spent on a train just about anywhere in Switzerland can rank as a
memorable trip-capper.

From its famous efficiency, to its unique mingling of the
modern and the traditional, to its flat-out spectacular scenery,
Switzerland delights the Swiss...and their visitors.

ZÜRICH

Zürich is one of those cities that tourists tend to skip right through. Since it's a transportation hub, people fly in or change trains here, but don't give stopping a serious thought. The local graffiti jokes: *Zürich = zu reich, zu ruhig* ("too rich, too quiet"). But even though you won't find a hint of Swiss Miss in Switzerland's leading city—and with limited time, I'd certainly spend it up in the mountains—Zürich is surprisingly comfortable and enjoyable for a quick visit.

Zürich was founded by the Romans as a customs post (in prehistoric times, people lived on pilings near the shores of Lake Zürich). Roman Turicum eventually became Zürich. It gained city status in the 10th century, and by the 19th century it was a leading European financial and economic center. Today, it's home to the world's largest gold marketplace and the fourth-largest stock exchange (after New York, London, and Tokyo). Assuming you've got the money to enjoy it, Zürich is by many measures the world's most livable city. Its 370,000 people (1 million in greater Zürich) are known for their wealth and hard work. Zürich is the only place in Switzerland where you'll see men in ties running in the streets.

Planning Your Time

While Luzern and Bern provide more charming urban experiences, Zürich is worth a quick visit. With two weeks in Switzerland, I'd spend a day here. Begin by visiting the impressive Swiss National Museum, then wander along the river, using my self-guided walk, and take a river/lake cruise. With less time, do only the self-guided walk; with more time, take your pick of the many museums.

Orientation to Zürich

Zürich sprawls around the northern tip of the long, skinny Lake Zürich (Zürichsee). The grand Bahnhofstrasse cuts through Zürich's glitzy shopping center—a 15-minute walk along here connects the train station and the country's top historical museum (Swiss National Museum) with the lakefront. Across the Limmat River is the Niederdorf neighborhood, a vibrant, cobbled, Old World zone of colorful little shops, cafés, and restaurants.

Tourist Information

A helpful TI is located in the great hall of the train station (under the fat blue angel; May–Oct Mon–Sat 8:00–20:30, Sun 8:30–18:30; Nov–April Mon–Sat 8:30–19:00, Sun 9:00–18:30; tel. 044-215-4000, www.zuerich.com). Pick up their city guide and map, browse the racks of brochures, and ask about their daily walking tours.

For a whirlwind visit, consider the **ZürichCARD**, which covers transportation by train, tram, bus, and boat (including trips to the airport and up to the Uetliberg viewpoint); admission to 37 museums (usually permanent exhibits only); half off the city walking tour; and "welcome drinks" in many restaurants (19 SF/24 hrs, 38 SF/72 hrs, sold at TI). The one-day card will pay for itself if you do the walking tour and at least one museum in a day. The TI also sells a 24-hour transit pass (8 SF).

Tours: You can see Zürich on a **guided walk** (similar to the self-guided walk in this chapter; 2 hrs, 20 SF, half-price with Swiss Pass or ZürichCARD; leaves from TI mid-April–Oct daily at 15:00, Sat–Sun also at 11:00, Nov–March Wed and Sat–Sun only at 11:00). There's also a **bus tour** (2 hrs, 33 SF, daily at 9:45, 12:00, and 14:00 year-round). The TI has details on both tours.

Arrival in Zürich

By Train: The slick train station (with a TI, lockers, and shopping mall—see beginning of self-guided walk, later) is on the north end of downtown; to reach most of my recommended hotels, cross the Walche-Brücke bridge in front of the station.

By Plane: From Zürich Airport, catch a train to the station downtown (6.10 SF, 15 min, departs every 10 min 5:00–24:00) rather than take a 50–60-SF taxi ride. For more on the airport, see page 63.

Getting Around Zürich

On the trams and buses, a ticket good for one short ride (within five stops) costs 2.50 SF (1-hour ticket for 4 SF, 24-hour transit pass for 8 SF, www.zvv.ch). You can buy tram/bus tickets from ticket machines at stops, at public-transit booths (marked ZVV), and at the train station. You can't buy tickets onboard, and you'll face an 80-SF fine if you're caught without one. All transportation is covered by the Swiss Pass and ZürichCARD, mentioned earlier.

Helpful Hints

Medical Help: The **Permanence** drop-in clinic on the main floor of the train station offers on-the-spot medical aid (daily 7:00–22:00, Bahnhofplatz 15, tel. 044-215-4444). There's also a dentist on the lower level.

Bikes: A city program called "Züri rollt" allows you to borrow a bike for free (must leave passport and 20-SF deposit, May–Oct daily 8:00–21:30, across from train station, next to the Swiss National Museum; other locations around town have roughly the same hours—look for *Züri rollt* or *Velogate* signs). Popular bike paths line the lake from Zürich. For more info, ask the TI or visit www.zuerirollt.ch.

Laundry: There is no central launderette in town, but many hotels will do laundry by request for a fee.

Internet Access: Internetcafe.ch is a five-minute walk from the station (Mon–Fri 7:00–23:00, Sat 8:00–23:00, Sun 10:00–22:00, Uraniastrasse 3, tel. 044-210-3311, www.internet cafe.ch).

Self-Guided Walk

Welcome to Zürich

This handy walking tour is the perfect orientation for travelers blitzing Zürich from the train station. It crisscrosses the river, connecting the city center's main sights en route to the boat dock for a lazy lake-cruise finale (or a quick tram ride back to the station). Allow about an hour for the walk.

Train Station

Zürich's central station has a great energy. This major European hub handles 2,000 trains a day, including InterCity expresses to many major capitals. Built in 1870, its vast main hall was once lined with tracks. Today, it's a farmers' market (Wed 10:00–20:00) and community hall—busy with concerts, exhibitions, and even "beach" volleyball. The station sits above a vast underground modern shopping mall that's open late, even on Sundays (Mon–Fri until 21:00, Sat–Sun until 20:00).

Above you, find the fat blue angel, Zürich's "Guardian Angel," protecting all travelers. The angel has been here since 1997 to celebrate the 150th anniversary of the Swiss rail system. To the angel's right, just across the street, is the **Swiss National Museum.** It's the best museum in town, offering an essential introduction to Swiss history (described later, under "Sights in Zürich"). To maximize your education, tour this museum before starting the walk.

• *From the station hall, follow the six white lines that lead to Bahnhofplatz (also well-signed). The station fronts Zürich's main shopping boulevard...*

Bahnhofstrasse

Mile-long Bahnhofstrasse, stretching from the train station to the lake, is lined with all the big-name shops (though it's become a bit "hamburgerized" in recent years). Cross the street (watch for silent streetcars), but before heading on down, look back at the station.

The facade of the station is a huge triumphal **arch,** built in 1871 to symbolize the triumph of industry. In the Industrial Age, Zürich emerged as Switzerland's leading city. Presiding over all this triumph is Helvetia, the personification of Switzerland. The Helvetii were the Celtic tribe that the Romans defeated in 15 B.C. to gain control of what is now Switzerland. Romans described them as "very good warriors with an affinity for bright and shiny metal." Helvetia was adopted as a symbol of the Swiss confederation in 1848, when the diverse cantons that banded together to create Switzerland needed some symbol of unity to transcend all their linguistic and regional differences. Helvetic ethnic heritage is the one thing all Swiss cantons have in common. (The "CH" you see on Swiss bumper stickers stands for the Latin "Confoederatio Helvetica.")

Helvetia is flanked by allegories of river travel (the goddess sitting on the boat) and rail travel (another goddess sitting on a train), reminding us that Zürich has long been a transportation hub. Zürich's river, the Limmat, starts from the lake and eventually flows into the Rhine and then (in Rotterdam) out to sea.

The statue of **Alfred Escher** honors the man who spearheaded the creation of the infrastructure that allowed the country to function efficiently within its mountains, and connected Switzerland with the rest of Europe. Many Swiss trace their nation's strong economy and ethos of efficiency to this man.

• *Start strolling down Bahnhofstrasse. In two blocks (on the right), you'll see...*

Pestalozzi Park

The only park along this pedestrian- and tram-only boulevard is dedicated to Zürich's most important teacher, Johann Heinrich

Welcome to Zürich Walk

1. Train Station
2. Bahnhofstrasse
3. Pestalozzi Park
4. Police Department
5. Schipfe Street
6. Lindenhof
7. St. Peter's Church
8. Roman Bath & Weinplatz
9. Rathausbrücke
10. Conditorei Schober
11. Grossmünster
12. Fraumünster
13. Paradeplatz
14. Lake Zürich

Pestalozzi (1746–1827). He promoted the notion, still prevalent in today's Switzerland, that a good education should be available for everyone—not only for sons of rich families. Parks like this are rare in central Zürich because of sky-high property values, which are among the most expensive in the world.

In the park's far corner gurgles a copy of a Parisian **Wallace Fountain.** If you have a big head, good luck getting a drink from here. More than 1,200 fun and fresh fountains are sprinkled around town, spouting water that's as good as bottled mineral water (the city regularly checks its quality). This is a blessing in a town where restaurants charge for a glass of tap water. Tourist brochures brag that Zürich is Europe's most "fountainous" city.

From Pestalozzi Park to Lindenhof: From the park, head left a couple of blocks to the Limmat River. Then go right onto Werdmühlestrasse, and head toward Werdmühleplatz (following signs to *Stadtpolizei*), and make a short stop at the **Police Department,** facing the river (open daily 9:00–11:00 & 14:00–16:00). Don't be shy—show your ID and enter for a free peek at a fine example of Swiss Jugendstil: an amazing wall and ceiling painting by Swiss artist Augusto Giacometti. (If the building is closed, you can get a good look from the always-open lobby—but no photos are allowed.) Giacometti's famous *Hall of the Flowers* (*Blüemlihalle*, 1926), awash in vibrant orange and red, reflects the relief and joy the artist felt when World War I ended. (Augusto's nephew, Alberto, is the more famous Giacometti, much appreciated for his tall, skinny statues.)

From here, walk along the river upstream toward the church spires. Without crossing the river, take the stairs down to the boardwalk below the Heimatwerk Swiss folk-crafts shop. Back when the city's trade depended on river traffic, this small riverside street, called **Schipfe,** was Zürich's harbor. Today it retains its old river-merchant ambience. You'll pass a fun riverside eatery (the recommended Restaurant Schipfe 16) and an arcade.

• *Twenty yards before the ugliest bridge in Switzerland, head up the stairs for two blocks, and then climb to the right up Pfalzgasse. You'll enjoy a great view from another park...*

Lindenhof

Important forts and strategic buildings stood on this hilltop square from Roman times through the Carolingian era. The statue commemorates the local women who cleverly defended the town in 1292. Their men were engaged in another battle. The Habsburgs circled the city, ready to attack. The women put on armor and made like a big, rowdy army, tricking the Habsburgs into thinking the whole city was prepared to attack.

When Zürich became a free city in the 13th century, the

townspeople destroyed the fort here and established a law forbidding any new construction. The citizens realized that whoever lived on this hill would rule over the city—and they didn't want any more rulers. Today, this is a people's square, where locals relax under linden trees (for which the square is named) and enjoy the commanding city view. You're atop a moraine of glacial debris (see page 39).

Survey Zürich beyond its river. The **university** (behind the green spire) is the largest in Switzerland, with 25,000 students. Left of that is Zürich's renowned **technical college,** the ETH (Eidgenössische Technische Hochschule, or Federal Institute of Technology), with 15,000 students. The ETH has graduated 25 Nobel Prize winners, including Albert Einstein and Wilhelm Röntgen (who discovered X-rays). The ETH terrace offers a great city viewpoint (which you can visit later by riding the little Polybahn funicular). Lining the far side of the river, the **Niederdorf** is the lively restaurant, café, and bar district. On a clear day, you can see the Alps behind the twin domes.

• *Take the stairs at the back of the park, just left of the chess players, down to Strehlgasse, and go left on Glockengasse, around the Golden Bell. Continue down tiny Robert-Walser-Gasse toward St. Peterhofstatt. You'll pass a characteristic eatery, Reblaube Gaststube, made famous by visits from Goethe in 1779. He'd meet here for long, wine-fueled discussions with the minister of...*

St. Peter's Church (St. Peterskirche)

Founded in the seventh century, this church—Zürich's oldest—has one of Europe's largest clock faces (28 feet in diameter). The town watchman used to live above the clock. If he spotted a fire, he would ring the alarm and hang a flag out of the window facing the blaze. This system seems to have worked—Zürich never suffered a devastating fire. In the 18th century, this church's preacher, Johann Kaspar Lavater (1741–1801), was so well loved that people reserved their seats for Sunday Mass.

From St. Peter's Church to the Grossmünster: Continue past the

Switzerland's Zwingli Reformation

Today's Evangelical Reformed Church of Switzerland was founded by Huldrych Zwingli (1484–1531), who preached in Zürich from 1519 through 1531. A follower of the humanist philosopher Erasmus of Rotterdam, Zwingli believed that the true foundation of the church was based on preaching the Holy Scriptures freely—in the people's language, rather than in Latin. In 1522, most of German-speaking Switzerland embraced Zwingli's ideas...and that required leaving the Roman Catholic Church.

In 1517, when Zwingli was 33, German church reformer Martin Luther posted his revolutionary *95 Theses* (which questioned the practice of selling forgiveness, salvation, church offices, and so on). Within two years, sellers of indulgences were refused entry to Zürich. As the Reformation swept Switzerland, things heated up. In 1523, rioters were storming churches, and authorities called for an orderly removal of all images in Zürich houses of worship (except stained-glass windows, which were destroyed).

The new, reformed Swiss church let priests marry. (Zwingli, like Luther, promptly took advantage of this freedom.) Fancy Masses were replaced by simple services. At Zürich's main church, the Grossmünster, preachers studied Latin, Greek, and Hebrew in order to translate the Bible into the people's German. In 1531, the Zwingli Bible (the first complete Bible translated into German) was published. It's still used today (like the King James Bible is in English).

Zwingli gave the Swiss church an unusual austerity: no altar, no pictures, and for a while, not even any music. Church services focused on preaching. Holy Communion was celebrated only on holidays. This puritanical simplicity permeated Swiss society in general. Zwingli was no fan of the "separation of church and

church on Schlüsselgasse and take the first left, down the narrow Thermengasse ("Bath Lane"). Look under your feet through the grid at the lit-up excavations of a **Roman bath,** discovered by accident in 1984. You're standing over studs that elevated the floor, which was heated from below.

The lane empties out on **Weinplatz,** a wine market of centuries past (notice the grape-picker on the fine little fountain). A wall mural inside the Barchetta bar shows the medieval river action circa 1570, including a mill on the bridge that raised drinking water to pipes that led to nearby buildings. (Note the dock here for the "river bus"—described later, under "Sights in Zürich.")

The city's oldest bridge, the **Rathausbrücke,** goes back to Roman times, but now looks more like a concrete pier. Cross the bridge, passing the 17th-century, Renaissance-style City Hall, which faces a fancy Neoclassical police station, and walk a block uphill to Marktgasse, the gateway to the bustling Niederdorf neighborhood.

state." Pushing for a theocracy, he established an ironclad city law: The government's duty was to oversee public worship, and only preaching that was true to the Bible was to be tolerated.

But Zwingli's reforms were by no means universally supported. Oh, it was a mess: Switzerland's Protestant movement split over baptism. Luther and Zwingli split over the Eucharist (is Christ's body really *in* the bread, or there only in a spiritual sense?). And, as old-school Catholics predicted, putting the Bible into the hands of regular people brought chaos—enabling every Tom, Dick, and Hans to "carve his own path to hell." Switzerland was embroiled in a religious civil war, as Protestant cantons fought Catholic ones. In 1531, while fighting as a "citizen soldier," Zwingli was killed in battle. His friend and partner Heinrich Bullinger succeeded him as the leader of German-speaking Swiss Protestantism.

Bullinger collaborated with John Calvin as Swiss Protestantism matured. The Protestant focus on preaching promoted the translation and interpretation of the Bible. Everyone was reading the Bible directly, which promoted literacy. The Reformation provided a basis for the autonomous community spirit, strong work ethic, and high literacy of a prosperous Switzerland for the future. The Swiss church became a place where equals would meet and worship God. Zwingli's heritage included transferring the notion of social charity from being a church phenomenon to being the social welfare responsibility of any self-respecting modern state. The foundations of Swiss democracy and its present social policies are rooted in Zwingli's teaching. And these Swiss reformers planted the seeds of what became the Presbyterian Church in the United States.

To the left runs Niederdorfstrasse, which was the leading commercial street before the old city wall was torn down to create Bahnhofstrasse. The Starbucks a block down from here faces the charming square. The **Niederdorf**—a district of colorful streets, fun shopping, restaurants, and nightlife—continues on from here. You can explore this area now...or, better yet, tonight (you'll find some dining suggestions later, under "Eating in Zürich").

To continue our walk, go in the opposite direction (right), heading up **Münstergasse.** Dada enthusiasts will know that in 1916, at the Cabaret Voltaire (#26), this "anti-art" art movement was born. At #19, pop into Schwarzenbach, which still advertises "merchandise from the colonies" out front and sells things the old-fashioned way inside (in loose bags, by the weight). Inhale. Pick up 100 grams of dried bananas from Togo or some Thai sticks...of coconut, of course. Across the street, Zürich's popular **Conditorei Schober,** a riot of silk flowers, serves famously good (and expensive) hot chocolate and champagne truffles.

• *Farther up the street is the "big cathedral" (literally)...*

Grossmünster

It was here that Huldrych Zwingli—whose angry religious fervor made Martin Luther seem mellow—sparked the Reformation in German-speaking Switzerland. The

domes of its towers (early examples of Neo-Gothic) are symbols of Zürich. They were rebuilt following a 1781 fire, and after much civic discussion, were left a plain stone color. Step inside and sit down. Let the strength and purity of the 12th-century Romanesque architecture have its way with you. The simple round arches seem strong, and the wide triumphal arch separating the nave from the altar makes you feel like a winner. The impact of the architecture is made stronger because it's uncluttered—Zwingli's reforms led to a clean sweep of Catholic decor in 1519.

In the front are three **choir windows** by Augusto Giacometti (c. 1933). Mary and the Baby Jesus (at her feet) meet two of the three kings bearing their gifts, while angels hover above with offerings of flowers. In the **crypt** (stairs below altar), you'll see an original 15th-century statue of Charlemagne (a copy now fills its niche on the river side of the church exterior). The church is free and open daily (March–Oct 9:00–18:00, Nov–Feb 10:00–17:00, pick up English story of the Swiss Reformation). For 2 SF and 200 steps, you can enjoy a sweeping city view from atop the tower (Mon–Sat 9:15–17:00, Sun 12:30–17:00).

Leaving the church, go right and into the corner, where a door leads to a fine Romanesque **cloister** ringed with fanciful 12th-century carvings (free, Mon–Fri 9:00–18:00, closed Sat–Sun). Upon entering, take eight steps to the left and meet the sculptor (self-portrait on the highest arch).

• *Cross the river to another tall-steepled church.*

Fraumünster

This was founded as an abbey church for a convent in 853, when Zürich was little more than a village. The current building, which sits on the same footprint as its Carolingian predecessor, dates from 1250. With the Reformation of Zwingli, the church was taken by the Zürich town council in 1524 and—you know the drill— gutted to fit Zwingli's taste. Today, it's famous for its windows by Chagall, described in the "Fraumünster's Chagall Windows" sidebar on page 52 (Mon–Sat 9:00–12:00 & 14:00–18:00, Sun 14:00–18:00, occasional evening concerts).

From the Fraumünster to Lake Zürich: From the church, Poststrasse (continuing away from the river) takes you back to Bahnhofstrasse and the busy **Paradeplatz.** Survey the scene: The train station is a 10-minute walk to your right, and the lake is a few minutes to your left, down the classiest stretch of Bahnhofstrasse. You're facing Sprüngli, Zürich's top café for the

past century. Its "Luxemburgerli" *macarons*—little cream-filled, one-inch *macaron*-meringue hamburgers—are a local favorite (you can buy just a couple; if you buy 100 grams, you'll get a selection of 12). The café upstairs offers elegant finger-sandwich lunches. To the right is Credit Suisse, with a luxurious ground floor full of fancy shops worth a look. A bit farther (at #31) is the fine little Beyer watch museum (the watchmaker's personal collection is in the basement of his watch shop; 5 SF, Mon–Fri 14:00–18:00, closed Sat–Sun).

• *Turning left, follow Bahnhofstrasse to the boats and riverside terrace at Bürkliplatz. We'll finish this walk at...*

Lake Zürich (Zürichsee)

Lake Zürich is 17 miles long, 2.5 miles wide, and—because it's relatively shallow—warm enough for swimming in the summer. From here, you can enjoy the lakeside promenade (a fine strolling path 3 miles in either direction; left is sunnier and more interesting) or a short cruise. To go back to the station, catch tram #11 (from the inland side, across the street) or the riverboat-bus (both boat options described next).

Sights in Zürich

Cruises on Limmat River and Lake Zürich—You have two basic boat-ride options: 1) small, low-floating buses that take local commuters and joy-riding visitors up and down the river and to points nearby on the lake; and 2) big, romantic lake ships taking tourists on longer rides around Lake Zürich. All boats leave from Bürkliplatz (lake end of Bahnhofstrasse) and are covered by railpasses (but a cruise costs a flexi-day, which is fine if you're already using that day for a train trip to or from Zürich). None of the boats comes with commentary.

The low-to-the-water riverboat-buses (designed to squeeze

Fraumünster's Chagall Windows

The Fraumünster's claim to fame is its collection of 30-foot-tall stained-glass windows by Marc Chagall (1887–1985), the Russian-born French artist. Chagall gave an exhibit in Zürich in 1967. It was such a hit that the city offered the world-famous artist a commission. To their surprise, the 80-year-old Chagall accepted. Chagall designed the windows to stand in the church's spacious choir (zone behind the altar; underutilized in Protestant-style worship)—a space where he intuitively felt his unique mix of religious themes could flourish.

For the next three years, Chagall threw his heart and soul into the project, making the sketches at his home on the French Riviera, then working in close collaboration with a glassmaking factory in Reims, France. After the colored panes were made, Chagall personally painted the figures on with black outlines, which were then baked into the glass. Chagall spent weeks in Zürich overseeing the installation and completion.

His inimitable painting style—deep colors, simple figures, and shard-like Cubism—is perfectly suited to the medium of stained glass. Blending Jewish and Christian traditions, Chagall created a work that can make people of many faiths comfortable.

The five windows depict Bible scenes, culminating in the central image of the crucified Christ. From left to right, they are as follows:

1. The Prophets (red): The prophet Elisha (bottom) looks up to watch a horse-drawn chariot carry his mentor Elijah off to heaven. Farther up, Jeremiah (blue in color and mood) puts his hand to his head and ponders the destruction of wicked Jerusalem. Up in heaven (top), a multicolored, multifaceted God spins out his creation, sending fiery beams down to inspire his Prophets on earth. This window is artificially lit, as it's built into an interior wall.

2. Jacob (blue—Chagall's favorite color): Jacob (bottom, in deep purple amid deep blue) dreams of a ladder that snakes up to heaven, with red-tinged angels ascending and descend-

under the bridges) make a one-hour loop around the Zürich end of the lake and down the river to the train station and Swiss National Museum (2/hr, daily mid-April–mid-Oct generally 10:00–20:30, schedule posted at pier 6, buy ticket on boat; 4 SF for any ride, short or long; free with 24-hr transit pass, ZürichCARD, or Swiss Pass; www.zvv.ch). These buses can be handy for connecting the lake and the Swiss National Museum.

The big, touristy, lake-only boats are run by the Lake Zürich Navigation Company (8 SF for basic 1.5-hour trip, April–Oct daily 2/hr 11:00–19:30, Nov–March daily at 13:00 and 14:30 only, www.zsg.ch). They also offer longer trips, jazz and dinner cruises, and ing, symbolizing the connection between God above and Jacob's descendants (the Children of Israel) below.

3. Christ (green): The middle, and biggest, window depicts the central figure in God's plan of salvation—Jesus Christ, who, as the Messiah, fulfills the promises of the Old Testament prophets. Mother Mary suckles baby Jesus (bottom) amid the leafy family tree of Jesus' Old Testament roots. The central area is an indistinct jumble of events from Christ's life, leading up to his crucifixion. The life-size ascendant Christ is crucified in a traditional medieval pose, but he's surrounded by a circle that seems to be bearing him, resurrected, to heaven. Chagall signed and dated the work (1970).

4. Zion (yellow): King David (bottom right) strums his harp and sings a psalm, while behind him stands his mistress Bathsheba, who gave birth to Solomon, the builder of Jerusalem's temple. At the end of history, an angel (top) blows a ram's horn, announcing the establishment of a glorious New Jerusalem, which descends (center), featuring rust-colored, yellow, and green walls, domes, and towers.

5. The Law (blue): Moses, with horns of light and the Ten Commandments (top), looks sternly down on lawbreaking warriors on horseback wreaking havoc. At the bottom, an angel (in red) embraces the prophet Isaiah (very bottom) and inspires him to foretell the coming of the Messiah (in red, above the angel).

Everyone comes away with a different interpretation of this complex work, which combines images from throughout the Bible. The tall, skinny windows seem to emphasize the vertical connection between heaven above and earth below, both bathed in the same colored light. Some think Chagall used colors symbolically: Blue and green represent the earth, while red and yellow are heavenly radiance. But all recognize that the jumble of images—evoking the complexity of God's universe—reaches its Point Omega in the central window, celebrating the idea of salvation through Christ's crucifixion.

so on. The ticket kiosk is near pier 3; boats depart from piers 1 through 6.

▲**Swiss National Museum (Schweizerisches Landesmuseum)**—This massive museum, in a Neo-Gothic castle next to the train station, presents a wide range of Swiss historical artifacts, from the Stone Age to the present. In the late 19th century, it was clear that the world was changing, and the Swiss wanted to protect their unique heritage. A national competition was held, and Zürich (promising to provide a piece of land, pay for construction, and donate an impressive collection) won the privilege of hosting the country's National Museum. The quirky 1898 building is a

ZÜRICH

Switzerland's Clear-Headed Drug Policy

Like many of its neighbors, Switzerland has a progressive drug policy that aims to reduce the overall harm to its society, rather than focus on punishing users. Even by European standards, the country's approaches to soft and hard drugs are unusually pragmatic.

In 2002, Switzerland legalized marijuana use. When polls showed that more than 30 percent of the country had used marijuana, the parliament decided to decriminalize the drug, rather than criminalize a third of its population. But, while not wanting to clog its prisons with petty pot smokers, the country doesn't want to be known as another Holland, either. So the law remains a bit ambiguous: The Swiss can possess and use pot, but they can't sell it. Each spring, there's a push for stricter control. Word gets out that Switzerland is no haven for pot, and then things ease up.

Unlike marijuana, hard drugs remain absolutely illegal. Still, Swiss laws treat addicts as people needing medical help, rather than as criminals. Even in classy Zürich, you can see evidence of this policy. For instance, across the river from the station, on the far side of the Walche-Brücke bridge, there's a big, yellow, nondescript vending machine selling safe, government-subsidized syringes to heroin junkies. Go ahead, buy a box—it's about the cheapest souvenir you can purchase in Zürich.

mish-mash of architectural themes from around the country, and the slick new wing, which opened in 2009, resembles the vaulted sanctuary of a church. While some parts of this huge museum are fairly entertaining, especially in the new wing, on the whole it's not very well-presented. Most exhibits are dry and fairly old-school—they do little to bring Swiss history to life or make it easier to understand. However, now that the new wing's complete, the museum is rearranging its collection, which may improve the experience

Here are a few highlights: In the archaeology exhibit area on the ground floor, gold treasures and other finds are set among watercolors and models that hint at life in ancient times. You'll also find an exhibit on weapons, uniforms, and military equipment; Switzerland's largest collection of costumes, traditional garments, and decorative textiles; and pre-Reformation church art (all the fancy stuff the Protestants gutted from churches so they could concentrate). A Zwingli room focuses on the Reformation in Switzerland, and model living rooms show you how the Swiss lived from medieval times through the 19th century.

Cost, Hours, Location: 10 SF, covered by Swiss Pass, Tue–Sun 10:00–17:00, Thu until 19:00, closed Mon, audioguide-5 SF, borrow the English handout at the front desk for certain exhibits, mandatory bag check in lockers behind gift shop across from the entrance—2-SF deposit, Museumstrasse 2, good café in courtyard that leads into Platzspitz Park, tel. 044-218-6511, www.musee-suisse.ch.

Platzspitz Park—What used to be a riverside hangout for drug addicts has been cleaned up, and—apart from a rusty needle here and there—is now a safe, friendly place for a scenic picnic (free, daily 6:00–21:00, behind train station and Swiss National Museum, clean WC). From here, you can take a riverboat-bus down the river and around the lake (described earlier).

Kunsthaus Zürich—Switzerland's top collection of modern art includes works by Swiss artists (Alberto Giacometti, Johann Heinrich Füssli, and Ferdinand Hodler) as well as international greats such as Munch, Picasso, Kokoschka, Beckmann, Corinth, Monet, and Chagall. The younger generation is also represented, with pieces by Rothko, Merz, Twombly, Beuys, Bacon, and Baselitz (14 SF, free on Wed, not covered by Swiss Pass, open Wed–Fri 10:00–20:00, Tue and Sat–Sun 10:00–18:00, closed Mon; English audioguide, mandatory bag check downstairs in lockers—2-SF deposit, café; tram #3, #5, #8, or #9, or bus #31 to Kunsthaus stop, Heimplatz 1; tel. 044-253-8484, www.kunsthaus.ch).

Rietberg Museum—Filling historic villas set in a beautiful park, this museum houses art from Asia, Africa, the Americas, and the South Pacific (16 SF, covered by Swiss Pass, Tue and Fri–Sun 10:00–17:00, Wed–Thu 10:00–20:00, closed Mon, English audioguide-5 SF, tram #7 to Museum Rietberg stop, Villa Wesendonck, Gablerstrasse 15, tel. 044-206-3131, www.rietberg.ch).

Zürich Zoo—With 360 species, an impressive Madagascar rain forest hall, and a huge indoor exhibit, the city's zoo is a kid-friendly, fun place to see locals at play (22 SF, daily March–Oct 9:00–18:00, Nov–Feb until 17:00, tram #6 from Bahnhofstrasse in front of the station, direction: Zoo, ride to last stop, Zürichbergstrasse 221, tel. 084-896-6983, www.zoo.ch).

Uetliberg—If you want to see Zürich from above, take the excursion train that climbs from the main train station to this little mountain peak, high atop the city and lake. Buy your ticket at the station, then go downstairs to find the little red-orange S10 train on track 2 (16 SF round-trip, runs 6:30–24:00, 2–3/hr, 20 min, www.zvv.ch). From the Uetliberg station, it's a moderately steep, 10-minute climb up a paved pedestrian road to a hotel and a tall observation tower overlooking the city. The view is particularly striking at sunset. Sunny summer weekends bring hordes of local families with strollers. You can do the whole trip in about 1.5 hours.

Sleeping in Zürich

High season in Zürich is May, June, September, and October. About 10 days a year, festivals and conventions send prices higher.

My listings are near the train station, ideal for those passing through or leaving on an early-morning train or plane (train to airport: 6.10 SF, 15 min, leaves every 10 min). Your hotel may include the hotel tax in its price or charge you an extra 2.50 SF per person, per night. If I add "cable Internet" to the listing, it means you can access the Internet in your room with a cable, provided you have your own laptop. In this business-oriented city, rooms may be cheaper on weekends.

East of the Limmat River
Across the River from the Train Station

With this efficient, handy neighborhood as your home base, you're a quick stroll away from the train station, Swiss National Museum, riverboat dock, a huge underground mall of services and shops (under the station), and the Niederdorf restaurant and nightlife zone (down Stampfenbachstrasse). To reach these hotels, exit the train station from the huge hall with the "Guardian Angel" sculpture and the TI. Cross the river on the Walche-Brücke bridge, and use the map on page 57 to find your hotel.

$$ Hotel Bristol, run by Martin Hämmerli and his friendly staff, offers 56 modern, cozy rooms an eight-minute walk from

---

Sleep Code

(1 SF = about $1, country code: 41)
S = Single, **D** = Double/Twin, **T** = Triple, **Q** = Quad, **b** = bathroom, **s** = shower only. Unless otherwise noted, credit cards are accepted, English is spoken, and breakfast is included.

To help you sort easily through these listings, I've divided the rooms into three categories, based on the price for a standard double room with bath:

  $$$ Higher Priced—Most rooms 200 SF or more.
    $$ Moderately Priced—Most rooms between 140–200 SF.
     $ Lower Priced—Most rooms 140 SF or less.

Zürich Hotels and Restaurants

ZÜRICH

❶ Hotel Bristol	❽ Walhalla Hotel	⓯ Commihalle Rest.
❷ Hotel Leoneck	❾ To Seestrasse	⓰ Zeughauskeller
❸ Hotel Arlette	Apts. Drei Könige	⓱ Hiltl Veggie Rest.
❹ Hotel Alexander	❿ To easyHotel	⓲ Manora Cafeteria
❺ Hotel du Théâtre	⓫ Café Zähringer	⓳ Rest. Bauschänzli
❻ Alexander	⓬ Kantorei Rest.	⓴ Rest. Schipfe 16
Guest House	⓭ Wirtschaft Neumarkt	㉑ Internet Café
❼ City Backpacker	⓮ Rest. Swiss Chuchi	㉒ Free Bikes (3 Kiosks)
Hotel Biber		

the station. This is a business-quality place with family-run warmth. The staff at the reception desk are helpful and happy to answer travel questions (Sb-150–175 SF, small Db-160–195, big Db-190–240 SF, Tb-210–260 SF, Qb-230–285 SF, superior Qb-280–360 SF, 5 percent discount if you reserve direct and show this book, pay Internet access, pay cable Internet, laundry-15 SF, Stampfenbachstrasse 34, tel. 044-258-4444, fax 044-258-4400, www.hotelbristol.ch, info@hotelbristol.ch).

$$ Hotel Leoneck offers 80 modern yet kitschy, bovine-themed rooms at a good price. The hotel, with its cheery lobby and fine attached Crazy Cow restaurant (daily 6:30–22:30, www.crazy cow.ch), somehow manages to make Swiss cows seem cool. Enjoy the moo-velous mural in your room (Sb-120–170 SF, Db-170–230 SF, Tb-230–280 SF, Qb-280–320 SF, family rooms, ask for a 10 percent Rick Steves discount when you reserve, breakfast-17 SF, half the rooms are non-smoking, many have balcony, elevator, free Internet access and cable Internet, some street noise—ask for quieter back room, Leonhardstrasse 1, tel. 044-254-2222, fax 044-254-2200, www.leoneck.ch, info@leoneck.ch, Herr Gold). From the Walche-Brücke bridge, it's a 12-minute uphill walk, or take tram #6 or #10 from the station (direction: Bahnhof Oerlikon, two stops to Haldenegg, look for Crazy Cow restaurant). You can also take tram #10 directly from the airport (30 min).

$$ Hotel Arlette is a bit forgettable, but its 30 rooms are comfortable, functional, and centrally located in a quiet neighborhood (Sb-135–185 SF, Db-175–250 SF, pay Internet access, pay Wi-Fi, Stampfenbachstrasse 26, tel. 044-252-0032, fax 044-252-0923, hotel.arlette@bluewin.ch, Schlotter family).

In the Niederdorf

The atmospheric, cobblestoned old town of Zürich lies across the river and a short walk from the station. During the day, it's busy with shoppers and workers on lunch breaks; at night, the restaurants and clubs keep the pedestrian streets vibrant. To reach the Niederdorf on foot from the train station, cross the Bahnhofbrücke bridge, go through the square called Central (again, beware the silent streetcars), and head to the right along Niederdorfstrasse.

$$$ Hotel Alexander is a good business-class hotel in a very central location offering a decent value (Sb-150–180 SF, Db-200–230 SF, extra bed-30 SF, 10 percent discount if you show this book, air-con, Wi-Fi, Niederdorfstrasse 40, tel. 044-251-8203, fax 044-252-7425, www.hotel-alexander.ch, info@hotel-alexander.ch).

$$$ Hotel du Théâtre occupies a renovated little trapezoid-shaped theater. The 50 thespian-themed rooms are small but luxurious, with triple-paned windows that keep out tram noise. The breakfast room/lounge overlooks the Polybahn funicular (Sb-

150–215 SF, Db-200–240 SF, breakfast-18 SF, Wi-Fi, Seilergraben 69, Centralplatz, tel. 044-267-2670, www.hotel-du-theatre.ch, info@hotel-du-theatre.ch).

$$ Alexander Guest House is the annex to (and one block away from) the Hotel Alexander, listed earlier. Its 20 rooms, all with twin beds, are basic and uninspiring, but they're also clean, quiet, and perfectly good (Sb-95–130 SF, Db-140–180 SF, extra bed-25 SF, ask for a 10 percent Rick Steves discount when you book, contact through Hotel Alexander—listed earlier—where you'll also have breakfast, Zähringerstrasse 16).

Hostel: **$ City Backpacker Hotel Biber,** buried right in the middle of the Niederdorf action three floors above a restaurant, offers the cheapest backpacker beds in the old center, with a cool ambience aimed at young travelers (65 bunks in 4- to 6-bed dorms for 35 SF each, S-73 SF, D-110 SF, towels-3 SF, sheets-3 SF, private rooms include sheets, no breakfast, pay Internet access, free Wi-Fi, lockers, kitchen, smoky lobby, terrace, street noise at night, no curfew, no membership needed, reception open daily 8:00–12:00 & 15:00–22:00, 8-minute walk to station at Niederdorfstrasse 5, tel. 044-251-9015, www.city-backpacker.ch, sleep@city-backpacker.ch).

West of the Limmat River
Near the Train Station
$$$ Walhalla Hotel, just behind the train station, has 48 modern, spacious rooms (Sb-170–200 SF, Db-235–275 SF, Tb-300–350 SF, family room-350–400 SF, cheaper on weekends, free Wi-Fi, Limmatstrasse 5, tel. 044-446-5400, fax 044-446-5454, www.walhalla-hotel.ch, walhalla-hotel@bluewin.ch). Their guest house annex, around the corner, rents 26 simpler but ample rooms for less (Sb-127–147 SF, Db-194–224 SF).

Farther from the Station
$$ Seestrasse Apartments Drei Könige offers studios with kitchenettes for a good price in a classy neighborhood near the Rietberg Museum. The units are in a stately Art Nouveau building rented out by the fancy Hotel Ascot down the street, and the lake is a five-minute walk away (Db-160–210 SF, cheaper by the week, pay Wi-Fi, Seestrasse 65, tel. 044-283-1777, www.seestrasse-apartments.ch, info@seestrasse-apartments.ch). From the station, take tram #7 to the Museum Rietberg stop, and cross the street to #65.

$ easyHotel is a decent value in this pricey town, with small, modern rooms located a bit away from all the sights but still only a 10–15-minute walk from the station. Although the base rate is strangely cheap (Sb/Db-70–95 SF), you'll pay a little bit for each additional service you want—breakfast, Wi-Fi, watching the TV in your room, room-cleaning service during your stay, and so on—which can add up (Zwinglistrasse 14, toll tel. 0900-327-994, www .easyhotel.com, zuerich@easyhotelschweiz.ch). From the station, take bus #31 (direction: Schlieren Zentrum) to the Kanonengasse stop, walk away from station one block down Kanonengasse, then right on Zwinglistrasse to #14.

Eating in Zürich

The Niederdorf is Zürich's dining district, and the traffic-free Niederdorfstrasse is its restaurant row. And though the count-less eateries lining this main drag don't offer the best values, the people-watching is hard to beat. Browse the street and survey the eating options (including many colorful ethnic places). All of these recommendations are within a few minutes' walk of this spine of Zürich's people zone. Many of the venerable guild houses—no longer economic powers—are now convivial tradi-tional restaurants.

East of the Limmat River
In the Niederdorf

Café Zähringer is an artsy, bohemian co-op with a passion for serving reasonably priced healthy food to people who take time to keep life in balance. Linger in the stay-awhile interior, or enjoy the leafy seating out on the square—a block from where Lenin lived before heading back to Russia (22–25-SF daily specials, always good veggie and vegan plates, organic produce, salads, also meat dishes and wok dishes, famously good coffee, daily until 24:00, Zähringerplatz 11, tel. 044-252-0500). You may happen to notice the sweet smell of an herb not on the menu.

Kantorei Restaurant serves well-presented modern Medi-terranean cuisine with an Italian touch in a classy but unpreten-tious setting. Sit inside or out on the quiet, atmospheric square next to a fountain (30–40-SF plates, 17–20-SF lunch specials, daily 11:30–14:00 & 18:00–23:00, proud of its wine list, good vegetables, Neumarkt 2, tel. 044-252-2727).

Wirtschaft Neumarkt, tucked away in the old town, offers creative international dishes and prides itself in using only healthy ingredients such as organic vegetables, salads, and additive-free meat, which justifies the higher prices. The interior is unremark-able—eat outdoors here. In good weather, the restaurant's long and fun-loving garden is packed with in-the-know locals eating well under chestnut trees. The upper garden is best, so it's usu-ally filled with diners who knew to make reservations (28–38-SF plates, lunch specials, Mon–Sat 11:30–14:00 & 18:00–24:00, closed

Sun, extensive wine list and good beer on tap, Neumarkt 5, tel. 044-252-7939).

Restaurant Swiss Chuchi is a busy place popular with tourists and locals for traditional cheese dishes. They offer a fun selection of cheese and meat fondues. The 25–30-SF fondue is splittable if you order another dish or a salad (daily 11:30–24:00, indoor and outdoor seating, follow your nose to Rosengasse 10 on Hirschenplatz, tel. 044-266-9666).

Across the River from the Train Station

Commihalle Restaurant, near several recommended hotels, is part of a popular Italian chain. Their 35-SF "Tavolata" special—ideal for big eaters—gets you an antipasto buffet, pasta dish, main meat dish, and dessert-buffet finale (available only Tue–Sat 18:30–21:30). The interior is plain but dressy, and there's outdoor seating (filling 17–25-SF pastas, no pizza, always a good vegetarian option, daily 11:00–24:00, Stampfenbachstrasse 8, tel. 044-250-5960).

West of the Limmat River
Off Bahnhofstrasse

Zeughauskeller fills an atmospheric 500-year-old armory with medieval battle gear (William Tell's crossbow?) and happy eaters enjoying typically Swiss cuisine. Their fun, accessible menu offers traditional meals, including lots of soft meats (but no cheese, which the Swiss don't like to smell unless they're eating it). *Kalbsgeschnetzeltes*—calf's liver with *Rösti* (30 SF)—is a house specialty and a local fave. There's outdoor seating, but the interior has all the character and stays cool even when it's hot (18–33-SF plates, daily until 23:00, plenty of beer and wine, kid-friendly, near Paradeplatz at Bahnhofstrasse 28—go down In Gassen lane to find entrance, tel. 044-211-2690).

Hiltl Vegetarian Restaurant is a popular treat for vegetarians. In 1898, Ambrosius Hiltl was fighting rheumatoid arthritis. His doctor said, "No more meat," so Ambrosius established the world's first vegetarian restaurant. Today his great-great-great-grandson Rolf carries on the family tradition. Historic photos decorate the walls, but the loyal clientele's attention is on the enticing buffet and friendly conversation. At dinner, along with the salad buffet, there's an Indian buffet (endorsed by Indian tourists). Fill your plate, which is sold by the weight—generally 23–28 SF per hearty meal. At lunch, the salad bar is cheaper, but with fewer Indian options. The à la carte menu comes with delightful salads, curries, and fancy fruit juices. Hiltl's food is legendary for its freshness and lack of preservatives (daily 6:00–23:00, 2 blocks off Bahnhofstrasse where it kinks at Sihlstrasse 30, tel. 044-227-7000).

Manora, a cafeteria at the Manor department store on

Bahnhofstrasse, is reliably good and fast. Choose between a fresh salad bar (big plate-10 SF) and a variety of main dishes (10–15 SF). It's popular with locals—eat early or late (Mon–Fri 9:00–20:00, Sat 9:00–17:00, closed Sun, fifth floor, Bahnhofstrasse 75).

Along the Limmat River

Restaurant Bauschänzli is both a fancy riverside restaurant and a sloppy beer garden (a block inland from the boat docks at Bürkliplatz). Filling a small island on the river, its fun-loving and popular self-serve restaurant offers Zürich's best beer-garden experience—like a Munich *Biergarten* without the kraut. Help yourself to the cheap salad bar and the beer and wine from big casks (grab the glass or carafe of your choice). *Citro* (lemonade) is mixed with lager to make a shandy (known here as a *Panaché*). *Süssmost* is apple juice. The garden is open daily in good weather May through mid-September (call ahead if it's raining), followed in fall by a raucous Oktoberfest (40-SF plates, daily 11:00–23:00, live Bulgarian folk band plays Euro-folk music daily as locals dance—15:00–17:00 & 19:15–22:30, Stadthausquai 2, tel. 044-212-4919, reserve only for the fine-dining restaurant).

Restaurant Schipfe 16, gorgeously and peacefully situated on the river with an old-town view, is part of a city-run organization providing work for hard-to-employ people. It was originally a soup kitchen, but the location was just too charming to stay that way, so it's now open to the general public. Don't expect polished service; instead, feel good that you're contributing to a worthy cause and enjoying healthy and decent food at a great price. The best seats are right along the river (lunch only, 20-SF two-course daily specials, Mon–Fri 10:00–16:00, closed Sat–Sun, Schipfe 16, tel. 044-211-2122).

Zürich Connections

From Zürich by Train to: Luzern (2/hr, 1 hr), **Interlaken** (at least hourly, 2–3 hrs, 1–2 transfers), **Bern** (2/hr, 1 hr), **Murten** (2/hr, 1.75 hrs, transfer in Bern, Fribourg, or Kerzers), **Appenzell** (2/hr, 1.75 hrs with transfer in Gossau or 2.25 hrs with transfer in St. Gallen), **Lausanne** (2/hr, 2.25 hrs), **Zermatt** (at least hourly, 3.5 hrs, 1–2 changes), **Chur** (2/hr, 1.25–1.5 hrs), **Lugano** (hourly, 2.75 hrs, half with easy change in Arth-Goldau), **Berlin** (roughly hourly, 8–9 hrs), **Munich** (4/day direct, 4.25 hrs, more with transfers), **Frankfurt** (4/day direct, 4 hrs, more with transfers), **Vienna** (2/day direct, 8 hrs, plus 1 night train, 9 hrs). Train info: toll tel. 0900-300-300 or www.rail.ch.

Zürich Airport

Smooth, compact, and user-friendly, Zürich Airport is an eye-opening introduction to Swiss efficiency. There are three levels: 1) train station on the bottom floor, with train info and ticket desk; 2) main level, with a top-end food court, Migros and Co-op supermarkets, fancy souvenir shops, post office (easy to mail things home—pack light), banks, ATMs, and lockers; and 3) upper level, with departures, TI, lockers, and Internet kiosks. Eateries and ATMs are plentiful before and after the security checkpoint. For flight information, call the automated toll number: 0900-300-313 (press 2 for English).

Upon arrival by plane, pick up a free baggage cart. The train station underneath the airport can whisk you about anywhere you'd want to go in Europe, including **downtown Zürich** (6.10 SF, 15 min, leaves every 10 min 5:00–24:00, much cheaper than the 50–60-SF taxi ride). Your train ticket into Zürich is good for the following two hours on all city public transportation.

Sleeping at the Airport: Since most of my recommended accommodations are near the station, and the train connection to the airport is so fast and frequent, there's little reason to sleep at the airport. But if you're catching an early-morning flight, consider the **$$$ Radisson Blu Hotel** (Db-from 195 SF, tel. 044-800-4040, radissonblu.com/hotel-zurichairport).

From Zürich Airport by Train to: Luzern (2/hr, 1.25 hrs, most with change in Zürich), **Interlaken** (2/hr, 2.25 hrs, transfer in Bern), **Bern** (2/hr, 1.25 hrs), **Murten** (hourly, 2 hrs, change in Bern), **Appenzell** (2/hr, 1.5 hrs with transfer in Gossau), **Lausanne** (2/hr, 2.5 hrs, some with change in Biel), **Zermatt** (at least hourly, 4.5 hrs, 1–2 changes), **Chur** (2/hr, 1.75–2 hrs, change at Zürich main station), **Lugano** (hourly, 3 hrs, 1–2 changes), **Munich** (4/day direct, 4–4.25 hrs, more with 3–4 changes, 4.75–5.5 hrs).

ZÜRICH

LUZERN
and CENTRAL SWITZERLAND

Luzern has long been Switzerland's tourism capital. Situated on the edge of a lake, with a striking alpine panorama as a backdrop, Luzern was a regular stop on the "Grand Tour" route of Europe during the Romantic era, entertaining visitors such as Mark Twain, Goethe, and Queen Victoria. And with a charming old town, a pair of picture-perfect wooden bridges, a gaggle of fine museums, and its famous weeping lion, there's still enough in Luzern to earn it a place on any Swiss itinerary.

Luzern also makes a fine home base for exploring the surrounding region, known as Central Switzerland (Zentralschweiz). A wide variety of boat trips, mountain lifts, and other excursions make fun day trips.

Planning Your Time

Many visitors home-base in Luzern for a week of side-trips. While I'd rather settle in the high country instead, Luzern is worth at least a full day and two nights. To get the most out of your day, begin with the TI's two-hour walking tour (daily May–Oct, Wed and Sat only Nov–April), or follow the self-guided walk in this chapter. Then hit the museums that might interest you most: Art buffs flock to the Rosengart Collection for its Picasso exhibit; gearheads will have a ball at the Swiss Transport Museum; and those interested in geology dig the Glacier Garden. In the late afternoon, take a peaceful boat trip on Lake Luzern, then wander the town's scenic bridges at sunset.

Luzern

Luzern (loot-SERN, sometimes spelled "Lucerne" in English) is a charming midsize city with about 60,000 residents (and a metropolitan area sprawling to almost 200,000). It sits where the Reuss River flows out of Lake Luzern (Vierwaldstättersee). South of the river is the train station and the bustling new town (Neustadt), and north of the river is the quaint, traffic-free old town (Altstadt). The river is spanned by a series of pedestrian bridges, including two classic wooden ones: the Chapel Bridge, with its famous stone water tower, and the Mill Bridge. Museums, restaurants, and hotels are scattered on both sides of the Reuss River.

Orientation to Luzern

Tourist Information

Luzern's helpful, modern TI is right inside the train station (mid-June–mid-Sept daily 8:30–19:30; May–mid-June and mid-Sept–Oct Mon–Fri 8:30–18:30, Sat–Sun 9:00–19:30; Nov–April Mon–Fri 8:30–17:30, Sat–Sun 9:00–13:00; Bahnhofstrasse 3, tel. 041-227-1717, phone not answered on weekends, www.luzern.org).

At the TI, pick up the free, informative *City Guide* (which you'll get stamped at your hotel for sightseeing discounts—see "Helpful Hints," later), and browse through their other literature. Confirm the details for their walking tour (described later, under "Tours in Luzern"). The TI also provides a free room-booking service (with some great last-minute deals) and sells tickets to various activities around town, such as boat trips. If you have kids (or are one), ask about the pedal boats.

The TI also sells the **LucerneCard,** which includes unlimited travel on local trains and buses (but not boats), as well as half off the walking tour and the entry fees to most local museums (19 SF/24 hrs, 27 SF/48 hrs, 33 SF/72 hrs). Buying this card makes sense only if you don't have a Swiss Pass (which already covers many Luzern attractions) and plan on doing a lot of sightseeing. For example, if you're going to the expensive Swiss Transport Museum and at least one other museum, a one-day LucerneCard pays for itself.

Arrival in Luzern

Luzern's train station is user-friendly. The TI is on the town side of the station, next to Burger King, just off track 3. Most other important services are down the escalators at the front of the tracks, in an underground shopping mall called RailCity. There you'll find the ticket desks, WCs, ATMs, lockers, a convenient self-service cafeteria, a long-hours grocery store, and lots of other shops and restaurants. If all the other stores in town are closed (such as on Sundays), head for RailCity.

For the quickest route into the old town, ride any escalator down into the underground RailCity and follow signs to *Altstadt* (to avoid having to cross the busy streets above).

In front of the train station is Bahnhofplatz (where buses fan out in every direction) and the pleasant lakefront.

Helpful Hints

Medical Help: Permanence is a welcoming drop-in medical clinic open 24/7 at the train station (downstairs in RailCity, near Co-op grocery store).

Visitors Card for Sightseeing Discounts: When you check into your Luzern hotel, have them stamp your *City Guide* tourist brochure (free at TI). This stamped brochure becomes a Visitors Card *(Gästekarte)* that gives you minor discounts at all of Luzern's museums. Remember to carry this brochure with you and ask for the discount when buying entrance tickets.

Internet Access: An Internet point is inside the **TI** (4 SF/10 min). The cheaper **Inside** is downstairs, in RailCity (3 SF/15 min, 8 SF/hr, Mon–Sat 9:00–22:00, Sun 10:00–21:00). Even cheaper is the city **library** *(Stadtbibliothek),* situated upstairs in the same building as the Bourbaki Panorama (4 SF/hr—which is also the minimum charge, 10-SF deposit for plastic card required, free Wi-Fi, Mon–Fri 11:00–18:30, Thu until 20:00, Sat 9:30–16:00, closed Sun, Löwenplatz 10, tel. 041-417-0707, www.bvl.ch). You'll also see other Internet signs scattered around town.

Post Office: The main post office *(Hauptpost)* is kitty-corner from the train station (Mon–Fri 7:30–18:30, Sat 8:00–16:00, closed Sun).

Cinema: In Switzerland, movies are shown in their original version with subtitles. The Bourbaki Panorama building has several screens.

Bike Rental: You can rent bikes at the train station and enjoy Luzern's delightful lakeside bike paths (25 SF/half-day, 33 SF/day, 5 SF less with Eurailpass or Swiss Pass; at SBB counter #21 downstairs in RailCity, www.sbb.ch/mobilitaet).

Laundry: Take your dirty laundry to **Jet Wasch** (17 SF wash and dry, Mon–Fri 8:00–12:00 & 14:00–18:00, Sat 9:00–16:00, closed Sun, Bruchstrasse 28, tel. 041-240-0151, www.jet wasch.ch). Ask nicely and they may deliver.

Water Fountains: Luzern is proud of its clean drinking water and its more than 200 public fountains, each with a fun design and spouting potable water. In the summer, you'll see locals take full advantage of these fountains, refilling their plastic water bottles again and again.

Getting Around Luzern

Except for the Swiss Transport Museum, all the sights, hotels, and restaurants recommended in this chapter are within easy walking distance from the station. The Swiss Transport Museum is a 30-minute walk around Lake Luzern. To get there without the hike, catch bus #6, #8, or #24, or take a boat (summer only) to the Verkehrshaus stop. Buses and all boats depart from Bahnhofplatz, in front of the train station. The TI's *City Guide* includes a map of bus routes. On the bus, the stops for all the major sights are announced.

Public transportation prices in Luzern depend on which zones you travel in; a single ticket within the primary zone (Zone 1) costs 2.80 SF. A short ride of up to six stops—which would cover the trip from the town center to the Swiss Transport Museum or the Lion Monument—costs 2 SF. A day pass is 10 SF. All public transit in Luzern is covered by the Swiss Pass (and, except for boats, by the LucerneCard). Transit info: www.vbl.ch.

Tours in Luzern

Walking Tour—A two-hour tour in both English and German is offered every morning in summer (18 SF, departs from TI at 9:45, daily May–Oct, only Wed and Sat Nov–April).

Tourist Train—A tacky little train does a 40-minute circuit of the city's sights, departing from Hotel Schweizerhof (12 SF, 25-SF combo-ticket also includes walking tour and saves 5 SF, buy tickets from driver, headphone commentary, daily Easter–Oct, runs hourly 10:00–19:00 June–Aug, less frequently outside summer, tel. 041-220-1100, www.citytrain.ch).

Local Guide—**Ursula Korner** is a good guide (160 SF/2 hrs, tel. 041-248-6048, ursula.korner@ko5ive.com). The TI has a list of other guides.

Self-Guided Walk

Reuss River Stroll

This self-guided orientation stroll will give you a brief overview of the town—you'll walk up along the Reuss (pronounced "royce") River, then across one of Luzern's famous wooden bridges, then back through the old town. Begin at Bahnhofplatz, the busy zone between the lake and the train station. Stand in front of the big stone arch.

Bahnhofplatz: This is the transportation hub of Luzern—and all of Central Switzerland. From the area in front of the

Luzern's Reuss River Stroll

station, buses zip you anywhere in town. Along the lakefront, you can catch a boat for a lazy cruise around Lake Luzern. And underneath you is the extensive RailCity shopping mall, honeycombed with pedestrian passageways leading to different parts of town. The big stone **arch** was the entrance of the venerable old train station—built in the late 19th

century when Switzerland became a top tourist spot, with Luzern as its main attraction. But it burned down in 1971 and was replaced with the modern station. Today, the arch hides vents for the huge underground parking lot below. This is a popular evening meeting spot for local teens.

• *The huge modern building with the big overhanging roof (on your right, with your back to the station) is the...*

Culture and Conference Center (Kultur-und-Kongresszentrum): This building, finished in 1998 by Parisian architect Jean Nouvel, features a concert hall that hosts the Luzern Festival, one of Switzerland's biggest music events (mid-Aug–mid-Sept, www.lucernefestival.ch). It also holds the **Luzern Museum of**

1. Bahnhofplatz
2. Culture & Conference Center
3. Chapel Bridge
4. Jesuit Church
5. Reuss River Weir System
6. Mill Bridge
7. Mühlenplatz
8. Weinmarkt Square
9. Hirschenplatz
10. Weggisgasse
11. Sternenplatz
12. St. Peter's Chapel & City View

LUZERN

Art (Kunstmuseum Luzern; described later, under "Sights in Luzern").

Lake water is pumped up, into, through, and out of this building; if you wander around its far side, you'll see open channels that go right through the middle of the structure (blocked by benches, so distracted tourists don't fall in), as well as a big pond. The architect claims this design recalls earlier times, when Luzern was swamplands...but it more likely recalls his own original plans for the building. Nouvel wanted to put the center out in the middle of the lake. When he was voted down by the people of Luzern, he decided to surround it with water anyway. The plaza under the roof (which reflects the lake and weather, further incorporating the building into the surrounding environment) is a busy community space popular for open-air concerts.

• *Now walk in the opposite direction from the conference center, across the busy street. Stroll Bahnhofstrasse along the river until you have a good view of Luzern's most famous landmark, the wooden...*

Chapel Bridge (Kapellbrücke): Luzern began as a fishing village. By the 13th century, traffic streaming between northern and southern Europe went through nearby Gotthard Pass, and Luzern became a bustling trading center. In the first half of the 14th century, this bridge was built at an angle, to connect the town's medieval fortifications. The bridge was part of the city defense system, so the "window" openings facing the lake are smaller than those on the inland side, giving defenders more cover. The octagonal stone **Water Tower** (Wasserturm) was built around 1300.

In the 17th century, the bridge was decorated with paintings depicting the development of the town, as well as its two patron saints. In 1993, a leisure boat moored under the bridge caught fire, and before long, Luzern's wooden landmark was in flames. (A plaque before the start of the bridge tells the story.) When you venture onto the bridge, you'll notice the wood is a lighter color—that is, newer—in the middle. Chapel Bridge was painstakingly rebuilt, but many of its famous paintings were lost. Those still remaining under the wooden roof at the ends of the bridge are restorations of the 17th-century originals; those in the middle were in storage during the fire and were therefore saved. Boats are no longer allowed under the bridge, it's now strictly non-smoking, and you'll notice tiny security cameras everywhere.

Wander out onto the bridge itself. Notice the colorful **paintings** overhead. The coats of arms on the paintings tell you which aristocratic families sponsored them. Painting #1 features a legendary and formidable giant, an icon of Luzern you'll see all over town. This big boy dates back to the Middle Ages, when mammoth bones discovered locally were mistakenly identified as the bones of a 15-foot-tall human giant. Painting #2 shows an angel shining a divine light on the place where the town would be born (and where, in the eighth century, a monastery was founded). The name "Luzern" is derived from the Latin word for "light." Painting #3 shows Luzern circa 1400—see how the bridge was already part of the city fortifications. Painting #6 shows a bigger city, as it looked in 1630. In the middle, a painting features the town's patron saint, Mauritius (a plaque midbridge tells why he matters to Luzern).

Paintings #9 and #10 are left charred black as a reminder of the tragic fire.

Any swans out? Locals say they originated as a gift from the French king Louis XIV, in appreciation for the protection his Swiss Guards gave him. Today, local children make sure the swans get their daily bread.

• *Now head back to the train-station end of the bridge, and continue up the river. Enter the big, white...*

Jesuit Church (Jesuitenkirche): This was the first major Baroque church in Switzerland (built 1666–1677; free entry, open daily 6:00–18:30). It's dedicated to the great missionary Francis

Xavier, a co-founder of the Jesuit order, who's shown on the facade baptizing Asians (depicted looking like American Indians).

Even though Luzern was a relatively small town back then, the pope wanted to establish a strong presence in Central Switzerland to empower the local Catholics during the tense times of the Protestant Reformation. The interior of the church once dripped with Baroque stucco. It's been retouched in the lighter Rococo style (c. 1750). Rich as it looks, there's no real marble here—what you see is stucco made from ground-up marble laid smoothly and economically upon a wooden foundation.

The decorations on the ceiling celebrate the life (and afterlife) of Xavier. After the missionary dies, you see him heaven-bound (in the center). In an exuberant setting that includes both this church and Luzern's landmark Chapel Bridge, the pope's representative and townsfolk gather to wish him Godspeed. Xavier's cart is pulled by an elephant, a leopard, and a camel, all commemorating his mission trips to the exotic Far East. Riding his chariot into heaven, he anticipates a hero's welcome. As the local music school uses the church pipe organ for practice, you may enjoy an impromptu concert.

In the second niche up on the right, you can meet the only Swiss saint: Brother Klaus, a 15th-century hermit monk who lived in the nearby mountains. He was a great peacemaker between the cantons and is considered the original Swiss isolationist. Since Klaus' time, Switzerland has employed this ethic of avoiding pointless entanglement in foreign squabbles. The statue wears Klaus' original robe. His walking stick is at his feet.

• *Back outside, continue strolling downriver toward Luzern's other wooden bridge. You'll pass the recommended Opus Restaurant and iron pedestrian bridge (at the narrowest crossing spot, marking the location of Luzern's first bridge in the 12th century). Stop at the spiky fence partially damming up the river.*

Reuss River Weir System: This big river flows out of the lake. Lake Luzern's main source of water is snowmelt, which trickles in from streams coming off the surrounding mountains. The water drains out of the lake here on its way to the Rhine. Luzern is

LUZERN

responsible for controlling the flow of water and preventing the flooding of lakeside villages by maintaining the lake level. In the mid-19th century, the city devised and built a simple yet ingenious extendable dam (*Nadelwehr*, "spiked weir"). When the water is highest (in the spring), they remove spikes to open the flow; as the summer wears on and the water level drops, they gradually broaden the dam to keep the flow steady. In the winter, they close the dam entirely to keep the lake level high enough for boats. Construction in the river is ongoing, as the city repairs the system. If you're an engineer, you'll want to study the information posted just before the Jesuit Church, or on the far side of the Mill Bridge.

• *Continuing along the river, you'll pass the Depot History Museum on your left (described later, under "Sights in Luzern") before coming to the wooden...*

Mill Bridge (Spreuerbrücke): Unlike the rebuilt Chapel Bridge, this one's original—and the city is determined to keep it that way (try to find the low-profile security cameras). Cross the bridge, appreciating the fine old 17th-century paintings. Painting #1 shows Luzern's favorite giant again, with the blue-and-white city and cantonal banners under the double eagle of the Holy Roman Empire—a reminder that the German emperor granted free status to the city. The flip side shows Judgment Day, with some going to heaven and others to hell. As you cross the bridge, notice that each painting includes a skeleton. Townsfolk crossed the bridge daily, and these scenes provided vivid reminders that nobody, in any walk of life, can escape death (an especially poignant message in times of war and plague, when these were painted). Like the other wooden bridge, this bridge was part of the city fortification—its downstream defending wall is higher.

Midway across is a little 16th-century chapel, built to guard against destruction by flood. A line of family crests acknowledges the volunteers who, over the years, have kept the chapel decorated according to the season. Since 1987, this has been the work of Frau Segesser. While you're paused here, notice the serious woodwork.

The wide stretch at the end of the bridge was to accommodate wagons delivering grain or whatever else was to be milled. Once upon a time, 10 mills churned here—this was the medieval industrial center of Luzern. The "Spreu" in the bridge's name means "chaff" (the sheath surrounding the wheat), which was separated from the wheat at the mill. You can see sketches of these mills as

LUZERN

you leave the bridge (on the red wall on the left). A turbine that generated power in 1889 sits quiet on the left, and the tradition of harnessing water power continues here. The stream of water spurting into the air (on the right) indicates that the modern hydroelectric plant—underwater beneath you—is engaged. It creates enough power for 1,000 households.

After crossing the bridge, turn right to find yourself in **Mühlenplatz.** This square, which is traffic-free in summer, marks the entrance to the old town (if weir construction is still underway during your visit, you may find this square torn up). The recommended, riverfront Hug bakery on your right is a good place for lunch or a snack. Across the square, a fun facade tells the story of the wine god Bacchus (to the right of the river murals, on the front of Fischer Stube, Mühlenplatz 11).

• *At the top of the square (under the Swiss Marilyn Monroe), head right on Kramgasse, then take the first left onto Weinmarktgasse, which leads to...*

Weinmarkt: In medieval Luzern, this square served as a marketplace for wine (as the name implies). The big mural on the decrepit green building at the top of the square looks like the Last Supper, but it's actually the Wedding Feast at Cana, where Jesus turned water into wine. On the right (as you face the mural), the facade of a now-gone pharmacy comes with a wise saying, *Amor medicabilis nvllis herbis* (roughly, "No medicine can cure a broken heart"). Across the square is a modern building with a secret message hiding in its strange zigzags. Start at the top left and read: W-E-I-N-M-A-R-K-T. The soldiers on the fine 15th-century fountain are there to remind visitors that this town is tough and strong.

• *Leave the square on the left side of the big mural. You'll walk several yards to...*

Hirschenplatz: This square hasn't always been a square—notice the footprints of two former buildings in the middle. It's named for the Hirschen ("Deer") Restaurant, with the elaborate golden sign. Across from that, try to guess who used to have a shop in the big green building. Yep—the jeweler (see all the rings?). Notice that, along with a happy cupid at the top, death is lurking again. To the right of that building, look for the painting of a famous German writer with the legend *"Goethe logierte hier 1779."* Goethe—the "German Shakespeare"—visited Luzern and stayed in a hotel on this corner. To the left of the building with the rings, the grand facade on the Dornach House, from 1899, celebrates the 400-year anniversary of the last battle against the Germans. Switzerland has enjoyed a durable understanding that there can be disagreements—but no wars—with its historically aggressive and militaristic neighbor to the north.

Continue out of the square onto the busy **Weggisgasse.** As you stroll, consider that every building in the old town—whether new or rebuilt—is required to offer residential apartments to prevent this historic zone from becoming only office space and touristy shops.

• *After two blocks, you'll come to the Manor department store, with the recommended, tasty, and convenient Manora self-service cafeteria on the top floor. Turn right after the Manor store and walk one block to...*

Sternenplatz: This tiny square is dominated by the colorful facade of the Restaurant Fritschi. The paintings feature symbols from Luzern's annual Mardi Gras celebration—the city's biggest event, called Fasnacht here. Pictured near the top of the building are the restaurant owners, Mr. and Mrs. Fritschi, celebrating Fasnacht by wearing masks and throwing oranges. Flanking them are their trusty servants, a nanny and a jester—who, in this case, bear a striking resemblance to the Fritschis. Below them is the story of Fasnacht: The cock calls at 5:00 in the morning the Thursday before Ash Wednesday (on the left), and the people get up to frighten winter away. Mr. and Mrs. Fritschi arrive on their wagon to kick off the festivities (on the right). Flying around the scene are oranges—traditionally tossed from the Fritschis to their adoring fans. Once rare here in winter, oranges are special to the festivities, as they mark the beginning of spring.

Continue down the street at the bottom of the square (Hans-Holbein-Gasse), and you'll come upon a colorful fountain with masks of Herr and Frau Fritschi and their servants. Continue to the riverfront, walking around **St. Peter's Chapel,** the namesake of Chapel Bridge—which you've arrived at once again. We finish our walk here, with the classic Luzern view: the Chapel Bridge and Water Tower, with Mount Pilatus hovering in the background.

• *From here you may want to take a...*

Lakefront Stroll: Consider walking from here along the lakefront, past the National Hotel toward the Swiss Transport Museum. The delightful pathway was built during the tourism boom in the 19th century, when this part of the bay was filled in and fancy resort hotels went up—giving this city the nickname "Monte Carlo of Switzerland." Simply follow the tree-lined waterfront promenade (Nationalquai) that begins near the Hofkirche (the big church with the pointy spires). Believe it or not, Luzern's wooden Chapel Bridge used to stretch all the way to that church.

Sights in Luzern

If you'll be doing a lot of sightseeing here, review your options for saving money: Many Luzern sights are covered by the Swiss Pass (as noted in this section); your hotel can stamp your *City Guide* brochure to turn it into a free Visitors Card that gives you minor discounts at many attractions; and the LucerneCard offers half-price entry to most of the major sights in town (for details, see "Tourist Information," earlier).

Museums

Luzern is charming enough that simply strolling the streets and bridges and cruising the lake would be enough for a happy day of sightseeing. But the city also offers some fine museums, especially if you're into modern art.

▲▲**Rosengart Collection (Sammlung Rosengart Luzern)**—In the 1930s and 1940s, wealthy resident Siegfried Rosengart palled around with all-star modern artists, financing and collecting their works. This museum displays the fruits of his labor. The building's three floors boast works from all the big names from the late 19th and early 20th centuries, with an emphasis on the art of Pablo Picasso and Paul Klee.

The first floor features an extensive **Picasso** collection, including 32 paintings and some 100 drawings, watercolors, and graphic and sculptural works. Near the Picassos are several dozen black-and-white candid photographs of the artist (from a rotating collection of 200), by American David Douglas Duncan. This exhibit makes the museum a ▲▲▲ experience for Picasso fans. I've seen a pile of Picassos, but never have I gotten as personal with him as I did here. Duncan's intimate photos of the artist and his family capture the very human personality of this larger-than-life genius. The photos—taken in Picasso's later years, and many featuring his wife Jacqueline—provide insight into his artistic process, as well as his lifestyle, showing him at work and at play. As a fly on the wall of his chaotic studio, you'll see Picasso in the bathtub, getting a haircut, playing dress-up, moving to a new house, horsing around with his kids, entertaining his guest Gary Cooper, and getting a ballet lesson from Jacqueline. The excellent English descriptions—which you must borrow when you buy your ticket—are essential for getting the stories behind the photos.

In the basement are 125 small works by **Paul Klee,** displayed chronologically by room number so you can follow the evolution of his career. Watch as Klee discovers colors and blossoms from a doodler and, at times, watercolor artist into a mature painter.

The museum also has works by Braque, Monet, Renoir, Miró, Chagall, Cézanne, Matisse, Modigliani, and Pissarro.

Cost, Hours, Location: 18 SF, covered by Swiss Pass, good English booklet-2.50 SF, otherwise you can borrow English info sheets, daily April–Oct 10:00–18:00, Nov–March 11:00–17:00, a few blocks from the train station in the new town up Pilatusstrasse at #10, tel. 041-220-1660, www.rosengart.ch.

▲Depot History Museum (Depot Historisches Museum Luzern)—This cluttered old museum is a "depot" for the accumulated bric-a-brac of Luzern's past (10 SF, covered by Swiss Pass, Tue–Sun 10:00–17:00, closed Mon, Pfistergasse 24, tel. 041-228-5424, www.hmluzern.ch).

The museum is in one of Luzern's oldest surviving buildings, which used to house military weapons and uniforms. Their collection is too big to display effectively, so they've come up with an innovative concept: Throw all of their archived stuff together and display it on three crowded floors. You'll wander through shelves of old weapons, stained-glass windows, sculptures, and old-fashioned tourism posters. The items are displayed without much rhyme or reason, and each is labeled with a barcode. You'll use a scanner (included with entry) to scan the item you're interested in. You can then read about its history in English on your handheld screen.

▲Swiss Transport Museum (Verkehrshaus)—This enormous complex, across the lake from the train station, includes hundreds of exhibits in several different buildings, covering virtually all modes of transportation. It's a fun excursion, but it's pricey, a bit dated (the giant country map is nothing when you've Google-Earthed), and a little overwhelming, demanding at least a half-day. If you're in town for only one day, I'd skip this and enjoy the museums and ambience in the old town. But if you have a second day, have your kids in tow, and are obsessed with trains, planes, and automobiles, this can be time well spent.

Getting There: From downtown, it's a 30-minute **walk** to the museum, most of it along a beautiful promenade (described earlier, under "Lakefront Stroll"; the museum is at Lidostrasse 5). This is a pleasant walk, even if you're not going to the museum. To make a faster beeline to the museum, take **bus** #6, #8, or #24 from the station, and get off at the Verkehrshaus stop (the stop is announced, plus you'll see the huge, barrel-shaped, can't-miss-it IMAX theater, covered by 2-SF short ride ticket). For a more scenic approach, catch a **boat** in front of the train station (also to Verkehrshaus; 10 SF round-trip, 2/hr, 10 min each way).

Cost: 27 SF, half-price with Swiss Pass. In addition to the exhibits, the museum has a wide variety of shows and demonstrations (pick up a schedule—and inquire about English-speaking events—as you enter). These include a planetarium show (included in entry price) and an IMAX theater (18 SF, www.imax.ch). Combo-tickets are also available (37 SF for museum plus IMAX).

Hours and Information: Daily April–Oct 10:00–18:00, Nov–March 10:00–17:00, IMAX shows 11:00–17:00, sometimes in evenings. Tel. 041-375-7575 or recorded info 0848-852-020, www.verkehrshaus.ch.

Touring the Transport Museum: Starting in the first building, you'll come across a 30-minute show about the Gotthard

Tunnel. Then you'll wander through endless halls of train engines and tram cars. As you exit, you'll be face-to-face with jetliners and surrounded by pavilions devoted to various vehicles (such as planes, cars, boats, motorcycles, spaceships, and high-mountain lifts). Many of the exhibits are interactive, such as the parasailing simulator, where you lie down on a smoothly gliding platform and peer down at the countryside below.

Upstairs in the boat and cable-car building, be sure to seek out the **Swissarena,** an enormous (more than 2,000 square feet) aerial photograph of Switzerland (follow signs that look like a Swiss map in a CBS-style eye). This photo map, spread out on the floor like laminated linoleum, is detailed enough to show virtually every single building within Switzerland's borders. Slide on the Swiss slippers, borrow a map and magnifying glass, and glide across Switzerland, looking for the places you've visited so far.

The new two-story **Road Transport Hall** has a warehouse stacked floor to ceiling with 80 vehicles dating from 1860 to 2005, including horse carriages, bicycles, and automobiles. At the interactive car theater, you can select the vehicle you want to see.

Other Luzern Museums—Music fans may want to venture out to the **Richard Wagner Museum,** housed in a building where the composer lived (6 SF, covered by Swiss Pass, mid-March–Nov Tue–Sun 10:00–12:00 & 14:00–17:00, closed Mon and off-season, a 10-minute walk along the lakefront, south of train station at Richard Wagner Weg 27, tel. 041-360-2370, www.richard-wagner-museum.ch). The **Luzern Museum of Art** (Kunstmuseum Luzern), in the lakefront cultural center by the train station, features special exhibits of contemporary art (16 SF, covered by Swiss Pass, Tue–Wed 10:00–20:00, Thu–Sun 10:00–18:00, closed Mon, Europaplatz 1, tel. 041-226-7800, www.kunstmuseumluzern.ch). The **Museum of Natural History** (Natur-Museum), with an emphasis on interactive exhibits, is great for kids (6 SF, covered by Swiss Pass, Tue–Sun 10:00–17:00, closed Mon, near the end of the Mill Bridge next to the Depot History Museum at Kasernenplatz 6, tel. 041-228-5411, www.naturmuseum.ch).

Near Löwenplatz

The following sights composed the original 19th-century tourist center of Luzern. They're clustered around Löwenplatz, a square that's a 10-minute walk from the old town (or a short bus ride across the river from the station; take bus #1, #19, #22, or #23 three stops from the train station, direction: Maihof, covered by 2-SF short ride ticket). This square remains the heart of touristy Luzern, with a must-see monument and a pair of tacky but fun attractions. If you're doing the Glacier Garden and Bourbaki Panorama, and you don't have a Swiss Pass or LucerneCard, you might as well buy the 17-SF **Lionpass,** which saves you 3 SF.

I've listed the museums in descending order of respectability (or ascending order on the international "tacky tourist trap" scale). When you get off the bus, you'll see the round Bourbaki Panorama across the street; the lion and the Glacier Garden are one long block farther up the hill, on a lane away from the busy street.

▲**Lion Monument (Löwendenkmal)**—This famous monument is an essential stop if you're visiting Luzern—if only because when

you get back home, everyone will ask you, "Did you see the lion?" The huge sculpture (33 feet long by 20 feet tall) is carved right into a cliff face, over a reflecting pool in a peaceful park (free, open sunrise to dusk). Though it's often over-run with tour groups, a tranquil moment here is genuinely moving: The mighty lion rests his paws on a shield, with his head cocked to one side, tears streaming down his cheeks. In his side is the broken-off end of a spear, which is slowly killing the noble beast. This heartbreaking figure repre-sents the Swiss mercenaries who were killed or executed defending the French king in the French Revolution. The inscription reads, *Helvetiorum fidei ac virtuti*—"To the loyalty and bravery of the Swiss."

▲**Bourbaki Panorama**—Here's your chance to get right in the middle of a great painting—literally. In the 19th century, before the dawn of cinema, modern people were hungry for visual enter-tainment. Uniform panorama theaters like this were built all over Europe and hosted various gigantic paintings, which were rolled up and taken on road trips. This 360-degree painting (a 33-foot-tall wraparound canvas with a circumference of 360 feet) tells the story of the culminating battle of the Franco-Prussian War. The 1.50-SF booklet explains it all and makes for a good souvenir (8 SF, covered by Lionpass combo-ticket and Swiss Pass; April–Oct Tue–Sun 9:00–18:00, Mon 13:00–18:00; Nov–March Tue–Sun

10:00–17:00, Mon 13:00–17:00; Löwenplatz 11, tel. 041-412-3030, www.bourbakipanorama.ch).

Upon arrival, request an English playing of the 12-minute soundtrack of the battle. Spend your waiting time enjoying the fine first-floor exhibit about 19th-century entertainment. When the English narration starts, be on the second-floor viewing platform to savor all 360 degrees of the dramatic conclusion of the Franco-Prussian War. For three days in February of 1871, the 87,000-man French Army—led by the panorama's namesake, General Bourbaki—trudged through the snow across the Swiss border. Once in Switzerland, they gave up their weapons and surrendered to the Swiss—who, the story goes, took excellent care of the French, nursing them back to health before sending them home.

The Bourbaki Panorama was painted by Edouard Castres, who was actually there (as a Red Cross volunteer) on that frigid morning. The 1881 painting was thoroughly refurbished in 2000, when several life-size figures were added to the foreground. Sound effects fill the hall while you view the painting. The museum exhibit gives more background on the Franco-Prussian War and Bourbaki's army, as well as details about this and other panorama paintings.

Glacier Garden (Gletschergarten)—This complex is a strange sort of mini-theme-park with an eclectic hodgepodge of exhibits, most loosely relating to alpine geology. Although it's very touristy, and the various pieces don't quite hang together (such as the fun but out-of-place Hall of Mirrors), it adds up to a pleasant, if overpriced, activity (12 SF, covered by Lionpass combo-ticket and Swiss Pass, daily April–Oct 9:00–18:00, Nov–March 10:00–17:00, Denkmalstrasse 4, tel. 041-410-4340, www.gletschergarten.ch).

Pick up the English info booklet as you enter, and follow the numbers on the confusing one-way path. First, you'll walk through the **glacier-grinded grounds** that give the museum its name. While geologists would get a thrill out of this, it was just a bunch of holes to me. Then you'll enter the **museum,** with exhibits about glacial processes and a dramatic slideshow that gives you an idea of what this area once looked like. The slideshow takes you back in time, starting 16,000 years ago—at the end of the last Ice Age, when Luzern was emerging from beneath the Reuss Glacier—to 20 million years ago, when this region was a subtropical sea. You'll see lots of rocks with fossils and with the tracks of former sea creatures. Downstairs are huge 3-D reliefs of late–18th-century Luzern, and the Alps and lakes of Central Switzerland. Back upstairs, you'll cross directly into the **Amrein's House,** an old chalet with some original furnishings and models of traditional Swiss buildings. As you leave, you have the option of hiking up the steep **Tower Walk,** which leads to another old chalet and an observation tower.

At the end, be sure to visit the **Hall of Mirrors.** This undeniably enjoyable attraction, made in 1896 for a national exhibition in Geneva, is a delightfully low-tech fun house. You'll grope your way through twisting corridors—with mirrors on all sides—decorated like a Disneyfied Alhambra. It's confusing, dizzying, and claustrophobic, but goofy fun. As you run into yourself (literally) again and again, you'll lament the poor sap who has to clean the smudge marks off all those mirrors (walk slowly and, if you don't mind looking foolish, with arms outstretched). As you leave, giggling and nauseated, you'll ask yourself: So, what exactly did that have to do with glaciers?

Alpineum—This disappointing attraction, overshadowed by its substantial gift shop, displays a handful of paintings and reliefs of famous Swiss mountain peaks and panoramas. These are the same views you'll see if you visit the peaks in person—but in a musty, outmoded, tourist-trap environment. The exhibit also includes English explanations and miniature models of traditional houses, trains, boats, people, and cows. Visit this only if you have a Swiss Pass, which gets you in for free (otherwise 5 SF, not covered by LionPass combo-ticket, April–Oct daily 9:00–12:30 & 13:30–18:00, closed Nov–March, Denkmalstrasse 11, tel. 041-410-6266, www.alpineum.ch).

Sleeping in Luzern

Luzern accommodations are expensive. I've listed one big, classic hotel (the Waldstätterhof), a handful of small, basic hotels, and two good backpacker options. The prices here are for high season (April–Oct); you'll pay marginally less off-season. These are all centrally located (except Backpackers Luzern). The city can be noisy at night, so ask for a room on a high floor.

$$$ Hotel Waldstätterhof is a grand old hotel across the street from the train station, with reasonable rates for its high level of comfort. Its 102 bright, spacious rooms come with all the amenities (Db-240–280 SF depending on size, pricier suites, Zentralstrasse 4, tel. 041-227-1271, fax 041-227-1272, www.hotel-waldstaetterhof.ch, info@hotel-waldstaetterhof.ch).

$$$ Hotel des Alpes is a good bet if you want to sleep right on the river in the old town. Its lobby hides above a busy restaurant, but the 45 rooms are fresh and modern, with new bathrooms. Pricier riverfront rooms come with beautiful views (riverview rooms: Sb-160 SF, Db-255 SF; back-side rooms: Sb-135 SF, Db-205 SF, less in winter; a few rooms have balconies for the same price, Furrengasse 3, tel. 041-417-2060, fax 041-417-2066, www.desalpes-luzern.ch, info@desalpes-luzern.ch).

Sleep Code

(1 SF = about $1, country code: 41)
S = Single, **D** = Double/Twin, **T** = Triple, **Q** = Quad, **b** = bathroom, **s** = shower only. Unless otherwise noted, credit cards are accepted, English is spoken, and breakfast is included.

To help you sort easily through these listings, I've divided the rooms into three categories, based on the price for a standard double room with bath:

$$$ Higher Priced—Most rooms 200 SF or more.
  $$ Moderately Priced—Most rooms between 100–200 SF.
    $ Lower Priced—Most rooms 100 SF or less.

$$ Hotel Baslertor and its cheaper annex, **Hotel Pension Rösli** (across the street), offer well-located rooms for various budgets. The Baslertor's 30 rooms, with old, dark furnishings, are more expensive and come in several sizes (Sb-100–150 SF, budget Db-100–150 SF, small Db-125–175 SF, medium Db-150–200 SF, large Db-175–225 SF, ask for 10 percent Rick Steves discount when you reserve and show book upon arrival, extra bed-25 SF, elevator, free Internet access in business center, free Wi-Fi, atmospheric breakfast room, plush public spaces, small, solar-heated swimming pool). The Rösli pension—an older building with lower ceilings—has six rooms with even older furnishings and no elevator (Db-100–150 SF). Both hotels charge 18 SF per person extra for breakfast. Roland runs a tight ship (with strict cancellation policies), staffing both hotels from the Baslertor reception desk (Pfistergasse 17, tel. 041-249-2222, fax 041-249-2233, www.baslertor.ch, info@baslertor.ch).

$$ Hotel Goldener Stern is a solid value, offering 16 perfectly acceptable rooms over a restaurant and with some street noise (Sb-100 SF, smaller top-floor D-120 SF, Db-150 SF, Tb-190 SF, Qb-220 SF, prices drop for longer stays or when slow, tiny elevator, pay Internet access, free Wi-Fi, church bells ring at night, Burgerstrasse 35, tel. 041-227-5060, fax 041-227-5061, www.goldener-stern.ch, hotel@goldener-stern.ch, Amrein family).

$$ Hotel Alpha, once a convent-run boarding house for village girls, is now popular with students. It offers 50 big, bright, institutional rooms, most with the toilet down the hall. Although it's located in a pleasant residential area, it still has some street noise from the nearby school and playing field—even at night (S-72 SF, twin D-104 SF, twin Db-144 SF, T-150 SF, comfy lounges and TV room, Zähringerstrasse 24, at intersection with Pilatusstrasse, tel. 041-240-4280, fax 041-240-9131, www.hotelalpha.ch,

Luzern Hotels & Restaurants

info@hotelalpha.ch). It's a 10-minute walk or an easy bus ride from the train station (take bus #1, #2, or #10, get off at Pilatusplatz, and walk 2 blocks).

$$ Jailhotel Löwengraben is a theme hotel renting clean but small, spare cells in the renovated former city prison on a nondescript street a few steps from the heart of the old town. As much an experience as a place to sleep, it has 133 beds in 56 cells (3 double beds, but the vast majority—logically—are twins). Cells, which can be a bit stuffy, come with cot-like beds, tiny barred windows, and reinforced doors—so it really does feel like a prison (except for the mod but teeny WCs). It's a fun experience, but hardly a good value, given how spartan the rooms are. It's noisy on weekends, as it's above a club. On the upside, the club waives its 15–20-SF cover charge for hotel guests—if you can't beat 'em, join 'em (S-70–98 SF, Sb-97–118 SF, D-100–122 SF, Db-126–153 SF, T-146–169 SF, Tb-175–205 SF, Qb-256 SF, people who actually did time here enjoy sleeping in the four wardens' suites-225–280 SF, less off-season; 10 percent discount if you reserve direct, mention this book, and show it upon arrival; non-smoking, Löwengraben 18, tel. 041-410-7830, fax 041-410-7832, www.jailhotel.ch, hotel@jailhotel.ch).

$ Backpackers Luzern is calm and well-run, sharing a modern, blocky building with student dorms *(Studentenheim)* in

1. Hotel Waldstätterhof
2. Hotel des Alpes
3. Hotel Baslertor & Hotel Pension Rösli
4. Hotel Goldener Stern
5. To Hotel Alpha
6. Jailhotel Löwengraben
7. To Backpackers Luzern
8. To Lion Lodge Lucerne
9. Hug Bakery/Café
10. Heini Bakery/Café
11. Opus Rest. & Wine Bar
12. Restaurant Rathaus Brauerei
13. Restaurant Taube
14. Nix in der Laterne Rest.
15. Restaurant Schiff
16. Manora Cafeteria
17. Launderette

a peaceful residential area a 15-minute walk south of the train station. The place has 30 rooms (each with a balcony), a pair of kitchens for guests, a welcoming lounge, no curfew, Internet access (8 SF/hr), and laundry (9 SF/load for full service). The walk to the center is mostly along the lake, through pretty parks and next to a fine beach (31 SF/person in 4-bed rooms, 38 SF/person in 2-bed rooms, D-70–76 SF, includes sheets, no breakfast, reception open 7:30–10:00 & 16:00–23:00, elevator, Alpenquai 42, tel. 041-360-0420, fax 041-360-0442, www.backpackerslucerne.ch).

$ Lion Lodge Lucerne is located in a new building near the Lion Monument (32–34 SF/person in 4- to 6-bed rooms, 36 SF/person in 2-bed rooms, D-72–86 SF, Db-90 SF, includes sheets, no breakfast, kitchen, pay Internet access, verandas, bus #1 to Wesemlinrain stop, then cross street to Zürichstrasse 57, tel. 041-410-0144, www.lionlodge.ch, info@lionlodge.ch).

Eating in Luzern

While eateries along the river are pricey and a bit touristy, if you have one evening in Luzern, that's where you'll make the best memories. Here's a selection of places with decent prices, many with great riverfront ambience.

Dining in Style

Opus, next to the big Jesuit Church, is both a trendy wine bar and a good restaurant. Pair your wine with meat, fish, and vegetarian dishes with international flair (25–38 SF); the lush and varied salad bar ("antipasti buffet"—a small plate piled high makes a light and healthy dinner for 17 SF); or your choice of dried meats and cheeses (21–31 SF, choose and cut your own fresh bread to go with it). They always have a couple dozen bottles of wine open and available by the glass. Sit in the upscale, colorful interior; in the candlelit and extremely romantic wine cellar; or out front, right on the river (open long hours daily, Bahnhofstrasse 16, tel. 041-226-4141, www.restaurant-opus.ch).

Romantic **Nix in der Laterne** has a white-tablecloth-dressy interior and great outside seats right on the fast-rushing river. In keeping with their philosophy of making everything from scratch using fresh seasonal ingredients, they offer a brief chalkboard menu that the waiter explains (50-SF 2-course dinners, 35-SF plates, 20-SF lunches, daily 11:00–24:00, reservations smart for dinner, Reusssteg 9, tel. 041-240-2543).

Traditional Swiss Sit-Down Restaurants

Restaurant Rathaus Brauerei is a lively microbrewery with an ideal riverfront location and a young, helpful staff. It's clearly a local favorite for its Seidel Rathausbier, brewed in such small quantities that you can only get it here. They serve their beer to ladies in a two-deciliter "elegant flute." Special seasonal brews are on the menu board, along with salads, "gourmet" pretzel sandwiches, 22–30-SF dishes, Swiss-style mac and cheese (21 SF), and the daily three-course special (24 SF, Mon–Sat, 35 SF on Sun)—available until it's sold out (open long hours daily, Unter der Egg 2, tel. 041-410-5257).

Restaurant Taube is popular for serving "grandma's cooking" (great spot for a good *Rösti*, 26 SF) and for its riverside seating (18-SF 2-course lunches, closed Sun, Burgerstrasse 3, tel. 041-210-0747).

Restaurant Schiff has scenic riverfront tables in the old town with good, traditional Swiss food, relatively reasonable prices, and a fun, accessible menu (plenty of salads, pizzas, most main dishes 25–35 SF, open long hours daily, music many evenings, across the river from Jesuit Church, Unter der Egg 8, tel. 041-418-5252).

Note that the **bakeries** listed below also have sit-down restaurants.

Fast and Affordable

Bakeries: Luzern has several bakery chains with many inviting branches that serve both take-away sandwiches and treats and light sit-down meals. Consider these two: **Hug Bakery/Café** has a cuddly location overlooking the river at the old-town end of the Mill Bridge, smack in the middle of the sightseeing action. People come for a drink, snack, or dessert, or to settle in for a meal. The selection includes basic traditional Swiss dishes (some plates come with *Rösti*, 20 SF) and two-course lunch deals (17 SF) to enjoy at outdoor tables with river views or in the splendid glassed-in terrace (Mon–Fri 7:00–19:00, Sat 7:00–17:00, Sun 10:00–17:00, may stay open later in good summer weather, Mühlenplatz 6). The cheap take-away salads, pastries, and sandwiches are made to order for the inviting riverside benches just a few steps away. The similarly priced **Heini Bakery/Café** has four locations in Luzern, including one in the old town half a block down from the Manor department store on Falkenplatz (Mon–Sat 7:00–18:30, Sun 9:00–18:00).

Self-Service Cafeteria: **Manora,** a cafeteria on the fifth floor of the Manor department store in the old town, is ideal for a tasty, efficient lunch. Choose between a fresh salad bar (big plate-11 SF) or a variety of main dishes (6–15 SF). In good weather, climb the stairs to the outdoor terrace, with great views over the rooftops of Luzern to the lake and Mount Pilatus. This place is packed with locals and very crowded during peak times—eat early or late, and send your travel partner up top to claim an outdoor table while you buy the food (Mon–Wed 9:00–18:30, Thu–Fri 9:00–21:00, Sat 8:00–16:00, closed Sun, non-smoking inside, smoking allowed on roof, Weggisgasse 5).

Luzern Connections

Luzern is marvelously well-situated in Switzerland, with convenient connections to anywhere in the country. Note that Luzern is on both the Golden Pass and the William Tell Express scenic rail lines (see the Scenic Rail Journeys chapter).

From Luzern by Train to: Zürich (2/hr, 1 hr), **Zürich Airport** (2/hr, 1.25 hrs, many with change in Zürich), **Bern** (2/hr, 1–1.5 hrs), **Interlaken** (hourly, 2–2.5 hrs), **Lausanne** (hourly direct, 2.25 hrs), **Appenzell** (2/hr, 2.75 hrs, change in Herisau or in Zürich and Gossau), **Lugano** (hourly, 2.5 hrs, half with change in Arth-Goldau), **Chur** (hourly, 2.25 hrs, change in Thalwil). Train info: toll tel. 0900-300-300 or www.rail.ch.

Central Switzerland: Day Trips from Luzern

Luzern is perched on the edge of a super-scenic lake and ringed by family-friendly mountain peaks that are easily conquerable for a price. All of this makes the city a perfect springboard for alpine excursions. The following side-trips—including a boat cruise, two different mountain lifts, and a hidden military fortress—are all popular excursions.

If you're home-basing in Luzern for several days, consider the **Tell-Pass.** This pass includes two days of free rides on lifts, boats, and several area train lines in a seven-day period, and half-price on the other five days (158 SF, or 126 SF with a Swiss Pass; buy at TIs, train stations, and boat docks; April–Oct only, www.tell-pass.ch). A longer version gives you five free days in a 15-day period, and half-price on the other ten days, for 210 SF (168 SF with Swiss Pass). A Tell-Pass doesn't make sense if you have a consecutive-day Swiss Pass (as opposed to a flexipass).

Possible Whirlwind Day Trip: This plan combines most of these adventures (the fortress, a mini-lake cruise, and the Pilatus mountain lift—up one side and down the other) into one jam-packed day trip. Note that the fortress is open only on weekends from April through October, so if you want to tour it, you'll have to do this trip on a summer Saturday or Sunday. Confirm all the schedules and logistics at the TI before embarking. First, take an early train or boat to Stansstad and tour Fortress Fürigen, then have lunch in Stansstad. Catch the 13:46 boat to Alpnachstad (23 min), then ride up the mountain on the Pilatus cogwheel train (departing 14:20, arriving at the summit at 14:50). When you're ready to return to Luzern, catch the gondola for the seven-minute ride down to Fräkmüntegg (4/hr, last departure at 18:00 July–Aug, at 17:15 April–June and Sept–Oct, at 16:15 Nov–March), where you have a chance to do the luge ride before changing to a smaller gondola down to Kriens (check for last scheduled run, 30-min ride, don't get off at Krienseregg). In Kriens, walk five minutes, following the white signs to *Luzern bus.* (You don't want the bus stop in front of the building.) Bus #1 gets you to Luzern's main station in 15 minutes. Whew!

Boats of Note: These boats can help you connect the excursions in this chapter: **Stansstad** (Fortress Fürigen) **to Alpnachstad** (where you catch the Pilatus cogwheel train; 7 boats/day, 23 min, 2 steamboats/day July–Aug, 10 SF); **Stansstad to Luzern** (9 boats/day, 1 hr, 2 steamboats/day July–Aug, 16.80 SF, 31 SF round-trip);

Alpnachstad to Luzern (7 boats/day, 1.5 hrs, 23 SF). While the bridge near Stansstad is under repair, the old-fashioned steamboats won't be running between Alpnachstad and Stansstad (but their modern counterparts will continue on those routes). For boat information, see www.lakelucerne.ch.

Lake Cruises

Lake Luzern (or Lucerne) is the English name for the lake, but the Swiss call it the Vierwaldstättersee—"Lake of Four Forest

Cantons," since it lies at the intersection of four of Switzerland's states (or cantons, as their political units are called).

This lake—the most touristed in Switzerland—has a variety of boat routes and destinations (33 stops in all). Cruises range from a one-hour sampler tour (around Luzern's "harbor") to a full-blown, six-hour exploration (to Flüelen, at the far end of the lake, and back again). Some routes are round-trip; on others, you'll get out, explore, and then take the next boat back. Romantics will want to hitch a ride on one of the five old-fashioned paddleboat steamers.

The easiest, most efficient trip is to boat across from the train station to the Swiss Transport Museum (Verkehrshaus, described earlier under "Sights in Luzern"; 10 SF round-trip, 2/hr, 10 min each way). In summer, a "castle cruise" makes one-hour (15.20 SF)

and two-hour (24 SF) round-trip sightseeing swings around the lake (3–4/day, Sun only in spring and fall, from piers 3 or 4). For most, the two-hour circle is about as much of a scenic cruise as the lake deserves. Another easy two-hour excursion is to take the boat from Luzern to Weggis or Vitznau (under Mount Rigi, across the lake; see "Mountain Lifts," later), then back to Luzern (31 SF round-trip to Weggis, 38 SF to Vitznau). You can buy tickets at the Luzern TI and get advice on which trip best fits your schedule.

Boats leave from the lake piers in front of the Luzern train station. They're operated by the Lake Lucerne Navigation Company (tel. 041-367-6767, www.lakelucerne.ch). Note that these boats are free with a Eurailpass or Swiss Pass. But remember that if you're using a flexipass, the boat trip costs a flexi-day. Doing the lake cruise on the day you arrive or depart—when you're already using a flexi-day for your train transportation—is a smart plan.

Mountain Lifts

There's no shortage of mountain lifts in Central Switzerland. I've described the two most famous and most accessible from Luzern: Mount Pilatus and Mount Rigi.

Mount Pilatus

Looming behind Luzern, Pilatus is a dramatic backdrop to the city, and also an enjoyable destination. While legend dictates that it's named for Pontius Pilate—whose body is supposedly in one of its lakes, kicking up a fuss if disturbed—it more likely comes from a Latin word meaning "cloudy." It's also said to be infested with dragons.

You can ascend Pilatus (to the overlook platform, at 7,000 feet, called "Pilatus Kulm") two different ways: by cogwheel train (the world's steepest, at 48 per-cent grade) or gondola (in three stages).

By Train: The cogwheel train leaves from the lakeside town of Alpnachstad—from Luzern, take the S5 train to Alpnachstad (2/hr, 20 min), or take the 1.5-hour boat (7/day, 22 SF). The cogwheel train runs mid-May–mid-Nov only (1–2/hr, daily 8:15–18:30, 30 min up, 40 min down; for the best views going up, take a downhill-facing seat on the right side, www.pilatus.ch).

By Gondola: The gondola leaves from the town of Kriens, virtually a suburb of Luzern (from in front of Luzern train station, take city bus #1 for 15 min to Kriens; gondola goes continuously, daily July–Aug 8:30–17:30, April–June and Sept–Oct until 16:45, Nov–March until 15:45, closes for maintenance mid-Oct–mid-Nov, www.pilatus.ch). From Kriens, you'll take a small gondola to Krienseregg (recreation area with trails and playground), then on to Fräkmüntegg (total trip 30 min).

At Fräkmüntegg, you'll have a chance to zip down Switzerland's longest luge ride, called "Dragon Speed" (8 SF, almost a mile long, good weather only, daily July–Aug 10:00–18:00, May–June and Sept–Oct 10:00–12:00 & 13:15–17:00, until 17:15 Sat–Sun with no midday break, www.rodelbahn.ch). At the fun Suspension Rope Park ("Seilpark"), you can test your agility high up on seven rope courses with varying degrees of difficulty (26 SF includes material and instruction; July–Aug daily 10:00–17:30; May–June and Sept–late Oct Tue–Sun 10:00–17:00, closed Mon; closed off-season, www.pilatus-seilpark.ch).

From Fräkmüntegg, it's another seven minutes in a bigger gondola to the observation platform at Pilatus Kulm.

Costs: A one-way segment to the top, no matter how you go, costs 32 SF; round-trip costs 64 SF (with your choice of cogwheel train or gondola for each leg; does not include your transportation between Luzern and the cogwheel train or gondola stations). Swiss Pass holders go for half-price (32 SF round-trip), and Eurailpass holders get a 30 percent discount (45 SF round-trip). When you buy your ticket, tell them which way you want to go up and down (it's most interesting to go up one way, down the other). Don't throw your ticket away when you board, as you'll have to scan it several times until you finally exit at the last station.

The handiest way to visit Pilatus from Luzern is with the popular **Golden Round Trip** package. This includes the bus to Kriens, the gondola up to Pilatus, the cogwheel train down to Alpnachstad, and a lazy, 1.5-hour boat trip back to Luzern (or the same route, reversed; 90 SF). The cheaper **Silver Round Trip** returns you to Luzern by train instead of boat (72 SF, both run May–mid-Oct only). Figure out the best route with the help of Luzern's TI, or check www.pilatus.ch (tel. 041-329-1111, fax 041-329-1112).

At the Summit: The summit (Pilatus Kulm) is a family fun zone with plenty of activities, including a "summer toboggan" (Switzerland's longest at more than a mile). Hotel Bellevue acts as the visitors' center, with a good information office, restaurants, a souvenir shop, and Internet terminals. Hotel Pilatus-Kulm hosts temporary exhibits. Its three restaurants have the original furnishings from 1889; there's also a modern self-service cafeteria. Check out the fancy WC: When you open a door, a red dragon claims the stall for you. The terrace below is full of free and comfortable deck chairs.

LUZERN

Hikes from Pilatus: These walks lead to great viewpoints. I've listed them roughly in order of difficulty, from easiest to most strenuous. All leave from the summit, Pilatus Kulm.

Two short **Dragonpaths** lead through tunnels to various viewpoints in the rock. These paths come with signs illustrating dragon tales by the famous Swiss artist Hans Erni.

A 10-minute hike takes you up to **Esel** ("Donkey," commemorating the pre-cable-car days, when Queen Victoria came up to Pilatus on the back of a donkey). Below, Esel hides an impressive part of Switzerland's anti-aircraft defense system. Find the gray, round structures within the imitation rock. Modern missiles behind the camouflage point to the skies. The biggest radar in Switzerland towers above Hotel Pilatus-Kulm in an off-limits military zone.

Hiking to **Tomlishorn** (35 min), you'll spot more camouflaged military installations. Stop at the yellow *Echo* sign and shout your message out to the world. Somebody out there keeps yelling it back.

A 1.5-hour hike leads to the 6,700-foot cross-capped summit of **Matthorn** (not Matterhorn). This hike is moderately strenuous—generally uphill, with lots of ups and downs. A visitors' book invites you to sign and leave your impressions on this breathtaking spot.

Sleeping at the Summit: You can spend the night on the summit of Pilatus. Linger outside to enjoy the views with the marmots and mountain goats...or head inside for the hotels' free nightly entertainment: movies and a disco on alternating nights. **$$ Hotel Bellevue** is a modern, round building with 28 rooms—clean and bright, with Nordic-style furniture (Sb-111 SF, Db-192 SF). **$$$ Hotel Pilatus-Kulm,** closed for renovation until August 2010, is a historic building from 1900 (Sb-190 SF, Db-240 SF). Both hotels come with a big breakfast, have Wi-Fi, and share contact information (tel. 041-329-1212, fax 041-329-1213, www.pilatus.ch, hotels @pilatus.ch).

Mount Rigi

This long, shelf-like mountain, across the lake from Luzern, provides sweeping views of Central Switzerland (and, on a clear day, Germany and France, too). Even though it's at a lower altitude than Pilatus (5,900 feet), this so-called "Queen of the Mountains" boasts the first cog railway in Europe and claims to offer the best vistas in the area. Compared with Mount Pilatus, Rigi has virtually no tour groups (since its summit hotel doesn't court them). Still, the top can be busy between 10:00 and 15:00. The mountain is laced with more than 60 miles of hiking trails and other attractions to while away an afternoon. You can even stay overnight at the Rigi Kulm Hotel (described later). From the Rigi Kulm station, it's a short, steep climb (10 min) past the hotel to the top of the mountain.

As with Pilatus, you have two ways to approach the topmost viewpoint, Rigi Kulm: by cogwheel train (from Arth-Goldau or Vitznau) or by cable car (from Weggis).

By Train: To go by cogwheel train, you have two options: from the town of Arth-Goldau ("behind" Rigi, accessible by train from Luzern) or from Vitznau (right on Lake Luzern, accessible by boat—but not train—from Luzern). The train from Luzern to Arth-Goldau takes 30 minutes; once there, you'll take the blue cogwheel train up to Rigi Kulm (40 min, departs hourly, coordinated with arrival of certain trains from Luzern, daily 8:00–18:10). You can also take the boat from Luzern to Vitznau (1 hour), then take a different, red cogwheel train from there up to Rigi Kulm (30 min, departs hourly, daily 8:35–22:05, for the best views sit on the side closest to the station).

By Cable Car: To go by cable car, take the boat from Luzern to Weggis (40 min), then board the cable car to Rigi Kaltbad (10 min, 2/hr, Mon–Fri 6:50–18:50, Sat–Sun 8:20–18:50); there you'll switch to the red cogwheel train from Vitznau that brings you the rest of the way up to Rigi Kulm.

Costs: As with Mount Pilatus, you can go up one way and down the other for maximum experience at the same price. Before ascending, figure out your complete route at the Luzern TI. No matter how you go, the price from the base of the mountain to Rigi Kulm is 37 SF one-way, 64 SF round-trip, plus the cost of getting from Luzern to the cogwheel train or cable-car stations (with a Swiss Pass, the whole trip is free, from Luzern all the way to the top of Rigi). The cogwheel train and cable-car prices are half-price with a Eurailpass; the train trip from Luzern to Arth-Goldau and the boat trips to Vitznau and Weggis are also included in your pass (but you'll have to use one of your flexi-days). Figure five to six hours for the total round-trip from Luzern. The schedules and prices listed here are for mid-March through November (less frequent in winter; confirm at Luzern TI, or check www .rigi.ch).

Sleeping at the Summit: Stay overnight and watch the sun rise, accompanied only by the sounds of the wind and the ringing of a few cow and goat bells. **$$$ Rigi Kulm Hotel** is a large, recently remodeled inn set just below the summit (Sb-140–195 SF, Db-220–310 SF, prices depend on room size and views, free Wi-Fi, café and restaurant, tel. 041-880-1888, fax 041-855-0055, www.rigikulm.ch, hotel@rigikulm.ch, Käppeli family).

Fortress Fürigen Museum of War History

The Fortress Museum of Fürigen (Festung Fürigen Museum zur Wehrgeschichte) shows you another face of the country and the reason why Switzerland was able to remain peaceful and neutral: its elaborate and secret system of bunkers and fortresses. Unfortunately, this fascinating exhibit is open only Saturday and Sunday, April through October.

Enter through an innocent-looking wooden barrack. The bunker is always chilly, but no worries: Visitors are loaned original Swiss Army coats. Put on your coat, grab the English brochure that explains each room, and you're on your way. The radio station was placed near the entrance to assure clear reception. The living quarters were gas-proof, complete with specially sealed doors and devices to monitor the air for poison. The museum is a petting zoo of 20th-century weaponry. Visitors can fiddle with and even aim guns, knowing all the ammo is now imaginary. Think of the photo op: you, in a Swiss military uniform, manning a cannon.

Historical photographs take you back to World War II. Fortress Fürigen was built in 1941 as part of a new military strategy: to protect Switzerland with fortresses hidden in the Alps, called *Réduitfestung* (roughly "shelter fortress"—see sidebar on opposite page). In case of a Nazi invasion, the Swiss government would retreat to a secret bunker in the Berner Oberland, and Swiss troops would abandon the border regions and gather around this alpine stronghold. Fortress Fürigen was meant to protect roads and rail lines that led from Luzern and Zürich along Lake Luzern into the Berner Oberland. This was one of a network of fortresses in the area. After World War II, they were retooled with a new focus: the threat of the Soviet Union and nuclear war.

Big guns in the fortress could shoot more than six miles, and machine guns protected the immediate access routes to the bunker. This fortress could house and feed 100 people for three weeks. But in 1990, with the end of the Cold War, the practical Swiss decommissioned the fortress, refit it with vintage WWII and early Cold War gear, and opened it to the curious public.

Cost, Hours, Information: 5 SF, covered by Swiss Pass. The museum is open only on weekends from late spring through early fall (April–Oct Sat–Sun 11:00–17:00, closed Mon–Fri and Nov–March). Tel. 041-618-7522, www.nidwaldner-museum.ch. Remember to pick up the loaner English booklet as you enter.

Getting There: Fortress Fürigen is near the lakefront town of Stansstad (on Kehrsitenstrasse), below the village of Fürigen, not far from Luzern. It's an easy trip from Luzern by **train** (6.20 SF one-way, 2/hr, 18 min, direction: Engelberg). From the train station in Stansstad, walk 15 minutes, following brown signs to *Festungsmuseum* or *Kehrsiten* (down Bahnhofstrasse to

Swiss Military Readiness

Strolling through a peaceful Swiss village—charming pastoral greenery studded with rustic farmhouses between an Alp and a lake—my friend walked with me to the door of a nondescript barn. He said, "Stand here," and slid open the door to reveal a solitary, mighty gun—pointing right at me. Crossing a field, kicking a stray soccer ball back to a group of happy grade-schoolers, we came to another barn. This time I noticed the "wooden" door was actually metal, with a clever paint job. Inside was a military canteen, now selling snacks to civilians, and a steel ladder leading down into a military-gray world that felt like a vast submarine. A network of passages, just big enough for heavily armed soldiers to race down single file, led to a series of gun barns and subterranean command rooms with charts locating other installations in the area.

Switzerland may be famous for its neutrality, but it's anything but lax defensively. Travelers marvel at how Swiss engineers have conquered their Alps with the world's most-expensive-per-mile road system. But no one designs a Swiss bridge or tunnel without also designing its destruction. Each comes with built-in explosives, so, in the event of an invasion, the entire country can be blasted into a mountain fortress.

Even today, you can't get a building permit without an expensive first-class bomb shelter worked into the plan. Old tank barriers (nicknamed "Toblerones" for their shape) stand ready to be dragged across the roads to slow any invasion. Sprawling hospitals are dug into mountains, still ventilated to be kept dry and ready for use. And halfway up alpine cliffs, Batcave-type doors can slide open, allowing fighter jets to zoom into action from hidden airstrips cut out of solid rock. If you're approaching a mountain pass by car, look for the explosive patches ominously checkering the roads near the summit.

But the end of the Cold War in 1989 brought changes even to neutral Switzerland. Western armies began cutting back on their military spending, and Switzerland followed suit, with deep cuts in its defense budget. The Swiss Army met its tighter budget in part by closing many of the 15,000 hidden fortresses that protected the country's strategic roads, train lines, and mountain passes. Some of the forts, such as Fortress Fürigen, have been turned into tourist attractions no more formidable than medieval castles.

Stanserstrasse, cross and follow signs, right on Achereggstrasse, left passing swimming-pool sign and tennis courts, and finally along the lake).

You can also get to Stansstad from Luzern by **boat** (9/day, 1 hour, plus 2 steamboats/day July–Aug—due to bridge repairs, steamboats may not be running, 16.80 SF one-way, 31 SF round-trip). From Stansstad's boat dock, walk 10 minutes up to the main street (Achereggstrasse) and keep left, following the brown signs for *Festungsmuseum.*

Drivers arriving in Stansstad can follow white signs to *Kehrsiten* for lakeside parking (1 SF/hr, free WC, 5-min walk along lake to museum entrance).

Near the Fortress Museum: Located in an old school, the Nidwaldner Museum is a military museum popular with WWII buffs (same price and hours as fortress, Mürgstrasse 12, www .nidwaldner-museum.ch).

BERN and MURTEN

Enjoy urban Switzerland in the charming, compact capital of Bern. Ramble the ramparts of Murten, Switzerland's best-preserved medieval town, and resurrect the ruins of an ancient Roman capital in nearby Avenches.

If you like cute, small towns (as I do), make Murten your home base. Otherwise, choose busier Bern.

Planning Your Time

On a quick trip, big Bern and little Murten—about a half-hour apart by train or car—are each worth a half-day. Either makes a fine day trip or overnight stop. Murten, while easy by train, is even better by car. With a car, I'd sleep in Murten.

Bern is a convenient stop between other destinations (such as going from the Berner Oberland to Murten or Zürich). If you're

day-tripping, put your bag in a locker at the Bern station, spend a few hours taking my self-guided "Welcome to Bern" walk and visiting some museums, then catch a late-afternoon train to your next stop. You could combine the destinations in this chapter by ending your busy Bern day in Murten, where you can spend the evening wandering the walls and savoring a lakeside dinner. In the morning, linger in Murten or move on to your next destination.

Bern

Stately but human, classy but fun, the Swiss capital gives you the most delightful look at urban Switzerland. Bern's top attractions are window-shopping and people-watching in lively market squares and along the streets lined with cozy, covered arcades. But there's more to this city: Enjoy Bern's excellent museums, quaint-for-a-capital ambience, and delightful river scene. In this city (and canton), look for flags "bearing" the symbol of the local mascot—a roaring bear.

The city, founded in 1191, has managed to avoid war damage and hasn't burned down since a great fire swept through in 1405. After the fire, wooden buildings were no longer allowed, and Bern took on its gray-green sandstone complexion (with stones quarried from nearby). During its 12th- and 13th-century growth spurt, the frisky town grew through two walls. Looking at the map of the city contained within a bend of the Aare River, you can get a sense of how it started with a castle at the tip of the peninsula, and expanded with a series of walls—each defending an ever-bigger city from its one land-accessible side. The clock tower marks the first wall (1218). A generation later, another wall was built (in 1256, at today's prison tower). The final wall—where today's train station sits—was built in 1344.

In 1353, Bern became the eighth canton to join the Swiss Federation. Its power ended with the conquest by Napoleon in 1798. But in 1848, Bern rose again to become the Swiss capital.

Today, the German-speaking town has about 130,000 people (two-thirds Protestant and one-third Catholic). Its pointy towers, sandstone buildings, and colorful fountains make Bern one of Europe's finest surviving medieval towns.

Orientation to Bern

User-friendly Bern is packed into a peninsula bounded by the Aare River. The train station is located where the peninsula connects to the mainland. From there, a handy main drag leads gradually downhill, straight through the middle of town past most of the major sights, to the tip of the peninsula (across a bridge and finally to the bear park).

Tourist Information

Start your visit at the TI, on the ground floor inside the **train station** (June–Sept daily 9:00–20:30; Oct–May Mon–Sat 9:00–18:30, Sun 10:00–17:00; tel. 031-328-1212, www.berninfo.com). Pick up a free map of Bern (and maps for any other Swiss cities you'll be visiting), and browse through their free brochures: general information booklet, museum guide, bus and walking tour info, transit map, quarterly events and exhibits listings, and informative leaflets on various sights. There's a second TI near the **bear park** (June–Sept daily 9:00–18:00; March–May and Oct daily 10:00–16:00; Nov–Feb Fri–Sun 11:00–16:00, closed Mon–Thu).

Arrival in Bern

By Train: Bern's bustling train station is a thriving multistory mall. The trains almost get lost. On the upper level, you'll find a Migros grocery store (daily 8:00–21:00) and a pharmacy (daily 6:30–22:00). The ground floor has lockers (6 SF) and WCs (2 SF, both near the TI in the far-back corner), and the lower level has a Co-op grocery store (daily 7:00–22:00). From the station, it's a 30-minute downhill stroll through the heart of town to the bear park and up to the rose garden. My "Welcome to Bern" self-guided walk, later in this chapter, lays out the most interesting route.

By Car: The old town is essentially car-free (only service vehicles and public transit allowed), so leave your car near the train station *(Bahnhof).* Drivers approaching by freeway should follow *Bern Zentrum* signs, then *Bahnhof,* and *Bahnhof Parking* to find the huge pay garage behind the station (45-min meter parking outside, all-day lot inside, 2–4 SF/hr, depending on time of entry). While not the cheapest option, it's the easiest for a quick visit. From here, you're just an escalator ride away from the TI and Switzerland's capital.

Helpful Hints

Blue Monday: Most of Bern's museums are closed on Monday.

Internet Access: The **TI** has an Internet terminal (12 SF/hr), and there are Internet cafés throughout the city. You can also get online at **Thalia Bookstore,** on the lower level of the Loeb department store on Spitalgasse, two blocks from the station (2 SF/15 min, pay at cashier, then take receipt to info desk near terminals behind escalators, Mon–Wed 9:00–19:00, Thu 9:00–21:00, Fri 9:00–20:00, Sat 8:00–17:00, closed Sun, tel. 031-320-2020).

Bookstore: Stauffacher is huge, with an entire floor of English books; a fine travel section; and an inviting café with a terrace, good salads, and Internet access (Mon–Fri 9:00–19:00, Thu until 21:00, Sat 9:00–17:00, closed Sun, a block from the train station at Neuengasse 34). They also have a branch on the lower level of the train station (Mon–Sat 7:00–22:00, Sun 9:00–22:00).

Laundry: Jet Wash is located at Dammweg 43 (self-service, 5–8 SF to wash, 6 SF to dry, Mon–Sat 7:00–21:00, Sun 9:00–18:00, get there on bus #20).

Bike Rental: The **"Bern rollt"** program offers free loaner bikes for a half-day during the summer at three very central locations: at the train station (on Milchgassli), near the train station (on Hirschengraben), and in the old center (on Zeughausgasse near Bärenplatz). Just leave your photo ID and a 20-SF deposit and take off with the bike of your choice (first 4 hours free, then 1 SF/hr, daily in summer 7:00–21:30, tel. 079-277-2857, www.bernrollt.ch). Try the "Swiss Flyer," a clever little electric-motor-powered bike, or even a scooter or skateboard. **Velostation,** also with a location at the station, rents bikes by the day (1 SF/hr, www.velostationbern.ch).

Local Guide: Marie-Therese Lauper is a charming and hard-working independent guide (mobile 079-700-0880, amth lauper@dplanet.ch).

Getting Around Bern

The city is walkable, though the buses and trams can be handy. A standard single ticket costs 3.80 SF, a shorter trip *(Kurzstrecke)* runs 2 SF, and a day pass is 12 SF. The bus info center is across Bubenbergplatz from the station (Mon–Fri 8:30–18:00, closed Sat–Sun, tel. 031-321-8844, www.bernmobil.ch). Buy tickets from the machines located at bus and tram stops (pay in cash; new planned machines will also take euros and bankcards).

Here's the best plan for exploring the town: Walk from the train station to the far end of town, then catch bus #12 back to the station (2 SF, bus runs about every 6 min). Note that in 2011, the bus and tram numbers in Bern will change.

Tours in Bern

Walking tours leave daily from April through October at 11:00 from the TI at the train station (1.5 hrs, 20 SF, German and English

together). A new tour, focusing on the bear as a heraldic symbol for the city, leads you from the train station to the bear park (departs at 13:30, check TI's website for tour dates—www.berninfo.com, 1.5 hrs, 20 SF). The TI also offers four-hour **iPod tours** (18 SF) and organizes **river rafting tours** by request (usually daily June–Sept, 55 SF, minimum of 4 people). You can raft from Bern's Kirchenfeldbrücke to Worblaufen (return by train), or from Thun (near Interlaken) to Bern.

Self-Guided Walk

Welcome to Bern

This orientation walk begins at the train station and ends at the bear park, at the far end of town. From the bear park, you can catch bus #12 or browse your way back to your starting point, which is the…

Train Station

The station is a bright and airy shopping center, with a TI (in the far-back corner), an exchange desk open long hours, and all the shops you could need.

Stepping outside, you enter the big square called Bahnhofplatz. The old town was sealed off here with a fortified wall, which was replaced in the 19th century by the train station. Today all city buses and trams come and go from the station.

Bern's vision is to create a car-less city. The city was ripped up and new tram lines were put in for the Euro 2008 soccer tournament. And the "Bern rollt" program provides free loaner bikes

BERN AND MURTEN

Welcome To Bern Walk

1. Train Station
2. Bärenplatz
3. Parliament Square
4. Terraces
5. Casino Concert Hall
6. Kornhausplatz
7. Zytglogge-Turm (Clock Tower)
8. Kramgasse Shops & Einstein House
9. Bern Cathedral
10. Münsterplattform
11. Nydegg Bridge
12. Bear Park
13. Old Tram Depot

(government-subsidized and staffed by otherwise difficult-to-employ people).

Across the square stands the **Heiliggeistkirche** (Holy Ghost Church). Notice its gray-green Bernese sandstone, quarried nearby, used for the church and surrounding buildings. It's porous and easily eroded by water. That's why Bern's buildings have their characteristic over-sized eves. These are newer buildings, but built with the same stone as the older buildings to maintain architectural harmony (mandatory under city law).

• *From the train station TI, cross Bahnhofplatz, walk 50 yards, and turn left (around the church) onto Spitalgasse. This marks the start of one long street (with four names). The spine of both the peninsula and our walk, this street rambles downhill through the heart of town to the bridge and bear park.*

Notice the first of Bern's 11 historic **fountains,** the Bagpiper. These colorful 16th-century fountains are Bern's trademark. The city commissioned them for many reasons: to brighten up the cityscape of gray stone buildings, to show off the town's wealth, and to remind citizens of great local heroes and events. They also gave local artists something to work on after the Reformation deprived them of their most important patron, the Catholic Church.

Shopping opportunities abound under the more than three

miles of arcades that line Bern's lanes. Stores run the gamut from affordable to high-end, where prices are so steep, there's no danger of buying anything—my kind of shopping (stores generally open Mon–Fri 9:00–18:30, Thu until 21:00, Sat 9:00–17:00, closed Sun). In German, the slang for the corridor under these arcades is *Rohr* (pipe). To stroll through the town is to *rohren* (go piping).

• *Continue* "rohren" *down Spitalgasse until you reach...*

Bärenplatz

In summer, a daily market is held on this square (busiest on Tue and Sat mornings). The street runs under the **Prison Tower** (Käfigturm)—once a part of the city wall (c. 1256). Renovated from 1641 to 1644, the tower served as a prison until 1897 (*Käfig* means "cage"). Notice how the hand on the clock really is a hand—and how it was built in a slower-paced era, when just an hour hand told time precisely enough. The bears on the tower are from Bern's coat of arms. Live ones await you at the end of this walk.

To the left (50 yards), you'll see the **Dutch Tower** (Holländerturm). Swiss soldiers were famous mercenaries who fought all over Europe. Returning from a battle in the Netherlands, the soldiers brought back the habit of smoking. But smoking was forbidden within the city walls of Bern, so they hid in this tower to smoke secretly. Locals joke that now that a new, modern-day smoking ban has come to Bern, this tower may regain its historic function.

Farther left at the far end of the square is a modern, controversial, and mossy **fountain** by the Swiss surrealist Meret Oppenheim. Made in 1983, it symbolizes growth and life, and is supposed to demonstrate communication between an object of art and the beholder. It worked well...too well, in fact, as most citizens immediately communicated their dislike and wanted it destroyed. But Bern's politicians proved braver than expected, and the fountain survived. Time has transformed Oppenheim's gray concrete column into a multicolored pillar decorated with moss, grass, and flowers. Locals like it only in the winter, when it's covered with ice. The grand building beyond the fountain—once the city orphanage—is the police station.

As each of the town's successive walls and moats was torn down, it provided Bern with vast, people-friendly swaths of land that function as elongated "squares"—popular today for markets and outdoor cafés. This is a top place to be seen in the evening.

• *With your back to the modern fountain, stroll to the end of Bärenplatz, filled with market stalls and lined with fun places to eat (see "Eating in Bern," later). The big building you'll see from the square is the...*

Parliament (Bundeshaus)

You may brush elbows with some high-powered legislators, but you wouldn't know it—everything looks very casual for a national capital. The fine granite plaza in front of the parliament (built in 2004 to replace a parking lot) is a favorite spot for demonstrations and markets. The 26-squirt fountain (one for each canton) is a real kid-pleaser (and makes for fun photos) on a hot summer day. Facing the square on the left is the Swiss National Bank—this country's Fort Knox, with half the Swiss gold stock buried under the square (the rest is in Zürich).

Standing in front of the parliament, check out the statuary. The woman on the top of the building represents political independence, the one on the left (under the "1291") stands for freedom, and the one on the right (1848) symbolizes peace.

Drop in to the welcome center at the back of the building, and pick up the generous literature on the Swiss government. Its bicameral system was inspired by the US Constitution, with one big difference: Executive power is shared by a committee of seven, with a rotating ceremonial president and a passion for consensus. This is a mechanism to avoid power grabs by any single individual...a safeguard that the Swiss love.

When parliament is in session, the galleries are open to the public, so you can watch the action (free, must leave ID at entrance, no photos). When parliament is not in session, you can take a guided hour-long tour of the building in English (free; tours run hourly Mon–Sat at 9:00, 10:00, 11:00, 14:00, 15:00, and 16:00, Thu also at 17:00, 18:00, and 19:00; sign up the day before by calling 031-322-8522, www.parlament.ch, besucherdienst @pd.admin.ch).

• *Continuing past the parliament info kiosk, walk around behind the parliament to the...*

Terraces

From here, you have a commanding view over the Aare River and Bern's biggest swimming pool, the **Marzilibad.** On a clear day, you can see the peaks of the Eiger, Mönch, and Jungfrau (see the Gimmelwald and the Berner Oberland chapter), and the far less imposing "mountain" of Bern, the **Gurten** (with the view tower poking up above its forested summit). The Gurten is the city's favorite recreation spot, offering music festivals in summer and very modest skiing opportunities for children in winter.

Follow the tree-lined pedestrian lane left a few hundred yards to Kirchenfeld Bridge. Stand at the center for great river views (many museums are just across the bridge; the best options are described later, under "Sights in Bern"). The **Casino** isn't for gamblers—it's the home of Bern's Symphony Orchestra.

• *With your back to the river, follow the tram tracks down another swath of land created by the removal of a city wall, to...*

Kornhausplatz

This square is ornamented by the colorful fountain of an **Ogre** (*Chindlifresser*, "child-eater"). Two legends try to explain this gruesome sight. It's either a folkloric representation of the Greek god Chronos, or a figure that was intended to scare children off the former city walls.

The building behind on the left used to be the granary and now houses the modern public library and the huge **Kornhauskeller** restaurant. If the restaurant is open, wander down the stairs and head inside. Once the vast city wine cellar, now an Italian restaurant (recommended later, under "Eating in Bern"), this cellar was built in high Baroque style (1718) and renovated with paintings inspired by the Pre-Raphaelites in 1897. The 12 columns show traditional costumes of Bernese women.

• *Back on Kornhausplatz, step under the clock tower where Marktgasse becomes Kramgasse to see the fancy clock ornamenting its downhill side.*

Zytglogge-Turm

Bern's famous clock tower was part of the original wall marking the first gate to the city (c. 1250). The clock, which dates back to 1530, performs four minutes before each hour: The happy jester comes to life, Father Time turns his hourglass, the rooster crows (in German, that's "kee-kee-ree-kee" rather than "cock-a-doodle-doo"), and the golden man on top hammers the bell. Apparently, this nonevent was considered entertaining five centuries ago.

To pass the time waiting for the action, read the TI's leaflet explaining what's so interesting about the fancy old clock (for example, the golden hour hand is an hour behind for half the year because of the modern innovation of Daylight Saving Time). You can determine the zodiac, today's date, and the stage of the moon—look at the black-and-gold orb. Enthusiasts can tour the medieval mechanics—early Swiss engineering at its best—and see the billows that enable the old rooster to crow (12 SF, 45-min tour, May–Oct daily at 14:30, buy ticket from guide).

Under the clock are the old regional measurements (Swiss foot, the bigger Bernese foot, and the *Elle*, or "elbow," which was the distance from the elbow to the fingertip) and the official meter and double meter. It took a strong man like Napoleon to bring consistency to measurements in Europe, and he replaced the many goofy feet and elbows of medieval Europe with the metric system used today (c. 1800).

• *Continue your stroll down the main drag. At this point you enter the older part of town, where bigger department stores are replaced by quainter shops and galleries on...*

Kramgasse

Bern has wide streets like this one, but not many squares. In the Middle Ages, craftsmen exhibited their goods on the sidewalks under simple roofs. Eventually, these were formalized, buildings were expanded, and arcades evolved. Today, though the arcades are privately owned, owners must keep them clean and allow public access.

Most shops are underneath the arcades, but don't miss the ones in the **cellars** that you can access only from the main road. The cellars, marked by old-time hatches, were originally for storing

BERN AND MURTEN

potatoes and coal, and later, wine. People said "merry Bern" was floating on wine, just as Venice was floating on water. The merry times ended in 1798, when the French invaded (and drank all the wine). The cellars were once again used for potatoes, and the city got a new nickname: "sad Bern." Napoleon's soldiers not only liberated Bern from its wine, but also from the tremendous treasury the city was known for. Napoleon used money looted from Bern to finance his Egyptian crusade.

The apartment that **Einstein** called home between 1903 and 1905, during several of his happiest and most productive years, is 200 yards from the clock tower (on the right, at Kramgasse 49). See period furniture, the original spiral staircase entrance, Einstein's Patent Office desk, photos, and manuscripts. The museum doesn't do much for me, but I guess everything's relative (6 SF; April–Sept daily 10:00–17:00; Feb–March and

Oct–mid-Dec Mon–Fri 10:00–17:00, Sat 10:00–16:00, closed Sun; closed mid-Dec–Jan; tel. 031-312-0091, www.einstein-bern.ch). Die-hard fans may also want to visit the Einstein Museum, located in the Historical Museum of Bern (described later, under "Sights in Bern").

• *Just below Einstein's apartment, 20 yards past the Samson Fountain, turn right and crawl through the narrow Münstergässchen to the...*

BERN AND MURTEN

Bern Cathedral

Bern's 15th-century Münster, Catholic-turned-Protestant, is capped with a 330-foot-tall tower, the highest in Switzerland (finished in 1893). The late-Gothic church was dedicated to St. Vincent of Zaragoza. During the Reformation, religious icons were destroyed by Protestants (an act called "iconoclasm"). The church wasn't originally so plain; it was once adorned with 26 separate little chapels and altars dedicated to Mary and various saints. An ornate screen separated the priests from the worshippers. When the Reformation came to town in 1528, however, all this was swept away—the iconoclasts believed that images distracted worshippers from focusing on God. The new center of attention was the pulpit, where Protestant preachers shared the word of God—not in Latin, but in the people's language.

This church's main portal, with its striking gold-leaf highlights, seems pretty un-Protestant. It probably survived because its theme, the Last Judgment, showed that no matter how rich you are or what rank you have in Church hierarchy, anyone can end up

Albert Einstein (1879–1955) in Bern

The man who changed how we see our universe made his greatest discoveries during the eight years he lived in Bern (1901–1909). Raised in Germany, Albert Einstein went to college in Zürich, hoping to land a job teaching math and physics. But the young grad's GPA and resume were mediocre, so he took a temp job instead in Bern's Patent Office, inspecting and registering inventions.

Twenty-three-year-old Albert and his new bride Mileva (his college sweetheart) rented a second-floor apartment at Kramgasse 49 (today's Einstein House), where Mileva soon gave birth to little Hans Albert. Einstein punched the clock at the Patent Office and spent his spare time reading, hiking the Bern countryside, and thinking. At night, he'd join with his mates—the self-named "Olympia Academy"—to smoke, drink beer, and talk math and philosophy. Outwardly, he led an ordinary life, but his thoughts were always on science's Big Questions. At home, in pubs, or at work he'd scribble down equations and ideas, filing them in his self-described "Department of Theoretical Physics"—a desk drawer in his office.

Then, one warm spring day, as Einstein walked on the outskirts of Bern, it all started coming together. So began his *annus mirabilis*—the miracle year of 1905—in which the 26-year-old unknown amateur physicist quickly wrote five papers that would shock and perplex the world. Published in a major physics journal, they touched on a variety of subjects—such as how molecules move and how light can appear as either a wave of energy or as a beam of tiny particles.

The most famous and unsettling paper, his theory of special relativity, described a world in motion. A person on a moving train and someone who's stationary see the world from different perspectives—that's the classic principle of relativity described by Galileo and Newton. But Einstein said there's an exception to the rule—light, whose speed always remains constant whether it's on a moving train or on the ground. So a person on a moving train and one at rest will never agree on what they observe...yet they're both right. The discrepancies only become obvious as the

in hell (an idea Protestants dug). Condemned people are popping in the flames like lottery balls. Notice the humorous details in the commotion of people heading to hell (especially what the little green devil is doing to the sinful monk).

Cathedral entrance is free (April–Oct Mon–Sat 10:00–17:00, Sun 11:30–17:00; Nov–March Mon–Fri 10:00–12:00 & 14:00–16:00, Sat 10:00–12:00 & 14:00–17:00, Sun 11:30–16:00; last entry 30 min before closing, audioguide-5 SF, photos allowed, tel. 031-312-0462, www.bernermuenster.ch). Climb the spiral staircase 210 feet above town for the view and the exercise (4 SF, 344 steps, train travels close to the speed of light. Then, while the person on the train thinks everything is normal, the one on the ground sees the train shrink, train clocks slow down, and the person on the train stops aging!

Einstein's papers initially drew little interest and a measure of skepticism. (Einstein did get a promotion in the Patent Office—from "technical expert third class" to "technical expert second class.") But over time, other physicists grasped the significance of Einstein's work, seeing how he took earlier findings, wove them together, and did the math that explained it all. Subsequent experiments proved that, in fact, even Einstein's most bizarre assertions were correct. Time on a fast-moving jet really does slow down (hence, those interminable intercontinental flights).

Einstein was invited to lecture at the local university, though he was still working nine-to-five at the Patent Office. In his spare time, he worked on his next project, general relativity. He theorized that gravity is not a force that attracts things but a curving of space—like a bowling ball on a soft mattress—that affects the motion of nearby objects. In 1909, Einstein's growing reputation won him a job offer to teach in Zürich, and he quit the Patent Office and left Bern for good.

Einstein would never again approach the creative level of his days in Bern. In 1922, he won the Nobel Prize for his work done during the 1905 *annus mirabilis*. Albert and Mileva split, and he remarried. When Hitler took power in Germany (1933), Einstein—a pacifist and a Jew—left Europe for America. His curly black hair had turned white, and his aging face became a pop-culture icon of genius—complete with pipe, moustache, basset-hound eyes, and halo of frizzy white hair.

In 1939, Einstein wrote a letter to President Roosevelt theorizing that the tiniest particle of matter could be converted into an enormous amount of energy. The principle was one he'd discovered back in 1905—that energy is equivalent to mass times the speed of light squared (a very big number). And so, $E = mc^2$ became the atomic bomb, from an idea hatched in the pubs and arcaded streets of Bern.

last entry 30 min before closing). Marie-Thérèse Lauper works up there, watching over the church, answering questions, and giving those with a ticket a fine city view and a chance to peek at her bells.

• *Head behind the cathedral to a terrace overlooking the river, the...*

Münsterplattform

Starting in the 14th century, this terrace was built from all kinds of "recycled" stones from older buildings. Archaeologists even unearthed some heads of statues that were victims of Reformation iconoclasts. Look down on the Aare (find the bear out on the breakwater). Notice the security nets beneath you. The platform used to be the favorite place for suicides—to the terror of the people living below. The Pavilion Café offers a scenic spot under a chestnut tree for a bite or a drink on a sunny day. The pavilion opposite is a tiny branch of the city library, providing park-goers with books, boules, and table tennis. This little park is frequented by pot smokers, and nobody seems to care. Behind the café, the "vertical tram" has been carrying locals up and down since 1896 (1.20 SF).

With your back to the river, return to the main drag (now called Gerechtigkeitsgasse) via Junkerngasse. On the **Fountain of Justice,** a blindfolded figure of Justice triumphs over the mayor, pope, sultan, and emperor. A few steps above the fountain, a grate reveals a bit of the stream that used to flow open down the middle of the peninsula, providing people with a handy disposal system.

• *From here, it's a straight stretch through the oldest part of town to the bridge at the end of the old town, called...*

Nydegg Bridge

Look downstream from the Nydegg Bridge. To your left is the site of the original town castle (now a church). The small bridge below is the oldest in Bern (and, until 1844, the only bridge crossing the Aare here). Above on the ridge, just behind and to the right of the pointy spire, is the Rosengarten restaurant (described at the end of this walk). And just upstream stands the site of the original Lindt chocolate factory, evoking an age when this stretch of river was lined with mills powering the industrial zone of Bern—tanneries, shipyards, lumber mills, and so on. The area is now routinely flooded when the river runs high. As you look upstream, notice the peaceful path along the left bank, a nice place for a walk.

• *Continue across the bridge to reach the...*

Bear Park (BärenPark)

The symbol of Bern is the bear, and some lively ones frolic along this new, terraced hillside, to the delight of locals and tourists alike.

Since 1857, Bern had been housing its bears in big, barren, concrete pits *(Bärengraben)*. But thanks to the agitation of the B.L.M. (Bear Liberation Movement), a reluctant city government was forced to replace the pits with posher digs. In the spring of 2009, the last of the pit bears died, and in October of 2009, three-year-old brown bears Finn (a male from Finland) and Björk (a female from Denmark) moved to this new space. Finn and Björk enjoy much better conditions than their forebears, including a fishing channel next to the river—though they can still access the larger pit, which is now a historic monument (free, circuit around park open daily 24 hours, shop open daily 8:30–16:30, bus #12, tel. 031-357-1515, www.baerenpark-bern.ch). For info on guided tours by bear keepers, call 031-357-1525.

• *Behind the bear park is the...*

Old Tram Depot

This depot hosts a tourist center (TI, brewery restaurant/café with terrace). Its excellent 3-SF "Bern Show," complete with an animated town model and marching Napoleonic-era soldiers, illustrates the history and wonders of Bern (20 min, uncomfortable benches, show in English once hourly—see schedule—or ask for a printed script; June–Sept daily 9:00–18:00; March–May and Oct daily 10:00–16:00; Nov–Feb Fri–Sun 11:00–16:00, closed Mon–Thu).

From here, a seven-minute hike up the moderately steep, cobbled pathway takes you to the rose garden and the recommended **Restaurant Rosengarten,** which offers a grand city view and basic, reasonably priced food.

From the Old Tram Depot, it's an easy trip on bus #12 back to the train station (2 SF). If wandering back through town, be sure to get off into the quieter side lanes, which have a fascinating and entertaining array of shops and little eateries.

Sights in Bern

▲▲**The Berner Swim and Marzilibad**—For something to write home about, join the local merchants, students, and carp in a float down the Aare River. The Bernese, proud of their very clean river and their basic ruddiness, have a tradition—sort of a wet, urban *paseo*. On summer days, they hike upstream 5 to 30 minutes, then float back down to the excellent (and free) riverside baths and pools (Marzilibad) just below the Parliament building.

The process is easy: Hike up the paved riverside sidewalk as far as you like, then take the steps leading into the water whenever you want to "put in." As you approach Marzilibad, just stroke over to the shore to grab one of the several poles placed to help people exit the river. The locals make it look easy, but this can be dangerous—the current is swift. If you miss the last pole, you're history.

If a float down the river is a bit much for you, enjoy the Marzilibad, a well-equipped public swimming pool and park with picnic spots, restaurant, lockers, wading pools, games, and more.

▲▲Museum of Fine Arts (Kunstmuseum)—Featuring 800 years of local art, this three-story museum offers a unique opportunity to see the best of Swiss artists, from romantic folk art to the Jugendstil movement. You'll find old masters in the basement, 19th-century works on the ground floor, and 20th-century stuff upstairs (7 SF, extra for temporary exhibits, covered by Swiss Pass, no English on wall captions but English sheet for temporary exhibits, Tue 10:00–21:00, Wed–Sun 10:00–17:00, closed Mon, no photos, 4 blocks north of station, Holdergasse 12, tel. 031-328-0944).

▲▲Paul Klee Center (Zentrum Paul Klee)—With his wavy building mirroring the wavy landscape of the Bern countryside, Italian architect Renzo Piano celebrates the creative spirit of Swiss-born artist Paul Klee (1879–1940). Klee wasn't just a great painter, he was an interdisciplinary explosion of creative energy. The center, which fosters music and theater as well as the visual arts, has

a mission: to bring art to the people. For instance, a huge zone is devoted to a children's creative workshop that includes painting and a shadow theater. Children's workshops are scheduled throughout the day (15 SF for 1-hour workshop at 12:00, 14:00, or 16:00, no advance reservations).

The Klee collection is in the building's middle wave. This cultural center keeps about 200 of Klee's pieces on display (out of a collection of 4,000). It's the best place in the world to experience and learn about this modernist painter of lively, almost childlike art. Artistically, you can't put Klee in a box. His paintings—mostly from the 1920s and 1930s—are playful yet enigmatic. Audioguides let you enjoy Klee's favorite music while you wander through the collection. His art is full of symbolism...or maybe we just think so. He experimented in pointillism, as you'll see in the piece *Ad Parnassum*.

Insula Dulcamara (Bittersweet Island) is a good example of Klee's enigmatic hieroglyph style. It's a puzzle—he pairs opposites: man, woman; air, water. It's 1938... is that a submarine on the horizon evoking the rise of fascism? Perhaps the black figures are death, floating in an eternal spring-like landscape. Kids love Klee, and they always teach the art snobs a thing or two with their interpretations.

Downstairs you'll find cafés, an art database, a movie about building the museum, a cozy hangout, and the children's workshop. Pick up a free English-language booklet when purchasing your ticket

Cost, Hours, Location: 18 SF for one exhibit, 22 SF for two, covered by Swiss Pass, audioguide-5 SF, Tue–Sun 10:00–17:00, closed Mon, take bus #12 from train station to Zentrum Paul Klee stop—6/hr, stops right at the center, Monument im Fruchtland 3, tel. 031-359-0101, www.zpk.org.

Einstein Museum—Fans of the genius will want to visit this new museum, which began as a temporary exhibit and now occupies the second floor of Bern's Historical Museum. Photos and exhibits depict Einstein's accomplishments and complicated personal life, within the context of the contemporary events of his time (18 SF, covered by Swiss Pass, audioguide-5 SF, Tue–Sun 10:00–17:00, closed Mon, across bridge from Parliament at Helvetiaplatz 5— take tram #3 or #5, tel. 031-350-7711, www.einsteinmuseum.ch).

Other Bern Museums—Near the Historical Museum are the Alpine, Communication, Natural History, Rifle, and Kunsthalle contemporary art museums—appealing mainly to visitors with those specific interests (the TI produces a good free pamphlet describing all the museums). The Natural History Museum is fun for kids (all covered by Swiss Pass, most open Tue–Sun 10:00–17:00, closed Mon, take tram #3 or #5 across the bridge, www.museen-bern.ch).

Sleeping in Bern

These places are listed in approximate geographical order from the train station. The first is a block south of it, and the rest are in the old town past Bärenplatz, about a 5–10-minute walk away.

$$$ Hotel National is well-located, with 46 fine rooms. It's a simple, old-school, hardwood-floor time warp of a place with a classic elevator. There's some street noise, and inward-facing rooms can be noisy on Friday and Saturday, so request a quiet room (S-65–90 SF, Ss-100–125 SF, D-130 SF, Ds-150–170 SF, 3–5-person family room with shower-235–300 SF, extra bed-30–45 SF, elevator, free Internet access, pay Wi-Fi, Hirschengraben 24, tel. 031-381-1988, fax 031-381-6878, www.nationalbern.ch, info@nationalbern.ch).

$$$ Hotel Continental has 40 bright and comfy Nordic-flavored rooms and a cheery breakfast room with a sun terrace (Sb-140–170 SF, Db-190–230 SF, Tb-240–270 SF, cheaper Fri–Sun,

Sleep Code

(1 SF = about $1, country code: 41)
S = Single, **D** = Double/Twin, **T** = Triple, **Q** = Quad, **b** = bathroom,
s = shower only. Unless otherwise noted, credit cards are
accepted, English is spoken, and breakfast is included.

To help you sort easily through these listings, I've divided
the rooms into three categories, based on the price for a
standard double room with bath:

$$$ Higher Priced—Most rooms 150 SF or more.
$$ Moderately Priced—Most rooms between 100–150 SF.
$ Lower Priced—Most rooms 100 SF or less.

elevator, save 15 SF by skipping breakfast, free Internet access,
pay Wi-Fi, Zeughausgasse 27, tel. 031-329-2121, fax 031-329-2199,
www.hotel-continental.ch, info@hotel-continental.ch).

$$$ Hotel Goldener Schlüssel is the oldest inn in down-
town Bern, but it's been completely renovated. Its 35 small, Euro-
style staterooms have modern sliding-glass-door bathroom pods.
The back rooms are quieter and more expensive, as the front rooms
facing Rathausgasse get café and disco noise from across the street
(Sb-138–160 SF, Db-178–220 SF, Db suite-290–360 SF, Tb-235–
275 SF, Qb-255–295 SF, extra bed-50 SF, elevator, free Internet
access, pay Wi-Fi, Rathausgasse 72, tel. 031-311-0216, fax 031-311-
5688, www.goldener-schluessel.ch, info@goldener-schluessel.ch).

$$ Backpackers Hotel Glocke rents the cheapest beds in the
old town, and your group always gets its own dorm. The two upper
floors have all private rooms (bunk in 6-bed dorm-34 SF, bed in
bunk-bed D-43 SF, S-72 SF, D with one big bed-108 SF, Db-140
SF, T-141 SF, Q-172 SF, includes sheets, towels-3 SF, dorms have
lockers and sinks, no breakfast but nice kitchen, non-smoking,
elevator, pay Internet access, free Wi-Fi in lounge, laundry, no
membership necessary, no curfew, reception open 8:00–11:00 &
15:00–22:00, 10-min walk from station at Rathausgasse 75, tel.
031-311-3771, fax 031-311-1008, www.bernbackpackers.com, info
@bernbackpackers.com).

$ Bern Youth Hostel is a big, institutional place below the
Parliament building near the river. It's well-run and adult-friendly
(dorm bed-37 SF, S-64 SF, D-92 SF, includes sheets and breakfast,
nonmembers pay 6 SF extra/night, dinner-14 SF, Internet access,
Wi-Fi, lockers, laundry, reception open 7:00–10:30 & 14:00–24:00,
Weihergasse 4, tel. 031-326-1111, www.youthhostel.ch/bern, bern
@youthhostel.ch).

Eating in Bern

Between the Station and Bärenplatz

Tibits, a busy self-service buffet in the train station building, offers a huge variety of vegetarian-only salads and sandwiches, plus two different hot dishes. Help yourself to a plate and pile it on. The price is by weight: An average helping will cost you about 20 SF (4 SF/100 grams, 7.50 SF for soup and bread, variety of sandwiches for 8 SF, fresh fruit juices for 7 SF, Mon–Thu 6:30–23:30, Fri–Sat 6:30–24:00, Sun 8:00–23:00, Bahnhofplatz 10, tel. 031-312-9111).

Gourmanderie Moléson is a long, skinny, classy bistro serving dishes with a French flair, including fondue, *tartes flambées* (Alsatian pies—25–29 SF), vegetarian meals, two-course lunch deals (30 SF), and dinner specials (26–35 SF). It has a dressy and very Swiss interior with tables that tumble out onto the street (Mon–Fri 11:30–14:30 & 18:00–23:30, Sat 18:00–23:30, closed Sun, Aarbergergasse 24, tel. 031-311-4463).

Restaurant della Casa, a traditional Swiss place with Old World ambience inside and tables on the sidewalk outside, has daily specials (22–25 SF) scrawled on chalkboards throughout. While not cheap, it's been a neighborhood favorite for generations. This is a cheese-free, yet traditional, Swiss restaurant (25–36-SF plates, Mon–Fri 10:30–23:30, Sat 9:00–15:00, closed Sun, between Parliament and the station at Schauplatzgasse 16, tel. 031-311-2142).

Restaurant Vatter is exclusively organic—serving mostly vegetarian, lots of Indian cuisine, and some meat dishes. It's a fresh, mod place with a terrace overlooking the lively Bärenplatz. The restaurant is above an organic produce store (25-SF plates, Mon–Fri 8:30–20:30, Sat 8:30–17:00, closed Sun, Bärenplatz 2, tel. 031-312-5171).

Ristorante Luce brings the cooking of Italy's Emilia Romagna region to Bern. With a venerable dining hall and great seating on the square, it's popular and known as a good value (hearty pastas-20 SF, salads, no pizzas, daily 11:30–14:00 & 18:00–23:00, Zeughausgasse 28, tel. 031-310-9999).

Around Kornhausplatz

Kornhauskeller, decorated with colorful mural paintings, is a splurge. It's in the palatial cellar of the old granary, originally built to house the state's wine cellar. This dressy, pricey Mediterranean place offers lunch specials and a fine antipasto bar for those on a budget. Make a meal out of the 19-SF or 27-SF plate, telling the man behind the buffet exactly what you'd like (35–60 SF plates, Mon–Sat 11:45–14:30 & 18:00–24:00, Sun 18:00–23:30, Kornhausplatz 18, tel. 031-327-7272).

Bern Hotels & Restaurants

1. Hotel National
2. Hotel Continental
3. Hotel Goldener Schlüssel
4. Backpackers Hotel Glocke
5. Bern Youth Hostel
6. Tibits Cafeteria
7. Gourmanderie Moléson
8. Restaurant della Casa
9. Restaurant Vatter
10. Ristorante Luce
11. Kornhauskeller Rest.
12. Restaurant Harmonie & Housi's Brot-Loube
13. Restaurant Rosengarten
14. Brewery Restaurant
15. Schwellenmätteli Rest.
16. Internet Access (in Loeb Dep't Store)
17. Stauffacher Bookstore
18. To Launderette
19. Free Bikes (3 Locations)

Near the Cathedral

Restaurant Harmonie, owned by the Gyger family since 1915, is one of the oldest and most traditional places in town. It offers filling Swiss cuisine and is the favorite lunch spot for the country's politicians (daily specials, 30–50 SF plates, closed Sat–Sun, Hotelgasse 3, tel. 031-313-1141).

Housi's Brot-Loube is the bakery next door to Restaurant Harmonie. Here you can pick up sandwiches (they'll warm them for you), salads, drinks, and pastries for a picnic at the nearby Münsterplattform (Mon–Fri 6:30–18:30, closed Sat–Sun, Münstergasse 74).

Near the Bear Park

Many finish their town walk at the bear park and have worked up an appetite. You have two fine options here.

Restaurant Rosengarten is good for city views. During the day, come for lunch, or for tea and cake with local grannies (19-SF two-course lunch special). At night you'll dine with couples enjoying the fresh seasonal menu (20–40-SF dinner plates, March–Nov daily 9:00–24:00, closed off-season, moderately steep walk up cobbled Aargauerstalden, or take bus #10 from the old town, tel. 031-331-3206).

Brewery Restaurant offers seating in their big, bright, and boisterous microbrewery, or on their leafy terrace overlooking the town and river. Quick and not too expensive, it's a local favorite, serving good-time food (fast and healthy 16–24-SF lunch plates, daily 11:00–24:00, in Old Tram Depot above the bear park, reserve in evening, tel. 031-368-1415).

On the Aare River

Schwellenmätteli Restaurant is a chance to join trendy locals for a meal or drink while sitting over the river. This mod restaurant/lounge has classy tables inside and out. At the tip of the pier is a lounge complete with sofas, mattresses, and a glass floor that lets you see the river racing underneath. The outdoor dining area and bar is open only in nice weather. The cuisine is modern Mediterranean, with some local trout (15-SF starters, 28–40-SF main dishes, daily 9:00–24:00, 15-min riverside stroll from bear park to Dalmaziquai 11, or take stairs and path below Kirchenfeld Bridge down to river, reservations smart for dinner, tel. 031-350-5001). Their Italian restaurant across the parking lot is also good.

Bern Connections

From Bern by Train to: Murten (hourly, 35 min), **Lausanne** (2/hr, 70 min), **Interlaken** (2/hr, 55 min, some with change in Spiez), **Luzern** (2/hr, 1–1.5 hrs), **Zürich** (2/hr, 1 hr), **Zürich Airport** (2/hr, 1.25 hrs), **Fribourg** in Switzerland (2/hr, 20 min), **Zermatt** (1–2/hr, 2.25 hrs, transfer in Visp), **Montreux** (2/hr, 1.5 hrs, transfer in Lausanne), **Lugano** (hourly, 3.75 hrs, transfer in Luzern or Zürich), **Appenzell** (hourly, 3 hrs, transfer in Gossau), **Munich** (roughly hourly, 5.75–6.25 hrs, 1–2 changes), **Frankfurt** (hourly, 4 hrs, some with change in Basel), **Freiburg** in Germany (hourly, 1.75–2.5 hrs, few direct, most with change in Basel), **Salzburg** (roughly hourly, 7–9 hrs, 1–4 changes), **Paris** (1–2/hr, 4.5–6 hrs, 1 direct train in morning and 1 in evening, otherwise 1–3 changes). Train info: toll tel. 0900-300-300 or www.rail.ch.

Route Tips for Drivers

Interlaken to Bern: From Interlaken, catch the autobahn (direction: Spiez, Thun, then Bern). Circle Bern on the autobahn, taking the fourth Bern exit, Neufeld Bern. Signs to *Bern Zentrum* take you to Bern *Bahnhof* (train station). Turn right just before the station into the Bahnhof Parkplatz (described earlier, under "Arrival in Bern").

Heading to Murten from Bern: From the station, drive out of Bern following signs for *Lausanne,* then follow the green signs to *Neuchâtel* and *Murten*. The autobahn ends 20 miles later, in Murten.

Murten

The finest medieval ramparts in Switzerland surround the 5,000 people of Murten (pronounced MOOR-ten; if you say MURR-ten, you might get a quizzical look). You're on the linguistic cusp of Switzerland: 25 percent of Murten speaks French; a few miles to the southwest, nearly everyone does (French-speakers call the town Morat).

Murten is a totally charming mini-Bern with lively streets, the middle one nicely arcaded with breezy outdoor cafés and elegant shops (many closed Mon). Its castle is romantic, overlooking Lake Murten and the rolling vineyards of gentle

Mont Vully in the distance. Spend a night here and have dinner with a local Vully wine, white or rosé. Murten is touristed, but seems to be enjoyed mostly by its own people.

Make time for nearby Avenches (see end of chapter). Though quaint today, the town was once a powerful Roman capital—as its ruins attest.

Orientation to Murten

Tourist Information

Murten's TI is just inside the city walls at the far end of town from the train station (Easter–Sept Mon–Fri 9:00–12:00 & 13:00–18:00, Sat–Sun 11:00–16:30, Oct–Easter shorter hours and closed weekends, Französische Kirchgasse 6, tel. 026-670-5112, www.murten tourismus.ch). Get a free map and walking guide, and ask about sights, biking, and boat trips.

Arrival in Murten

By Train: To reach the town from the station (a 5-min walk), exit to the right, take the first left, and walk up Bahnhofstrasse, then turn right through the town gate. Murten is a tiny town...and a delight on foot.

By Car: You can park overnight in the old town for free (18:00–10:00). During the day, don't park inside the gates; Murten's brown-clad parking cops are infamous. Park in the lot near the castle and Co-op supermarket (1.80 SF/hr, pay at machine inside by elevator). Get the latest advice on parking from your hotelier.

Helpful Hints

Internet Access: Try **A&A Computer** (12 SF/hr, Mon–Fri 9:00–12:00 & 14:00–19:00, Sat 9:00–16:00, closed Sun, shorter hours in winter, behind train station, past Peugeot garage, at Engelhardstrasse 6, tel. 026-670-0520). The TI has info on local Wi-Fi hotspots.

Post Office: It's across the street from the train station.

Laundry: There's none in town.

Local Guide: Mary Brunisholz, an American who married into this part of Switzerland, is an excellent guide with a car (150–200 SF/half-day, mobile 078-601-7040, mary.brunisholz @vtxnet.ch). The TI has a list of other guides.

Self-Guided Walk

Welcome to Murten

This introductory walk will give you the lay of the land and a lesson on the historic 15th-century Battle of Murten.

Murten

Key:

1. Hotel/Rest. Murtenhof & Krone
2. Hotel/Rest. Ringmauer
3. To Berger Farmhouse
4. Freiburger Falle Rest.
5. Restaurant Anatolia
6. Restaurant Eintracht
7. Grizzly's Restaurant
8. Pizzeria Taverna Italiana
9. Bar & Blumen Pub
10. Züger Bakery
11. Co-op Supermarket
12. Cinema
13. Library
14. Internet Access
15. Simonet Weapons Shop
16. Steps to Lake
17. Access to Ramparts

• *Start your walk just below the town's main gate at the public school, where you see a statue of the feisty local leader...*

Adrian von Bubenberg

Burgundy was the aggressive power of the day, and this Murten native stopped the power grab of the 15th century by beating Charles the Bold. Adrian von Bubenberg stood here and looked across the lake at the distant peaks of the Jura Mountains—the historic border between the Swiss and the French (more on the battle a little later).

The earliest Swiss clockmakers were from those Jura Mountains. Look at the **clock tower**—where's the little hand? As part of its lease, the restaurant below takes responsibility for hand-winding the clock each day, as it has since 1712. That's the Bern gate—so called because it opens up onto the road to Bern. The tiny grated window in the mighty door is a security window.

• *Rather than enter the gate, go right instead. Head along the outside of the wall, around the first turret, and look for the cannonballs, left in the wall to remind townsfolk of their incredible victory over the Burgundians—like an Alamo with a happy ending.*

Belly up to the...

Lakeview Terrace

Across the way is Mont Vully (mohn voo-yee)—one big vineyard and a mecca for lovers of Swiss white wine. The lowlands to the right—a rich former lakebed—are the heart of the fertile Three Lakes Region (lakes Biel, Neuchâtel, and Murten). The lush farmland is called the "vegetable garden of Switzerland" for its soil, which yields more than 60 varieties of produce.

The ancient Celtic Helvetii tribe recognized the fertility of this land and settled here. The Romans likewise made this land a priority in establishing their colony of Helvetia (the origin of Switzerland's official name, Confoederatio Helvetica).

• *Check out the small...*

French Church

Foreseeing a showdown with Burgundy, Adrian von Bubenberg had the town walls strengthened. As three-quarters of the townspeople were German-speaking, they took a vote and decided to tear down the French church to get more stones. (This little church was rebuilt for the French-speaking community six years after its big one was demolished.) As the Calvinist Reformation swept through Catholic Switzerland in the early 16th century, churches like this were stripped of their rich paintings, sculptures, and stained glass. The altar became a Bible on a table, and pulpits became the focus. The emphasis was teaching the word of God. In this church, about the only exceptions to the "no distractions" rule are the tiny stained-glass coats of arms—heraldry of the wealthy families who helped fund its construction.

• *From here, you'll walk across town. Walk past the TI, the clock tower, and up the lane to the library (on right, #31).*

Library

Notice that along with being a "Bibliothek," the library is also a "Ludothek." This means that parents can check out toys and games for their children, rather than spend their hard-earned money keeping massive places like Toys "R" Us in business. Across the street, the typically Bernese little **Web Husli** shows off its old-time loom. The door is perfect for short people—if you're under 5' 4", stand tall on the threshold. After a 14th-century fire burned down the wooden town, future building was limited to the characteristic yellow Jura stone (like the library). Around the corner (left), just past the town's morgue, is the public WC.

• *Continue straight ahead to the...*

German Church

Murten's German church, built in 1710, is also post–Reformation Protestant simple. As the town is on the border between two cantons (Bern and Fribourg), for 400 years its rule was shared: Every five years, it would flip between cantons. Arrangements like this didn't sit well with Napoleon, and around 1800, he made it firmly a part of nearby Fribourg.

Inside, notice the big stucco relief (center of ceiling) with two seals: the bear for Bern and the three castles for Fribourg. The Protestant passion for Bible study is also evident in this church. The pulpit was carved from a single trunk of oak in 1460. Explore the choir (circle of seats for big shots) behind the altar. Find Adrian von Bubenberg's seat. (Hint: The window above shows the war hero in red, with his victorious local yokels in their alpine red-knit hats...underdogs whupping the Burgundians.) Pull up the seat and rest on the misericord—a lazy but permissible alternative when everyone stands during a long service. Notice that the two prime seats do double duty (on the right hand of the preacher sat the leader of Bern or Fribourg—depending on who happened to be ruling that year). To computer gamers, the stained-glass depiction of the crucifixion feels proto-Tetris (c. 1926).

• *Leaving the church, hook left around the back. Finger the limestone and sandstone tombstones, quarried from Mont Vully for noble families.*

Then climb the creaky stairs onto the ramparts and walk about 50 yards.

Rampart Ramble

Murten's only required sightseeing is to scramble the ramparts (free, open daily until 21:00). Survey the town. Note the uniformity of Murten. Paint your place the wrong color, and you may be instructed to redo it—at your own expense. Scanning the countless chimneys, think of the enforced conformity that comes with living in a small town (and find the one oddball). Telephone and electricity wires are all underground. Look back at the roof of the German church. A color-blindness test is built into its tiles. (If you can find the six-sided "star of David"—not a Jewish symbol in this case, but recalling the star that guided the wise men to Bethlehem on the first Christmas—you're OK.)

• *Continue to the **tower**. Climb the steps for a commanding town and lake view.*

With your back to the lake, look inland and imagine the action on June 22, 1476. Mighty Charles the Bold, with his 20,000 well-armed Burgundians, was camped on the hill (with the divided forest) for 10 days, laying siege to the town of 2,000. Runners were sent out from the town to gather help. A makeshift army of about 10,000 villagers gathered on the hills to the left. Just as George Washington attacked when the Redcoats were celebrating Christmas, the Swiss swooped in as the Burgundians were still hungover from a big Midsummer Night's Eve bash. The Battle of Murten was fought in pouring rain—a muddy, bloody mess. Almost all 20,000 Burgundians were slaughtered—many driven into the lake with their armor to drown (try swimming in a coat of mail). For centuries, French bones would wash ashore. Charles the (no-longer-so-) Bold barely got away on a very fast horse.

This victory demonstrated to the Swiss the advantages of *E Pluribus Unum,* and the assemblage of the many still-fiercely independent Swiss cantons into the Helvetic Confederation snowballed. In this sweet little corner, an influential battle in European history had been fought. Burgundian power ebbed, and Europe got to know a new nation...Switzerland.

• *Walk a bit farther along the wall and descend at the next tower (across from Café–Pension Ringmauer).*

The stairs lead to a fine old **clock** mechanism from 1816. Once powering the big clock in the City Hall tower, it spent decades in a to-be-assembled pile (à la Ikea), gathering dust in an attic. An old local, recognizing a good challenge, reassembled it into perfect working order (1991). Notice how the gearbox powers three different clock faces, and how the old hand crank raises the stones that power the clock. The white face determines the clock's time, which rings on the quarter-hour.

• *Step outside the wall, where you'll see the Catholic church (1886), private gardens along the wall, and the different stages of the wall's construction.*

The first phase was built with large river stones, some arranged in a neat fishbone pattern. Later, the town ran out of money, and the next stage shows pebbles and rubble mixed with a rough concrete. And finally, when the town prospered again, they finished the wall with finely cut sandstone.

• *Walk back into town, stopping on the first corner at the fire station–turned-community-**cinema**.*

Local shareholders are thanked with their names on the door. Pop into the charming theater—80 plush, red seats. Notice what's playing tonight (see "Nightlife in Murten," later). At this corner, spin slowly, admiring the town's fine shutters.

• *Then, continue a block to the...*

Main Street

In the 19th century, Murten's townsfolk used one of three water fountains on this street. Enjoy the colorful store signs as they still hang out their shingles in the traditional fashion. Bakery and *pâtisserie* competition on this street is fierce. Drop into one for the local specialties: *Nidlechueche,* a sweet, doughy cream tart; and *Seelander Zwetschen,* a chocolate-covered prune truffle with liqueur.

Near the top of the main street, **Simonet Weapons** sells all the latest knives by Victorinox. There's the green "stay-glow," and even a model with a USB flash drive for the outdoorsman with a laptop. At the top of the street (#16), Murten's oldest house has fine paintings under its eaves. There's some nice *Schmuck* (jewelry) two doors to the right.

• *Farther to the right, at the top of town, step into...*

Murten Castle

The town castle, which houses the police station in a former prison (closed to the public), shows off an impressive gun from 1882 and a lovely lake view. The nearby museum is not worth your time or money, but steps lead from there down to the lake.

Activities in Murten

Lake Activities—To get down to Murten's lazy lakefront, find the access just past the castle, at Rathausgasse 17 (a block from Hotel Murtenhof), or go out the gate by the TI and take a left

BERN AND MURTEN

down the hill. Just past the grassy breakwater is Pantschau, a big park, which is flanked by cheap self-service eateries (such as La Chaloupe, with salad bar and crêpes) and the Beach House (with better lakeside seating). There's mini-golf, windsurfing gear rental and instruction, an open-air summer film fest, and a fine lakeside promenade. Buy tickets for cruises (described next) at the kiosk at Pier 1.

One-Hour Lake Murten Cruise (with Hiking Option): Boats go about six times a day through the summer (19 SF without stops, 23.60 SF with stopover privileges, covered by Swiss Pass, 4/day Oct–April, call to confirm off-season, tel. 032-329-8811 or 032-729-9600, www.navig.ch; TI can help).

Consider stopping in the small town of Praz on the French-speaking shore. From there you have two good options: You could hike through vineyards up Mont Vully—where a bench and a pretty lake and Alp views await—and return on the lake with your same ticket. Or you can walk from Praz back to Murten, clockwise around the lake (2 hrs, 9.60 SF for boat from Murten to Praz).

Half-Day Three Lakes Cruise: Consider sailing on all three of the region's lakes (connected by canals) and stopping at several small medieval villages along the way. Two boat companies make the trip once a day (3.25–4.25 hours each way, 51 SF for one-way ticket, 58-SF "day card" covers round-trip). One boat leaves from Murten at 10:00, arrives in the town of Biel at 14:10, then turns around immediately and heads back along the same route, leaving Biel at 14:20 and arriving in Murten at 18:20 (runs Tue–Sun late May–late Sept, tel. 032-729-9600, www.navig.ch). A different boat leaves Biel at 9:45 and arrives in Murten at 13:00. It returns from Murten at 14:30, giving you an hour or so in town, and docks in Biel at 18:20 (runs daily April–late Oct, tel. 032-329-8811, www.bieler see.ch/de). Ask at the TI if they (or the post office) have coupons—you may find ample boat-trip discounts—then buy tickets at the waterfront. You can condense this full-day trip by taking the boat one way and the train the other (2/hr, 1–1.25 hrs, 1–2 changes).

Swimming Pool—The Olympic-size public swimming pool is outside of town next to the lake, just past the castle (8 SF, daily mid-June–mid-Aug 9:00–21:00, spring and fall 9:30–19:00, closed in winter and spring, www.schwimmbad-murten.ch).

Biking—The Three Lakes region has 100 miles of signposted bike paths (well-described in the TI's brochures). Pick up a free map or buy a top-notch one at the TI. The best easy ride circles the lake and Mont Vully (through vineyards and, if you like, to the summit for a good view). You can rent **bikes** at train-station ticket counters (25 SF/half-day, 33 SF/day, 5 SF less with Eurailpass or Swiss Pass, includes helmets, daily 5:30–22:15, www.rent-a-bike .ch). Ask about being dropped off with your bike—or dropping off your bike—at another station, which opens up interesting options (7 SF extra, limited to a few stations).

Nightlife in Murten

Movies—Murten's cute little community co-op theater plays movies nightly (15 SF, Schulgasse 18). Movies are shown in their original language (capital letter indicates the soundtrack language, small letters indicate subtitles—e.g., "Efd" means "English with French and *Deutsch* subtitles").

The open-air cinema hosts a lakeside summer film festival with outdoor screenings of a different movie each night (early July–early Aug, details at TI).

Pubs—There are plenty of inviting pubs and nightclubs in town. The **Bar and Blumen** sells drinks with a lake view by night (between Hotel Murtenhof & Krone and Town Hall). The main street has an Irish bar and several other nightspots. The bar just outside the clock tower is popular with locals.

Sleeping in Murten

(1 SF = about $1, country code: 41)

This adorable town is no secret. July through mid-September (especially on weekends) is peak time—make a reservation and expect maximum prices. When price ranges are given in the hotel listings, it means that prices vary depending on the season, type of room, or view. The nearest youth hostel is in Avenches (see page 129).

$$$ Hotel Murtenhof & Krone, a worthwhile splurge, has 57 nicely appointed rooms—each a stylish mix of old and new. The Krone section of the hotel has smaller, plainer, less-expensive rooms and a cozy, spacious lounge. This place is well-run by the Joachim family—Theodore, Jutta, and their sons Marc and Ariste (Sb-120 SF, small Db-160 SF, big Db-240 SF, Tb-220–280 SF, family rooms, in mid-Sept–May ask for a 10 percent discount with this book, elevator, free Internet access, pay Wi-Fi, parking 18 SF/day, next to castle at Rathausgasse 1–5, tel. 026-672-9030, fax 026-672-9039, www .murtenhof.ch, info@murtenhof.ch). They have the best lakeview restaurant in town (described later, under "Eating in Murten").

$$ Hotel Ringmauer ("Ramparts") is friendly and characteristic, with a fun mix of modern decor in a traditional setting.

Showers and toilets are within a dash of all 14 rooms (S-65 SF, D-115 SF, Db-130 SF, T-155 SF, Q-175 SF, attached restaurant, near town wall farthest from lake, Deutsche Kirchgasse 2, tel. 026-670-1101, fax 026-672-2083).

$ Berger Farmhouse is the choice if "Green Acres is the place" for you—and if you have a car. Consider a night in a barn (literally) at the big, traditional Berger-Aegerter family farm. Frau Berger, who speaks German and French, fills a big room with six single beds (and can add up to four more). There's no plumbing—you use a bathroom in the family building next door. The place is generally empty, so you're likely to have it all to yourself—surrounded by hay, old farm tools, and the noise of animals (May–Nov only because there's no heat, 30 SF/bed with breakfast, she'll cook dinner for 15 SF by request, family deals, includes sheets but no towels, a third of the way to Avenches, a mile or so south of Murten, on the main road just before Greng, look for the sign, Lindenweg 2, tel. 026-670-1407).

Eating in Murten

Eating in Murten is a joy. I'd stroll the main drag up one side and down the other to survey the action before making a choice. For elegance and a lake view, it's the Murtenhof. There are several good options right on the lake a 10-minute walk down from the town center. Budget eaters can assemble a picnic at the Co-op grocery or find a salad bar. Bakeries make good sandwiches, but they close by about 18:00.

Anything called "Seelander" or mentioning "three lakes" is typical of this Three Lakes region. Traditional restaurants serve *Egli-Filets*, the very popular perch "from the lake" (these days actually caught in Bodensee—Lake Constance in English—up by the German border). As this is the "vegetable garden of Switzerland," restaurants pride themselves on offering good veggies. You'll want a glass of wonderfully smooth and refreshing white Vully (voo-yee) wine with your meal (about 4 SF/glass).

Restaurant Murtenhof, with a covered terrace giving diners a comfortable and classy lakeside setting regardless of the weather, serves "updated Three Lakes cuisine" and several vegetarian choices. Sipping a glass of local white wine with the right travel partner, while gazing across the lake at hillside vineyards as the sun sets, is one of Europe's fine moments. Their fresh and tasty "catch of the day" (while not *Egli*) actually *is* from the lake (19 SF). To be sure you get the limited lakeside seating, call in a reservation (salad bar, March–Nov Tue–Sun 11:00–23:00, closed Mon and Dec–Feb, tel. 026-672-9030). The occasional baaah-ing of sheep and goats from the field below the open windows adds a nice soundtrack to the rustic elegance.

Ringmauer Restaurant is a good bet for French cuisine and decadent desserts, offering both a dressy section (21–32-SF lunch plates, 36–55-SF dinner plates, 78-SF five-course fixed-price meal) and a cheaper zone (25–40-SF plates, 18-SF daily special). This local favorite has outdoor seating on a quiet, picturesque lane and serves top-end local wine by the glass (Tue–Sat 11:30–13:45 & 18:30–21:30, Sun 11:30–13:45 only, closed Mon, Deutsche Kirchgasse 2, tel. 026-670-1101).

Fun-loving **Freiburger Falle** serves all the old *Fribourgeoise* traditions, such as meat on a hot stone (36 SF), fondue, and so on, in a cellar under the main street. You'll eat under alphorns and castle-style chandeliers (closed Tue, find it hiding under the storm-cellar doors in front of the Irish pub at Hauptgasse 43, tel. 026-672-1222, Bruno Lüscher).

Restaurant Anatolia is a Turkish place with crayon-quality menus posted everywhere and rather high prices for ethnic food. Still, it has fresh ingredients, good cooking, and a charming owner, Mehmet. Eat indoors with the fine mural of Istanbul, or watch the main-drag action from an outside table (22–28 SF, daily 10:00–23:00 in summer, shorter hours off-season, Hauptgasse 45, tel. 026-670-2868).

Restaurant Eintracht serves local cuisine from a fun menu, including old-time chef specials. If there is a down-and-dirty, horse-meat-cookin' local hangout in town, this is it (17-SF lunch specials, 16–39-SF plates, half portions available, healthy specials, Mon–Tue and Thu–Sat 7:30–23:30, Sun 7:30–18:00, closed Wed, vineyard ambience or streetside seating, Hauptgasse 19, tel. 026-670-2240).

Grizzly's Restaurant, perfect for those in need of a quick trip back home, is a playful, enthusiastic place with an enticing menu of North American delicacies. The Yukon-chic interior comes with totem poles, buckskins, and rock and roll. The outside offers the finest seats on the main street (fresh salads, trappers' spare ribs, mussels, vegetarian options, Tue–Sat 11:00–23:30, closed Sun–Mon, reservations smart, Hauptgasse 24, tel. 026-670-0787). As the menu says, "If the meal's not ready in 10 minutes, it will be in 15. If it's not on the table in 15 minutes, have another beer."

Pizza: Murten has two pizzerias. The one on the main street has better views, but locals prefer **Pizzeria Taverna Italiana** for its better value (17-SF daily specials, 20-SF pizza and pasta, 15-SF pizzas to go, daily 10:00–14:00 & 17:00–22:00, near Hotel Murtenhof at Kreuzgasse 4, tel. 026-670-2122).

Bakeries: The main street has four bakeries, all with ample charm. **Züger** (at Hauptgasse 33) has a tearoom and offers daily indoor seating and pleasant outside seats. They have delicate, local-style, open-face sandwiches and a wide variety of salads for around 16 SF (Wed–Sat and Mon 6:45–18:30, Sun 7:45–18:30, closed Tue).

Supermarket: The giant **Co-op** (with a cafeteria) towers between the train station and city center (Mon–Thu 9:00–23:30, Fri–Sat 9:00–24:00, closed Sun).

Murten Connections

From Murten by Train to: Avenches (hourly, 10 min, direction: Payerne), **Bern** (hourly, 35 min), **Fribourg** in Switzerland (hourly, 30 min), **Lausanne** (hourly, 1.5 hrs, generally transfer in Fribourg, Payerne, or Neuchâtel), **Zürich** (2/hr, 1.75 hrs, transfer in Bern, Fribourg, or Kerzers). Train info: toll tel. 0900-300-300 or www .rail.ch.

Route Tips for Drivers
Murten to Lake Geneva (50 miles): The autobahn from Bern to Lausanne/Lake Geneva makes everything speedy (see the Lake Geneva and French Switzerland chapter). Murten and Avenches are 10 minutes off the autobahn. Broc, Bulle, and Gruyères are within sight of each other and the autobahn. It takes about an hour to drive from Murten to Montreux. The autobahn (direction: Simplon) takes you high above Montreux (pull off at great viewpoint rest stop) and Château de Chillon. For the castle, take the first exit east of the castle (Villeneuve). Signs direct you along the lake back to the castle.

Near Murten: Avenches

Avenches, four miles south of Murten, was once Aventicum, the Roman capital of Helvetia. Today, it's a quaint little town with an ancient theater taking a bite out of it. From the town spreads a vast field of sparse Roman ruins.

With a pleasant, small-town French ambience, Avenches (ah-vahnsh) is a quieter, less expensive place to stay than Murten. Just a few minutes away by train, it also makes an easy day trip. The **TI** (Mon–Fri 8:30–12:00 & 13:30–17:30, closed Sat–Sun, Place de l'Eglise 3, tel. 026-676-9922, www.avenches.ch) and the town are a seven-minute uphill walk from the station.

Roman Avenches
Aventicum was a Roman capital, with a population of 20,000. The Romans appreciated its strategic crossroads location, fertile land, and comfortable climate (several times voted "most livable place to retire"). While the population of today's Avenches could barely fill the well-worn ruins of their Roman amphitheater, Aventicum was

once one of the largest cities of the Roman Empire. Everything sits on Roman ruins, which were nearly quarried to oblivion over several centuries; the scant remains were finally spared in the 19th century. Today, things are carefully preserved. Metal detectors must be registered here. Mothers, knowing that turning

up anything ancient will bring on the archaeologists, yell at their kids, "Don't dig!" Even the benches on the main street are bits of a 2,000-year-old temple cornice.

There are five Roman sights: the amphitheater, a lone tower, a sanctuary and a theater in a field outside of town, and a museum.

The **amphitheater,** or arena, which once seated 18,000, is the largest Roman ruin in Switzerland (free, always open). Although the gladiator action is no more, it's still busy with an annual opera festival and other musical events. At the top of the amphitheater (just past the museum entrance), scan the surrounding countryside. All the farmland was once a walled Roman town of about 20,000 people. The **tower** on the ridge (on left)—the only one remaining of the original 73 towers—marks where the wall once stood. In the middle, past the lone standing column of the **sanctuary,** you can see the small **theater** ruins (described later).

The **Roman museum** fills a medieval tower attached to the amphitheater in town with three fascinating floors of Roman artifacts. Good students borrow the extensive English catalog, which affords a fairly intimate look at domestic life here back then. Don't miss the glass, mosaics, and a gold bust of Marcus Aurelius (A.D. 80) found in an old Roman sewer in 1939 (4 SF, covered by Swiss Pass; April–Sept Tue–Sun 10:00–12:00 & 13:00–17:00; Oct–March Tue–Sun 14:00–17:00; closed Mon year-round, tel. 026-675-1727).

Perhaps the best Aventicum experience is to spend some quiet time at sunset pondering the evocative **Roman theater** (Théâtre Romaine) and **sanctuary** in the fields, a half-mile walk out of town (free, always open, tiny free car park at the site). The single column marks "Du Cigognier"—nicknamed the "stork sanctuary" (c. 1700) for the stork nest it supported. The site was a quarry until the 19th century, so almost nothing remains.

Sleeping in Avenches

(1 SF = about $1, country code: 41)
$$$ Hotel Couronne is an Old World, three-star place with a modern interior. It sits grandly on the main square of little

Avenches, where Yves and Isabelle Faivre rent 21 charming, bright rooms (Sb-125–140 SF, Db-190–210 SF, Tb-270 SF, parking-20 SF/day, next to TI, tel. 026-675-5414, www.lacouronne.ch, couronne avenches@vtx.ch).

$ The Avenches **IYHF hostel,** the only hostel in the area, is a beauty (open April–mid-Oct). It's run by the Dhyaf family; has 3- to 10-bed rooms; and includes breakfast and linens, a homey TV room, table tennis, a big backyard, and a very quiet setting near the Roman theater (37 SF for dorm bed in 3-bed room, 35 SF in 4-bed room, 32 SF in 6- to 10-bed room, nonmembers pay 6 SF extra, lunch or dinner—15 SF, no curfew, reception open 7:00–9:30 & 17:00–22:00, Internet access, laundry, 3 blocks from center at medieval *lavoir,* or laundry, Rue du Lavoir 5, tel. 026-675-2666, fax 026-675-2717, www.youthhostel.ch/avenches, avenches @youthhostel.ch). If you're on a tight budget and have a car or railpass, this place is a great option.

GIMMELWALD
and the BERNER OBERLAND

Interlaken • Lauterbrunnen • Gimmelwald •
Mürren • Wengen

Frolic and hike high above the stress and clouds of the real world. Take a vacation from your busy vacation. Recharge your touristic batteries high in the Alps, where distant avalanches, cowbells, the fluff of a down comforter, the whistle of marmots, and the crunchy footsteps of happy hikers are the dominant sounds. If the weather's good (and your budget's healthy), ride a cable car from the traffic-free village of Gimmelwald to a hearty breakfast at the revolving Piz Gloria restaurant, 10,000 feet up on the Schilthorn. Linger among alpine whitecaps before riding, hiking, or paragliding down 5,000 feet to Mürren and home to Gimmelwald.

Your gateway to the rugged Berner Oberland is the grand old resort town of Interlaken. Near Interlaken is Switzerland's open-air folk museum, Ballenberg, where you can climb through original traditional houses gathered from every corner of this diverse country.

Ah, but the weather's fine and the Alps beckon. Head deep into the heart of the Alps, and ride the cable car to the stop just this side of heaven—Gimmelwald.

Planning Your Time

Rather than tackle a checklist of famous Swiss mountains and resorts, choose one region to savor: the Berner Oberland.

Interlaken is the region's administrative headquarters and transportation hub. Use it for business—banking, post office, laundry, shopping—and as a springboard for alpine thrills.

If the weather's decent, explore the two areas that tower above either side of the **Lauterbrunnen Valley,** south of Interlaken: On one side is the **Jungfrau** (and beneath it, the towns of Wengen and

Kleine Scheidegg), and on the other is the **Schilthorn** (overlooking the villages of Gimmelwald and Mürren).

For accommodations without the expense and headache of mountain lifts, consider the valley-floor village of **Lauterbrunnen.** But for the best overnight options, I'd stay on the scenic ridge high above the valley, in the rustic hamlet of **Gimmelwald,** or the resort town of **Mürren.** I've also listed some options in the resort of **Wengen** and a few other mountain towns. Ideally, spend three nights in the region, with a day exploring each side of the valley.

For the fastest look, consider a night in Gimmelwald, breakfast at the Schilthorn, an afternoon doing the Männlichen–Wengen hike, and an evening or night train out. What? A nature-lover not spending the night high in the Alps? Alpus interruptus.

Getting Around the Berner Oberland

For more than a century, this region has been the target of nature-worshipping pilgrims. And Swiss engineers and visionaries have made the most exciting alpine perches accessible....

By Lifts and Trains: Part of the fun—and most of the expense—here is riding the many mountain trains and lifts (gondolas and cable cars).

Trains connect Interlaken to Wilderswil, Grindelwald, Lauterbrunnen, Wengen, Kleine Scheidegg, and the Jungfraujoch. Lifts connect Wengen to Männlichen and Grund (near Grindelwald); Grindelwald to First; Lauterbrunnen to Grütschalp (where a train connects to Mürren); and the cable-car station near Stechelberg to Gimmelwald, Mürren, and the Schilthorn.

For an overview of your many options, study the "Alpine Lifts in the Berner Oberland" map on page 133 and the "What's What in the Berner Oberland" sidebar on page 134. Lifts generally go at least twice hourly, from about 7:00 until about 20:00 (sneak preview: www.jungfraubahn.ch or www.schilthorn.ch).

Beyond Interlaken, trains and lifts into the Jungfrau region are only 25 percent covered by Eurailpasses, without using a flexi-day; with the Swiss Pass, they're free up to Wengen or Mürren (uphill from there, Swiss Pass–holders pay half-price). Ask about discounts for early-morning and late-afternoon trips, youths, seniors, families, groups (assemble a party of 10 and you'll save about 25 percent), and those staying awhile. Generally, round-trips are double the one-way cost, though some high-up trains and lifts are 10–20 percent cheaper. It's possible to buy your entire package

Berner Oberland

Note: This birds-eye view looks **south**

Eiger 13,026'
Mönch 13,449'
Jungfrau 13,642'
JUNGFRAU-JOCH 11,300'
TUNNEL
SCHILTHORN 9,748'
BIRG 8,784'
KLEINE SCHEIDEGG 6,762'
GIMMEL-WALD 4,593'
GREAT HIKE
W.-ALP
STECHEL-BERG 3,025'
MÜRREN 5,381'
GRINDEL-WALD 3,393'
MÄNNLICHEN 7,317'
LIFT STN.
NICE WALK
GRUND
GRÜTSCHALP 4,879'
To First
WENGEN 4,180'
LAUTERBRUNNEN 2,612'
ISENFLUH
ZWEILÜTSCHINEN
SCHYNIGE PLATTE 6,454'
WILDERSWIL 1,916'
To Luzern
OST STN.
ISELTWALD
BRIENZ
Lake Brienz
Aare River
WEST STN.
To Bern
SPIEZ
Lake Thun
BALLENBERG OPEN-AIR MUSEUM
INTERLAKEN 1,860'
ST. BEATUS HÖHLEN CAVES

of lifts at once, but then you don't have the flexibility to change with the weather.

Popular local passes include the following:

The **Junior Card,** for families traveling with children, is a great deal, and pays for itself in the first hour of trains and lifts (20 SF/one child, 40 SF/two or more children, lets children under 16 travel free with at least one parent, buy at Swiss train stations).

The **Berner Oberland Regional Pass** is a good idea for those staying a week and exploring the region extensively (7-day version-230 SF, discount with Swiss Pass, includes 3 days of unlimited travel and 4 days of half-price fares on all trains, buses, and lifts—even all the way south to Gstaad and Brig, valid May–Oct, 15-day version-277 SF, www.regiopass-berneroberland.ch).

The **Jungfraubahnen Pass** is more limited in scope, covering six consecutive days of unlimited transportation in just the Jungfrau region. This pass covers all the trains, lifts, buses, and funiculars, with one exception: You pay half-price for the train between Kleine Scheidegg and the Jungfraujoch (200 SF, or 150 SF with Swiss Pass, valid May–Oct, tel. 033-828-7233, www.jungfraubahn.ch).

Alpine Lifts in the Berner Oberland

Cheaper round-trip fares to Schilthorn are available

JUNGFRAUJOCH 11,333'

Jungfrau ▲ 13,642'

GIMMELWALD 4,593'

STECHELBERG 3,025'

MÜRREN 5,361'

Mönch 13,449' ▲

LIFT STATION
Hourly Bus →
(4 Sf)

SCHILT-HORN 9,748'

43-2-20

Eiger ▲ 13,026'

66-2-50

TRÜMM. FALLS ■

10-2-20
(Laut.-Mürren)

ALLMENDHUBEL

KLEINE SCHEIDEGG 6,762'

LAUTERBRUNNEN 2,612'

8-2-10

GRÜTSCHALP 4,879'

24-3-30

6-2-15

N

30-2-55

24-4-10

WENGEN 4,180'

ISENFLUH 3,357'

GRINDEL-WALD 3,393'

36-2-30

MÄNNLICHEN 7,317'

10-2-35
(Interlaken E.-Grind.)

7-2-20 Inter. Ost to Lauterbrunnen
41-2-75 Inter. Ost to Kl. Scheidegg
107-2-140 Inter. Ost to Jungfraujoch

32-30-30

ZWEI-LÜTSCHINEN

SCHYNIGE PLATTE 6,454'

35-2-55

WILDERSWIL 1,916'

FIRST 7,113'

OST STN.

3-2-5

WEST STATION

To Bern

To Brienz

ISELTWALD

INTER-LAKEN 1,860'

To Thun

Lake Brienz

3-3-3

Lake Thun

To Brienz & Luzern ←

Interlaken Ost to Brienz

9-2-30

Note: Elevations in feet

Not to Scale

Code:
1st # = Approx. cost in Swiss
 Francs: 2nd class 1-way
2nd # = Trips per hour
3rd # = Duration of trip in min.

Notes:
Swiss Passes cover travel to Wengen and Mürren;
Eurail/other int'l passes cover travel only to Interlaken.
(Passes offer discounts beyond these points.)

Pick up Jungfrau Region Tarif brochure from Tourist Info
for current prices. Also check www.jungfraubahn.ch

BERNER OBERLAND

By Car: Interlaken, Lauterbrunnen, Isenfluh, and Stechelberg are all accessible by car. You can't drive to Gimmelwald, Mürren, Wengen, or Kleine Scheidegg, but don't let that stop you from staying up in the mountains; park the car and zip up on a lift. To catch the lift to Gimmelwald, Mürren, and the Schilthorn, park at the cable-car station near Stechelberg (2 SF/2 hours, 6 SF/day, cash only; see page 157 for more information). To catch the train to Wengen or Kleine Scheidegg, park at the train station in Lauterbrunnen (parking: 2 SF/2 hours, 10 SF/9–24 hours).

Helpful Hints in the Berner Oberland

Weather: The local economy lives by the weather. You're wise to be in touch. Ask at your hotel or the TI for the latest. A local TV station showing live video from the famous (and

What's What in the Berner Oberland

For such a small corner of the world, this region packs in a lot to experience. Here's a quick rundown of the place names you'll encounter.

Allmendhubelbahn (AHL-mehnd-hòo-behl-bahn): A classic old funicular from Mürren, leading to good hikes at the top (see page 169).

Ballenberg: Swiss Open-Air Folk Museum, on Lake Brienz (see page 141).

Berner Oberland: The mountainous part of the canton of Bern, sometimes referred to as the "Jungfrau region." Everything else on this list is in the Berner Oberland (also called "Bernese Oberland" in English).

Birg (beerg): Cable-car stop between Mürren and the Schilthorn, with a trail leading steeply down to Gimmelwald and more (see page 178).

Brienz (bree-ENTS): Lake on the east side of Interlaken (Brienzersee) and the namesake town on its shore.

First (feersht): Overlook point accessible by lift from Grindelwald; endpoint of hike from Schynige Platte (see page 186).

Gimmelwald (GIM-mehl-vahlt): Wonderfully rustic time-warp village overlooking the Lauterbrunnen Valley; good home-base option (see page 155).

Grindelwald (GRIN-dehl-vahlt): Expensive resort town, not to be confused with Gimmelwald.

Grütschalp (GRITSH-alp): Station at the top of the cable car from Lauterbrunnen. It's connected by train and a trail to Mürren (see page 184).

Interlaken (IN-tehr-lah-kehn): Big town at the "entrance" to the Berner Oberland; you'll go through here to get anywhere else in this chapter (see page 137).

Jungfrau, Mönch, Eiger (YOONG-frow, munkh, EYE-gehr): Literally "Maiden, Monk, Ogre," the three major peaks of the region, from right to left (the Jungfrau's the highest, at 13,642 feet).

Jungfraubahn (YOONG-frow-bahn): Company that runs all of the trains and lifts in the area (except for the Schilthorn cable cars).

Jungfraujoch (YOONG-frow-yoke): High-altitude (11,300 feet) observation deck near the Jungfrau peak, accessible by train from Kleine Scheidegg.

Kleine Scheidegg (KLY-neh SHY-dehk): Viewpoint with breath-taking Eiger, Mönch, and Jungfrau views; has several hotels and restaurants (see page 188), plus the train station that offers pricey rides to the Jungfraujoch (page 176).

Lauterbrunnen (LOUT-ehr-broo-nehn): Small town in the middle of the Lauterbrunnen Valley. From here, a cable car goes up to Grütschalp (with connections to Mürren and Gimmelwald), the train runs up to Wengen and Kleine Scheidegg, and the PostBus goes to Stechelberg and the Schilthornbahn lift. For hotels and restaurants, see pages 153–154.

Lauterbrunnen Valley: Valley at the heart of the Berner Oberland; most towns and activities in this chapter lie in or overlook this valley.

Männlichen (MEN-leekh-ehn): Lift station on a dramatic ridge separating the region's two valleys. Connected to Wengen and also to Grund (near Grindelwald) by lifts; also the starting point of an easy hike to Kleine Scheidegg with nonstop mountain views (see page 184).

Mürren (MIH-rehn): Pleasant resort town near Gimmelwald, midway up the Schilthorn cable-car line; a good high-mountain home base for those who find Gimmelwald too small and rustic (see page 165).

Schilthorn (SHILT-horn): The 10,000-foot peak across the Lauterbrunnen Valley from the Jungfrau, reached by cable car from near Stechelberg (in the valley), Mürren, and Gimmelwald; features spectacular views and the Piz Gloria revolving restaurant made famous by James Bond (see page 175).

Schilthornbahn: Cable-car company that operates the lift on the west side of the Lauterbrunnen Valley near Stechelberg, connecting the valley floor with Gimmelwald, Mürren, Birg, and the Schilthorn.

Schynige Platte (SHIH-nih-geh PLAH-teh): High-altitude observation point near the entrance to Lauterbrunnen Valley, reached by funicular from Wilderswil; starting point of a long but scenic hike to First (see page 186).

Sefinen Valley (seh-FEE-nehn): Branches off the Lauterbrunnen Valley beyond Stechelberg and Gimmelwald; good for a hike (see page 181).

Stechelberg (SHTEH-khehl-behrk): Village where the road ends at the upper end of the Lauterbrunnen Valley, about a mile beyond the Schilthornbahn cable-car station (for accommodations, see page 188).

Thun (toon): Lake to the west of Interlaken (Thunersee) and its namesake town on the lake.

Trümmelbach Falls (TRIM-mehl-bahkh): Striking series of waterfalls near Lauterbrunnen (see page 151).

Wengen (VAYNG-ehn): Resort town on Jungfrau side of Lauterbrunnen Valley; on the train line between Lauterbrunnen and Kleine Scheidegg (see page 173).

Wilderswil (VIHL-dehrs-vihl): Village near entrance of the Lauterbrunnen Valley; on the train line between Interlaken and Lauterbrunnen; has funicular to Schynige Platte and trailhead to First (see page 186).

most expensive-to-reach) peaks plays just about wherever you go. For the latest weather, you can also check www .swisspanorama.com (entire area), www.jungfraubahn.ch (for Jungfraujoch), or www.schilthorn.ch (for Schilthorn peak).

Closed Days: On Sundays and holidays (including the lesser-known religious holidays), small-town Switzerland is quiet. Hotels are open and lifts and trains run, but many stores are closed.

Off-Season Closures: Note that at higher altitudes many hotels, restaurants, and shops are closed between the skiing and hiking seasons: from late April until late May, and again from mid-October to early December.

Rainy-Day Options: When it rains here, locals joke that they're washing the mountains. If clouds roll in, don't despair. They can roll out just as quickly. With good rain gear and the right choice of trail, you can thoroughly enjoy a hike in the rain, with surprise views popping out all around you as the clouds break. Some good bad-weather options are the North Face Trail, the walk from Mürren or Allmendhubel to Grütschalp, the Sefinen Valley hike, and the Lauterbrunnen Valley walk. Also consider a visit to Trümmelbach Falls or the Lauterbrunnen Valley Folk Museum. All of these options are described in this chapter.

Local Guidebook: For an in-depth look at the area's history, folk life, flora, fauna, and for extensive hiking information, consider Don Chmura's *Exploring the Lauterbrunnen Valley* (sold throughout the valley, 8 SF).

Visitors Cards *(Gästekarten):* The hotels in various towns issue free visitor's cards that include measly discounts on some sights. Though these cards won't save you much, you can ask at your hotel for the details.

Skiing: The Berner Oberland is a great winter-sports destination, with good snow on its higher runs, incredible variety, relatively reasonable prices, and a sense of character that's missing in many swankier resort areas. You can even swish with the Swiss down the world's longest sledding run (9 miles long, out of Grindelwald, only open when snow's good). Three ski areas cluster around the Lauterbrunnen Valley: Mürren-Schilthorn (best for expert skiers), Kleine Scheidegg-Männlichen (busiest, best variety of runs), and Grindelwald-First (best for beginners and intermediate skiers, but lower elevation can make for iffier snowpack). Lift tickets cost around 60 SF a day, including the Sportspass Jungfrau, which covers all three areas (see www.jungfrauwinter.ch for prices and info). For more tips, see the Switzerland in Winter chapter.

Interlaken

When the 19th-century Romantics redefined mountains as something more than cold and troublesome obstacles, Interlaken became the original alpine resort. Ever since, tourists have flocked to the Alps "because they're there." Interlaken's glory days are long gone, its elegant old hotels eclipsed by the new, more swanky alpine resorts. Today, its shops are filled with chocolate bars, Swiss Army knives, and sunburned backpackers.

While European jet-setters are elsewhere, Interlaken is cashing in on a huge interest from India and the Arab world. Indians come to escape their monsoon season—especially in April and May—and to visit places they've seen in their movies. (The Alps often stand in for Kashmir, which is less accessible to film crews.) There's even a restaurant called "Bollywood" atop the Jungfraujoch. People from the hot and dry Arabian Peninsula come here just to photograph their children frolicking in the mist and fog.

Orientation to Interlaken

Efficient Interlaken (pop. 5,500) is a good administrative and shopping center. Take care of business, give the town a quick look, and view the live TV coverage of the weather higher up (at the TI)... then head for the hills.

Tourist Information

The TI has good information on the region (June Mon–Fri 8:00–18:00, Sat 8:00–16:00, closed Sun; July–Aug Mon–Fri 8:00–19:00, Sat 8:00–17:00, Sun 10:00–12:00 & 17:00–19:00; Sept Mon–Fri 8:00–18:00, Sat 9:00–13:00, closed Sun; shorter hours Oct–May; under the 18-story skyscraper on the main street between West and Ost train stations, a 10-min stroll from either, Höheweg 37; tel. 033-826-5300, www.interlaken.ch). The *You Want It All* booklet is an almanac covering everything you need in Interlaken (except for some events, which are covered more thoroughly in the monthly entertainment guide). There's no point in buying a regional map, as good mini-versions of the map are included in various free transportation and hiking brochures.

Arrival in Interlaken

Interlaken has two train stations: Ost (East) and West. All trains stop at both stations. If heading for higher-altitude villages, get off at the Ost station. For hotels in Interlaken, get off at the West station. The West station also has a helpful and friendly information center for in-depth rail questions (Mon–Fri 9:00–12:00 &

BERNER OBERLAND

13:30–18:30, Sat 9:00–12:00 & 13:30–17:00, closed Sun, tel. 058-327-4750, www.bls.ch; ticket windows open daily 6:40–19:00). Ask about discount passes, special fares, railpass discounts, and schedules for the scenic mountain trains. There's an exchange booth next to the ticket windows. A post office with a cluster of phone booths is a few blocks away.

It's a pleasant 20-minute walk between the West and Ost stations, an easy, frequent train connection (2–3/hr, 3.40 SF), or a quick trip on the bus (5/hr, 10 min, 3.40 SF, tel. 058-448-2008, www.postauto.ch). From the Ost station, private trains take you deep into the mountainous Jungfrau region (see "Interlaken Connections," page 148).

Helpful Hints

Laundry: Friendly Helen Schmocker's **Wäscherei** has a change machine, soap, English instructions, and a delightful riverside location (self-service daily 7:00–22:00—6 SF/load; full service Mon–Fri 8:00–12:00 & 13:30–18:00, Sat until 16:00, closed Sun, drop off in the morning and pick up that afternoon—12 SF/load; from the main street take Marktgasse over two bridges to Beatenbergstrasse 5, tel. 033-822-1566).

Bike Rental: You can rent bikes at either train station on weekdays but not weekends (11.50 SF/2 hours, 25 SF/half-day, 33 SF/day, 5 SF less with Eurailpass or Swiss Pass, Mon–Fri 8:00–17:00, later drop-off possible, closed Sat–Sun, www.rentabike.ch).

Self-Guided Walk

Welcome to Interlaken

Most visitors use Interlaken as a springboard for high-altitude thrills (and rightly so). But the town itself has history and scenic charm and is worth a short walk. This 45-minute stroll circles from the West train station down the main drag to the big meadow, past the casino, along the river to the oldest part of town (historically a neighboring town called Unterseen), and back to the station.

• *From the West train station, walk along...*

Bahnhofstrasse: This main drag, which turns into Höheweg as it continues east, cuts straight through the town center from the West train station to the Ost station. The best Swiss souvenir shopping is along this stretch (finer shops are on the Höheweg stretch, near the fancy hotels). At the roundabout is the handy post office (with free public WCs). Just behind the post office, on Marktgasse, the hardware store stocks real cowbells (both ornate and plain). At Höheweg 2, the TV in the window of the Schilthornbahn office shows the weather up top.

BERNER OBERLAND

Interlaken

1 Hotel Lötschberg,
Guest House Susi's B&B
& Sirinya's Thai Rest.

2 Sunny Days B&B

3 Hotel Aarburg &
Launderette

4 Katy's Lodge B&B

5 Villa Margaretha

6 Backpackers' Villa
(Sonnenhof)

7 Balmer's Herberge &
Metro Bar

8 Happy Inn Lodge

9 Restaurant Bären

10 Goldener Anker

11 Città Vecchia

12 Benacus Wine Bar & Rest.

13 Metropole Hotel's "Top O'Met"

14 Restaurant Schuh

15 Funny Farm Bar

16 Migros Supermarket/Cafeteria

17 Co-op Supermarket/Cafeteria

18 Town History Museum/
Museum of Tourism

19 Vertical Sport

The 18-story **Metropole Hotel** (a.k.a. the "concrete shame of Interlaken") is by far the town's tallest building. Step right into the lobby and ride the elevator to the top for a commanding view of the "inter-laken" area, and gaze deep into the Jungfrau region to the scenic south. A meal or drink here costs no more than one back on earth. Consider sipping a drink on its outdoor view terrace (or come back tonight—it's open very late).

• *On your right is...*

Höhematte Park: This "high meadow," or Höhematte (but generally referred to simply as "the park"), marks the beginning of Interlaken's fancy hotel row. Hotels like the Victoria-Jungfrau hearken back to the days when Interlaken was *the* top alpine resort (late 19th century). The first grand hotels were built here to enjoy the views of the Jungfrau in the distance. (Today, the *jung Fraus* getting the most attention are next door, at Hooters.)

The park originated as farmland of the monastery that pre-dated the town (marked today by the steeples of both the Catholic and Protestant churches—neither are of any sightseeing interest). The actual **monastery site** is now home to the courthouse and county administration building. With the Reformation in 1528, the monastery was shut down, and its land was taken by the state. Later, when the land was being eyed by developers, the town's leading hotels and business families bought it and established that it would never be used for commercial buildings (a very early exam-ple of smart town planning). There was talk of building a parking lot under it, but the water table here, between the two lakes, is too high. (That's why the town cemetery is up on the hillside.) Today, this is a fine place to stroll, hang out on the park benches or at Restaurant Schuh, and watch the paragliders gracefully land.

From the park, turn left onto the grounds of **Casino Kursaal,** where, at the top of each hour, dwarves ring the toadstools on the flower clock. The Kursaal, originally a kind of 19th-century fat farm, is now both a casino (passport but no tie required to enter) and a convention center.

• *Follow the path left of the Kursaal to the river (huge public swimming pool just over the river). Walk downstream under the train track and cross the pedestrian bridge, stopping in the middle to enjoy the view.*

Aare River: The Aare River is Switzerland's longest. It connects Lake Brienz and Lake Thun (with an 18-foot altitude difference—this short stretch has quite a flow). Then it tumbles out of Lake Thun, heading for Bern and ultimately into the Rhine. Its level is controlled by several sluices. In the distance, a church bell tower marks a different parish and the neighborhood of Unterseen, which shares the town's name, but in German: Like the word *Interlaken, Unterseen* means "between the lakes." Behind the spire is the pointy summit of the Niesen (like so many Swiss peaks, capped with a restaurant and accessible by a lift). Stroll downstream along the far side of the river to the church spire. The delightful riverside walk is lined by fine residences. Notice that your Jungfrau view now includes the Jungfraujoch observation deck (the little brown bump in the ridge just left of the peak).

• *At the next bridge, turn right to the town square lined with 17th-century houses on one side and a modern strip on the other.*

Unterseen: This was a town when Interlaken was only a mon-astery. The church is not worth touring. A block away, the (gener-ally empty) **Town History Museum/Museum of Tourism** shows off classic posters, fascinating photos of the construction of the Jungfraujoch, and exhibits on folk life, crafts, and winter sports—all well-described in English (5 SF, May–mid-Oct Tue–Sun 14:00–17:00, closed Mon and mid-Oct–April, Obere Gasse 26).

Return to Station: From Unterseen, cross the river on Spielmatte, and you're a few minutes' walk from your starting point. On the second bridge, notice the border between the two towns, or parishes, marked by their respective heraldic emblems (each with an ibex, or wild mountain goat). A block or so later, on the left, is the Marktplatz. The river originally ran through this square. The town used to be called "Aaremühle" ("Aare mill") for the mill that was here. But in the 19th century, town fathers made a key marketing decision: Since "Aaremühle" was too difficult for English tourists to pronounce, they changed the name to "Interlaken." Judging from the throngs of tourists on the main drag, it worked.

Sights near Interlaken

▲▲Swiss Open-Air Folk Museum at Ballenberg

Across Lake Brienz from Interlaken, the Swiss Open-Air Museum of Vernacular Architecture, Country Life, and Crafts in the Berner Oberland is a rich collection of more than 100 traditional and historic buildings brought here from every region of the country. All the houses are carefully furnished, and many feature traditional craftspeople at work. The sprawling 50-acre park, laid out roughly as a huge Swiss map (Italian Swiss in the south, Appenzell in the east, and so on), is a natural preserve providing a wonderful setting for this culture-on-a-lazy-Susan look at Switzerland.

The Thurgau house (#621) has an interesting wattle-and-daub (half-timbered construction) display, and house #331 has a fun bread museum and farmers' shop. There are daily events and demonstrations (near the east entry), hundreds of traditional farm animals (like very furry-legged roosters, near the merry-go-round in the center), and a chocolate shop (under the restaurant on the east side).

An outdoor cafeteria with reasonable prices is inside the west entrance, and fresh bread, sausage, mountain cheese, and other goodies are on sale in several houses. Picnic tables and grills with free firewood are scattered throughout the park.

The little wooden village of Brienzwiler (near the east entrance) is a museum in itself, with a lovely pint-size church.

Cost, Hours, Information: 18 SF, covered by Swiss Pass. A RailAway combo-ticket, available at both Interlaken stations, includes transportation to and from Ballenberg and your admission (39 SF from Interlaken West station, 36 SF from Interlaken

BERNER OBERLAND

Ost, add 17.40 SF to return by boat instead). The houses are open daily mid-April–Oct 10:00–17:00, but the grounds and restaurants stay open until 18:00 (last bus to Brienz train station leaves Ballenberg east/west entrances at 18:00/18:07). Pick up a daily craft demonstration schedule at the entry, and buy the 2-SF map/guide so you'll know where you are. The more expensive picture book is a better souvenir than guide. Guided two-hour tours in English must be booked well in advance (11 SF, tel. 033-952-1030, www.ballenberg.ch).

Getting There from Interlaken: Take the train from either of Interlaken's train stations to Brienz (2/hr, 30 min, 9 SF one-way from West station or get the RailAway combo-ticket—described above). From the Brienz station, catch a bus to Ballenberg (10 min, 3.40 SF one-way; leaves Ballenberg east entrance on the hour, then picks up at west entrance at :07 after the hour). Consider returning from Brienz by boat (boat dock next to train station, one-way to Interlaken Ost-25 SF).

Boat Trips

"Interlaken" is literally "between the lakes" of Thun and Brienz. You can explore these lakes on a lazy boat trip, hopping on and off as the schedule allows (free with Swiss Pass or Eurailpass but uses a flexi-day, schedules at TI or at travel center in West station). The boats on Lake Thun (5/day in summer, 2/day spring and fall, 5-hour round-trip, 61 SF) stop at the St. Beatus Höhlen caves (30 min away, described next) and two visit-worthy towns: Spiez and Thun. The boats on Lake Brienz (5/day July–Aug, 2–4/day off-season, 3-hour round-trip, 43 SF) stop at the super-cute village of Iseltwald and at Brienz (easy bus and train connections back to Interlaken from Brienz, near Ballenberg Open-Air Folk Museum—described later).

The **St. Beatus Höhlen caves** on Lake Thun can be visited with a one-hour guided tour (18 SF, 2/hr, Easter–mid-Oct daily 10:30–17:00, closed mid-Oct–Easter, tel. 033-841-1643, www.beatushoehlen.ch). The best excursion plan: Ride the bus from Interlaken (1–2/hr, 20-min ride, 4.80 SF, line #21—direction: Thun, departs West station at :19 past the hour); tour the caves; take the short, steep hike down to the lake; and return by boat (12 SF one-way, 30 min to Interlaken).

Adventure Sports

High-Adrenaline Trips—For the thrill-seeker with money, several companies offer trips such as rafting, canyoning (rappelling down watery gorges), bungee jumping, and paragliding. Costs range from 150 SF to 190 SF. Interlaken's two dominant companies are **Alpin Raft** (tel. 033-823-4100, www.alpinraft.com) and

Outdoor Interlaken (tel. 033-826-7719, www.outdoor-interlaken .ch). Other companies are generally just booking agents for these two outfits. For an overview of your options, visit www.inter lakenadventure.com or study the racks of brochures at most TIs and hotels (everyone's getting a cut of this lucrative industry).

Several years ago, two fatal accidents jolted the adventure-sport business in the Berner Oberland, leading to a more professional respect for the risks involved. Companies have very high standards of safety. Statistically, the most dangerous sport is mountain biking. Enjoying nature up close comes with risks. Adventure sports increase those risks dramatically. Use good judgment.

Less-Risky Alternatives—**Vertical Sport** has a breathtaking indoor rock-climbing facility, where you can snack or enjoy a nice cup of hot chocolate while watching hotshots practice their gravity-defying skills (Tue–Fri and Sun 9:00–18:00, Sat 9:00–16:00 or until 22:00 in bad weather, closed Mon, private lessons for beginners by the hour, at the back of the park across from Hotel Savoy at Jungfraustrasse 44, tel. 033-823-5383, www.verticalsport.ch).

Outdoor Interlaken's Seilpark offers five rope courses of varying difficulty and height in a forest, giving you a tree-top adventure through a maze of rope bridges and zip lines (37 SF, family deals, must weigh between 44 and 264 pounds; June–Aug daily 10:00–18:00; April–May and Sept–Oct Mon–Fri 13:00–18:00, Sat–Sun 10:00–18:00; closed Nov–March; from Interlaken West station, it's a 15-min walk—head right up Rugenparkstrasse and into the park, then look for signs; tel. 033-826-7719, www .outdoor-interlaken.ch).

Castles

A few impressively well-kept and welcoming old castles in the Interlaken area are worth considering for day trips by boat, bus, or car.

Thun Castle (Schloss Thun), built between 1180 and 1190 by the Dukes of Zähringen, has a five-floor historical museum offering insights into the cultural development of the region over a period of some 4,000 years. From the corner turrets of the castle, you are rewarded with a spectacular view of the city of Thun, the lake, and the Alps (8 SF; April–Oct daily 10:00–17:00; Nov–Jan Sun only 13:00–16:00; Feb–March daily 13:00–16:00; tel. 033-223-2001, www.schlossthun.ch).

Hünegg Castle (Schloss Hünegg), in Hilterfingen (farther along Lake Thun, toward Interlaken), contains a museum exhibiting furnished rooms from the second half of the 19th century. The castle is situated in a beautiful wooded park (8 SF, mid-May–mid-Oct Mon–Sat 14:00–17:00, Sun 11:00–17:00, closed off-season, tel. 033-243-1982, www.schlosshuenegg.ch).

BERNER OBERLAND

Oberhofen Castle (Schloss Oberhofen), also on Lake Thun, is ideal for those interested in gardens. Its beautifully landscaped park with exotic trees is a delight (free, mid-May–mid-Oct daily from 10:00 until dusk, closed off-season). The museum in the castle depicts domestic life in the 16th–19th centuries, including a Turkish smoking room and a medieval chapel (10 SF, mid-May–mid-Oct Mon 14:00–17:00, Tue–Sun 11:00–17:00, closed off-season, tel. 033-243-1235, www.schlossoberhofen.ch).

Nightlife in Interlaken

Youthful Night Scenes—For counterculture with a reggae beat, check out **Funny Farm** (past Balmer's Herberge hostel, in Matten). The young frat-party dance scene rages at the **Metro Bar** at Balmer's (bomb-shelter disco bar, with cheap drinks and a friendly if loud atmosphere). And if you're into **Hooters,** you won't have a hard time finding it.

Mellower After-Dark Hangouts—The first three options are also described later, under "Eating in Interlaken": For a stylish wine bar with local yuppies, check in at the **Benacus Piazza del Vino** on the square in Unterseen. To nurse a drink with a view of the park, the outdoor tables at **Restaurant Schuh** are the place to be. The **"Top O'Met"** bar and café has great indoor and outdoor view seating with reasonable prices, 18 floors above everything else in town (in the Metropole Hotel skyscraper, open nightly until late). **Hotel Oberland** (near the post office) often has live alpine music in its restaurant/bar.

Sleeping in Interlaken

I'd sleep in Gimmelwald, or at least Lauterbrunnen (20 min by train or car). Interlaken is not the Alps. But if you must stay here...

$$$ Hotel Lötschberg, with a sun terrace and 21 rooms, is run with lots of thoughtful touches by English-speaking Susi and Fritz (Sb-130 SF, Db-172 SF, big Db-192 SF, extra bed-35 SF, family deals, closed Nov–mid-April, elevator, pay Internet access, free Wi-Fi, free laundry machines, free loaner bikes; lounge with microwave, fridge, and free tea and coffee; 3-min walk from West station: leaving station, turn right, after Migros at the circle go left to General-Guisan-Strasse 31; tel. 033-822-2545, fax 033-822-2579, www.lotschberg.ch, hotel@lotschberg.ch). Energetic Fritz organizes guided adventures (guests can go tandem paragliding with Fritz at a discount, 140 SF, about 20 SF cheaper than any other deal in town).

$$ Guest House Susi's B&B is Hotel Lötschberg's no-frills, cash-only annex, offering three nicely furnished, cozy rooms

Sleep Code

(1 SF = about $1, country code: 41)
S = Single, **D** = Double/Twin, **T** = Triple, **Q** = Quad, **b** = bathroom,
s = shower only. Unless otherwise noted, credit cards are accepted, English is spoken, and breakfast is included.

To help you sort easily through these listings, I've divided the rooms into three categories, based on the price for a standard double room with bath:

$$$ Higher Priced—Most rooms 150 SF or more.
  $$ Moderately Priced—Most rooms between 90-150 SF.
    $ Lower Priced—Most rooms 90 SF or less.

and four apartments with kitchenettes (Sb-115 SF, Db-145 SF; apartment-130 SF/2 people, 220 SF/4–5 people; hotel closed Nov–mid-April but apartments available with 5-night stay, same contact info as Hotel Lötschberg, above).

$$ Sunny Days B&B, a homey, nine-room place in a quiet residential neighborhood, is run by Dave from Britain (Sb-98–110 SF, Db-120–158 SF, prices vary with size of room and view, extra bed-about 40 SF, less in winter, 1-night stay-20 SF extra, pay Internet access in lobby, pay Wi-Fi; exit left out of West station and take first bridge to your left, after crossing two bridges turn left on Helvetiastrasse and go 3 blocks to #29; tel. 033-822-8343, www.sunnydays.ch, mail@sunnydays.ch).

$$ Hotel Aarburg offers 10 plain, peaceful rooms over a restaurant in a beautifully located but run-down old building a 10-minute walk from the West station (Sb-75 SF, Db-130 SF, 10 SF more in July–Aug, 2 doors down from launderette at Beatenbergstrasse 1, tel. 033-822-2615, fax 033-822-6397, hotel-aarburg@quicknet.ch).

$$ Katy's Lodge B&B is a funky old house in a quiet, handy location. It's not cozy, but it rents seven basic rooms at a good price (Db-90–108 SF, T-114–126 SF, Qb-140–160 SF, 6-bed room-228 SF; discount offered with cash and this book: 10 percent off for 3 or more nights; garden, playground, 3-min walk from West station, across from Hotel Lötschberg at Bernastrasse 7, tel. 033-821-0963, www.katys-lodge.ch, katyslodge@bluewin.ch).

$$ Backpackers' Villa (Sonnenhof) Interlaken is a creative guest house run by a Methodist church group. Renovated in 2009, it's fun, youthful, and great for families, without the frat-party scene of Balmer's Herberge (listed below). Travelers of any age feel comfortable here (dorm bed in 2- to 7-bed room with free locker, sheets, and towel-37–45 SF, S-79 SF, Sb-91 SF, D-98 SF,

Db-118 SF, T-135–153 SF, Tb-165 SF, Q-164–180 SF, Qb-196 SF, includes breakfast, some Jungfrau-view balconies, kitchen, garden, movies, small game room, pay Internet access, free Wi-Fi, laundry, free admission to public swimming pool/spa, no curfew, no membership required, open all day, reception open 7:00–23:00, free use of public buses—bus #2 runs from hostel to either station, 10–15-minute walk from stations, across the park from the TI at Alpenstrasse 16, tel. 033-826-7171, fax 033-826-7172, www.villa .ch, mail@villa.ch).

$ Villa Margaretha, run by English-speaking Frau Kunz-Joerin, offers the best cheap beds in town. It's like Grandma's big Victorian house on a residential street. Keep your room tidy, and you'll have a friend for life (D-90 SF, T-135 SF, Q-180 SF, the three rooms share one big bathroom, 2-night minimum, apartment for 2–3 people-1,000 SF/week, closed Oct–April, cash only, no breakfast served but dishes and kitchenette available, lots of rules to abide by, go up small street directly in front of West station to Aarmühlestrasse 13, tel. 033-822-1813, www.villa-margaretha .com, info@villa-margaretha.com).

$ Balmer's Herberge is many people's idea of backpacker heaven. This Interlaken institution comes with movies, table tennis, a launderette, bar, restaurant, free Wi-Fi, pay Internet access, tiny grocery, kitchen, bike rental, swapping library, excursions, bus pass, shuttle-bus service (which meets important arriving trains), and friendly, hardworking staff. This little Nebraska, a hive of youthful fun and activities, is home for those who miss their fraternity. It can be a mob scene, especially on summer weekends (bunk in 6- to 12-bed dorm-29 SF, S-45 SF, D-77 SF, T-104 SF, Q-138 SF, includes sheets and breakfast, open year-round, emailed reservations recommended 5 days in advance for private rooms, Hauptstrasse 23, in Matten, 15-min walk from either train station, tel. 033-822-1961, fax 033-823-3261, www.balmers.com, mail @balmers.ch). They also have private rooms in an adjacent guest house (Db-130 SF, Tb-165 SF, Qb-220 SF).

$ Happy Inn Lodge, above the lively, noisy Brasserie 17 restaurant, has 16 cheap backpacker rooms and two new doubles with private baths (bed with bedding in 4- to 8-bed dorm-22–24 SF, S-32–60 SF, D-64–80 SF, Db-84–104 SF, T-78–108 SF, Q-104–144 SF, breakfast-8 SF, no membership required, no curfew, pay Internet access, free Wi-Fi, bus pass, 5-min walk from West station at Rosenstrasse 17, tel. 033-822-3225, fax 033-822-3268, www .brasserie17.ch, info@happyinn.com).

Eating in Interlaken

In Unterseen, the Old Town Across the River

Restaurant Bären, in a classic low-ceilinged building with cozy indoor and fine outdoor seating, is a great value for *Rösti,* fondue, raclette, fish, traditional sausage, and salads (20–30-SF plates including fondue for one, Cordon Bleu is popular, open daily 11:30–14:00 & 17:30–22:00, closed Mon for lunch and all day off-season; from West station, turn left on Bahnhofstrasse, cross the river, and go several blocks to Seestrasse 2; tel. 033-822-7526).

Goldener Anker is *the* local hangout—smoky, with a pool table and a few unsavory types. If you think Interlaken is sterile, you haven't been to the "Golden Anchor." Jeannette serves and René cooks, just as they have for 25 years. This place, with its "melody rock and blues" ambience, sometimes hosts small concerts, and has launched some of Switzerland's top bands (hearty 15–25-SF salads, fresh vegetables, 3 courses for 20 SF, daily from 16:00, Marktgasse 57, tel. 033-822-1672).

Città Vecchia serves decent Italian with seating indoors or out, on a leafy square (16–22-SF pizzas, 20–28-SF pastas, 30–40-SF plates, daily 11:30–14:00 & 17:30–23:30, closed Tue Oct–April, on main square in Unterseen at Untere Gasse 5, tel. 033-822-1754).

Benacus Wine Bar and Restaurant is a snooty, trendy spot serving Euro-Asian modern cuisine and tapas with a good list of open wines (28–38-SF plates, closed Sun–Mon, Stadthausplatz, tel. 033-821-2020).

On or near Interlaken's Main Drag (Höheweg)

Interlaken's main drag, Höheweg, is lined with eateries. Asian, American, and Arab group tourism cuts into the local ambience, but you have plenty of options.

Sirinya's Thai Restaurant is run by charming Sirinya, who serves great Thai dishes and popular spring rolls at reasonable prices (19–24-SF plates, Tue–Sat 16:00–23:30, Sun 11:00–22:00, closed Mon, at the recommended Hotel Lötschberg, General-Guisan-Strasse 31, tel. 033-821-6535).

Metropole Hotel's "Top O'Met," capping Interlaken's 18-story aesthetic nightmare, is actually a decent café/restaurant serving traditional and modern food at down-to-earth prices. For just 6 SF, you can enjoy a glass of wine and awesome views from an indoor or outdoor table (25-SF lunch deals include 2 courses and a drink, daily 11:30–24:00, Höheweg 37, just step into the Metropole Hotel and go up the elevator as far as you can, tel. 033-828-6666).

Restaurant Schuh retains its grand-café ambience on the best real estate in town (at the corner of the park, across from Metropole Hotel and TI). The interior is a big tour-group food

BERNER OBERLAND

fight, but there's no better place to nurse a drink or coffee and watch the paragliders float into the park (live schmaltzy music, newspapers, Höheweg 56, tel. 033-822-9441).

Cheap Eats

Interlaken's two big supermarkets sell picnic supplies and also have reasonable self-service restaurants: **Migros** is across the street from the West station (Mon–Thu 8:00–18:30, Fri 8:00–21:00, Sat 7:30–17:00, closed Sun), while the **Co-op** is across the river from the West station, on your right (same hours as Migros). The only grocery store open late at night is **Co-op Pronto** (daily 6:00–22:30, 30 yards west of TI on Höheweg).

Interlaken Connections

If you plan to arrive at Zürich Airport and want to head straight for Interlaken and the Alps, see page 63 in the Zürich chapter. Note that Interlaken is connected to Luzern and Montreux (on Lake Geneva) via the Golden Pass scenic rail route (see the Scenic Rail Journeys chapter).

There are a few long-distance trains from Interlaken—you'll generally transfer in **Bern** (for Bern connections, see page 116). Train info: toll tel. 0900-300-300 or www.rail.ch.

From Interlaken Ost by Train to: Lauterbrunnen (2/hr, 20 min), **Bern** (2/hr, 55 min, some with change in Spiez), **Spiez** (3/hr, 25 min), **Brienz** (1–2/hr, 20 min), **Zürich** and **Zürich Airport** (2/hr, 2–3 hrs, most with transfer in Bern or Spiez), **Luzern** (hourly, 2–2.5 hrs), **Lugano** (hourly, 4.75 hrs, 1–2 changes), **Zermatt** (1–2/hr, 2.25 hrs, transfer in Spiez and Visp).

From Interlaken to the Lauterbrunnen Valley

To reach the heart of the valley, drive or take the train to Lauterbrunnen (train leaves twice an hour from Interlaken Ost station, 20 min). You cannot drive to Gimmelwald (park at the cable-car station near Stechelberg and ride up on the lift; see "Getting to Gimmelwald" on page 157) or to Mürren, Wengen, or Kleine Scheidegg (park in Lauterbrunnen and take the cable car to Mürren or the train to Wengen/Kleine Scheidegg). For more details, see "Lauterbrunnen Valley Connections" on page 155.

Lauterbrunnen

Lauterbrunnen is the valley's commercial center and transportation hub. In addition to its train station and cable car, the one-street

town is just big enough to have all the essential services (bank, post office, bike rental, launderette, and so on)—plus several hotels. It's idyllic, in spite of the busy road that slices it in two. Sitting under sheer cliffs at the base of the valley, with its signature waterfall spurting mightily out from the cliff (floodlit at night),

Lauterbrunnen is a fine springboard for Jungfrau and Schilthorn adventures. But for spending the night, I still prefer Gimmelwald or Mürren, perched on the ledge above the valley.

Orientation to Lauterbrunnen

Tourist Information

Stop by the friendly TI to check the weather forecast, use the Internet (1 SF/6 min), find out about guided walks and events, and buy hiking maps or any regional train or lift tickets you need (June–mid-Sept daily 9:00–12:00 & 13:00–18:00, Sat–Sun until 18:00, shorter hours off-season, located near the Co-op grocery, tel. 033-856-8568, www.mylauterbrunnen.com).

Arrival in Lauterbrunnen

The slick, modern train station has lockers and is across the main street from the cable-car station. Go left as you exit the station to find the TI. Drivers can find parking in the large multistory pay lot behind the station (2 SF/2 hours, 10 SF/9–24 hours, www.jungfraubahn.ch).

Helpful Hints

Medical Help: Dr. Bruno Durrer, who has a clinic near the Jungfrau Hotel (look for *Arzt* sign), is good. He and his associate both speak English (tel. 033-856-2626, answered 24/7).

Internet and Laundry: Two places within a short walk of each other in the town center compete for your coins: The **Valley Hostel** is automated (Internet access-2.50 SF/15 min, launderette-5 SF/load, includes soap, May–Oct daily 9:00–21:00, shorter hours Nov–April, don't open dryer door until machine is finished or you'll have to pay another 5 SF to start it

Lauterbrunnen

To Trümmelbach Falls, Schilthorn Cable Car (to Gimmelwald & Mürren) & Stechelberg Village via Road

To Trümmelbach Falls, Schilthorn Cable Car (to Gimmelwald & Mürren) & Stechelberg Village via Trail

Staubbach Waterfall

Weisse

FOLK MUSEUM

To Wengen, Kleine Scheidegg & Jungfraujoch

Lütschine

MAIN DRAG

To Wengen

To Grütschalp & Train to Mürren

To Grütschalp & Train to Mürren

POST

TRAIN STATION

CABLE-CAR STATION

River

To Isenfluh

To Interlaken & Grindelwald

Not to Scale

Note: Train station to church is a 5 min. walk

BERNER OBERLAND

1. Hotel Restaurant Silberhorn
2. Hotel Staubbach
3. Valley Hostel
4. Chalet im Rohr
5. Matratzenlager Stocki
6. Mountain Holiday Park-Camping Jungfrau
7. Schützenbach Retreat
8. Hotel Restaurant Oberland
9. Hotel Restaurant Jungfrau
10. Pub Horner
11. Co-op Grocery
12. Internet Cafés/ Launderettes (2)
13. Bike Rental
14. Alpia Sports Shop

again, tel. 033-855-2008); **Airtime** is fully staffed (Internet access-10 SF/hr, pay Wi-Fi, self-service laundry-10 SF/load, full-service laundry-25 SF/load, May–Oct daily 9:00–19:00, shorter hours Nov–April, café sells homemade goodies and English-language paperbacks, also books adventure sports, tel. 033-855-1515, www.airtime.ch). The word's out on their aptly named "world-famous" brownies.

Grocery Store: The **Co-op** is on the main street (Mon–Fri 8:00–12:00 & 14:00–18:30, Sat 8:00–12:00 & 13:30–17:00, closed Sun).

Bike Rental: You can rent mountain bikes at **Imboden Bike** on the main street (25 SF/half-day, 35 SF/day; full-suspension—45 SF/half-day, 65 SF/day; daily July–Aug 8:30–20:00, Sept–June 9:00–18:30 except closed for lunch 12:00–13:00 Oct–May, tel. 033-855-2114, www.imboden-bike.ch).

Sports Gear: You can rent hiking boots, skis, and snowboards at the **Alpia Sports** shop (Mon–Fri 8:00–12:00 & 14:00–18:00, Sat–Sun 10:00–12:00 & 16:00–18:00, shorter hours in fall and closed in May, at Hotel Crystal, tel. 033-855-3292, www .alpiasport.ch).

Activities in and near Lauterbrunnen

Hikers' Loop from Lauterbrunnen—If you're staying in Lauterbrunnen, consider this ambitious but great day plan: Ride the cable car to Grütschalp, walk along the ridge to Mürren, take the cable car up to the Schilthorn and back down to Mürren, ride the funicular up to Allmendhubel, take the North Face Walk to Gimmelwald, take the lift down to the Stechelberg station, catch the PostBus to Trümmelbach Falls, and walk through the valley back into Lauterbrunnen. Make it more or less strenuous or time-consuming by swapping lifts and hikes (all described later in this chapter). Or rent a mountain bike and do a wheeled variation on this (parking your bike in Mürren for the Schilthorn trip).

▲**Trümmelbach Falls**—If all the waterfalls have you intrigued, sneak a behind-the-scenes look at the valley's most powerful, Trümmelbach Falls (11 SF, daily July–Aug 8:30–18:00, April–June and Sept–mid-Nov 9:00–17:00, closed mid-Nov–March, tel. 033-855-3232, www.truemmelbach.ch). It's about halfway between Lauterbrunnen and the Schilthornbahn station (about a 45-minute walk from either one, at a

BERNER OBERLAND

leisurely pace). To save time, you can take the PostBus to the falls from either place. Once there, you'll ride an elevator up through the mountain and climb through several caves (wet, with lots of stairs, and—for some—claustrophobic) to see the melt from the Eiger, Mönch, and Jungfrau grinding like God's bandsaw through the mountain at the rate of up to 5,200 gallons a second (that's 20,000 liters—nearly double the beer consumption at Oktoberfest). The upper area is the best; if your legs ache, skip the lower falls and ride down on the elevator.

▲▲**Cloudy-Day Lauterbrunnen Valley Walk**—Try the easy trails and pleasant walks along the floor of the Lauterbrunnen Valley. For a smell-the-cows-and-flowers lowland walk—ideal for a cloudy day, weary body, or tight budget—take the PostBus from Lauterbrunnen town to the Schilthornbahn station near Stechelberg (left of river) and follow the riverside trail back for three basically level miles to Staubbach Falls, near the town church (you can reverse the route, but it's a very gradual uphill to Stechelberg). A trail was recently cut into the cliff to take visitors up "behind" Staubbach Falls (at the uphill end of Lauterbrunnen town). But the trail stops short of the actual falls, and you'll feel betrayed after making the short climb—I'd skip it.

There's a fine paved, car-free riverside path all the way along the valley (popular with bikers). Detour to Trümmelbach Falls (described earlier) en route (it's about a 45-minute walk from the Schilthornbahn station to Trümmelbach Falls, and another 45 minutes to Lauterbrunnen). In this "Valley of Many Waterfalls" (literally), you'll see cone-like mounds piled against the sides of the cliffs, formed by centuries of rocks hurled by tumbling rivers.

If you're staying in Gimmelwald, try this plan: Take the Schilthornbahn lift down to the Stechelberg station (5 min), then walk to Trümmelbach Falls (45 min), then on to Lauterbrunnen (45 min). To return to Gimmelwald from Lauterbrunnen, take the cable car up to Grütschalp (10 min), then either walk to Gimmelwald (1.5 hours) or take the train to Mürren (10 min). From Mürren, it's a downhill walk (30 min) to Gimmelwald. (This loop trip can be reversed, or started in any point along the way—such as Lauterbrunnen or Mürren.)

Lauterbrunnen Valley Folk Museum (Talmuseum Lauterbrunnen)—This interesting museum shows off the local folk culture and two centuries of mountaineering from all the towns of this valley. You'll see lots of lace, exhibits on cheese and woodworking, cowbells, and classic old photos (free with "visitor's card" given by local hotels, 3 SF otherwise, mid-June–mid-Oct Tue and Thu–Sun 14:00–17:30; closed Mon, Wed, and off-season; English handout, just over bridge and below church at the far end of Lauterbrunnen town, tel. 033-855-3586 or 033-855-1388, www.talmuseumlauterbrunnen.ch).

Hang Out with Base-Jumpers—In recent years, the Lauterbrunnen Valley has become an El Dorado of base-jumping (parachuting off cliffs), and each season thrill-seekers hike to the top of a cliff, leap off—falling as long as they can (this provides the rush)—and then pull the ripcord to release a tiny parachute, hoping it will break their fall and a gust won't dash them against the walls of the valley.

Locals generally have little respect for the base-jumpers, whom they consider reckless. But to learn more, talk with the jumpers themselves, who congregate at the **Pub Horner,** at the upper end of town (near the waterfall). This is the grittiest place in Lauterbrunnen, providing cheap beds and meals for base-jumpers and the only real after-dark scene. Locals, base-jumpers, and stray tourists gather here in the pub each evening (9 rooms, bunks-32 SF, D-64–86 SF, cheaper apartments, no breakfast, free Wi-Fi and Internet access for customers, BBQ dinner in summer, dancing nightly from 22:00 upstairs, tel. 033-855-1673, www.hornerpub .ch, mail@hornerpub.ch, run by Gertsch Ferdinand). Their kitchen sells cheap pastas and raclette, and puts out a nightly salad bar (8–14-SF meals).

Sleeping in Lauterbrunnen

(2,612 feet, 1 SF = about $1, country code: 41)
$$$ Hotel Silberhorn is a big, formal, 32-room, three-star hotel that still manages to feel family-run. It has generous public spaces and a recommended, elegant-for-Lauterbrunnen restaurant just above the quiet lift station across from the train station. Almost every double room comes with a fine view and balcony. They're in the midst of remodeling their rooms, so ask for a newer room for the same price (Sb-89–109 SF, Db-159–179 SF, bigger "superior" Db-180–209 SF, pay Internet access, free Wi-Fi in lobby, tel. 033-856-2210, www.silberhorn.com, info@silberhorn.com).

$$ Hotel Staubbach, a big, Old World place—one of the first hotels in the valley (1890)—is being lovingly restored by hard-working American Craig and his Swiss wife, Corinne. The staff is friendly, and the hotel has the casual feel of a national park lodge, with 30 simple and comfortable rooms that are being updated. It's family-friendly, there's a kids' play area, and the parking is free. Rooms that face up the valley have incredible views, though you may hear the happy crowd across the meadow at Pub Horner or the church bells chiming on the hour (S-90–100 SF, Sb-120 SF, D-110–120 SF, Db-140 SF, Tb-190 SF, Qb-220–240 SF, 10 SF extra per room for 1-night stays, 20 SF extra for balcony rooms with valley view, closed Nov–mid-April, elevator, free Wi-Fi, 4 blocks up from station on the left, tel. 033-855-5454, fax 033-855-5484, www.staubbach.com, hotel@staubbach.com). Guests can watch a DVD of my TV show on the region in the lounge.

$ Valley Hostel is practical and comfortable, offering 70 inexpensive beds for quieter travelers of all ages, with a pleasant garden and the welcoming Abegglen family: Martha, Alfred, Stefan, and Fränzi (D with bunk beds-60 SF, twin D-70 SF, beds in larger family-friendly rooms-25 SF/person, breakfast-5 SF, most rooms have no sinks, kitchen, 16-SF cheese fondue on request for guests 18:00–20:00, Internet access, Wi-Fi, coin-op laundry, 2 blocks up from train station, tel. & fax 033-855-2008, www.valleyhostel.ch, info@valleyhostel.ch).

$ Chalet im Rohr—a creaky, old, woody firetrap of a place—has oodles of character (and lots of Asian groups and paragliders). It offers 50 beds in big one- to four-bed rooms that share six showers (27 SF/person, no breakfast, cash only, common kitchen, free Wi-Fi, across from church on main drag, tel. & fax 033-855-2182, www.chaletimrohr.ch, bookings@chaletimrohr.ch, Elsbeth von Allmen-Müller).

$ Matratzenlager Stocki is rustic and humble, with the cheapest beds in town (15 SF with sheets in easygoing little 25-bed co-ed dorm with kitchen, closed Nov–Dec, across river from station, tel. 033-855-1754, Frau Graf).

$ *Camping:* Two campgrounds just south of town provide 15–35-SF beds (in dorms and 2-, 4-, and 6-bed bungalows, sheets-5 SF, kitchen facilities, cash only, big English-speaking tour groups). **Mountain Holiday Park-Camping Jungfrau,** romantically situated beyond Staubbach Falls, is huge and well-organized by Hans. It also has fancy cabins and mobile homes you can rent by the week (tel. 033-856-2010, www.camping-jungfrau.ch). **Schützenbach Retreat,** on the left just past Lauterbrunnen toward Stechelberg, is a simpler campground (tel. 033-855-1268, www.schuetzenbach.ch).

Eating in Lauterbrunnen

At **Hotel Restaurant Oberland,** Mark (Aussie) and Ursula (Swiss) Nolan take pride in serving tasty, good-value meals from a fun menu. It's a high-energy place with lots of tourists and a huge front porch good for lingering into the evening (17-SF pizzas, 20–25-SF main courses, traditional Swiss dishes, daily 11:30–21:00, tel. 033-855-1241).

Hotel Restaurant Jungfrau, along the main street on the right-hand side, offers a wide range of specialties, including fondue and *Rösti,* served by a friendly staff. Their terrace has a great valley view (daily 12:00–14:00 & 18:00–21:00, tel. 033-855-3434, run by Brigitte Melliger).

Hotel Restaurant Silberhorn is the local choice for a fancy meal out. Call to reserve a view table (14-SF salad plate, 23–35-SF main dishes, daily from 18:00, classy indoor and outdoor seating, above the cable-car station, tel. 033-856-2210).

Lauterbrunnen Valley Connections

The valley-floor towns of Lauterbrunnen and Stechelberg have connections by mountain train, bus, and cable car to the traffic-free villages, peaks, and hikes high above. Prices and trip durations given are per leg unless otherwise noted.

From Lauterbrunnen by Train to: Interlaken (2/hr, 20 min, 7 SF), **Wengen** (2/hr, 15 min, 6.20 SF), continues to **Kleine Scheidegg** (hourly, 30 min, 24 SF), where you change to a different train to reach the **Jungfraujoch** (2/hr, 50 min, 66 SF) or **Grindelwald** (2/hr, 30 min, 32 SF).

By Cable Car to: Grütschalp (2/hr, 10 min), where you can catch a train to **Mürren** (2/hr, 10 min); total trip time 30 min, total cost 10.20 SF.

By PostBus to: Schilthornbahn cable-car station (hourly, 15 min, 4 SF, covered by Swiss Pass), continues to **Stechelberg town** (hourly, 5 min, 4 SF).

By Car to: Schilthornbahn cable-car station (10-min drive, parking lot: 2 SF/2 hours, 6 SF/day, cash only).

From Schilthornbahn Cable-Car Station near Stechelberg to: Gimmelwald (2/hr, 5 min, 5.60 SF), continues to **Mürren** (2/hr, 10 min, 5.60 SF) and the **Schilthorn** (2/hr, 20 min, 43 SF). The cable car runs up from the valley station—and down from Mürren—at :25 and :55 past the hour (5:55–19:55; after 19:55, runs only once an hour until 23:55). From Gimmelwald to both Mürren and the valley station, the cable car runs at :00 and :30 (6:00–20:00; after 20:00 runs only once an hour until 24:00).

Gimmelwald

Saved from developers by its "avalanche zone" classification, Gimmelwald was (before modern tourism) one of the poorest places in Switzerland. Its traditional economy was stuck in the hay, and its farmers—unable to make it in their disadvantaged trade—survived only on a trickle

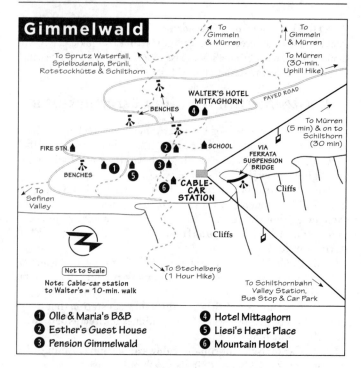

Gimmelwald

To Gimmeln & Mürren

To Gimmeln & Mürren

To Mürren (30-min. Uphill Hike)

To Sprutz Waterfall, Spielbodenalp, Brünli, Rotstockhütte & Schilthorn

WALTER'S HOTEL MITTAGHORN

PAVED ROAD

BENCHES

4

To Mürren (5 min) & on to Schilthorn (30 min)

FIRE STN.

2 SCHOOL

VIA FERRATA SUSPENSION BRIDGE

BENCHES

1 **3**

5 **6**

CABLE-CAR STATION

Cliffs

To Sefinen Valley

Cliffs

Not to Scale

Note: Cable-car station to Walter's = 10-min. walk

To Stechelberg (1 Hour Hike)

To Schilthornbahn Valley Station, Bus Stop & Car Park

1 Olle & Maria's B&B
2 Esther's Guest House
3 Pension Gimmelwald

4 Hotel Mittaghorn
5 Liesi's Heart Place
6 Mountain Hostel

of visitors and on Swiss government subsidies (and working the ski lifts in the winter). For some travelers, there's little to see in the village. Others (like me) enjoy a fascinating day sitting on a bench and learning why they say, "If heaven isn't what it's cracked up to be, send me back to Gimmelwald."

Take a walk through the town. The huge, sheer cliff face that dominates your mountain views is the Schwarzmönch ("Black Monk"). The three peaks above (or behind) it are, left to right, Eiger, Mönch, and Jungfrau. While Gimmelwald's population dropped in the last century from 300 to about 120 residents, traditions survive. Most Gimmelwalders have one of two last names: von Allmen or Feuz. They are tough and proud. Raising hay in this rugged terrain is labor-intensive. One family harvests enough to feed only about 15 cows. But they'd have it no other way, and, unlike the absentee-landlord town of Mürren, Gimmelwald is locally owned. (When word got out that urban planners wanted to develop Gimmelwald into a town of 1,000, locals pulled some strings to secure the town's bogus avalanche-zone building code. Today, unlike nearby resort towns, Gimmelwald's population is the same all year.) Those same folks are happy the masses go to touristy and commercialized Grindelwald, just over the Kleine Scheidegg ridge. Don't confuse Gimmelwald and Grindelwald—

they couldn't be more different.

Thanks to the leadership of the village teachers (Olle and Maria) and their son (Sven), Gimmelwald now has a helpful little website (www.gimmelwald.ch), where you can check out photos of the town in different seasons, get directions for 11 of the best hikes out of town, and see all the latest on activities and rooms for rent.

Getting to Gimmelwald

To get from Lauterbrunnen to Gimmelwald, you have two options:

1. Schilthornbahn Cable Car: The faster, easier way—best in bad weather or at the end of a long day with lots of luggage— is to drive. It's 10 minutes from Lauterbrunnen (or 30 minutes from Interlaken) to the Schilthornbahn cable-car station near Stechelberg (parking lot: 2 SF/2 hours, 6 SF/day, cash only).

If you don't have a car, ride the PostBus from Lauterbrunnen to the Schilthornbahn station (4 SF, 15 min, departs hourly—coordinated with arrival of train in Lauterbrunnen, www.postauto.ch).

From the Schilthornbahn station, the cable car whisks you in five thrilling minutes up to Gimmelwald (5.60 SF, 2/hr at :25 and :55 past the hour 5:55–19:55, at :55 only 19:55–23:55; Gimmelwald is the first stop). Note that the Schilthornbahn cable car is closed for servicing for a week in early May and also from mid-November through early December. If you're here during this time, you'll ride the cargo cable car directly from the valley floor up to Mürren, where a small bus shuttles you down to Gimmelwald.

2. Grütschalp Cable-Car and Mürren Train: The more scenic route is to catch the cable car from Lauterbrunnen to Grütschalp, where a special vintage train will roll you along the incredibly scenic cliffside to Mürren (total trip from Lauterbrunnen to Mürren: 30 min, 10.20 SF, www.jungfraubahn.ch). From there, either walk to the middle of Mürren and take a left down a moderately steep paved path 30 minutes to Gimmelwald, or walk 10 minutes across Mürren to catch the cable car down to Gimmelwald (5.60 SF).

Self-Guided Walk

Welcome to Gimmelwald

Gimmelwald, though tiny, with one zigzag street, offers a fine look at a traditional Swiss mountain community.

• *Start this quick walking tour at the...*

Cable-Car Station: When the lift came in the 1960s, the village's back end became its front door. Gimmelwald was, and still is, a farm village. Stepping off the cable car and starting up the path, you see a sweet little hut (pictured on next page). Set on stilts to

BERNER OBERLAND

Swiss Cow Culture

Traditional Swiss cow farmers could make more money for much easier work in another profession. In a good year, farmers produce enough cheese to break even—they support their families on government subsidies. (Throughout the Alps, various governments support traditional farming as much for the tourism as for the cheese.) But these farmers have made a lifestyle choice to keep tradition alive and live high in the mountains. Rather than lose their children to the cities, Swiss farmers have the opposite problem: Kids argue about who gets to take over the family herd.

The cows' grazing ground can range in elevation by as much as 5,000 feet throughout the year. In the summer (usually mid-June), the farmer straps elaborate ceremonial bells on his cows and takes them up to a hut at high elevations. The cows hate these big bells, which weigh upward of 10 pounds and can cost more than 2,000 SF apiece—a proud investment for a humble farmer. When the cows arrive at their summer home, the bells are hung under the eaves.

These high-elevation summer stables are called "alps." Try to find some on a Berner Oberland tourist map (e.g., Wengernalp, Grütschalp, or Schiltalp). The cows stay at the alps for about 100 days. The farmers hire a team of cheesemakers to work at each alp—mostly hippies, students, and city slickers eager to spend

keep out mice, the hut was used for storing cheese (the rocks on the rooftop here and throughout the town are not decorative—they keep the shingles on through wild storms). Behind the cheese hut stands the village schoolhouse. In Catholic Swiss towns, the biggest building is the church. In Protestant towns, it's the school. Gimmelwald's biggest building is the school (2 teachers share 1 teaching position, 17 students, and a room that doubles as a chapel when the Protestant pastor makes his monthly visit). Don't let Gimmelwald's low-tech look fool you: In this school, each kid has his or her own website. Up and across from the station, just beyond the little playground, is the recommended Mountain Hostel.

three summer months in the mountains. Each morning, the hired hands get up at 5:00 to milk the cows; take them to pasture; and make the cheese, milking the cows again when they come home in the evening. In summer, all the milk is turned into alp cheese (it's too difficult to get it down to the market in liquid form). In the winter, with the cows at lower altitudes, the fresh milk is sold as milk.

Every alp also has a resident herd of pigs. Cheesemaking leftovers (*Molke,* whey) can damage the ecosystem if thrown out—but pigs love the stuff. (The pigs parade up with the cows, but no one notices.) Cheesemakers claim that bathing in whey improves their complexion...but maybe that's just the altitude talking.

Meanwhile, the farmers, glad to be free of their bovine responsibilities in summer, turn their attention to making hay. The average farmer has a few huts at various altitudes, each surrounded by small hay fields. The farmer follows the seasons up into the mountains, making hay and storing it above the huts. In the fall, the cows come down from the alps and spend the winter moving from hut to hut, eating the hay the farmer spent the summer preparing for them.

Throughout the year you'll see farmers moving their herds to various elevations. If snow is in the way, farmers sometimes use tourist cable cars to move their cows. Every two months or so, Gimmelwald farmers bring together cows that aren't doing so well and herd them into the cable car to meet the butcher in the valley below.

• *Walk up the lane 50 yards, past the town's Dalí-esque art gallery (the shower in the phone booth), to Gimmelwald's...*

"Times Square": The yellow alpine "street sign" shows where you are, the altitude (1,370 meters, or 4,470 feet), how many hours *(Std.)* and minutes it takes to walk to nearby points, and which tracks are serious hiking paths (marked with red and white, and further indicated along the way with red and white patches of paint on stones). You're surrounded by buildings that were built as duplexes, divided vertically right down the middle to house two separate families. The writing on the post office building is a folksy blessing: "Summer brings green, winter brings snow. The sun greets the day, the stars greet the night. This house will keep you warm. May God give us his blessings." The date indicates when it was built or rebuilt (1911). Gimmelwald has a strict building code: for instance, shutters can only be painted certain colors.

• *From this tiny intersection, walk away from the cable-car station and follow the town's...*

BERNER OBERLAND

Main Street: Walk up the road. Notice the announcement board: one side for tourist news, the other for local news (e.g., deals on chainsaw sharpening, upcoming shooting competitions). Cross the street and peek into the big new barn, dated 1995. To the left of the door is a cow-scratcher. Swiss cows have legal rights (e.g., in the winter, they must be taken out for exercise at least three times a week). This big barn is built in a modern style. Traditionally, barns were small (like those on the hillside high above) and closer to the hay. But with trucks and paved roads, hay can be moved more easily, and farm businesses need more cows to be viable. Still, even a well-run big farm hopes just to break even. The industry survives only with government subsidies (see "Swiss Cow Culture" sidebar, previous pages). Small as Gimmelwald is, it still has daily mail service. The postman comes down from Mürren each day (by golf cart in summer, sled in winter) to deliver mail and pick up letters at the communal mailbox (outside the recently shuttered post office). As you wander, notice private garden patches. Until recently, most locals grew their own vegetables—often enough to provide most of their family's needs.

• *Go just beyond the next barn. On your right is the...*

Water Fountain/Trough: This is the site of the town's historic water supply. Local kids love to bathe and wage water wars here when the cows aren't drinking from it. Detour left down a lane about 50 yards (along a wooden fence and then past pea-patch gardens) to the next trough and the oldest building in town, Husmättli, from 1658. (Most of the town's 17th-century buildings are on the road zigzagging below town.) Study the log-cabin construction. Many are built without nails. The wood was logged up the valley and cut on the water-powered village mill (also below town). Gimmelwald heats with wood, and since the wood needs to age a couple of years to burn well, it's stacked everywhere.

• *Back on the paved road, continue uphill.*

Twenty yards along, on the left, the first house has a bunch of scythes hanging above the sharpening stone. Farmers pound, rather than grind, the blade to get it razor-sharp for efficient cutting. Feel a blade...carefully.

A few steps farther, notice the cute cheese hut on the right (with alpine cheese for sale). Its front is an alpine art gallery with nail shoes for flower pots. Nail shoes grip the steep, wet fields—this is critical for safety, especially if you're carrying a sharp scythe. Even today, farmers buy metal tacks and fasten them to boots. The hut is full of strong cheese—up to three years old.

Look up. In the summer, a few goats are kept here (rather than in the high alp) to provide families with fresh milk (about a half-gallon per day per goat). The farmers fence off the fields, letting the goats eat only the grass that's most difficult to harvest.

On the left (at the *B&B* sign) is the home of Olle and Maria, the village schoolteachers. Maria runs the Lilliput shop (the "smallest shop with the greatest gifts"—handmade delights from the town and region; just ring the bell and meet Maria). Her children—Sven, Sara, and Carina—do a booming trade in sugar-coated almonds.

• *Fifty yards farther along is the...*

Alpenrose: At the old schoolhouse, you might see big ceremonial cowbells hanging under the uphill eave. These swing from the necks of cows during the procession from the town to the high Alps (mid-June) and back down (mid-Sept). If the cows are gone, so are the bells—hanging from similar posts under the eaves of mountain huts in the high meadows.

• *At the end of town, pause where a lane branches off to the left, leading into the dramatic...*

Sefinen Valley: All the old homes in town are made from local wood cut from the left-hand side of this valley (shady side, slow-growing, better timber).

• *A few steps ahead, the road switches back at the...*

Gimmelwald Fire Station: The *Föhnwacht Reglement* sheet, posted on the fire-station building, explains rules to keep the village from burning down during the fierce dry wind of the Föhn season. During this time, there's a 24-hour fire watch, and even smoking cigarettes outdoors is forbidden. Mürren was devastated by a Föhn-caused fire in the 1920s. Because villagers in Gimmelwald—mindful of the quality of their volunteer fire department—are particularly careful with fire, the town has not had a terrible fire in its history (a rare feat among alpine villages).

Check out the other posted notices. This year's Swiss Army calendar tells reservists when and where to go (in all four official Swiss languages). Every Swiss male does a 22-week stint in the military, then a few days a year in the reserves until about age 30. The *Schiessübungen* poster details the shooting exercises required this year. In keeping with the William Tell heritage, each Swiss man does shooting practice annually for the military (or spends three days in jail).

• *Take the...*

High Road to Hotel Mittaghorn: The resort town of Mürren hovers in the distance. And high on the left, notice the hay field with terraces. These are from WWII days, when Switzerland, wanting self-sufficiency, required all farmers to grow potatoes. Today, this field is a festival of alpine flowers in season (best at this altitude in May and June).

• *Our walk is over. From Hotel Mittaghorn, you can return to Gimmelwald's "Times Square" via the path with the steps cutting downhill.*

Nightlife in Gimmelwald

Evening fun in Gimmelwald is found at the **Mountain Hostel** (offering a pool table, Internet access, lots of young Alp-aholics, and a good chance to share information on the surrounding mountains) or Walter's bar at **Hotel Mittaghorn.** From almost anywhere in Gimmelwald, you can watch the sun tuck the mountaintops into bed as the moon rises over the Jungfrau. If this isn't your idea of nightlife, stay in Interlaken.

Sleeping in Gimmelwald

(4,593 feet, 1 SF = about $1, country code: 41)

Gimmelwald is my home base in the Berner Oberland. To inhale the Alps and really hold them in, you'll sleep high in Gimmelwald, too. Poor and pleasantly stuck in the past, the village has only a few accommodations options—all of them quirky and memorable. Rates include entry to the public swimming pool in nearby Mürren (at the Sportzentrum, described on page 166). Factor the cable-car cost (5.60 SF per ride from Stechelberg or Mürren) into your accommodation costs. The cable car goes up and down twice an hour (up from the valley floor and down from Mürren at :25 and :55 past the hour 5:55–19:55, at :55 only 19:55–23:55; from Gimmelwald to both Mürren and the valley runs 6:00–20:00 at :00 and :30, on the hour 20:00–24:00). Be warned: You'll meet a lot of my readers in this town. This is a disappointment to some; others enjoy the chance to be part of a fun extended family.

$$ At **Olle and Maria's B&B,** the Eggimanns rent two rooms—Gimmelwald's most comfortable—in their quirky but alpine-sleek chalet. Maria and Olle, who job-share the village's only teaching position and raise three kids of their own, offer visitors a rare and intimate peek at this community (D-130 SF, Db with kitchenette-190 SF for 2 or 200 SF for 3 people, optional breakfast-20 SF, 3-night minimum, cash only, guarantee your reservation in advance with a check or PayPal, last check-in preferred by 21:00, free Wi-Fi, laundry service; from cable car, continue straight for 200 yards along the town's only road, B&B on left; tel. 033-855-3575, oeggimann@bluewin.ch).

$$ **Esther's Guest House,** overlooking the village's main intersection, rents seven clean, basic, and comfortable rooms, three of which have private bathrooms (S-50–70 SF, big D-120 SF, Db-120 SF, big T-140 SF, Tb-170–180 SF, Q-180 SF, Qb-190–200 SF, family room with private bath for up to 5 people-230 SF, cash preferred, breakfast-15 SF, 2-night minimum, pay Internet access, free Wi-Fi, low ceilings, fine guests' kitchen, tel. 033-855-5488, fax 033-855-5492, www.esthersguesthouse.ch,

BERNER OBERLAND

info@esthersguesthouse.ch). Esther also rents two four-person **apartments** with kitchenettes next door (150–160 SF for 2 people, 210–220 SF for 4 people, extra bed-30 SF, 3-night minimum, check website for details).

$$ Pension Gimmelwald is an old farmhouse converted into a family-style inn, with 12 simple rooms, a six-bed dorm, and the town's only restaurant. Its terrace, overlooking the Mountain Hostel, has gorgeous views across the valley (bed in 6-bed dorm-25 SF, S-60 SF, D-100 SF, T-150 SF, Q-185 SF, less in winter, open June–Oct and mid-Dec–mid-April, breakfast-12 SF, 2-min walk up from cable-car station, tel. 033-855-1730, www.pension gimmelwald.com, twnewark@yahoo.com, Englishman David).

$ Hotel Mittaghorn is a classic creaky, thin-walled, alpine-style place with a superb view of the Jungfrau Alps. It's run by Walter Mittler, a Swiss gentleman in his late 80s, with help from trusty Tim. The hotel has three rooms with private showers (first-come, first-served) and four rooms that share a coin-operated shower (open April–Oct, S-54 SF, D-86 SF, T-129 SF, 6-SF surcharge per person for 1-night stays, cash only, simple but hearty 15-SF dinner at 19:30 by reservation only, free Internet access, a five-minute climb up the path from the village center, tel. 033-855-1658, www.ricksteves.com /mittaghorn, mittaghorn@gmail.com). Please don't contact the hotel when it's

closed (Nov–March). To make a reservation, wait until April 1 (or later) to book by phone or email; it's also necessary to reconfirm by phone the day before your arrival. If no one's there when you arrive, look for a card in the hallway directing you to your room.

$ Liesi's Heart Place is run by the former proprietor of Pension Gimmelwald, who now rents a little suite in her home with a view and terrace. Liesi loves to help guests celebrate special occasions (Db-80–110 SF, Tb-110–150 SF, Qb-150–180 SF with 2-night stay, laundry, pleasant garden with grill, reserve by email and reconfirm 2–3 days before arrival, credit card number required to reserve but cash only to pay, located near Chalet Huusmätteli, tel. 033-855-1662, www.liesisheartplace.ch).

$ Mountain Hostel is a beehive of activity, as clean as its guests, cheap, and friendly. The hostel has low ceilings, a self-service kitchen, a mini-grocery, a bar, a free pool table, laundry, free Internet access and Wi-Fi, and healthy plumbing. It's mostly a college-age crowd; families and older travelers will probably feel more comfortable elsewhere. Petra Brunner has lined the porch with flowers. This relaxed hostel survives with the help of its guests. Read the signs, respect Petra's rules, and leave it tidier than you found it—bus your plates and clean the kitchen. This is one of those rare spots where a congenial atmosphere spontaneously combusts as the

piano plays, and spaghetti becomes communal as it cooks. If you've shown up without a reservation, check the front desk for Petra's sign-up sheet, where she lists any available beds for the night. This is not the place for your own private kegger; there is a fun bar on the premises, but brining your own alcohol is discouraged (26 SF per bed in 6- to 15-bed rooms, includes sheets, showers-1 SF, no breakfast, free Wi-Fi, laundry, good pizzas sold in the evening, open mid-April–mid-Nov, 20 yards up the trail from lift station, reserve with credit card through website or by phone after 18:00, tel. 033-855-1704, www.mountainhostel.com, info@mountain hostel.com).

Eating in Gimmelwald

The only restaurant in town is at **Pension Gimmelwald,** dishing up good food indoors or out on its glorious view terrace. They serve local, organically farmed meat and cheese, salads, and even make their own *Rösti* (13–22-SF main dishes, Tue–Sat 12:00–15:00 & 18:00–21:00, Sun 12:00–18:00, closed Mon). The **Mountain Hostel** has a decent members' kitchen and makes great pizzas in the evenings (14 SF, non-guests welcome). **Hotel Mittaghorn** serves dinner only to its guests (15 SF).

Consider packing in a **picnic** meal from the larger towns. Mürren, a five-minute cable-car ride or a 30-minute hike up the hill, has good restaurants and a grocery (see "Eating in Mürren," later). If you need a few groceries and want to skip the hike to Mürren, you can buy the essentials—noodles, spaghetti sauce, and candy bars—at the Mountain Hostel's reception desk, or check out the little store at Pension Gimmelwald. Local farmers post signs to sell their produce.

Mürren

Pleasant as an alpine resort can be, Mürren is traffic-free and filled with bakeries, cafés, souvenirs, old-timers with walking sticks, employees enjoying incentive trips, and Japanese tourists making movies of each other. Its chalets are prefab-rustic. With help from a cliffside train, a funicular, and a cable car, hiking options are endless from Mürren. Sitting on a ledge 2,000 feet above the Lauterbrunnen Valley, surrounded by a fortissimo chorus of mountains, the town has all the comforts of home (for a price) without the pretentiousness of more famous resorts.

Historic Mürren, which dates from 1384, has been overwhelmed by development. Still, it's a peaceful town. There's no full-time doctor, no police officer (they call Lauterbrunnen if there's a problem), and no resident priest or pastor. (The Protestant church—up by the TI—posts a sign showing where the region's roving pastor preaches each Sunday.) There's not even enough business to keep a bakery open year-round (Mürren's bakery is open mid-June–Sept and Dec–April)—a clear indication that this town is either lively or completely dead, depending on the season. (Holiday population: 4,000. Permanent residents: 400.) Keep an eye open for the "Milch Express," a tiny cart that delivers fresh milk and eggs to hotels and homes throughout town.

Orientation to Mürren

Mürren perches high on a ledge, overlooking the Lauterbrunnen Valley. You can walk from one end of town to the other in about 10 minutes.

There are two ways to get to Mürren: on the train from Grütschalp (10 min, connects by 10-min cable car to Lauterbrunnen, 30-min total trip) or on the Schilthornbahn cable car from near Stechelberg (in the valley), which stops at Gimmelwald, Mürren, and continues up to the Schilthorn. The train and cable-car stations (which both have WCs and lockers) are at opposite ends of town.

Tourist Information: Mürren's TI can help you find a room and gives hiking advice (July–mid-Sept Mon–Sat 8:30–19:00, Thu until 20:00, Sun 8:30–18:00, less off-season, above the village, follow signs to *Sportzentrum*, tel. 033-856-8686, www.my muerren.ch).

BERNER OBERLAND

Helpful Hints

R & R: The slick **Sportzentrum** (sports center) that houses the TI offers a world of indoor activities. The pool is free with the regional visitor's card given by local hotels (July–mid-Sept Mon–Sat 8:30–19:00, Thu until 20:00, Sun 8:30–18:00; pool and sauna generally opens at 10:00 Tue–Wed and Fri, otherwise at 13:00; shorter hours off-season, closed May and Nov–mid-Dec, www.muerren.ch/sportzentrum). In season, they offer squash, mini-golf, table tennis, and a fitness room.

Money: There's an ATM by the Co-op grocery in the middle of town. You can change money at the TI.

Internet Access: Connect at the **TI** (5 SF/15 min), at the **cable-car station** inside an old gondola (5 SF/15 min), or at the **Eiger Guesthouse** (4 SF/20 min, daily 8:00–23:00, across from the train station).

Laundry: Hotel Bellevue has a slick and modern little self-service launderette in its basement (5 SF/wash, 5 SF/dry, open 24/7).

Bike Rental: You can rent mountain bikes at **Stäger Sport** (25 SF/half-day, 35 SF/day, includes helmet, daily 9:00–18:00, closed late Oct–mid-May, in middle of town, tel. 033-855-

To Birg & Schilthorn

ALLMENDHUBEL

To Grütschalp

FUNICULAR

SPORT-
ZENTRUM

To Grütschalp &
Lift Down to
Lauterbrunnen

TRAIN
STATION

Cliffs

❶ Alpin Palace Hotel

❷ Hotel Alpina &
Edelweiss Cafeteria

❸ Hotel/Rest. Bellevue
& Launderette

❹ Hotel/Restaurant
Jungfrau

❺ Hotel/Restaurant
Blumental

❻ Eiger Guesthouse

❼ Chalet Fontana

❽ Chalet Helvetia

❾ Chalet Böbs

❿ Stägerstübli
Restaurant

⓫ Bar Bistro

⓬ Tham Chinese
Restaurant

⓭ Co-op Grocery

Note:
Cable-car station to train
station = 10-min. walk

Not to Scale

2355, www.staegersport.ch). There's a bigger bike-rental place in Lauterbrunnen (Imboden Bike, described on page 151). Use caution on rough stretches.

Mürren Massage: Sabina Kulicka is very strong—and she knows how to iron out your back after a good hike (90 SF/hr, lots of options, daily 8:00–21:00, in Hotel Alpenruh, tel. 033-855-4538, mobile 079-527-0832).

Skiing: The Mürren-Schilthorn ski area is the Berner Oberland's best place for experts, especially those eager to tackle the famous, nearly 10-mile-long Inferno run. The runs on top, especially the Kanonenrohr, are quite steep and have predictably good snow; lower areas cater to all levels, but can be icier. For rental gear, try the friendly, convenient **Ed Abegglen** shop (best prices, next to recommended Chalet Fontana, tel. 033-855-1245), **Alfred's Sporthaus** (good selection and decent prices, between ski school and Sportzentrum, tel. 033-855-3030), or **Stäger Sport** (one shop in Sportzentrum and another on the lower road near cable-car station, tel. 033-855-2330). For more info on skiing and snowboarding, see the Switzerland in Winter chapter.

Self-Guided Walk

Welcome to Mürren

Mürren has long been a top ski resort, but a walk across town offers a glimpse into its past. This stroll takes you through town on the main drag, from the train station (where you'll arrive if coming from Lauterbrunnen) to the cable-car station, then back up to the Allmendhubel funicular station.

• *Start at the...*

Train Station: The first trains pulled into Mürren in 1891. (A circa-1911 car is permanently parked at the Grütschalp station.) A display case inside the station displays an original car from the narrow-gauge, horse-powered line that rolled fancy visitors from here into town. The current station, built in 1964, comes with impressive engineering for heavy cargo. Look out back, where a small truck can be loaded up, attached to the train, and driven away.

• *Wander into town along the main road (take the lower, left fork).*

Stroll Under the Alpin Palace Hotel: The towering Alpin Palace Hotel was the "Grand Palace Hotel" until it burned in 1928. Its Jugendstil Hall is the finest room in Mürren. The small wooden platform on the left—looking like a suicide springboard—is the place where snow-removal trucks dump their loads over the cliff in the winter. Look back at the meadow below the station: This is a favorite grazing spot for chamois (the animals, not the rags for washing cars). Ahead, at Edelweiss Hotel, step to the far corner of the restaurant terrace for a breathtaking view stretching from the big three (Eiger, Mönch, and Jungfrau) on the left to the lonely cattle farm in the high alp on the right. Then look down.

Haus Montana is the spot where Kandahar ski boots were first made in 1933 (to give the necessary support to daredevils racing from the Schilthorn to the valley floor in Mürren's infamous Inferno race). Today, the still-respected Kandahar boots are made in nearby Thun.

• *Continue toward...*

"Downtown" Mürren: You'll pass the main intersection (where the small service road leads down to Gimmelwald) and the only grocery store in town (Co-op). The tiny fire barn (labeled *Feuerwehr*) has a list showing the leaders of the volunteer force and their responsibilities. The old barn behind it on the right evokes the time, not so long ago, when the town's barns housed cows. Imagine Mürren with more cows than people, rather than with more visitors than residents.

• *Reaching the far end of Mürren, you come to the...*

Cable-Car Station: The first cable car (goes directly to the valley floor) is for cargo, garbage, and the (reputedly) longest bungee jump in the world. The other takes hikers and skiers up to the Schilthorn and down to the valley via Gimmelwald.

• *Hiking back along the high road, you'll enter...*

Upper Mürren: You'll pass Mürren's two churches, the Allmendhubel funicular station and the Sportzentrum (with swimming pool and TI).

• *Consider riding the...*

Allmendhubelbahn Funicular: A quaint-looking but surprisingly rewarding funicular (from 1912, renovated in 1999) carries nature-lovers from Mürren to Allmendhubel, a perch offering a Jungfrau view that, though much lower, rivals the Schilthorn. At the station, notice the 1920s bobsled. The restaurants here (full- and self-service) have awesome views. Allmendhubel is particularly good for families. At 7.40 SF one-way (12 SF round-trip, 6 SF with Swiss Pass), it's cheaper than the Schilthorn (mid-June–mid-Oct runs every 20 min, daily 9:00–17:00, tel. 033-855-2042 or 033-856-2141, www.schilthorn.ch). The restaurant overlooks a great playground, and the entertaining children's hike—with rough and thrilling, kid-friendly alpine rides along the way—departs from here. This is also the departure point for the North Face hike and walks to Grütschalp (see "Hikes and Biking" on page 176).

• *Our walk is finished. Enjoy the town and the views.*

Activities in Mürren

During ski season and the height of summer, the Mürren area offers plenty of activities for those willing to seek them out. In July and August, you can enjoy occasional folkloric evenings (some Wednesdays, at the Sportzentrum), morning tours of flowers and wildlife (Sun at 9:00, meet at Allmendhubel station, 12 SF includes funicular ride up, 1.5 hours, led by Othmar from Hotel Bellevue—call him at 078-604-1401), and weekly yoga lessons by Denise (off Chalet Fontana, mobile 078-642-3485). Ask at your hotel or the TI for the latest. In spring and fall, Mürren is pretty dead.

If you have a bit of climbing experience—and want to get your heart pumping—**Klettersteig Via Ferrata** provides licensed guides to lead you down a vertigo-inducing via ferrata course (mountain climbing on an iron cable) from Mürren to Gimmelwald. Climbers are attached to a 1.4-mile-long steel cable as they traverse sheer cliffs, swinging rope bridges, and impossibly steep ladders. Reservations are smart (95 SF includes equipment, minimum 4 people, mid-June–Oct, takes 3 hours, tel. 033-821-6100, www.klettersteig-muerren.ch, info@be-je.ch).

BERNER OBERLAND

Nightlife in Mürren

Eiger Guesthouse is a popular sports bar–type hangout with pool tables, games, Internet stations, and a Scottish host (Alan) who stocks lots of whiskies. **Stägerstübli** is another good place to congregate. **Hotel Bellevue,** with its elegant alpine-lounge ambience, is also good for a drink. (All of these places are further described next, under "Sleeping in Mürren" or "Eating in Mürren.")

Sleeping in Mürren

(5,381 feet, 1 SF = about $1, country code: 41)
Prices for accommodations are often higher during the ski season. Many hotels and restaurants close in spring, roughly from Easter to early June, and may also shut down any time between late September and mid-December.

$$$ Hotel Alpina is a simple place with 24 comfortable rooms and a concrete feeling—a good thing, given its cliff-edge position (Sb-85 SF, Db-160 SF, Tb-200 SF, Qb-220 SF, most rooms with awesome Jungfrau views and balconies, prices less off-season and without a view, outside of mid-June–mid-Aug ask for a 10-SF/night Rick Steves discount, family rooms, pay Internet access, free Wi-Fi, homey lounge, exit left from train station and walk 2 min, tel. 033-855-1361, fax 033-855-1049, www.muerren.ch /alpina, alpina@muerren.ch; Cecilia, her cheerful son Roger, and his wife, Agripina).

$$$ Hotel Bellevue has a homey lounge, solid woodsy furniture, a great view terrace, the hunter-themed Jägerstübli restaurant, and 17 great rooms at fair rates—most with balconies and views (Sb-105–145 SF, Db-170–190 SF, special deals with this book in June, Db-150 SF if staying 2 nights or more in Sept–Oct, free Internet access and Wi-Fi, tel. 033-855-1401, fax 033-855-1490, www.muerren.ch/bellevue, bellevue-crystal@bluewin.ch, Ruth and Othmar Suter).

$$$ Hotel Jungfrau offers 29 modern and comfortable rooms and an apartment for up to 6 people (Sb-95–120 SF, Db-180–220 SF, lower prices are for nonview rooms, elevator, laundry service-15 SF, pay Wi-Fi, downhill from TI/Sportzentrum, tel. 033-856-6464, fax 033-856-6465, www.hoteljungfrau.ch, mail@hotel jungfrau.ch, Anne-Marie and Andres).

$$$ Hotel Blumental has 16 older but nicely furnished rooms and a fun game/TV lounge (Sb-75–80 SF, Db-150–170 SF, 10 percent cheaper in Sept–Oct, higher prices are for July–Aug, outside of July–Aug book direct and ask for a 10 percent Rick Steves discount, pay cable Internet, attached restaurant listed under "Eating

in Mürren," tel. 033-855-1826, fax 033-855-3686, www.muerren
.ch/blumental, blumental@muerren.ch; Ralph and Heidi, fourth
generation in the von Allmen family). Their modern little chalet
out back rents six rooms (Db-130–160 SF, includes breakfast in
the hotel).

$$ Eiger Guesthouse offers 12 good budget rooms. This
friendly, creaky, easygoing home away from home was renovated
in 2009 (S-70 SF, Sb-80–95 SF, D-100–120 SF, Db-130–160 SF,
bunk Q-160–180 SF, Qb-200–240 SF; special with this book:
D-90 SF with a 2-night minimum year-round—making this
about the best deal going for cheap beds in July–Aug; closed late
Oct–Nov and for one month after Easter, free Wi-Fi, game room,
terrace, across from train station, tel. 033-856-5460, fax 033-856-
5461, www.eigerguesthouse.com, info@eigerguesthouse.com,
well-run by Scotsman Alan and Swiss Véronique). The restaurant
serves good, reasonably priced dinners (18–25 SF).

$ Chalet Fontana, run by charming Englishwoman Denise
Fussell, is a rare budget option in Mürren, with simple, crispy-
clean, and comfortable rooms (S-45–55 SF, D-75–85 SF, large
D-95 SF, T-125 SF, price varies with size of room, 5 SF cheaper
without breakfast, cash only, closed Nov–April, fridge in common
kitchen, across street from Stägerstübli restaurant in town cen-
ter, mobile 078-642-3485, www.chaletfontana.ch, chaletfontana
@muerren.ch). If no one's home, check at the Ed Abegglen shop
next door (tel. 033-855-1245, off-season only). Denise also rents
a family apartment with kitchen, bathroom, and breakfast (two
bedrooms with 3 beds each, 130 SF/2 people, 160 SF/3 people, 200
SF/4 people, 260 SF/6 people).

$ Chalet Helvetia, run by Etmé Hunziker, offers a homey,
clean two-bedroom apartment with bathroom, kitchen, separate
entrance, and balcony from 40 SF per person (up to 4 people, no
breakfast, 2-night minimum, laundry service-10 SF/load, 200
yards below cable-car station on path to Gimmelwald on right, tel.
033-855-4169, mobile 079-234-7867, chalet.helvetia@quicknet.ch).

$ Chalet Böbs, with terrific views, is the last house in Mürren
on the road to Gimmelwald (at the sign, walk up the path to the
right, and it's on the left). Kitty and Albert, an alphorn player, rent
three apartments with kitchens: one that sleeps two people and
two that sleep up to five people—each with a double bed, bunk
bed, and a twin bed (Sb-70 SF, Db-90 SF, Tb-130 SF, Quad or
5b-150 SF, 3-night minimum, tel. 033-855-1463, mobile 078-633-
6091, boebs@quicknet.ch, www.boebs.ch).

BERNER OBERLAND

Eating in Mürren

Many of these restaurants are in or near my recommended hotels. Outside of summer and ski season, it can be hard to find any place that's open (ask around).

Stägerstübli is everyone's favorite Mürren diner. It's the only real restaurant not associated with a hotel. Located in the town center, this 1902 building was once a tearoom for rich tourists, while locals were limited to the room in the back—which is now the nicer area to eat. Sitting on its terrace, you know just who's out and about in town (18–35-SF lunches and dinners, big portions, lovely lamb, daily 11:30–21:00, closed first week of Sept, Lydia).

Bar Bistro has inexpensive light meals and impressive views (Mon–Wed 9:00–19:00, Thu–Sat 9:00–20:00, closed Sun, at the Sportzentrum, overlooking the ice rink).

Tham Chinese Restaurant is a humble place with good food that brings spice to the local eating scene (Thai and Chinese dishes, daily 12:00–20:00, near the train-station end of town on the lower road, tel. 033-856-0110).

Hotel Blumental specializes in typical Swiss cuisine, but also serves fish, international, and vegetarian dishes in a stony and woody dining area (15–29-SF specials, 21–31-SF fondue served for one or more, 14-SF pastas, daily from 16:30, tel. 033-855-1826).

Restaurant Hotel Jungfrau is a dressy ski lodge with a modern octagonal dining room and a fine view terrace. The salad bar (11 SF per plate or 17 SF all-you-can-eat) is always excellent, and 45 SF buys you a four-course meal (23-SF cheese fondue—minimum 2 people, veggie options, nightly 18:00–21:30, on upper road downhill from TI/Sportzentrum, tel. 033-856-6464).

Edelweiss cafeteria offers self-serve lunches and restaurant dinners with the most cliff-hanging dining in town—the views are incredible (pizzas, hearty salads, sandwiches; self-service until 17:00, then full service; next to the recommended Hotel Alpina).

Hotel Bellevue's restaurant is atmospheric, with three dining zones: view terrace, elegant indoor area, and the Jägerstübli—a cozy, well-antlered hunters' room guaranteed to disgust vegetarians. This is a good bet for game, as they buy chamois and deer direct from local hunters (lamb or game-34–44 SF, cheaper options as low as 15 SF, mid-June–Oct daily 11:30–14:00 & 18:00–21:00, closed off-season, tel. 033-855-1401).

The **Co-op** is the only grocery store in town, with good picnic fixings and sandwiches (Mon–Fri 8:00–12:00 & 13:45–18:30, Sat until 17:00, closed Sun). Given restaurant prices, this place is a godsend for those on a tight budget.

Wengen

Wengen—a bigger, fancier Mürren on the east side of the valley—has plenty of grand hotels, many shops, tennis courts, mini-golf, and terrific views. This traffic-free resort is an easy train ride above Lauterbrunnen and halfway up to Kleine Scheidegg and Männlichen, and offers more activities for those needing distraction from the scenery. (But hiking is better from Mürren and Gimmelwald.) Note that many Wengen shops take lunch very seriously, and close down for at least an hour around noon.

The **TI** is two blocks from the station: Go up to the main drag, turn left, and it's on the left. They have info on guided walks, short hikes, and local Internet cafés and Wi-Fi hotspots, and they sell hiking maps (daily in summer 9:00–18:00 except closed Sun 12:30–13:30, closed Sat–Sun mid-Oct–mid-Dec, coin-op Internet access-1 SF/3 min, tel. 033-855-1414, www.mywengen.ch).

If you're here in the winter to ski the Keine Scheidegg-Männlichen slopes, Wengen makes the best home base. Rent your gear from **Molitor Sport + Mode,** still run by the family of founder and famous ski racer Karl Molitor (who's now 90). Even if you're not renting a thing, stop in to see the cool old photos, gear, and Karl's medals on display, which add up to a mini-ski-racing museum (on Wengen's main drag, on the left past Männlichen cable-car station, tel. 033-855-2131). Other rental shops include **Alpia Sport** (right above train station, tel. 033-855-2626) and **Central-Sport** (on the main drag, past post office, tel. 033-855-2323).

The **Co-op grocery** here is great for picnic fixings, and is larger than most groceries in the area (Mon–Sat 8:00–18:30, closed Sun).

Sleeping and Eating in Wengen

(4,180 feet, 1 SF = about $1, country code: 41)

Above the Train Station

$$$ **Hotel Berghaus,** in a quiet area a five-minute walk from the main street, offers 19 rooms above a fine restaurant specializing in fish (Sb-92–125 SF, Db-184–250 SF, 5 percent discount with this book and cash, elevator, pay Internet access, pay Wi-Fi, open June–Sept and late Dec–Easter, tel. 033-855-2151, fax 033-855-3820, www.berghaus-wengen.ch, info@berghaus-wengen.ch, Fontana family). At the train station, you can dial #114 on the hotel phone to request a free pickup. Or, to walk to the hotel from the main drag, head up the street across from Hotel Bernerhof,

bear right at the fork, go 200 yards more past the church, and it's on the left.

$$$ Hotel Schönegg, on Wengen's main drag, is a centrally located splurge, decorated with antiques and old wood (Sb-120–140 SF, Db-240–280 SF; all rooms have balconies and great views, cozy family room with fireplace, free Wi-Fi, good restaurant with big terrace, look for big light-yellow hotel above main drag one block past TI, tel. 033-855-3422, fax 033-855-4233, www.hotel -schoenegg.ch, mail@hotel-schoenegg.ch, Herr Berthod und Frau Steiner).

Below the Train Station

$$ Bären Hotel, run by friendly Therese and Willy Brunner, offers 14 tidy rooms, some with perky, bright-orange bathrooms. Their restaurant is bright and inviting, offering garden-fresh Swiss cuisine (daily specials for 16.50 SF; Sb-70–90 SF, Db-140–150 SF, Tb-180–240 SF, pricier in winter, dinner-20 SF more, family rooms, free Internet access and Wi-Fi, kids' playroom, tel. 033-855-1419, fax 033-855-1525, www.baeren-wengen.ch, info @baeren-wengen.ch). From the station, cross the street to the Co-op grocery, turn right and go under the rail bridge, and follow the road down the hill—the hotel will be on your right.

$$ Clare and Andy's Chalet (Trogihalten) offers three rustic, low-ceilinged rooms (1-room studio: Sb-56 SF, Db-90 SF; 2-room suite: Sb/Db-106 SF, Tb-149 SF, Qb-188 SF; 4-room flat: Tb-159 SF, Qb-192 SF, 5 people-240 SF, 6 people-294 SF, 7 people-327 SF; breakfast-15 SF, no restaurant but dinner by request-35 SF, 4-night minimum preferred, prices higher for shorter stays, cash only, all rooms with balconies, tel. & fax 033-855-1712, mobile 079-423-7813, www.chaletwengen.ch, info@chaletwengen .ch, Clare is English, Andy is Swiss). From the station, follow the main street until Hotel Bernerhof, then turn left and follow the paved downhill path. Stay straight on the gravel path where the pavement curves, and look for the British flag up on the right.

More in the Berner Oberland

Lifts and Trains

Enjoying at least one of the two high-altitude thrill rides described here is an essential Berner Oberland experience.

▲▲▲The Schilthorn and a 10,000-Foot Breakfast

The Schilthornbahn cable car carries skiers, hikers, and sightseers effortlessly to the 10,000-foot summit of the Schilthorn, where

the Piz Gloria station awaits, with a solar-powered revolving restaurant, shop, and panorama terrace. At the top, you have a spectacular panoramic view of the Eiger, Mönch, and Jungfrau mountains, lined up on the horizon.

As you ascend in the cable car, keep an eye on the altitude meter. Ask at the Schilthorn station for a cable-car souvenir decal.

Linger on top. Head out to the terrace, where information boards identify each peak, and directional signs point hikers toward some seriously steep downhill climbs. Watch paragliders set up, psych up, and take off, flying 45 minutes with the birds to distant Interlaken. Walk along the ridge out back. This is a great place for a photo of the mountain-climber you. Youth hostelers—not realizing that rocks may hide just under the snow—scream down the ice fields on plastic-bag sleds from the Schilthorn mountaintop. (There's an English-speaking doctor in Lauterbrunnen—see page 149.)

Inside, Piz Gloria has a free "touristorama" film room with a "Multi-Vision" slide show and explosive highlights from the James Bond thriller that featured the Schilthorn, *On Her Majesty's Secret Service*. (To start either of the 10-min video clips, press the 007 or "Multi-Vision" button on the column in the middle of the room.)

You can ride up to the Schilthorn and hike down, but it's tough. (Hiking *up* from Gimmelwald or Mürren is easier on your knees...if you don't mind a

BERNER OBERLAND

5,000-foot altitude gain.) For information on **hikes** from lift stations along the Schilthorn cable-car line, see "Hikes and Biking" on page 177. My favorite "hike" from the Schilthorn is simply along the ridge out back, to get away from the station and be all alone on top of an Alp.

Cost, Hours, Information: You can ride to the Schilthorn and back from the Stechelberg station on the valley floor (92 SF), Gimmelwald (83 SF), or Mürren (72 SF). Snare a 25 percent discount for early and late rides (roughly before 9:00 and after 15:30) and in spring and fall (roughly May and Oct). Travelers with a Swiss Pass (who get half off) or with a Eurailpass (25 percent discount) might as well go whenever they like, because you can't double up discounts. Lifts go twice hourly, and the ride from Gimmelwald (including two transfers) to the Schilthorn takes 30 minutes. You can park your car at the valley station near Stechelberg (2 SF/2 hours, 6 SF/day, cash only). For more information, including current weather conditions, see www.schilthorn .ch or call 033-826-0007.

Breakfast at 10,000 Feet: The "007 Breakfast Buffet" is huge (27.50 SF, 8:00–11:00, save a little money by buying the combo cable-car ticket—92 SF, 59 SF with Swiss Pass, but you must leave from the Stechelberg station by 8:55). The restaurant also serves hot dishes all day at prices that don't rise with the altitude (around 20 SF).

▲▲▲Jungfraujoch

The literal high point of any trip to the Swiss Alps is a train ride through the Eiger to the Jungfraujoch. At 11,300 feet, it's Europe's highest train station. (If you have a heart or lung condition, you may want to check with your doctor before making this ascent.) The ride from Kleine Scheidegg takes about an hour (sit on the right side for better views), including two five-minute stops at stations actually halfway up the notorious North Face of the Eiger. You have time to look out windows and marvel at how people could climb the Eiger—and how the Swiss built this train track more than a hundred years ago. The second half of the ride takes you through a tunnel inside the Eiger (some newer train cars run multilingual videos about the history of the train line).

Once you reach the top, study the Jungfraujoch chart to see your options (many of them are weather-dependent). There's a restaurant, a history exhibit, an "ice palace" (a cavern with a gallery of ice statues), and a 20-minute video that plays continuously. A

BERNER OBERLAND

tunnel leads outside, where you can summer ski (33 SF for gear and lift ticket), sled (free loaner discs with a 5-SF deposit), or hike an hour across the ice to Mönchsjochhütte (a mountain hut with a small restaurant). An elevator leads to the Sphinx observatory for the highest viewing point, from which you can see the Aletsch Glacier—Europe's longest, at nearly 11 miles—stretch to the south. Remember that your body isn't used to such high altitudes. Signs posted at the top remind you to take it easy.

You can combine one of the best hikes in the region—from Männlichen to Kleine Scheidegg—with your trip up to the Jungfraujoch (see page 184).

Cost, Hours, Information: The first trip of the day to the Jungfraujoch is discounted; ask for a Good Morning Ticket, and leave the top by 12:30 (Nov–April you can get Good Morning rates for the first or second train and return any time that day; train runs all year; round-trip fares to Jungfraujoch: from Lauterbrunnen-161 SF, or 137 SF for first trip—about 7:00; from Kleine Scheidegg-109 SF, or 85 SF for first trip—about 8:00; confirm times and price, 25 percent discount with Swiss Pass and Eurailpass, railpass holders get a better deal than Good Morning Ticket and can't combine discounts). Pick up a leaflet on the lifts at a local TI (www.jungfraubahn.ch). If it's cloudy, skip the trip; for a terse trilingual weather forecast from the Jungfraujoch, call 033-828-7931.

Hikes and Biking

This area offers days of possible hikes. Many are a fun combination of trails, mountain trains, and cable-car rides. I've listed them based on which side of the Lauterbrunnen Valley they're on: west (the Gimmelwald/Mürren/Schilthorn side) or east (the Jungfrau side).

On the Gimmelwald (West) Side of the Lauterbrunnen Valley
Hikes from the Schilthorn
Several tough trails lead down from the Schilthorn, but most visitors take the cable car round-trip simply for the views (see "Lifts and Trains," earlier). If you're a serious hiker, consider walking all the way down (first hike) or part of the way down (second hike) back into Gimmelwald. Don't attempt to hike down from

BERNER OBERLAND

Gimmelwald Area Hikes

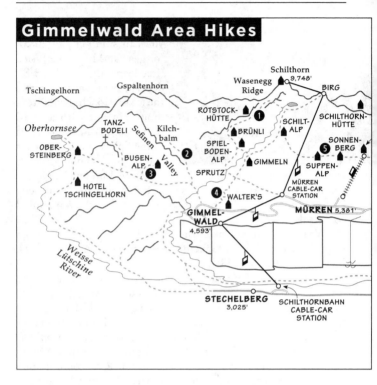

the Schilthorn unless the trail is clear of snow. Adequate shoes and clothing (weather can change quickly) and good knees are required. (If you want to visit the Sprutz Waterfall on your way to Gimmelwald, see page 183.)

From the Top of the Schilthorn (very difficult)—To hike downhill from the Piz Gloria revolving restaurant at the peak, start at the steps to the right of the cable, which lead along a ridge between a cliff and the bowl. As you pass huge rocks and shale fields, keep an eye out for the painted rocks that mark the scant trail. Eventually, you'll hit the service road (a ski run in the winter), which is steep and not very pleasant. Passing a memorial to a woman killed by lightning in 1865, you come to the small lake called Grauseeli. Leave the gravel road and hike along the lake. From there, follow the trail (with the help of cables when necessary) to scamper along the shale in the direction of Rotstockhütte (to Gimmelwald, see next hike) or Schilttal (the valley leading directly to Mürren; follow *Mürren/Rotstockhütte* sign painted on the rock at the junction).

▲▲Birg to Gimmelwald via Brünli (moderately difficult)— Rather than doing the very long hike all the way back down into Gimmelwald, I prefer walking the easier (but still strenuous) hike

Bietenhorn

Not to Scale

ALLMENDHUBEL

MÜRREN
TRAIN
STATION

WINTEREGG

GRÜTSCHALP
4,879'

*Staubbach
Falls*

CAMPING
JUNGFRAU

LAUTER-
BRUNNEN
2,612'

To
Inter-
laken

CAMPING
SCHÜTZENBACH

*Trümmelbach
Falls*

To Wengen &
Kleine Scheidegg

❶ Birg to Gimmelwald
via Brünil

❷ Up Sefinen Valley
to Kilchbalm

❸ Gimmelwald-
Tanzbodeli-
Obersteinberg-
Stechelberg/
Gimmelwald

❹ Sprutz Waterfall

❺ North Face Trail
from Allmendhubel

❻ Allmendhubel/
Mürren to
Grütschalp

❼ Allmendhubel to
Grütschalp via
Winteregg

Note: Elevation in feet

from the intermediate cable-car station at Birg. This is efficiently combined with a visit to the Schilthorn (from Schilthorn summit, ride cable car halfway down, get off at Birg, and hike down from there; buy the round-trip excursion early-bird fare, which is cheaper than the Gimmelwald–Schilthorn–Birg ticket, and decide at Birg whether you want to hike or ride down).

The most interesting trail from Birg to Gimmelwald is the high one via Grauseeli lake and Wasenegg Ridge to Brünli, then down to Spielbodenalp and the Sprutz Waterfall. Warning: This trail is quite steep and slippery in places, and can take four hours. Locals take their kindergartners on this hike, but it can seem dangerous to Americans unused to alpine hikes. Do not attempt this hike in snow, which you might find at this altitude even in the peak of summer. (Get local advice.)

From the Birg lift station, hike toward the Schilthorn, taking your first left down and passing along the left side of the little Grauseeli lake. From the lake, a gravelly trail leads down rough switchbacks (including a stretch where the path narrows and you can hang onto a guide cable against the cliff face) until it levels out. When you see a rock painted with arrows pointing to Mürren and Rotstockhütte, follow the path to Rotstockhütte (traditional old

Hiking in the Berner Oberland

This region is a wonderful place to hike, and I've listed my favorite excursions. The super-scenic walk from Männlichen to Kleine Scheidegg is the best of all worlds: It's both dramatic and relatively easy. The hike from Schynige Platte to First is spectacular, but much more challenging, as is the hike from the Birg cable-car station down to Gimmelwald—don't try either of these in bad weather. In case of rain, the lower hikes (North Face Trail from Allmendhubel; the walk from Mürren or Allmendhubel to Grütschalp; the Sefinen Valley hike from Gimmelwald; and the stroll along the Lauterbrunnen Valley) are better bets.

To do any serious hiking, you should invest in a good hiking map. Hikers can get specifics at the Mürren TI or from hoteliers. For a description of six diverse hikes on the west side of Lauterbrunnen, pick up the free *Mürren–Schilthorn Hikes* brochure. This 3-D overview map of the Mürren mountainside makes a useful and attractive souvenir. For the other side of the valley, get the *Wandern Jungfraubahnen* brochure, which also has a handy 3-D overview map of hiking trails (both brochures free at stations, hotels, and TIs).

Once under way, don't mind the fences (although be aware that wires can be solar-powered electric); a hiker has the right of way in Switzerland. Don't forget a water bottle and some munchies. Trails are well-marked, with yellow signs listing destinations and the estimated time it'll take you to walk there. Refer to maps (within this chapter) as you read about the hikes.

Weather Concerns: Locals always seem to know the weather report (as much of their income depends on it). Clouds can roll

farm with light meals and drinks, mattress loft with cheap beds), traversing the cow-grazed mountainside.

For a thrill, follow Wasenegg Ridge. It's more scary than dangerous if you're sure-footed and can handle the 50-foot-long "tightrope-with-handrail" section along an extremely narrow ledge with a thousand-foot drop. This trail gets you to Brünli with the least altitude drop. (The safer, well-signposted approach to Brünli is to drop down to Rotstockhütte, then climb back up to Brünli.) The barbed-wire fence leads you to the knobby little summit, where you'll enjoy an incredible 360-degree view and a chance to sign your name on the register stored in the little wooden box.

A steep trail winds directly down from Brünli toward

in anytime, but skies are usually clearest in the morning. All over the region, TV sets are tuned to the local weather station, with real-time views from all the famous peaks. The same station airs a travelogue on the region each evening at about 21:30. You can also check the weather at www.swisspanorama.com.

Snow: In the Berner Oberland, snow can curtail your hiking plans, even in July (the Männlichen lift doesn't even open until the first week in June). Before setting out on any hike, get advice from a knowledgeable local. Well into the spring, and sometimes also in early fall, the high trails (Männlichen to Kleine Scheidegg, Schynige Platte to First, and anything from Schilthorn or Birg) are likely to be impassable.

Wildlife: As hunting is not allowed in the vicinity of any lifts, animals find safe havens in places you're likely to be. Keep an eye out for chamois (called *Gemsen* here)—the sure-footed "goat antelopes" that live at the top of the treeline and go a little lower when hungry. Spotting an ibex—a wild goat with horns, scrambling along the rocky terrain—is another Berner Oberland thrill. You'll also encounter marmots—big alpine mice (like 2-pound squirrels) who get really fat each summer, planning to sleep underground for six months through the winter. These burrowing rodents are fun to watch, and if you sit still, they don't see you. You'll hear them whistle. Your best viewing place is above Allmendhubel, in the meadow above the highest hut in Blumental.

Nordic Walking: You may wonder about the Germans you'll see with their walking sticks (*Alpenstock*). This is trying to be the next craze: Nordic walking. Enthusiasts claim Nordic walking is an all-body workout, activating 90 percent of your muscles and burning a third more calories than "normal" walking, while cutting way back on the strain on your back and knees when going downhill. To do it right requires proper instruction. Sticks can be rented at some outdoor shops.

Gimmelwald and soon hits a bigger, easier trail. The trail bends right (just before the farm/restaurant at Spielbodenalp), leading to Sprutz. Walk under the Sprutz Waterfall, then follow a steep, wooded trail that deposits you in a meadow of flowers at the top side of Gimmelwald.

Hikes from Gimmelwald

▲**Up Sefinen Valley to Kilchbalm (very easy)**—An easy trail from Gimmelwald is up the Sefinen Valley (Sefinental). This is a good rainy-weather hike, as you can go as far as you like. After two hours and a gain of only 800 feet, you hit the end of the trail and Kilchbalm, a dramatic bowl of glacier fields. Note that snow can make this trail unsafe, even into the summer (ask locally for information), and there's no food or drink along the way.

From the Gimmelwald fire station, walk about 100 yards down the paved Stechelberg road. Leave it on the dirt Sefinental road, which becomes a lane, then a trail. You'll cross a raging river and pass a firing range where locals practice their marksmanship (Fri and Sat evenings; the *danger of fire* sign refers to live bullets). Follow signs to Kilchbalm into a forest, along a river, and, finally, to the glacier fields.

▲Gimmelwald–Tanzbodeli–Obersteinberg–Stechelberg/ Gimmelwald (more difficult, for good hikers)—This eight-hour, 11-mile hike is extremely rewarding, offering perfect peace, very few people, traditional alpine culture, and spectacular views. (There's no food or drink for five hours, so pack accordingly.) The trail can be a bit confusing, so this is best done with a good, locally purchased map.

About 100 yards below the Gimmelwald firehouse, take the Sefinental dirt road (described in previous listing). As the dirt road switches back after about 30 minutes, take the right turn across the river and start your ascent, following signs to *Obersteinberg*. After 1.5 hours of hard climbing, you have the option of a side-trip to Busenalp. This is fun if the goat-and-cow herder is there, as you can watch traditional cheesemaking in action. (He appreciates a bottle of wine from hikers.) Trail markers are painted onto rocks—watch carefully. After visiting Busenalp, return to the main path.

At the *Obersteinberg 50 min/Tanzbodeli 20 min* signpost, head for Tanzbodeli ("Dancing Floor"). This is everyone's favor-ite alpine perch—great for a little romance or a picnic with breathtaking views of the Obersteinberg valley. From here, you enter a natural reserve, so you're likely to see chamois and other alpine critters. From Tanzbodeli, you return to the main trail (there's no other way out)

and continue to Obersteinberg. You'll eventually hit the Mountain Hotel Obersteinberg (see "Sleeping in Obersteinberg," later; American expat Vickie will serve you a meal or drink).

From there, the trail leads to Mountain Hotel Tschingelhorn (see "Sleeping in Obersteinberg," later). About an hour later, you hit a fork in the trail and choose where you'd like your hike to end: back to Gimmelwald (2 hours total) or Stechelberg (near the bottom of the Schilthornbahn cable car, 1.5 hours total).

▲**Sprutz Waterfall (moderately difficult)**—The forest above Gimmelwald hides a powerful waterfall with a trail snaking behind it, offering a fun gorge experience. While the waterfall itself is not well-signed, it's on the Gimmelwald–Spielbodenalp trail. It's steep, through a forest, and can be very slippery when wet, but the actual crossing under the waterfall is just misty.

The hike up to Sprutz from Gimmelwald isn't worth the trip in itself, but it's handy when combined with the hike down from Birg and Brünli (described earlier) or the North Face Trail (see next listing). As you descend on either of these two hikes, the trail down to Gimmelwald splits at Spielbodenalp—to the right for the forest and the waterfall; to the left for more meadows, the hamlet of Gimmeln, and more gracefully back into Gimmelwald.

Hikes from Mürren/Allmendhubel
▲▲**North Face Trail from Allmendhubel (easy and family-friendly)**—For a pleasant, mainly downhill, two-hour hike (4

miles, from 6,385 feet to 5,375 feet)—with some stretches that can be challenging if you're not in shape—ride the Allmendhubel funicular up from Mürren (much cheaper than Schilthorn, good restaurant at top, see page 169). From there, follow the well-signed route, which loops counterclockwise around to Mürren (or cut off at Spielbodenalp, near the end, and descend into Gimmelwald via the Sprutz Waterfall). As this trail doesn't technically start at Allmendhubel, you'll start by following signs to *Sonnenberg*. Then just follow the blue signs. You'll enjoy great views, flowery meadows, mountain huts, and a dozen information boards along the way, describing the fascinating climbing history of the great peaks around you.

Along the trail, you'll pass four farms (technically "alps," as they are only open in the summer) that serve meals and drinks. Sonnenberg was allowed to break the all-wood building code with concrete for protection against avalanches. Suppenalp is quainter. Lean against the house with a salad, soup, or sandwich and enjoy the view. Just below Suppenalp is a new little adventure park with zip lines and other kid-pleasing activities.

Notice how older huts are built into the protected side of rocks and outcroppings, in anticipation of avalanches. Above Suppenalp, Blumental ("Flower Valley") is hopping with marmots. Because hunters are not allowed near lifts, animals have learned that these

BERNER OBERLAND

are safe places to hang out—giving tourists a better chance of spotting them.

The trail leads up and over to a group of huts called Schiltalp (good food, drink, and service, and a romantic farm setting). If the poles under the eaves have bells, the cows are up here. If not, the cows are still at the lower farms. Half the cows in Gimmelwald (about 100) spend their summers here. In July, August, and September, you can watch cheese being made and have a snack or drink. Thirty years ago, each family had its own hut. Labor was cheap and available. Today, it's a communal thing, with several families sharing the expense of a single cow herder. Cow herders are master cheesemakers and have veterinary skills, too.

From Schiltalp, the trail winds gracefully down toward Spielbodenalp. From there you can finish the North Face Trail (continuing down and left through meadows and the hamlet of Gimmeln, then back to Mürren, with more historic signposts), or cut off right (descending steeply through a thick forest and under the dramatic Sprutz Waterfall into Gimmelwald—see Sprutz Waterfall, previous page, for details).

▲**Allmendhubel/Mürren to Grütschalp (fairly easy)**—For a not-too-tough two-hour walk with great Jungfrau views, ride the funicular from Mürren to Allmendhubel (6,344 feet) and walk to Grütschalp (a drop of about 1,500 feet), where you can catch the train back to Mürren. An easier version is the lower Bergweg from Allmendhubel to Grütschalp via Winteregg and its cheese farm. For a super-easy family stroll with grand views, walk from Mürren just above the train tracks either to Winteregg (40 min, restaurant, playground, train station) or through even better scenery on to Grütschalp (1 hour, train station), then catch the train back to Mürren.

Hikes on the Jungfrau (East) Side of the Lauterbrunnen Valley

▲▲▲**Männlichen–Kleine Scheidegg (easy and with dramatic views)**—This is my favorite easy alpine hike (2.5 miles, 1.5 hours, 900-foot altitude drop to Kleine Scheidegg). It's entertaining all the way, with glorious Jungfrau, Eiger, and Mönch views. (Remember, that's the Young Maiden being protected from the Ogre by the Monk.) Trails may be snowbound into June; ask about conditions at the lift stations or local TIs (see "Jungfraujoch," under "Lifts and Trains" on page 175).

If the weather's good, start off bright and early. From the Lauterbrunnen train station, take the little mountain train up to Wengen. Sit on the right side of the train for great valley and waterfall views on your way up to Wengen. In Wengen, buy a picnic at the Co-op grocery across from the station, walk across town, and catch the lift to Männlichen, located on the top of the ridge high above you. Note that the lift can be open even if the trail is closed; if the weather is questionable, confirm that the Männlichen–Kleine Scheidegg trail is open before ascending. Don't waste time in Wengen if it's sunny—you can linger back here after your hike.

Riding the gondola from Wengen to Männlichen, you'll go over the old lift station (inundated by a 1978 avalanche that buried a good part of Wengen—notice there's no development in the "red zone" above the tennis courts). Farms are built with earthen ramps on the uphill side in anticipation of the next slide. The forest of avalanche fences near the top was built after that 1978 avalanche. As you ascend you can also survey Wengen—the bright red roofs mark new vacation condos, mostly English-owned and used only a few weeks a year.

For a detour that'll give you an easy king- or queen-of-the-mountain feeling, turn left from the top of the Wengen–

Männlichen lift station, and hike uphill 10 minutes to the little peak (Männlichen Gipfel, 7,500 feet).

Then go back to the lift station (which has a great kids' area) and enjoy an hour's walk—facing spectacular alpine panorama views—to Kleine Scheidegg for a picnic or restaurant lunch. To start the hike, leave the Wengen–Männlichen lift station to the right. Walk past the second Männlichen lift station (this one leads to Grindelwald, the touristy town in the valley to your left). Ahead of you in the distance, left to right, are the north faces of the Eiger, Mönch, and Jungfrau; in the foreground is the Tschuggen peak, and just behind it, the Lauberhorn. This hike takes you around the left (east) side of this ridge. Simply follow the signs for Kleine Scheidegg, and you'll be there in about an hour—a little more for gawkers, picnickers, and photographers. You might have to tiptoe through streams of melted snow—or some small snow banks, even well into the summer—but the path is well-marked, well-maintained, and mostly level all the way to Kleine Scheidegg.

About 35 minutes into the hike, you'll reach a bunch of benches and a shelter with incredible unobstructed views of all three peaks—the perfect picnic spot. Fifteen minutes later, on the left, you'll see the first sign of civilization: Restaurant Grindelwaldblick (the best lunch stop up here, open daily, closed Dec and May, described on page 188). Hike to the restaurant's fun mountain lookout to survey the Eiger and look down on the

BERNER OBERLAND

Kleine Scheidegg action. After 10 more minutes, you'll be at the Kleine Scheidegg train station, with plenty of lesser lunch options (including Restaurant Bahnhof, described on page 188).

From Kleine Scheidegg, you can catch the train up to "the top of Europe" (see Jungfraujoch information on page 176), take the train back down to Wengen, or hike downhill (gorgeous 30-min hike to Wengernalp station, a little farther to the Allmend stop; 60 more steep minutes from there into Wengen). The alpine views might be accompanied by the valley-filling mellow sound of alphorns and distant avalanches. If the weather turns bad or you run out of steam, catch the train at any of the stations along the way. After Wengernalp, the trail to Wengen is steep and, though not dangerous, requires a good set of knees. The boring final descent from Wengen to Lauterbrunnen is knee-killer steep—catch the train instead.

▲▲Schynige Platte to First (more difficult)—The best day I've had hiking in the Berner Oberland was when I made this demanding six-hour ridge walk, with Lake Brienz on one side and all that Jungfrau beauty on the other. Start at Wilderswil train station (just outside Interlaken), and catch the little train up to Schynige Platte (6,560 feet; 2/hr, 55 min, 35 SF). The high point is Faulhorn (8,790 feet, with its famous mountaintop hotel). Hike to a small mini-gondola called "First" (7,110 feet), then ride down to Grindelwald and catch a train back to your starting point, Wilderswil. Or, if you have a regional train pass (or no car but endless money), take the long, scenic return trip: From Grindelwald, take the lift up to Männlichen (2/hr, 30 min, 36 SF), do the hike to Kleine Scheidegg and down to Wengen (described above), then head down into Lauterbrunnen.

For a shorter (3-hour) ridge walk, consider the well-signposted Panoramaweg, a loop from Schynige Platte to Daub Peak.

The alpine flower park at the Schynige Platte station offers a delightful stroll through several hundred alpine flowers (free, June–Sept daily 8:30–18:00, www.alpengarten.ch), including a chance to see edelweiss growing in the wild.

Lowa, a leading local manufacturer of top-end hiking boots, has a promotional booth at the Schynige Platte station that provides free loaner boots to hikers who'd like to give their boots a try. They're already broken in, but bring thick socks (or buy them there).

If hiking here, be mindful of the last lifts (which can be as early as 16:30). Climbing from First (7,113 feet) to Schynige Platte (6,454 feet) gives you a later departure down and less climbing. The TI produces a great Schynige Platte map/guide narrating the train ride up and describing various hiking options from there (available at Wilderswil station).

Mountain Biking

Mountain biking is popular and accepted, as long as you stay on the clearly marked mountain-bike paths. You can rent bikes in

Mürren (Stäger Sport, see page 166) or in Lauterbrunnen (Imboden Bike, see page 151). The Lauterbrunnen shop is bigger, has a wider selection of bikes, and is likely to be open when the Mürren one isn't. On trains and cable cars, bikes require a separate ticket.

The most popular bike rides include the following:

Lauterbrunnen to Interlaken: This is a gentle downhill ride on a peaceful bike path across the river from the road (don't bike on the road itself). You can return to Lauterbrunnen by train (13 SF total for bike and you). Or rent a bike at either Interlaken station, take the train to Lauterbrunnen, and ride back.

Lauterbrunnen Valley (Between Stechelberg and Lauterbrunnen town): This delightful, easy bike path features plenty of diversions along the way (several listed under "Activities in and near Lauterbrunnen" on page 151).

Mürren to Winteregg to Grütschalp and Back: This fairly level route takes you through high country, with awesome mountain views.

Mürren to Winteregg to Lauterbrunnen: This scenic descent, on a service road with loose gravel, takes you to the Lauterbrunnen Valley floor.

Mürren–Gimmelwald–Sefinen Valley–Stechelberg–Lauterbrunnen–Grütschalp–Mürren: This is the best ride, but it's demanding—with one very difficult stretch where you'll likely walk your bike down a steep gulley for 500 yards. You'll take the cable car from Lauterbrunnen up to Grütschalp.

More Sleeping and Eating
in the Berner Oberland

I'd sleep in Gimmelwald, Mürren, or Lauterbrunnen. But you could also consider the following places.

BERNER OBERLAND

Sleeping and Eating at or near Kleine Scheidegg

(6,762 feet)

This high settlement above the timberline is where you catch the train up to the Jungfrau. All of these places serve meals. Confirm prices and availability before ascending. Note that the last train down to Wengen leaves Kleine Scheidegg at 18:30.

$$$ Hotel Bellevue des Alpes, lovingly maintaining a 1930s elegance, is a worthwhile splurge. Since the 1840s, five generations of von Allmens have run this classic old alpine hotel (subsidized by the family income from Trümmelbach Falls). The hallway is like a museum, with old photos (Sb-220–260 SF, Db-370–530 SF, includes breakfast and sumptuous 5-course dinner, open only mid-June–mid-Sept, tel. 033-855-1212, fax 033-855-1294, www.scheidegg-hotels.ch, welcome@scheidegg-hotels.ch).

$$ Restaurant Bahnhof invites you to sleep face-to-face with the Eiger (dorm bed-51 SF with breakfast, 70 SF also includes dinner; D-170 SF with breakfast and dinner; in the train station building, tel. 033-828-7828, www.bahnhof-scheidegg.ch, info @bahnhof-scheidegg.ch).

$ Restaurant Grindelwaldblick, a 10-minute hike from the train station, is more charming, romantic, and remote than Restaurant Bahnhof (38 SF/bed in 8- to 20-bed rooms, includes sheets and breakfast, closed Nov and May, tel. 033-855-1374, fax 033-855-4205, www.grindelwaldblick.ch). The restaurant, with a great sun terrace and a cozy interior, sells good three-course lunches (14–25 SF) and 25-SF dinners.

Sleeping in Stechelberg

(3,025 feet)

Stechelberg is the hamlet at the end of the road up the Lauterbrunnen Valley; it's about a mile beyond the Schilthornbahn lift that goes up to Gimmelwald, Mürren, and the Schilthorn (it's a five-minute PostBus ride or a 20-minute trail walk between the lift station and the village). Beyond Stechelberg lies the rugged Rear Lauterbrunnen Valley, the edge of the Jungfrau-Aletsch-Bietschhorn nature reserve—the most glaciated part of the Alps.

$$ Hotel Stechelberg, at road's end, is surrounded by waterfalls and vertical rock, with a garden terrace, a good restaurant, and 16 quiet rooms—half in a creaky old building, half in a concrete, no-character new building (D-86–110 SF, Db-130, Db with balcony-168 SF, T-147 SF, Tb-186 SF, Q-180 SF, Qb-234 SF, bus stops here 1–2/hr, free Wi-Fi, tel. 033-855-2921, fax 033-855-4438, www.hotel-stechelberg.ch, hotel@stechelberg.ch, Marianne and Otto).

$ The **Alpenhof** fills a former "Nature Friends' Hut" with cheap beds. Creaking like a wooden chalet built in 1926 should, and surrounded by a broad lawn, it provides a good, inexpensive base for drivers and families (28 SF/bed in 2- to 6-bed rooms, each group gets a private room, breakfast-12 SF, tel. 033-855-1202, www.alpenhof-stechelberg.ch, alpenhof@stechelberg.ch, Diane and Marc). From the Hotel Stechelberg, go up the paved path, go right at the fork, and cross the river; it's on your left.

Sleeping in Obersteinberg
(5,900 feet)
Here's a wild idea: **$$ Mountain Hotel Obersteinberg** is a work-ing alpine farm with cheese, cows, a mule shuttling up food once a day, and an American (Vickie) who fell in love with a mountain man. It's a 2.5-hour hike from either Stechelberg or Gimmelwald. They rent 12 primitive rooms and a bunch of loft beds. There's no shower, no hot water, and only meager solar-panel electricity. Candles light up the night, and you can take a hot-water bottle to bed if necessary (S-85 SF, D-166 SF, includes linen, sheetless dorm beds-68 SF; these prices include breakfast and dinner, with-out meals S-37 SF, D-74 SF, dorm beds-20 SF; closed Oct–May, tel. 033-855-2033). The place is filled with locals and Germans on weekends, but it's all yours on weekdays. Why not hike here from Gimmelwald and leave the Alps a day later?

If you like the idea of a hut on this hike, but also like electric-ity, try **$$ Mountain Hotel Tschingelhorn,** 15 minutes closer to Stechelberg (similar prices, tel. 033-855-1343, www.tschingel horn.ch).

Sleeping in Isenfluh
(3,560 feet)
The PostBus takes you up on a spectacular road, through a long and narrow tunnel to the tiny hamlet of Isenfluh, which is even smaller than Gimmelwald and offers better views (bus departs from Lauterbrunnen train station almost hourly—times posted at stop, 15 min, 4 SF one-way).

$$$ Hotel Restaurant Waldrand has a decent restaurant (including great fresh salads) and five reasonably priced rooms (Sb-85 SF, Db-170 SF, Tb-190 SF, cash only, includes breakfast, tel. 033-855-1227, fax 033-855-1392, www.hotel-waldrand.ch, info @hotel-waldrand.ch, Vreni and Urs Werthmüller).

BERNER OBERLAND

ZERMATT and the MATTERHORN

There's just something about that Matterhorn, the most recognizable mountain on the planet. Anyone who says, "You've seen one mountain, you've seen them all" hasn't laid eyes on this pointy, craggy peak. The Matterhorn seems to have a nearly mystical draw for people—it's the Stonehenge of Switzerland.

Oh, and there's a town, too. Zermatt, a little burg of about 5,600 people, might well be the most touristy resort in Switzerland. While there are pockets of traditional charm, virtually everyone you meet in Zermatt earns a living one way or another from those who flock here for a peek at the peak. Aside from the stone quarries you'll pass on the way into town, tourism is Zermatt's only industry.

Be warned that Zermatt is a one-mountain town. If you have time for only one mountainous region on your trip, I'd suggest the more interesting Berner Oberland over Zermatt (for specifics, see sidebar). Many visitors find Zermatt touristy and overrated, especially considering its inconvenient location (at the end of a long dead-end valley in the southwest corner of the country). And if you make the long trek and find only cloudy weather, there's little else to do...other than wish for a T-shirt that reads, "I went all the way to Zermatt and didn't even see the lousy Matterhorn."

Planning Your Time

On a two-week trip in Switzerland, I'd suggest two nights and the better part of two days in Zermatt if the weather's good. (To check the weather, call the Zermatt TI at tel. 027-966-8100, www.zermatt.ch.) For efficient sightseeing, arrive or leave on the Glacier Express; it's an all-day, cross-country scenic train ride to Chur,

Zermatt vs. the Berner Oberland

If your time is limited and you're going to only one alpine hideaway in Switzerland, the Berner Oberland offers far more high-mountain travel thrills than the Zermatt area (see the Gimmelwald and the Berner Oberland chapter). But if you're trying to make up your mind, here are a few comparisons.

The Berner Oberland is relatively easy to reach, thanks to its more central location in the country and its good rail connections to Bern and Luzern. Zermatt is farther off the beaten track, at the end of a dead-end valley near the Italian border—and the final approach by train (from Brig) is run by a private company, not covered by a Eurailpass (though it is covered by a Swiss Pass).

Zermatt is essentially one town focused on a single mountain. The Berner Oberland is an entire alpine region, with many towns and villages to visit—from the bustling administrative center of Interlaken to the tiny, traditional village of Gimmelwald. In Zermatt, most accommodations options are in the town itself. But in the Berner Oberland, you have your choice of places to sleep—in a resort town or humble hamlet; in the valley or on a ledge overlooking the mountains.

As for sightseeing, the best part of the Berner Oberland is the Lauterbrunnen Valley, with great high-altitude attractions

on both sides (the Jungfraujoch on one side, the Schilthorn on the other), plus other enjoyable lifts, towns, and hikes. Zermatt doesn't have nearly the same diversity. Budget travelers appreciate the Berner Oberland's cheaper accommodations and the discount given on mountain lifts to Eurailpass-holders (unlike in Zermatt).

Both areas are touristy, but there are more traditional tidbits of the authentic Swiss countryside in the Berner Oberland than in Zermatt. The Berner Oberland also offers a wider variety of activities than Zermatt. On a rainy day, you can poke around one of the traditional villages (like Gimmelwald) or the bigger town of Interlaken, or walk through the thundering Trümmelbach Falls.

You can tell where my heart lies. Still, if you've seen the Berner Oberland already, or if you want to sample two different mountain areas of Switzerland, Zermatt is worth a visit. And the Matterhorn is really something else—it's the reason this place is known around the world.

which has good connections to Zürich and elsewhere in northeast Switzerland (see the Scenic Rail Journeys chapter).

Orientation to Zermatt

Zermatt (elevation 5,265 feet) lies at the end of the valley called Nikolaital, along the Mattervispa River in the shadow of the mighty Matterhorn (14,690 feet, "Cervino" in Italian).

The train station is at the bottom of town, a few steps from the main drag, Bahnhofstrasse. As you stand in front of the station with the tracks at your back, the heart of the village is to your right. Lifts to thrilling Matterhorn viewpoints leave from near the train station: The train up to Gornergrat is across the street and to your left; the station for the underground train/gondola/cable car to Rothorn is a few blocks ahead and to the left along the river; and the gondola/cable car station up to Klein Matterhorn is through the village to your right across the river (about three-quarters of a mile away). Details on all of these are listed in this chapter.

Zermatt brags that its streets are traffic-free. Well, not quite. Electric cars (big golf carts) buzz around the streets like four-wheeled Vespas, some with surprisingly aggressive drivers. Watch your step.

Addresses are generally not used in this small town. To find your hotel, use the map in this chapter, follow the free map from the TI, look for signs, or ask a local.

Tourist Information

Zermatt's TI is right at the train station (mid-June–Sept daily 8:30–18:00 except closed for lunch Sun 12:00–13:30; Oct–mid-June Mon–Sat 8:30–12:00 & 13:30–18:00, Sun 9:30–12:00 & 16:00–18:00; tel. 027-966-8100, www.zermatt.ch). They offer two handy, free resources: an extremely detailed map that labels every building in town, and a thick information booklet with lift schedules and prices, hikes, and almost anything you could think to ask about (all info is also posted on their extremely detailed website). You can also buy hiking maps here, including a detailed 1:25,000 map for serious hikers (25 SF) and a good hiking guide (25 SF). If you're traveling with kids, ask for their booklet of activities for *Kinder*.

Arrival in Zermatt

Zermatt's small train station is conveniently located in the middle of town; the TI is immediately to the right as you leave the tracks, and you'll also stumble on to a stand of Elektro-taxis right out front.

Cars are not allowed in Zermatt. Drivers park in the huge lot at Täsch, a few miles before Zermatt (13.50 SF/day), then take the

Zermatt

To Täsch & Brig

Note: Many roads in Zermatt are unmarked

TRAIN STATION

6 BUSES TO LIFTS

GORNERGRAT STATION

12 **14** GETWINGSTRASSE

BAHNHOFSTRASSE

OBERE MATTEN

SUNNEGGA STATION

To Rothorn

14

HOFMATTSTRASSE

ENGLISH CHURCH

POST

13

OBER-HAUSEN

1

ALPINE CENTER

14

TRIFTWEG

HINTERDORF-STRASSE

2

9

BACHSTRASSE

BRUNNMATTGASSE

4

MATTERHORN MUSEUM

Cemetery

RIEDSTRASSE

HOF

CATHOLIC CHURCH

AM BACH

KIRCHSTRASSE

10

5

NEBEN BACH

11

OBER-DORF

OBERDORFSTRASSE

SCHLUHMATTSTRASSE

Matterispa River

SCHLUHMATTSTRASSE

STEINMATTE

To Zmutt

3

8

7

To Gornergrat

100 meters

100 yards

To Klein Matterhorn Lift (Bergbahn)

Luchre **B**

SCHLUHMATTEN

1 Hotel Romantica
2 Hotel/Rest. Le Mazot
3 Hotel Jägerhof
4 Hotel Tannenhof
5 Hotel Weisshorn
6 Hotel Bahnhof
7 Youth Hostel

8 Matterhorn Hostel
9 Whymper-Stube Rest.
10 Restaurant du Pont
11 Pizza Roma
12 Co-op Grocery
13 Migros Grocery
14 Laundries (3)

ZERMATT

shuttle train into town (runs every 20 min 6:00–22:30, then hourly until 1:00 in the morning, Thu–Sun runs hourly 23:00–6:00, 7.60 SF one-way, www.matterhornterminal.ch and www.mgbahn.ch).

Getting Around Zermatt

Even though Zermatt is "traffic-free," your feet aren't your only transportation option. Two different electric **bus** lines depart across from the train station: One line goes to the Bergbahn, the lift station for Klein Matterhorn (about 2/hr, 2.50 SF, or free with lift ticket), and the other goes to the hamlet perched above that station, called Winkelmatten (1–2/hr, 3.20 SF). The buses are marked with their destination and make a few stops along the way before heading back to the station (when they're marked *Bahnhof*).

You can also hire your own **Elektro-taxi** (about 12 SF to anywhere in the heart of town, extra charge for luggage and rides at night, taxi stand in front of train station, or call **Taxi Zermatt,** tel. 027-967-3333, mobile 084-811-1212).

Helpful Hints

Walking Tour: A free, one-hour village walking tour in English is offered once a week from June through September (usually Wed, confirm details at the TI). This is a good rainy-day option.

Internet Access: You'll see coin-op Internet stations all over town. The going rate is about 12 SF per hour.

Laundry: Waschsalon Doli is nice and central (20 SF to have them wash and dry a small load, Mon–Sat 8:30–12:00 & 14:00–19:00, closed Sun, tel. 027-967-5100). To find it from the station, take the first left past McDonald's, turn right at the tennis courts, and go down the steps at their sign. Other launderettes in town include **Tip Top** (Hofmattstrasse 30, tel. 027-967-8181) and **Womy Express** (in the Viktoria Center mall across from train station, tel. 027-967-3242).

Skiing: Zermatt's high elevation and variety of runs—and the chance to actually ski or snowboard from Switzerland to Italy—make it deservedly popular. Summer skiing is an option at Matterhorn Glacier Paradise (first lift starts at about 8:00, last lift stops around 14:00—after that the snow's too slushy, late April–late Nov, limited area in mid-summer). A one-day lift ticket will run you about 78 SF; equipment rents for about 45 SF, and snow-wear rental adds another 30–35 SF. Ask at the TI for details.

In the winter, beginners and intermediate skiers head for Gornergrat and the Matterhorn Glacier areas; more advanced skiers prefer Schwarzsee, Rothorn, and especially Stockhorn, with its mogul-filled "freeride" runs (generally open mid-Jan–

Easter). The Sunnegga area has a mix of easy and challenging runs.

Rental shops in town include **Matterhorn Sport** (several branches, one near Sunnegga lift, another at Bahnhofstrasse 78, tel. 027-967-2956, www.matterhornsport.ch), **Bayard Sport + Fashion** (also has several branches, including one on Bahnhofplatz, tel. 027-966-4950, www.bayardzermatt.ch), and **Dorsaz-Sport** (near Matterhorn Glacier lift, tel. 027-966-3810, www.dorsaz-sport.ch). For lift-ticket prices, see www.matterhornparadise.ch; for more tips, read the Switzerland in Winter chapter.

Sights in Zermatt

The town itself is short on attractions. On rainy days, the TI can only shrug, poignantly promote the Matterhorn Museum, or suggest that you go swimming in one of the big hotel pools.

Wander the Town—Zermatt is charming enough, despite its single-mindedness about catching the tourist dollar. The streets are lined with chalet after chalet. Just off the main drag, you'll spot small stands of traditional shacks set on stone stilts to keep out mice (called *mazots;* look for them around Hotel Romantica, or near the river in the Hinterdorf area). You'll also spot a handful of churches, including the big landmark Catholic church (can't miss it on Bahnhofstrasse). Its cemetery has lovingly tended graves adorned with flowers and lit by glowing votive lanterns at night. A smaller English church (built for the many British mountaineers who have flocked to this region) is above and behind the Matterhorn Museum.

▲▲Matterhorn Museum—It may be the outdoors that brings you to Zermatt, but this museum is the town's best indoor activity, and it's worth a visit on a rainy day. Most of the newly spruced-up museum is underground, as it's meant to look like an archeological dig where you can unearth the history of Zermatt and its famous mountain, with a focus on the 19th century. Pick up the free English flier and walk downstairs, through the reproductions of an old hotel, church, barn, and other buildings from Zermatt's past. Listen for the fun sound effects. The displays show typical furnishings, tools, and stuffed alpine fauna, as well as exhibits on the city's mountaineering history. You'll find out why Teddy Roosevelt climbed the famous peak before he was president. The reliefs of

What's What in Zermatt

Bergbahn: Lift station in Zermatt for Klein Matterhorn.

Blauherd: Upper station on the Sunnegga-to-Blauherd gondola; lower station on the Blauherd-to-Rothorn cable car, with good access to hikes, including the Marmot hike.

Findelnbach: Station stop on the train from Zermatt up to Gornergrat.

Fluhalp: Small settlement known for its good restaurant, accessible by hike from the Blauherd station.

Furi: Upper station on the gondola from Zermatt; lower station on a different gondola to Schwarzsee and a cable car to Trockener Steg.

Glacier Palace: Free sight at Klein Matterhorn; a cavern dug into a glacier with ice sculptures and exhibits.

Gorner Glacier: Glacier that lies between Gornergrat and Klein Matterhorn.

Gornergrat: Viewpoint (10,270 feet) between Klein Matterhorn and Rothorn. At the upper station of a train from Zermatt, it offers views of the Gorner Glacier, Matterhorn, and Monte Rosa.

Gourmetweg ("Gourmet Path"): Hike from Sunnegga down to Zermatt via Findeln through larch forests.

Hinterdorf: Attractive old quarter of Zermatt by the river, with antique chalets and traditional *mazots* (buildings on stone stilts).

Klein Matterhorn: At 12,530 feet, the highest cable-car station in Europe, with great views of the Alps; always snow-covered.

Matterhorn: Mountain peak whose shape forms the textbook example of a "horn," indicating that bowl-shaped valleys

the mountain (and surrounding region) offer a helpful topographic perspective. There's a morbid room displaying artifacts found after deadly accidents, and a room dedicated to July 14, 1865—the day the Matterhorn was finally conquered by a team of seven climbers. (Tragically, four of them died on the descent, when one of them fell, dragging three others to their deaths.) Be sure to check out the display case (near the restrooms) that holds a collection of Matterhorn memorabilia and products (10 SF, covered by Swiss Pass, audioguide-5 SF; July–Sept daily 11:00–18:00; April–June and Oct daily 14:00–18:00; Dec–March Mon–Sat 15:00–19:00, closed Sun; closed Nov; under glass dome at Kirchplatz 11, across from the big Catholic church, tel. 027-967-4100, www.matterhornmuseum.ch).

Goat Parade—A charming and unusual little event takes place each day in summer, as a small flock of local "blackneck" goats are herded through the center of town on the way to pasture (daily (cirques) were carved into the peak by several glaciers on all sides.

Monte Rosa: Tallest peak in Switzerland (15,200 feet).

Murmelweg ("Marmot Path"): Hike from Blauherd down to Sunnegga through marmot habitat.

Nikolaital Valley: Deepest valley in Switzerland, with the town of Zermatt at its upper end.

Riffelalp: Station stop on the train from Zermatt up to Gornergrat.

Riffelberg: Station stop on the train from Zermatt up to Gornergrat.

Riffelsee: Lake below the Rotenboden station.

Rotenboden: Station stop on the train from Zermatt up to Gornergrat.

Rothorn: Upper station of the Blauherd-to-Rothorn cable car, offering quintessential views of the Matterhorn.

Schwarzsee: Alpine lake at an elevation of 8,470 feet and a gondola station; the closest you can (easily) get to the Matterhorn.

Stafel: Village along the hike from Schwarzsee down to Furi.

Stellisee: Alpine lake along a hike from Blauherd.

Sunnegga: Upper station on the underground funicular from Zermatt and the lower station of the Sunnegga-to-Blauherd gondola; offers good access to hikes.

Trockener Steg: Upper station on the Schwarzsee-to-Trockener Steg gondola; lower station on the Trockener Steg-to-Klein Matterhorn cable car.

Winkelmatten: Cliff-hanging neighborhood above the Bergbahn lift station in Zermatt.

July–mid-Aug at around 9:00 and back home again at about 17:00). These furry goats, which are unique to the surrounding Upper Valais region, have a black head and shoulders, a white rear end, and long horns.

High-Mountain Excursions from Zermatt

You have four options for lifts up and out of Zermatt:

1. A cable-car ride to the highest lift station in Europe, **Klein Matterhorn** (not the "real" Matterhorn).

2. A side spur off the Klein Matterhorn line leading to **Schwarzsee,** with some of the closest views you'll get of the Matterhorn.

3. An underground funicular, then gondola, then cable car to **Rothorn,** with classic Matterhorn views.

4. A train up to **Gornergrat,** for good views down on a glacier. The first trip leads to a snowy wonderland, year-round skiing

ZERMATT

Zermatt Area

slopes, and a cave carved into the ice. The other three will take you to pristine pastures with alpine lakes and Matterhorn vistas. (For more details, see the "What's What in Zermatt" sidebar.)

Pass Prices: If the weather's clear and your pockets are deep, consider springing for a **Peak Pass,** which gives you unlimited access to all of these lifts; unfortunately, the minimum length of the pass is three days, so it's a bad value for a one- or two-day visit (3 days-183 SF, 4 days-208 SF, 5 days-232 SF). The **Panoramic Pass,** available only from mid-June to mid-September, is a better deal for a short visit; it covers Klein Matterhorn, Schwarzsee, and Rothorn, but not Gornergrat (1 day-122 SF, 2 days-140 SF). The **Hiking Pass** gives you unlimited access to lifts up to (but not above) Trockener Steg, Schwarzsee, Blauherd, and Riffelberg (3 days-138 SF, or 104 SF with Swiss Pass). You can purchase any of these passes at lift stations or local train stations.

Individual Tickets: Buy individual tickets directly at the lift stations. Some passes offer afternoon discounts on individual fares to Klein Matterhorn, Schwarzsee, or Rothorn—always ask (about 15 percent, valid after 13:30, mid-June–late Sept). Eurailpass holders do not get a discount on Zermatt lifts, but Swiss Pass

MATTERHORN
14,690'

To Cervinia,
Italy →

Glacier

Furgg
Glacier

TROCKENER
STEG

HÖRNLIHÜTTE

SCHWARZSEE
8,470'

SCHÖNBIELHÜTTE

FURGG

STAFEL

ZMUTT

Note:
This bird's eye view
looks south

Not to Scale

holders pay half-price. For more information, see www.matterhorn paradise.ch.

For Skiers: Note that the descriptions and prices in this section apply only to the summer season. If you're a skier, ask the Zermatt TI about specifics for your visit.

▲▲Klein Matterhorn (12,530 feet) and Schwarzsee (8,470 feet)

To really get your high-altitude high, zip up to the highest cable-car station in Europe, at Klein ("Little") Matterhorn. From way up here, the Matterhorn is just one of many cut-glass peaks—this is your best chance for a bird's-eye panorama of the Alps without hiking. But note that some visitors are disappointed by this particular view because it's not the classic Matterhorn profile on all the postcard racks (for that, head to Rothorn, explained later).

The trip up to Klein Matterhorn has three parts. First, you'll take a small, six-seat gondola on a six-minute ride over pretty glacier-carved foothills to the Furi station. From Furi you'll take a larger cable car up to Trockener Steg. (You can also take a different gondola from Furi to Schwarzsee—described below.) Finally, you'll board the last cable car up to Klein Matterhorn; on the left are great views down on glaciers and across to the Gornergrat train station. All the way up, you'll see plenty of ski lifts and picturesque little chalets. The area around Klein Matterhorn stays snow-covered all year long, making it a popular place for summer skiers.

Once up top, nonskiers have two sightseeing options: the observation deck and the Glacier Palace. As you leave the lift, follow the hall branching to the left, and take the elevator to the **observation deck** (12,200 feet). Exit the elevator and walk another 100 steps up to stunning panoramas. On a clear day, you can see Italy and France (including Mont Blanc, Europe's highest peak).

If you follow the hall from the lift all the way to the end, you'll reach the Panorama Bar and the exit. Go outside and walk

a few steps downhill to the low-profile entrance of the **Glacier Palace,** marked *Gletschergrotte* (free, daily 9:30–15:45). This place brags that it's the "highest glacial grotto in the world"—a claim that must make other high-altitude glacial grottos seethe with envy. The "Palace" is basically a big hole dug into the glacier, allowing you to walk deep inside. As you wander, you'll see ice sculptures (including the Matterhorn and some flowers encased in ice) and some lackluster exhibits about glaciers, local wines, and "glacier fleas" (a.k.a. "springtails," little bugs that live up here). You can also wriggle into an actual crevasse.

Rather than going all the way to Klein Matterhorn, you could take the gondola from Furi to the alpine lake **Schwarzsee.** Though a much lower elevation (8,470 feet), this area is the closest you can get to the Matterhorn (though it lacks the big-picture alpine panorama that the other lift excursions offer). You can also do this on your way back down from Klein Matterhorn (when you reach Furi, follow signs to *Schwarzsee* instead of *Zermatt;* 32 SF round-trip for just this segment from Furi to Schwarzsee and back to Furi, 21 SF one-way). Several popular hiking trails lead from here back down to the valley (see below).

Hikes: You won't find any hiking paths from the very top of Klein Matterhorn, since it's covered with snow year-round. The best hike on this series of lifts is at Schwarzsee. From the Schwarzsee lift station, the hike directly down to Furi is quite steep; a longer but easier and more enjoyable route is to hike down to Stafel, then on to Furi. Downhill from Furi is the **Ricola Herb Garden,** one of six company gardens that feature the 13 medicinal herbs in Ricola cough drops. It's a 15-minute walk down from Furi or a 30-minute walk up from Zermatt, in the hamlet of Blatten (always open, best July–Sept, near Restaurant Blatten, www. ricola.ch). From Furi you can catch the gondola back to Zermatt (or continue to Zermatt on foot). Plan on the better part of a day for the full Schwarzsee-Furi-Zermatt hike; easier hikes elsewhere in the region are described later.

Cost: Zermatt to Klein Matterhorn costs 90 SF round-trip (58 SF one-way; with Swiss Pass, 53 SF round-trip or 29 SF one-way); Zermatt to Schwarzsee is 47 SF round-trip (30 SF one-way, half-price with Swiss Pass, ask about afternoon discount). If you plan to do both, the Peak and Panoramic passes cover this combo-trip and more.

Hours: The lifts up to Klein Matterhorn are open daily year-round (generally Sept–late June 8:30–17:50, late June–Aug 7:00–16:30). If the weather's iffy, confirm that the entire route (all the way to Klein Matterhorn) is open before you ascend—upper segments can close if it's too windy. The gondola from Furi to Schwarzsee doesn't run in late spring or late fall (late June–Aug 8:00–16:30, Sept–mid-Oct and late Nov–early May 8:30–16:30, closed early May–mid-June and mid-Oct–late Nov, www .zermatt.ch).

Location: The elevator to the Klein Matterhorn station is about three-quarters of a mile upriver from the train station (simply follow the river, or catch an electric bus marked *Klein Matterhorn* or *Schwarzsee* in front of the Gornergrat train station, across from the main train station, 2/hr).

▲▲Rothorn (10,180 feet)

While actually farther away from the famous peak than the other lifts I've described, Rothorn offers *the* classic Matterhorn view. When Matt Lauer wanted the best shot of the Matterhorn to broadcast on the *Today* show, he came here (and brought along some alphorn players). It's also less crowded than Gornergrat. The passage up to Rothorn has three parts: first, an underground funicular to Sunnegga (eight cold minutes, bring a sweater), then a gondola to Blauherd, and, finally, a cable car to Rothorn. All along the way are typical glacial lakes, offering a picturesque foreground for your Matterhorn photos.

Hikes: You have plenty of easy options for walking around the lakes up here. Get details at the TI before you ascend. Perhaps the best is the mostly level hike from the Blauherd station, around the Rothorn peak, past the Stellisee, to the restaurant at Fluhalp, then back again. If only the Sunnegga funicular is open, it's still worthwhile to go for the hiking and a great view of the Matterhorn (15 SF one-way). Try the 40-minute Murmelweg ("Marmot Path")

ZERMATT

up to Blauherd—for a good chance of spotting these fuzzy mountain mammals—or hike from Sunnegga down to Zermatt. The Gourmetweg hike (allow 1.25 hours) takes you through larch forests, and the path is covered with soft, fragrant pine needles.

Cost, Hours, Location: 64 SF round-trip, 41 SF one-way, half-price with Swiss Pass; if going up after 13:30, ask about afternoon discount. You can get to Rothorn or Blauherd only between mid-June and mid-Sept (daily 8:30–16:30); the lower segment, to Sunnegga, is open longer (late May–early Nov). The whole shebang is open again December through April, when the mountain is ready for skiers. The station for the underground funicular from Zermatt is across the river from the train station, just downstream from the Gornergrat train tracks.

▲▲Gornergrat (10,270 feet)

This viewpoint is somewhere between Klein Matterhorn and Rothorn—both geographically and in terms of your experience. A train takes you from Zermatt up to Gornergrat in about 35 minutes, with stops at other stations along the way (Findelbach, Riffelalp, Riffelberg, and Rotenboden). On the way up, sit on the right-hand side for good Matterhorn vistas. At Gornergrat you'll enjoy a sweeping alpine panorama with great views of the Matterhorn (though it's not the perfect profile that you see from

Rothorn). What's distinctive about Gornergrat is that it offers the best views of the Gorner Glacier that runs between it and Klein Matterhorn. It also gets you up close to the *other* big mountain in the neighborhood, which is actually taller than the Matterhorn: Monte Rosa. This towering behemoth is the highest point in Switzerland (15,200 feet).

Hikes: The best option is to take the train from Gornergrat back to the Rotenboden station, where you can enjoy the pretty Riffelsee lake. Then walk down to the Riffelberg station and take the train back into Zermatt.

Cost, Hours, Location: 76 SF round-trip, 38 SF one-way, half-price with Swiss Pass, ask about afternoon discount. Two or three trains an hour leave mid-June–Sept, starting at about 7:00 and ending at about 19:00 (fewer trains and shorter hours off-season, tel. 027-921-4711, www.gornergrat.ch). The Gornergrat train station is right across the street from Zermatt's train station.

Other Mountain Activities

Aside from hiking and views, adventure-seekers have even more opportunities for alpine thrills near Zermatt. **Tandem paragliding** is an expensive but unforgettable experience, best from Rothorn (about 190 SF; Air Taxi/Air Born, tel. 027-967-6744, www.paragliding-zermatt.ch; or Alpine Adventures, tel. 027-967-2100, www.alpine-adventures-zermatt.com). The hills above Zermatt are laced with great **mountain-bike** paths (get specifics from TI). For skiing options, see "Helpful Hints," earlier.

Sleeping in Zermatt

Little Zermatt has more than a hundred hotels—and all of them are expensive. This is a resort town, plain and simple, where even the budget bunks cost big bucks. I've scrutinized the options and presented you with the best deals I could find. I've listed peak summer rates (generally highest July–Aug). You'll pay less at most places in shoulder season (June and Oct), and more during ski season (Dec–mid-Jan). When there's a range, higher prices are for busy times, and lower prices are when it's slow (unless otherwise noted). Many hotels close in the shoulder season (as early as mid-April). They reopen beginning in early May, but some stay on vacation until late June. Of course, several hotels are open year-round.

$$$ Hotel Romantica, a scenic block up from the main street, offers 15 rooms in a flower-dappled chalet surrounded by old-fashioned huts. If you like all those huts, consider sleeping in one—this hotel has converted two of them into accommodations. Both have tiny interiors with two stories: sitting room and modern bathroom downstairs, loft bedroom upstairs. Choose between the very low-ceilinged and rustic hut (cozy and romantic) or the

---

Sleep Code

(1 SF = about $1, country code: 41)
S = Single, **D** = Double/Twin, **T** = Triple, **Q** = Quad, **b** = bathroom, **s** = shower only. Unless otherwise noted, credit cards are accepted, English is spoken, and breakfast is included.

    To help you sort easily through these listings, I've divided the rooms into three categories, based on the price for a standard double room with bath:

  $$$ Higher Priced—Most rooms 150 SF or more.
    $$ Moderately Priced—Most rooms between 110-150 SF.
      $ Lower Priced—Most rooms 110 SF or less.

hut with more modern finishes (Sb-85–98 SF, Db-160–210 SF, huts-220 SF, prices depend on demand and length of stay, free Wi-Fi, tel. 027-966-2650, fax 027-966-2655, www.reconline.ch /romantica, romantica.zermatt@reconline.ch, Cremonini family).

$$$ Hotel Le Mazot has nine cozy, renovated rooms—four with Matterhorn-view balconies—in a central but quiet location next to the river and above an intimate restaurant (S-65 SF, Db-140–170 SF, Tb-170–200 SF, open late May–Oct only, Hofmattstrasse 23, tel. 027-966-0606, www.lemazotzermatt.ch, le.mazot@reconline.ch).

$$$ Hotel Jägerhof has 48 homey rooms with new bathrooms and lots of charm. It's a little farther from the center, across the river toward the Klein Matterhorn lift station (Sb-88 SF, Db-176 SF, Tb-238 SF, Qb-300 SF, some doubles have balconies, elevator, pay Internet access, free Wi-Fi, fitness room, tel. 027-966-3800, fax 027-966-3808, www.hoteljaegerhofzermatt.ch/home.php, jaegerhof@zermatt.ch, Perren family).

$$ Hotel Tannenhof is a great value hiding a few steps off the main drag behind a fancy hotel that steals the Matterhorn views. Its 23 rooms are small, tight, and woody, without much character, but the location is good and the place is well-run (S-55 SF, Sb-80 SF, D-100 SF, Db-120–130 SF, T-120 SF, pay Internet access and Wi-Fi, Englischer Viertel 3, tel. 027-967-3188, fax 027-967-3173, www.rhone.ch/tannenhof, hotel-tannenhof@rhone.ch, Schaller family).

$$ Hotel Weisshorn offers 16 basic but comfortable rooms over a restaurant, right in the heart of town. The rooms are nothing special (even the three with balconies), but the rates are reasonable (S-61 SF, Sb-76 SF, D-106–120 SF, Db-134–160 SF, T-159 SF, Am Bach 6, tel. 027-967-1112, fax 027-967-3839, www.holidaynet.ch /weisshorn, welcome@weisshorn-zermatt.ch).

$$ Hotel Bahnhof, with 17 tidy alpine-style rooms (and three dorm rooms) is in a 1902 building so completely remodeled that it feels brand-new. The basement features a relaxing lounge, a dining room, and a large guests' kitchen (often dominated by big groups). Rooms without baths have Matterhorn-view balconies. It's well-run, but management is offsite at night—so if the younger crowd comes back late after partying, you're on your own. It's conveniently located across the street from the train station (dorm bed-40 SF, S-70–80 SF, Sb-80–90 SF, D-100–110 SF, Db-110–145 SF, Qb-210–245 SF, no breakfast, nice showers, handy coin-op laundry facilities, free Wi-Fi, lockers, tel. 027-967-2406, fax 027-967-7216, www.hotelbahnhof.com, welcome @hotelbahnhof.com).

$ Zermatt's official **Youth Hostel** is sparkling new. It looks over town from a perch high above the river, and offers views of the Matterhorn. The hostel is slick and super-modern, with key cards and bathrooms inside most rooms (or down the hall). The hostel is an especially good deal since the rates include breakfast and dinner—a real plus in expensive Zermatt (prices per person: in 8-bed room-50 SF, in 6-bed room with bathroom-53 SF, in 4-bed room without bathroom-58 SF, in 4-bed room with bathroom-61 SF, in twin D-61 SF, in D with one big bed-76 SF, in Db with one big bed-86 SF, all rates include sheets, pay Internet access and Wi-Fi, no age limit, no curfew, Staldenweg 5, tel. 027-967-2320, fax 027-967-5306, www.youthhostel.ch/zermatt, zermatt@youthhostel.ch). From the station, take the bus marked *Winkelmatten* to the Luchre stop (3.20 SF); the hostel is a steep hike up from there (follow the signs with the international hostel symbol).

$ Matterhorn Hostel is a more low-key, easygoing place overlooking the river. Its mission is to provide cheap beds in an expensive town, and it delivers. The floor plan is claustrophobic, with not an inch of wasted space: 10 dorm rooms with graffiti decor are upstairs (some with Matterhorn-view balconies); the lounge and showers are in the basement; and a tiny Internet nook (free access) is tucked under the spiral staircase (bed in 6- to 8-bed dorm-34 SF, in 4-bed room-39 SF, in 2- or 3-bed room-44 SF, cash preferred, ask for a discount if you stay 4 or more nights off-season, breakfast-7 SF, towel rental-2 SF, sheets-3.50 SF, free Wi-Fi, closed 10:00–16:00, or 11:00–16:00 in peak season, Schluhmattstrasse 32, tel. 027-968-1919, fax 027-968-1915, www.matterhornhostel .com, info@matterhornhostel.com). It's a 15-minute walk from the train station on the way up to the Klein Matterhorn lift station, above the river. Take the bus to the Bergbahn/Klein Matterhorn lift station (2.50 SF), then take the elevator up to the cable-car station and walk several blocks down the hill. It's on the left, next to Sparky's restaurant.

Eating in Zermatt

Zermatt's restaurants are as expensive as its hotels. If there's a cheap snack bar–type place here, I haven't found it (unless you count McDonald's). But the town has several handy bakeries and grocery stores for buying a picnic, and the streets are lined with restaurants featuring garish signs, interchangeable menus, and high prices. Simply wander down the main drag (Bahnhofstrasse) and pick the place that looks best. I ate well without breaking the bank at the eateries listed here. The first two are obvious and touristy (with Japanese signs outside), but the prices and food are acceptable, and you may see locals mixed in with the out-of-towners.

Whymper-Stube, named for the first brave soul to conquer the Matterhorn, specializes in cheese dishes—that means fondue (about 25 SF per person) and raclette (8 SF per serving, two servings is enough for most). While American and Japanese tourists photograph each other eating fondue, six barstools in the corner are warmed by local regulars (kitchen open daily 12:00–14:00 & 18:00–22:00 but fondue and cold dishes are served daily 11:00–22:00, friendly staff, on Bahnhofstrasse, on the right just before the big church, tel. 027-967-2296).

Restaurant du Pont claims to be the oldest restaurant in town. Note that it doesn't claim to be the best. Its ambience—with low ceilings and Swiss folk sayings on the walls—beats the food (fondue for two-44 SF, *Rösti* for about 15 SF, daily 12:00–22:00, on Bahnhofstrasse at end of square with big Catholic church, tel. 027-967-4343).

Pizza Roma offers a good value, a friendly staff, and an escape from the worst tourist hordes. Dine in the warm, woody interior or outside on the sidewalk (16–22-SF daily specials, good 17–27-SF wood-fired pizzas, 17–24-SF pasta dishes, daily 18:30–22:30; from Bahnhofstrasse, turn left on Kirchstrasse just before the big Catholic church—it's on the right a few blocks up the hill after you cross the river; tel. 027-967-3229).

Grocery Stores: Co-op is across from the train station (Mon–Sat 8:00–19:00, closed Sun). **Migros** is across from the tennis courts on Hinterdorf Strasse (Mon–Sat 8:30–18:30, closed Sun).

Zermatt Connections

Zermatt is at the end of the dead-end Nikolaital Valley, which you can only reach on a private rail line. This train, operated by the Matterhorn Gotthard Railway (www.mgbahn.ch), connects Zermatt to Visp and Brig hourly (1.25 hrs, second-class fares: 34 SF one-way, 68 SF round-trip, covered by Swiss Pass, not covered or discounted by Eurailpass). In Brig, the Matterhorn Gotthard Railway station is just across the street from the Swiss Rail station. From here you can easily connect to destinations all over the country. If you're connecting to Lake Geneva (Lausanne or Montreux), you'll save time changing trains in Visp, which lies between Zermatt and Brig (Zermatt–Lausanne via Visp: 1–2/hr, 3 hrs total). Train info: toll tel. 0900-300-300 or www.rail.ch.

From Brig or Visp by Train to: Bern (1–2/hr, 1 hr, via Visp), **Zürich** (1–2/hr, 2.25 hrs, via Visp, some with transfer in Bern), **Lausanne** (1–2/hr, 1.75 hrs; faster to transfer in Visp), **Interlaken Ost** (1–2/hr, 1.25 hrs, transfer in Spiez), **Luzern** (1–2/hr, 2.25–2.5 hrs, transfer in Bern or Olten).

By Glacier Express to Eastern Switzerland: In summer, four trains depart Zermatt daily and arc scenically on high-altitude tracks over the middle of Switzerland to the east. All of these Glacier Express trains go through **Chur** (6 hrs), and some continue to **Davos** or **St. Moritz** (8 hrs total to either). In winter, there's one train per day in each direction. These trains do not require a transfer in Brig. For more details, see the Scenic Rail Journeys chapter.

APPENZELL

Welcome to cowbell country. In the moo-mellow and storybook-friendly Appenzell region, you'll find the warm, intimate side of the land of staggering, icy Alps. With just one percent of Switzerland's territory and one percent of its population, the little canton of Appenzell stubbornly celebrates its way of life. You'll see its symbol everywhere: a scary bear walking upright, yielding its sharp claws and teeth. And yet the people here are mellow and welcoming. You'll savor Appenzell's cozy, small-town atmosphere.

Appenzell is Switzerland's most traditional region...and the butt of jokes because of it. Entire villages meet in town squares like Appenzell town's Landsgemeindeplatz to vote (an event featured on most postcard racks). Until 1989, the women of Appenzell couldn't vote on local issues. Lately, the region has become more progressive. In 2000, its schools were the first to make English—rather than French—the mandatory second language. However, it still clings to some of its old ways. For example, each of Switzerland's cantons gets to choose whether to implement smoking bans, and Appenzell has left it up to each business owner (which means that many restaurants here will give you a whiff of the old Europe).

A gentle beauty blankets this region of green, rolling hills, watched over by the 8,200-foot peak of Mount Säntis (Appenzell's highest point). As you travel, you'll enjoy an ever-changing parade of finely carved chalets, colorful villages, and cows moaning, "Milk me." While farmers' bikini-clad daughters make hay, old ladies with scythes walk the steep roads, looking as if they just pushed the Grim Reaper down the hill. When locals are asked about Appenzeller cheese, they clench their fists as they answer,

"It's the best." (It is, without any doubt, the smelliest.)

If you're here in late August or early September, there's a good chance you'll get in on (or at least have your road blocked by) the ceremonial procession of flower-bedecked cows and whistling herders in formal folk costumes. The festive march down from the high pastures is a spontaneous move by the herding families, and when they finally do burst into town (a slow-motion Swiss Pamplona), locals young and old become children again, running joyously onto the streets.

Planning Your Time

On a two-week trip through Switzerland, save a day for the Appenzell region. This pastoral area offers a good first look at Switzerland—but would be anticlimactic after the rugged Berner Oberland or Matterhorn. If you have only a week or less in Switzerland, skip the subtle charms of Appenzell and head instead for the high mountains.

In the Appenzell region, I prefer overnighting up on Ebenalp to really get away from it all. But if that mountaintop retreat's rustic accommodations and steep hikes aren't your cup of tea, consider the comfort of sleeping in Appenzell town, which is also a more efficient base for getting around the region.

Getting Around Appenzell

Appenzell is a breeze by **car**—you could see everything in this chapter in one (very busy) day. Notice that the attractions in Stein and Urnäsch and the Kronberg luge ride form a handy little loop to the west of town. The lift up to Ebenalp is just to the south.

Appenzell town is a convenient public-transportation hub. Regional narrow-gauge trains are operated by Appenzeller Bahnen (www.appenzellerbahnen.ch). From Appenzell town, a very handy **train** runs hourly (2/hr during morning and evening rush hour), connecting most destinations I describe. It goes from Appenzell south to Wasserauen (base of Ebenalp lift, 14 min); the same train runs west from Appenzell, stopping at Gontenbad (one end of the Barefoot Walk, 3 min), Jakobsbad (luge ride and other end of the Barefoot Walk, 9 min), Urnäsch (folk museum, 17 min), then north to Herisau (33 min; change here to reach St. Gallen or Luzern), and Gossau (40 min; change here to reach Zürich or St. Gallen).

Regional **buses** also connect towns several times a day; for schedules, check with the TI or the post office.

Appenzell Region

The one destination in this chapter not well covered by public transportation is Stein (with its cheesemaking showcase and folk museum). Appenzell's shuttle service, **PubliCar,** takes passengers to locations not serviced by buses (for Appenzell to Stein, figure about 8.50 SF, or 3 SF with Swiss Pass or Appenzell Card). To reserve, inquire at the TI or post office, or call 0848-553-060.

Appenzell Town

In this authentically Swiss town, kids play "barn" instead of "house," while Mom and Dad watch yodeling on TV. The town center is a painfully cute pedestrian zone lined with some of Switzerland's most colorful housefronts. This is a great spot to simply let your pulse slow and enjoy Swiss small-town life. The big square of Landsgemeindeplatz—at the far end of Hauptgasse from the town church and TI—is where residents gather the last Sunday of each April to vote on local issues by show of hands.

(The rest of the year, it's a parking lot.) A fountain on the square shows an Appenzeller raising his hand to be counted.

Appenzell town is touristy, sure. But from watching the locals robustly greet each other in the streets or laugh over a local beer in the pubs, it's clear this is also a real, living town.

Orientation to Appenzell

Tiny Appenzell town clusters along its main street, Hauptgasse, which runs from the bridge over the Sitter River to the biggest square, Landsgemeindeplatz. From the middle of this colorful drag, Postgasse heads south to the train station. You can walk from one end of town to the other in about 10 minutes.

Tourist Information

The TI is on the main street at Hauptgasse 4 (May–mid-Oct Mon–Fri 9:00–12:00 & 13:30–18:00, Sat–Sun 10:00–12:00 & 14:00–17:00; mid-Oct–April Mon–Fri 9:00–12:00 & 14:00–17:00, Sat–Sun 14:00–17:00; tel. 071-788-9641). For information on the greater Appenzell region, call 071-898-3300 or check out www.appenzell.ch.

If you stay for several days in the region, you'll receive an **Appenzell Card** from your hotel that covers all local train trips (on trains operated by Appenzeller Bahnen, as far as St. Gallen), free rides on three different cable cars, free admission to local museums, a free ride on the Kronberg luge, a discounted rate on the PubliCar shuttle service (3 SF), and more (though the details of exactly what's covered by this card are subject to change from year to year). The card is free of charge, but only if you're staying three nights or longer. Hotels and some smaller pensions offer the card; ask when you reserve.

Arrival in Appenzell Town

From the **train** station—possibly Switzerland's cutest—walk straight ahead up Postgasse to Postplatz, then follow Poststrasse up to Hauptgasse, where you'll run directly into the TI.

If arriving by **car,** ask your hotel about parking. If you're just day-tripping here, leave your car in the free lot by the brewery (in the blue zone, you're limited to one hour; the white zone is unlimited). Walk across the bridge and veer right onto the main drag,

Appenzell Town

To ③, Stein & Wasserauen (Lift to Ebenalp)
To Urnäsch & ⑫
GAS STATION
BREWERY
FOUNTAIN
Landsgemeinde-platz
LIBRARY & CITY HALL
CHURCH
Kronen-garten
APPENZELL MUSEUM & ⓘ
WC
Adlerplatz
FOUNTAIN
Postplatz
To ⑩
200 Meters
200 Yards
POST
TRAIN STATION
MUSEUM LINER
To Kunsthalle Ziegelhütte & ⑧

Streets: ZIELSTR., HAUPTGASSE, STERNGASSE, MARKTGASSE, HAUPT-GASSE, ENGELGASSE, KAUGASSE, POSTSTR., GERBERSTR., ALTEWEISS, WEISSBADSTRASSE, WUHRESTRASSE, JAKOB-SIGNER-STRASSE, BANKGASSE, POSTGASSE, GINGELSTR., HOFERBAD, GUTERSTR., SITTERSTRASSE, GAISERSTRASSE, River, Sitter

❶ Hotel Adler
❷ Restaurant Hotel Traube
❸ To Haus Lydia & Gästezimmer Koller-Rempfler
❹ Restaurant Marktplatz
❺ Gasthaus Hof
❻ Hotel/Restaurant Appenzell
❼ Lokal Restaurant
❽ To Gasthaus Freudenberg
❾ Internet (Hotel Säntis)
❿ To Wasserauen/Ebenalp Cable Car (by foot)
⓫ To "Barefoot Walk," Kronberg Luge & Jakobsbad (by foot)
⓬ To Neff Bike Rental

Hauptgasse. You'll see a large church on your right, with the TI and Appenzell Museum just past it.

Helpful Hints

Blue Monday: Appenzell's museums are closed on Monday, but hiking and biking are good any day the sun shines. The Kronberg luge (in Jakobsbad) runs every day, unless it's raining.

When the Cows Come Home: If you're here at the right time, you might luck into seeing the festive procession of cows heading up to the high-mountain pastures (*Alpfahrt*, generally late May–early June) or returning from a summer high in the Alps (*Alpabfahrt*, generally late Aug–early Sept). Unfortunately, the cows don't give much advance notice—announcements of the event pop up around town just a few days ahead. If you want to be sure to fit some cows into your itinerary, you can catch them in the Appenzell cattle show, usually the first Tuesday in October. For more on the cow culture of the Swiss Alps, see the sidebar on page 158.

Internet Access: Use the computers at the library on the church square (3 SF/30 min, Tue and Thu 9:30–11:30 & 14:00–17:00, Wed 14:00–17:00, Fri 16:30–20:00, Sat 9:30–11:30, closed Sun–Mon). **Hotel Säntis** has a stand-up computer in its lobby (5 SF/30 min, free for guests, Landsgemeindeplatz 3).

Post Office: It's in front of the train station (Mon–Fri 7:30–12:00 & 13:30–18:00, Sat 8:00–11:00, closed Sun).

Bike Rental: You can rent wheels at the train station (20 SF/ half-day, 25 SF/day, return bike by 18:30). Most hotels rent bikes or can arrange a rental for you. For mountain bikes, go to the garage of **Elmar Neff,** a five-minute walk beyond Landsgemeindeplatz (20 SF/half-day, 30 SF/day, Mon–Fri 7:30–12:00 & 13:15–18:30, Sat 7:30–12:00 & 13:15–16:00, closed Sun, Hauptgasse 58, tel. 071-787-3477).

Sights in Appenzell

The Appenzell region has three folk museums—one in Appenzell town, another in Stein, and a third in Urnäsch. All are good, and they're different enough that visiting all three is worth considering if you have ample time and interest. To be more selective, weigh these differences: Stein's is the biggest, the most modern-feeling, and probably the best-presented, but also the most difficult to reach (especially without a car); Urnäsch's is the most atmospheric, as it's actually in a creaky old house; and Appenzell town's is the most convenient and a good all-around look at the region (and is especially strong on local costumes), but lacks a bit of the charm of the other two.

In Appenzell Town

▲**Appenzell Museum**—The folk moo-seum above the TI provides a fine look at the local cow culture. Buy your ticket, borrow the English translations, ride the elevator to the sixth floor, and work your way down. The collection of traditional costumes on the top floor is excellent. Wandering through the rest of the exhibits, you'll see old flags and banners, reconstructed rustic rooms, woodcarvings,

19th-century peasant art, handmade embroidery, and (oddly) an Egyptian coffin. One thought-provoking room displays boards called *Rebretter*, which were used to lay out the body of a recently deceased loved one. The boards were painted with the name and information of the deceased and, after the burial, displayed on the family's house (7 SF, covered by Swiss Pass; April–Oct daily 10:00–12:00 & 14:00–17:00; Nov–March Tue–Sun 14:00–17:00, closed Mon; Hauptgasse 4, tel. 071-788-9631).

▲**Folk Music**—Free folk music concerts take place every Thursday (mid-June–mid-Oct) at 18:30 in City Hall, and every Wednesday at 20:00 at Hotel Hof Weissbad (about 2 miles out of town, on the way to Wasserauen, tel. 071-798-8080). You may also find live music at local restaurants—ask at the TI.

Modern Art Museums—Appenzell has two modern/contemporary-art exhibits in great settings: **Museum Liner** is a silver-clad modern building right behind the train tracks (Unterrainstrasse 5, tel. 071-788-1800), and **Kunsthalle Ziegelhütte** is a bit farther out, at Ziegeleistrasse 14 (tel. 071-788-1860). Each one costs 9 SF, but a 15-SF combo-ticket gets you into both (also covered by Swiss Pass; April–Oct Tue–Fri 10:00–12:00 & 14:00–17:00, Sat–Sun 11:00–17:00, closed Mon; Nov–March Tue–Sat 14:00–17:00, Sun 11:00–17:00, closed Mon; www.museumliner.ch).

Hiking

Appenzell makes a good home base for hiking, with gentle hills and pastoral scenery all around. The TI can suggest several easy walks in the region. I recommended two possibilities here.

Appenzell to Wasserauen—This two-hour walk, which takes you to the foot of the Ebenalp cable car (described on page 221), begins near the parish church in Appenzell and leads you along the creek through meadows and forests. The path is well-marked. Once you reach Wasserauen, you can take the cable car up to Ebenalp, or simply hop on the train back to Appenzell.

Barefoot Walk (Barfussweg)—This 1.5-hour walk between Jakobsbad and Gontenbad offers a surprising and unusual experience...yes, with your shoes off. The trail leads over meadows, through creeks, and on stretches of asphalted road, in a tranquil valley roughly parallel to the Appenzell-Urnäsch road and rail line. Two specially designed fountains along the way will refresh your feet. The path was inspired by the philosophy of 19th-century therapist Sebastian Kneipp, who sought to treat medical conditions with water of different temperatures and pressures.

   To get from Appenzell town to the trailhead, take the train to Jakobsbad (1–2/hr, 9 min, trailhead right across the street from the train station and the Kronberg luge ticket office—described later), and do the barefoot walk to Gontenbad. From Gontenbad, you can ride the train back to Appenzell (3 min), or keep on walking (another 45–60 min).

Near Appenzell Town

▲Stein

The unassuming, hill-capping village of Stein has two worthwhile attractions, side-by-side: A cheese production facility with a visitors center, and arguably the region's best folk museum. Remember that Stein is very difficult to reach by public transportation; if you don't have a car, use the PubliCar service (described on page 210).

Appenzeller Demonstration Cheese Dairy (Appenzeller Schaukäserei)—This facility is where the Appenzeller brand—a major local producer—makes its cheese and explains the process to visitors (free, daily April–Oct 8:30–18:30, Nov–March 8:30–17:30, tel. 071-368-5070, www.showcheese.ch). It's fast, smelly, and user-friendly. As you enter, pick up the English description of the cheesemaking process ("From Milk to Cheese"), and ask about the next English showing of the 10-minute video (which treads a fine line between informative and promotional). Large, colorful displays trace the cheesemaking process, and you can peer down into the production facility (cheese is generally being made 9:00–17:00—most interesting when they pour the contents of the giant vat into the long line of wheel molds). You'll learn how the special pungent flavor of Appenzeller cheese comes from an age-old, secret-recipe herbal brine mixture that's lovingly rubbed on each wheel as it ages. Down the long hallway, watch hundreds of wheels of cheese silently age. Then head into the tasting area, where you can nibble on the various types of Appenzeller brand cheese. The ladies at the cheese counter love to cut it so you can sample it. Notice how the age affects the aroma and taste. The dairy also sells yogurt and cold drinks (the boxes of iced tea are cheap), and the restaurant serves powerful cheese specialties.

Appenzell Folklore Museum (Appenzeller Volkskunde Museum)—This excellent museum offers a modern, well-presented look at the folk culture in these parts (7 SF, covered by Swiss Pass, Tue–Sun 10:00–17:00, closed Mon, tel. 071-368-5056, www.appenzeller-museum.ch). Borrow the essential English translations at the entry, then explore the three floors of exhibits. The ground floor is dedicated to local customs and lifestyles. The replica of the alpine cheesemaking hut is occasionally used for

APPENZELL

live demonstrations. There's a huge collection of cowbells, which, according to the explanation, are used for various purposes: to scare off evil spirits, to make the lead cow easier to follow in processions, to more easily find a lost cow..."and anyway, cows like them." Upstairs is an art collection entitled "Peasant Painting 1600–1900," with everything from huge murals from the sides of barns to delicate oil paintings to miniature wood carvings—virtually all of them featuring pastoral countryside scenes of cheese-making huts, cows, and rolling meadows. Each of the "naive" (untrained) artists who created these works is explained in a short bio, which brings the collection to life. You'll see great examples

of the brightly painted traditional regional furniture (also easy to find in local hotels and restaurants). The basement shows off more furniture pieces (in the replica of a traditional bedroom, notice how the colorful paint makes the furniture stand out from the plain wooden walls). But the focus here is on two other local crafts: weaving and embroidery. The exhibit explains how embroidery gradually evolved from simple handmade to machine-made, as it went from a craft to an actual industry. The rustic loom and the giant embroidery machine are sometimes used for demonstrations.

A visit to this museum is best on Sundays, when **demonstrations** are going on (cheesemaking starts at 13:00, most interesting around 14:45); you might also see some action on summer Wednesdays. If you're interested in one of these demos, call ahead to ask when is the best time to come.

▲Urnäsch

This appealing one-street town has Europe's cutest museum. The **Museum of Appenzell Customs** (Appenzeller Brauchtums-

museum), on the town square, brings this region's folk traditions to life (6 SF, covered by Swiss Pass; April–Oct Mon–Sat 9:00–11:30 & 13:30–17:00, Sun 13:30–17:00; Nov–March Mon–Sat 9:00–11:30, closed Sun; tel. 071-364-2322, www.museum -urnaesch.ch). It's displayed on

four floors of two adjacent, different-as-day-and-night buildings. Though the new building is slick and mostly used for temporary exhibits, the 400-year-old, aptly named "Old House" has low ceilings, dramatically sloping funhouse floors, and lots of creaks. Warm and homey, it's a happy little honeycomb of Appenzeller culture—you'll feel like a local invited you over to his house for a visit. First ask to watch an English showing of the 20-minute movie that explains four of the major regional festivals. The most memorable is Silvesterchläus—the Appenzell New Year, celebrated on January 13 per the old Julian calendar. On this date, local men celebrate by putting on gigantic, cartoonish headdresses and giant cowbells. You'll see some of those actual costumes—and others— then twist your way up through the tiny halls and staircases, pausing to look at replicas of local rooms, collections of handicrafts and tools, and other slices of Appenzell life. On the top floor of the new building, don't miss the music room, where you can try your hand at traditional musical instruments, including a hammered dulcimer and a coin-in-a-bowl (which, in the right hands, is more musical than you might think). There's no English, and barely any German, but it's still fun to explore.

Kronberg Luge Ride (Bobbahn)

Between Appenzell and Urnäsch, in the village of Jakobsbad, you can enjoy a bobsled ride that runs on steel rails from May through October. Each sled has seatbelts and can carry two people. Two handles at the side allow you to control the speed: push to accelerate, pull to brake. Respect the *Bremsen!* signs—which suggest when to brake—and don't come too close to the sled in front of you. The luge doesn't run in rainy weather; if the skies look iffy, call ahead to check. One ride lasts about seven minutes (9 SF per sled for adults—two adults can share one sled, 6 SF per sled for kids—ditto, 81 SF/10 rides, 153 SF/20 rides, 270 SF/40 rides, multiple-ride cards shareable; July–Oct daily 9:00–18:00; May– June Mon–Fri 9:00–17:00, Sat–Sun 9:00–18:00; closed Nov–April except might run on good-weather weekends—call to ask; tel. 071-794-1289, www.kronberg.ch). As part of the same entertainment zone, you'll also find a chairlift and a high-ropes course. Note that Jakobsbad is a very easy side-trip by train from Appenzell (1–2/hr, 9-min trip, luge just across the tracks from the train station).

Sleeping in Appenzell Town

Sleep in touristy Appenzell town if you want comfort—but for a rustic, high-altitude thrill, I love the low-tech, no-shower dorms at Ebenalp (described later). Appenzell town is small, and the hotels are central. All hotels offer the Appenzell Card to guests who stay at least three nights. When I've listed a range, it's based on season; the highest prices are for July through September. The *Privatzimmer* are a 10- to 20-minute hike from the town center.

Sleep Code

(1 SF = about $1, country code: 41)
S = Single, **D** = Double/Twin, **T** = Triple, **Q** = Quad, **b** = bathroom, **s** = shower only. Unless otherwise noted, credit cards are accepted, English is spoken, and breakfast is included.

    To help you sort easily through these listings, I've divided the rooms into three categories, based on the price for a standard double room with bath:

  $$$ Higher Priced—Most rooms 130 SF or more.
   $$ Moderately Priced—Most rooms between 50–130 SF.
    $ Lower Priced—Most rooms 50 SF or less.

Hotels

$$$ Hotel Adler, above a delicious café/bakery with the best croissants in town (Tue–Thu 7:30–19:30, closed Wed), is in a building that dates from 1562. The hotel has two types of rooms: modern or traditional Appenzeller (with lamps imitating the local farmer headwear). Helpful Franz Leu, proud to be an Appenzeller, has turned the halls and traditional rooms of his hotel into a museum of regional art and culture (Sb-95–110 SF, Db-180–200 SF, suite-240–260 SF, elevator, free Internet access and Wi-Fi, non-smoking, Herr Leu can arrange bike rentals for guests, between TI and bridge on Adlerplatz, tel. 071-787-1389, fax 071-787-1365, www.adlerhotel.ch, info@adlerhotel.ch).

$$$ Restaurant Hotel Traube, just off Hauptgasse near Landsgemeindeplatz, rents seven cozy, tastefully decorated, modern rooms above a fine restaurant. The friendly Hunziker family has welcomed guests here for three generations, and they still do it with style (Sb-90–110 SF, Db-160–180 SF, free Wi-Fi, non-smoking, Marktgasse 7, tel. 071-787-1407, fax 071-787-2419, www.hotel-traube.ch, info@hotel-traube.ch). Don't confuse Hotel Traube ("grape" in German) with the similarly named Hotel Taube ("dove") nearby.

Privatzimmer

To experience a pleasant Swiss suburban neighborhood, consider the following B&Bs, just east of Appenzell's pedestrian zone. To reach them from the town center (TI/town church), cross the bridge, pass the Mercedes-Esso station, then take the next right. You'll reach Koller-Rempfler first (just a few houses down), then—after another 500 yards or so—Haus Lydia.

$$ Haus Lydia, a six-room, Appenzell-style home filled with tourist information and a woodsy folk atmosphere, is on the edge of town and includes a garden and a powerful mountain view. (That's Ebenalp on the horizon.) Its crisp, nicely decorated rooms are a fine option if you have a car or don't mind a 20-minute walk from the town center (Sb-70 SF, Db-110 SF, great breakfast, pay Internet access and Wi-Fi, Eggerstandenstrasse 53, tel. 071-787-4233, fax 071-787-8633, www.hauslydia.ch, contact@hauslydia.ch, friendly Frau Mock-Inauen). She also rents a roomy apartment by the week (Db-82–89 SF, breakfast extra).

$$ Gästezimmer Koller-Rempfler is a classic Germanic guest house renting four old-fashioned but comfortable rooms (Db-100–105 SF, Tb-140–150 SF, cash only, Eggerstandenstrasse 9, tel. 071-787-2117, niklauskoller@hotmail.com, Margaret and Niklaus speak just enough English).

Eating in Appenzell

In Appenzell, menus and prices are similar from place to place—it's fairly expensive but good local cuisine, usually featuring (surprise) the heavenly but oh-so-smelly Appenzeller cheese. The Appenzeller beer is tasty, famous, and about the only thing cheap in the region. Many top restaurants cluster around the big square called Landsgemeindeplatz (where Appenzellers vote). Eateries that permit smoking do so with a vengeance; if you need a smoke-free place, tune into which places I note are non-smoking. All restaurants are open daily from about 8:00 to 24:00 unless otherwise noted.

Restaurant Hotel Traube, at the recommended hotel of the same name, combines fresh ingredients to create a wide selection of Swiss and Appenzeller meals. Sit outside on the terrace, or in the woody dining room (with a non-smoking section). Their affordable "small dishes," for 10–20 SF, are plenty filling (19–37-SF main dishes, vegetarian options, Tue–Sun 9:00–24:00, closed Mon, Marktgasse 7, tel. 071-787-1407).

Restaurant Marktplatz is filled with locals playing cards in a genuine Appenzeller atmosphere. Enjoy the beautifully detailed inlaid tables and the wood-carved wall panels. This place prides itself on having been the first non-smoking restaurant in Appenzell (22–34-SF main dishes, closed Thu and early July–early Aug, on small parking lot across from Landsgemeindeplatz fountain, walk around white building with horse head, tel. 071-787-1204).

Gasthaus Hof, which feels particularly local, offers a bewildering variety of specials (from "vitamin corner" to cold dishes to the *Fitnessteller*). There's a sprawling beer garden out back. In the cozy dining room, the unforgettable aroma of Appenzeller cheese is trumped only by the cigarette smoke (most dishes 15–30 SF, tel. 071-787-4030).

APPENZELL

Hotel Appenzell fills a formal dining room that feels like a genteel café. They have a seasonal menu and specialize in vegetarian dishes, though they also serve meat dishes (20–33-SF main dishes, Tue closed until 14:00, at corner of square closest to TI, tel. 071-788-1515).

Lokal is modern, Italian, and the opposite of every other eatery in Appenzell. This low-key café serves made-to-order focaccia sandwiches, crêpes, and gelato for takeaway or to eat in the mod interior or out front (6-SF crêpes, 6–11-SF sandwiches, Sun and Tue 13:00–19:00, Wed–Thu 9:00–19:00, Fri–Sat 9:00–22:00, closed Mon, am Schmäuslemarkt, tel. 071-787-0115).

With a View over Town: **Gasthaus Freudenberg** has reasonably priced meals and sweeping panoramas over Appenzell's rooftops from outdoor tables. If you'd like to dine with a view, it's worth the steep, 15-minute uphill walk or short drive from the town center (22–26-SF fixed-price meals are a good deal, 21–38-SF salad-and-meat *Fitnessteller*, 15–20-SF veggie dishes, closed Wed and Nov; go under train station, turn right, and follow yellow *Freudenberg* signs through a residential zone, then up through the hills; tel. 071-787-1240). Drivers can follow the yellow *Freudenberg* signs from near the train station.

With a Grand Alpine View: If you're heading up to Ebenalp for a hike in the afternoon, consider sticking around for an early dinner at **Berggasthaus Aescher,** which begins serving at 17:30. But carefully note the last lift down; outside of summer, this isn't a practical option if you need to return to Appenzell to sleep (unless you want to hike down). For details on the lift and the restaurant, see the "Ebenalp" section, later.

Appenzell Connections

For taking the train to destinations within this chapter, see "Getting Around Appenzell" on page 209. Remember that for connections beyond the Appenzell region, you'll generally change in either Herisau or Gossau.

From Appenzell Town by Train to: Zürich (2/hr, 1.75 hrs with change in Gossau, 2.25 hrs with change in St. Gallen), **Chur** (hourly, 2–2.5 hrs, 1–3 changes, easiest via St. Gallen), **Luzern** (2/hr, 2.75 hrs, change in Herisau or in Gossau and Zürich), **Bern** (hourly, 3 hrs, transfer in Gossau), **Interlaken** (hourly, 4.5 hrs, 2 transfers including Gossau or St. Gallen and Zürich or Bern), **Lausanne** (2/hr, 5 hrs, transfer in Gossau or St. Gallen), **Munich** (3/day, 4.5 hrs, transfer in St. Gallen). Train info: toll tel. 0900-300-300 or www.rail.ch.

Ebenalp

This mountain features wonderful views and a cliff-hanging, family-run hut, providing a "hills are alive" thin-air alternative to Appenzell town. From Wasserauen— five miles south of Appenzell town by road or rail line—ride the lift up to Ebenalp (5,380 feet), a high, rocky ridge that drops off to vertical cliffs on the southern side. On the way up, you'll get a sneak preview of Ebenalp's cave church and the cliffside boardwalk that leads to the guest house (near the top, left side). From the top you'll enjoy a sweeping view north all the way to Lake Constance (Bodensee). Though this excursion is doable in so-so weather, clear skies really enhance the Ebenalp experience—ask in Appenzell before you head up to the mountain, or check the webcam at www.ebenalp.ch. In any weather, sturdy shoes and rain gear are recommended—the weather can change in the blink of an eye.

Leaving the lift, look for *Wildkirchli* and *Aescher* signs pointing to the 12-minute hike down to the mountain hut. First you'll hike steeply down under the cables, then you'll hook right and venture downhill through a prehistoric cave. It's slippery and

dimly lit, so watch your step and use the railing—trust me, you'll soon return to daylight. As you emerge into the light, you'll pass a hermit's home (a tiny museum, always open) and the 400-year-old Wildkirchli cave church (hermit monks lived there 1658–1853), before following the cliff-hugging path to a 170-year-old weathered-shingle guest house built snugly against the mountain. Originally a hut housing farmers, goats, and cows, it evolved into a guest house for pilgrims coming to the monks for spiritual guidance. Today, the recommended Berggasthaus Aescher welcomes tourists, offering cheap dorm beds and hot, hearty plates of *Rösti*.

The region is a hit with hikers who make the circuit of mountain hotels. There are 24 hotels, each a day's hike apart. All originated as alpine farms. Of these, Berggasthaus Aescher is the oldest and smallest.

APPENZELL

From Ebenalp's sunny cliffside perch, you can almost hear the cows munching on the far side of the valley. Only the paragliders, like neon jellyfish, tag your world as 21st-century. In the distance, nestled below Säntis peak, are the isolated Seealpsee ("Lake-Alp Lake") and the recommended Berggasthaus Seealpsee.

Hikes from Berggasthaus Aescher: The trail beyond Berggasthaus Aescher leads to a pair of rugged hikes that are worth considering: Down to the alpine lake called Seealpsee (and

Ebenalp

To Gais

To Stein

APPENZELL TOWN

To Gontenbad, Jakobsbad & Urnäsch

STEINEGG

WEISSBAD

Ebenalp 5,380'

To Brülisau & Hoher Kasten

To Säntis

CAVE

WASSERAUEN

Seealpsee

Note: Appenzell Town to Wasserauen = 5mi / 8km

Not to Scale

❶ Berggasthaus Ebenalp
❷ Berggasthaus Seealpsee
❸ Berggasthaus Aescher

eventually all the way down to Wasserauen), or up for a steep-but-scenic route back to the Ebenalp lift.

The hike down to **Seealpsee,** which takes a little over an hour, is steep but rewarding: Take a left at the first fork beyond Berggasthaus Aescher. After some initial knee-jarring switchbacks, the trail gets easier, and as it flattens out, a fork to the right leads in about 10 minutes to the lake. To reach Wasserauen (45 min) and the train back to Appenzell, retrace your steps till you reach the nearest fork, but this time take the other path (to the right), which turns into a narrow road.

To **return to the Ebenalp lift** from Berggasthaus Aescher, you can retrace your steps through the cave (allow 25 minutes for this uphill hike). Or, for a different and more strenuous return, you can hike up around the back of the mountaintop: As you leave the Berggasthaus, continue straight on the path (skipping the first fork in the trail, which leads down to Seealpsee). After the fork, the path winds you steeply uphill, eventually arriving back at the top of the Ebenalp lift.

Getting There: First, a train takes you from Appenzell to Wasserauen (1–2/hr, 14 min). Then, across the road from the

Wasserauen station, the Ebenalp lift carries hikers to the summit and back every 15 minutes (19 SF up, 27 SF round-trip, half-price with Swiss Pass, trip takes about 7 min, daily July–Aug 7:30–19:00 but extended until at least 20:00 in mid-July–early Aug, June and Sept 7:30–18:00, late May and Oct 7:30–17:30, Dec–Easter 8:30–17:00, closed for 2 weeks in both April and Nov for maintenance, free and reportedly safe parking at lift, pick up the free hiking map before you ascend, tel. 071-799-1212, www.ebenalp.ch).

Sleeping and Eating on Ebenalp

Although Appenzell town offers all the predictable comforts, hardy travelers enjoy overnighting on Ebenalp instead. You'll live by the lift schedule (see above), the facilities are limited (only rain-water), and reaching any of these accommodations involves some steep hiking. But it's an unforgettable place to sleep.

$$$ Berggasthaus Seealpsee is on the idyllic alpine See-alpsee, a hike up a private road from the Wasserauen train station (loft dorm beds with sheets-35 SF, D-110 SF, Db-130 SF, showers-3 SF, closed Nov–March, tel. 071-799-1140, fax 071-799-1820, www.seealpsee.ch, berggasthaus@seealpsee.ch, Meier family).

$$$ Berggasthaus Ebenalp sits atop the mountains just above the lift. Its refurbished rooms are booked long in advance for Saturdays, but are otherwise empty (4-, 6-, or 8-bed dorms with comforters-37 SF per person; D-118 SF, coin-op rainwater shower-4 SF, tel. 071-799-1194, Sutter family).

$ Berggasthaus Aescher (see photo on page 221) promises a memorable experience. The 170-year-old house has only rainwater and no shower. Friday and Saturday nights sometimes have great live music, but are often crowded and noisy, with up to 40 people, and parties going into the wee hours. July and August are pretty busy, but otherwise, Monday through Thursday, you'll normally get a small, woody dorm to yourself. The hut is actually built into the cliff; its back wall is the rock itself. You can study this alpine architecture from the toilet. Sip your coffee on the deck, sheltered from drips by the gnarly overhang 100 feet above. The guest book goes back to 1940, there's a fun drawer filled with an alpine percussion section, and the comfortable dining/living room is filled with happy hikers dining on *Rösti* and sipping coffee spiked with schnapps and topped with whipped cream. Claudia can show you rock-climbing charts. For a strenuous 45-minute pre-dinner hike, copy the goats: Take the high trail toward the lake, circle clockwise up toward the peak and the lift, then hike down the way you originally came (dorm bed-40 SF, includes breakfast and comforter, no towels or showers available, dinner-14–22 SF, no credit cards but euros and traveler's checks accepted, closed Nov–April, 12 min by

APPENZELL

steep trail below top of lift, tel. 071-799-1142, www.aescher-ai.ch, reservations by phone only, run by Claudia and Beny Knechtle-Wyss and their five children—Bernhardt-age 25, Reto-24, Lukas-21, Lilian-20, and Dominik-18—plus 35 sheep, 20 rabbits, five chickens, three pigs, and a dog). Lunch is served 11:30–15:00, and dinner from 17:30, but you can get a coffee anytime.

Near Appenzell: Liechtenstein

Appenzell is just an hour away from the tiny and touristy country of Liechtenstein. This quirky remnant of medieval feudal politics is truly landlocked, without a seaport, or even an airport. Liechtensteiners—who number about 35,000—speak German, are mostly Catholic, and have a stubborn independent streak. Women weren't given the vote until 1984.

Liechtenstein is not worth going out of your way for (unless you collect stamps—postal or passport), but it's a no-brainer detour if you happen to be driving south from Appenzell toward Chur or the Upper Engadine (Pontresina/St. Moritz). Heading south on the A13 expressway, the road actually skirts Liechtenstein just across the Rhine (the border). For a 30-minute detour, exit at Buchs and turn toward Schaan. After crossing the border (without stopping, or likely even noticing), you'll wind up in the town of Schaan. Follow signs (south/right) toward Vaduz, the capital of the Principality of Liechtenstein (Fürstentum Liechtenstein, or FL for short on its sleek black license plates).

Low-key Vaduz, with about 5,000 people, feels basically like a mid-sized Swiss town. Its pedestrianized main drag is lined with modern art and hotels bordering a district of slick office parks. Like other "micro-countries," Liechtenstein offers businesses special tax and accounting incentives. Many European companies locate here to take advantage of its low taxes.

Once in Vaduz, you'll find various parking lots and garages along the main street, Äulestrasse. Try to park directly under the looming castle. If you park at the Marktplatz garage, you can simply walk one block up to the pedestrian zone called Städtle, where you'll run right into the TI (at #37, daily 9:00–17:00, a second kiosk is set up at the big bus parking lot the same hours Easter-Sept, tel. from Switzerland 00-423/239-6300, www.tourismus.li). The TI will stamp your passport for 3 SF. If you have more time, go for a stroll along enjoyable Städtle street. Use Swiss francs or euros to buy a postcard and some Liechtenstein stamps to send to the collector in your life (1.80 SF postage to for a postcard to the US... but be sure to write and send it before leaving the country).

The billionaire prince, who looks down on his six-by-twelve-mile country, wields more real political power in his realm than any other member of European royalty. The Liechtenstein family purchased this piece of real estate from the Holy Roman Emperor. In 1719, the domain was granted principality status, answering only to the emperor. In 1806, during the age of Napoleon, Liechtenstein's obligations to the Habsburg emperor disappeared, and the country was granted true independence.

The Liechtenstein princes, who lived near Vienna, saw their country merely as a status symbol, and at first didn't even bother to visit. In fact, it wasn't until the 20th century that the first Liechtenstein prince actually lived here. Later, after World War I, tough times forced the principality to enter into an economic union with Switzerland. To this day Liechtenstein enjoys a close working relationship with its Swiss neighbors.

The prince's striking castle, a 20-minute hike above Vaduz, is closed to the public, but there's a fine view from the grounds (find the trail near Café Burg). After that visit, you'll quickly run out of things to do. No problem—just head back to Switzerland. Continue south through town on Äulestrasse, turn right at the well-marked *Schweiz* sign, cross back over the Rhine, and you're back in Switzerland (and the A13 expressway)...ready to check another country off your list. Or, if you're headed northeast toward Austria, head back north through Schaan, then up to Feldkirch.

LAKE GENEVA
and FRENCH SWITZERLAND

Lake Geneva, in the southwest corner of the country, is the Swiss Riviera. Separating France and Switzerland, the lake is surrounded by Alps and lined with a collage of castles, museums, spas, resort towns, and vineyards. Elegant French-style villas—with bright colors, frilly balconies, and characteristic mansard roofs—give it an air of gentility. Its crowds, therefore, are understandable. This area is so beautiful that Charlie Chaplin and Idi Amin both chose it as their second home.

French is the predominant language at Lake Geneva ("Lac Léman" in French, "Genfersee" in German). To establish a better connection with the locals, see the "French Survival Phrases" in the appendix, *s'il vous plaît*.

Skip the big, dull city of Geneva; instead, sleep in fun, breezy Lausanne. Explore the romantic Château de Chillon and stylishly syncopated Montreux. If time allows, delve deeper into the French Swiss countryside, which offers up chocolates, vineyards, Gruyère cheese, a mountaintop glacier, and a fine folk museum.

Planning Your Time

On a quick trip, you can get a good overview of Lake Geneva's highlights in a day or less. Lausanne makes the best home base. If you're in a hurry, make a beeline for Château de Chillon. With more time, lazily float your way between Lausanne and Chillon on a scenic boat cruise, and get lost in Lausanne's old town and unique museums (the Olympic and l'Art Brut museums are best).

On a longer trip, the French Swiss countryside to the north (especially around the town of Gruyères) is worth exploring. This is most convenient by car, especially if you're driving between Lake Geneva and points north (Bern, Murten, or the Berner Oberland), but it's doable by train. You can also get a good taste of this countryside on the convenient "Chocolate Train" excursion that departs from Montreux (described on page 251).

Getting Around Lake Geneva

Trains easily connect towns along Lake Geneva. Take the faster Direct trains if you're going between larger cities, such as Lausanne or Montreux, or the slower Régional or REV trains if you're heading for a smaller destination, such as Château de Chillon.

Boats carry visitors to all sights of importance. Daily boat trips (4/day in each direction May–Sept, fewer in shoulder season, virtually none late Oct–Easter) connect Lausanne with Vevey (60 min, 18.20 SF), Montreux (80 min, 23.40 SF), and Château de

Chillon (90 min, 25 SF). First class costs about a third more and gets you passage on the deck up top, where you should scramble for the first-come, first-served chairs. You can sail free with a Eurailpass or Swiss Pass, but it uses up a travel day of a flexipass; to avoid giving up a day just for the cruise, you could take an afternoon cruise on the same day you arrive by train in the morning (tel. 0848-811-848, www.cgn.ch).

Study the schedule (available at TIs and boat ticket windows) to find a cruise that appeals to you—you have a variety to choose from. For just a quick hop on the water, the short cruise between Montreux and Château de Chillon is fun (8.60 SF, 15 min). The pretty town of Vevey gives you the most scenic one-hour boat ride from Lausanne or a 30-minute ride from Chillon, and makes an enjoyable destination. Evian-les-Bains, immediately across from Lausanne, is the French spa town famous for its mineral water. The boats there are filled with people ready to enjoy its spa and tour its mineral-water facilities (31 SF round-trip, about hourly, 35 min, passport required).

Lausanne

Lausanne is the most interesting city on the lake, proudly dubbing itself the "Olympic Capital" (it's been home to the International Olympic Committee since 1915). Amble along the serene lakefront

promenade, stroll through the three-tiered, colorful old town, explore the sculptures at Olympic Park, and visit the remarkable Collection de l'Art Brut. Take a peek at the Gothic Cathedral, and climb its tower for the view.

The Romans founded Lausanne on the lakefront—but with the fall of Rome and the

rise of the barbarians, the first Lausanners fled for the hills, establishing today's old town. The Roman site was abandoned (scant ruins today), but in the age of tourism, the waterfront—a district called Ouchy—thrived. So the city has a design problem that goes back 1,500 years: two charming zones separated by a nondescript residential/industrial urban mess. Thankfully, the waterfront and the old town are easily linked by a steep, handy Métro line.

Lausanne has the energy and cultural sophistication of a larger city, but is home to only 125,000 people (300,000 in greater Lausanne). A progressive city government (with a mayor from the Green Party) that subsidizes art and culture, and a university with plenty of foreign students carbonate the place with a youthful spirit. That spirit shows itself in Lausanne's notoriety as a haven for inline skating and skateboarding.

Orientation to Lausanne

The tourist's Lausanne has two parts: 1) The lakefront **Ouchy** (oo-shee), with a breezy resort ambience and the Olympics Museum; and 2) the **old town district,** with creaky Old World charm and other fine museums, directly uphill from the lake. The "old town district" is divided roughly into two adjacent parts: the true "old town," or *vieille ville* (vee-yay veel), near the cathedral; and the "city center," or *centre-ville*, with my favorite hotels and restaurants. The train station is located between Ouchy and the old town, and everything's connected by the slick Métro.

Be careful to pronounce Lausanne correctly (loh-ZAHN), and don't confuse it with Luzern.

Lausanne

PALAIS DE BEAULIEU

COLLECTION DE L'ART BRUT

AVE. DES BERGIÈRES

AVE. DE BEAULIEU

PONT CHAUD.

RUE TERREAUX

FLON

AVE. J. GONIN

AVE. RUCHONNET

PRÉ DU MARCHÉ

AVE. VINET

RUE DE LA BORDE

AVE. L. VULLIEMIN

To Croisettes

HERMITAGE

BOIS DE SAUVABELIN

RUE DE BUGNON

See Old Lausanne Walk Detail Map

R. TUNNEL

Riponne-M. Béjart

Place de la Riponne

CASTLE

VIEILLE VILLE

R. DR ROUX

CATHEDRAL

CITY HISTORY MUSEUM

CENTRE-VILLE

MERC.

R. CENTRALE

PONT BESSIÈRES

Parc Mon-Repos

R. LANG.

HIGH PED. BRIDGE

Lausanne-Flon

Place de l'Europe

Place St. François

RUE DU GRAND-PONT

R. DU PETIT-CHÊNE

AVE. DU THÉÂTRE

AVE. STE. LUCE

TRAIN STATION

POST

Lausanne-Gare

AVE. DE LA GARE

AVE. OLIVIER

BLVD.

GRANCY

Crêt de Montriond

AVE. DE LA HARPE

Métro Line #2

Montriond

AVE. D'OUCHY

AVE. DE MONTCHOISI

AVE. DE LELYSÉE

Jordils

OUCHY

Parc Olympique

OLYMPIC MUSEUM & PARK

Parc du Denantou

To Geneva

AVE. DE RHODANIE

Ouchy

Place du Port

QUAI D'OUCHY

To Vevey & Montreux

To Geneva

BOAT TICKET OFFICE

Lake Geneva

500 meters

500 yards

To Geneva

To Evian, France

To Montreux & Château de Chillon

1 Aux Bonnes Choses Bakery
2 Migros Grocery
3 Café du Vieil-Ouchy

Tourist Information

Lausanne has two TIs: One is in the train station (daily 9:00–19:00), and the other is at the lakefront Ouchy Métro stop, in a blue pavilion (daily April–Sept 9:00–19:00, Oct–March 9:00–18:00, tel. 021-613-7373, www.lausanne-tourisme.ch).

At either TI, ask about **walking tours** in English (10 SF, free for students, 1.5 hrs, May–Sept Mon–Sat usually at 10:00 and 14:30, in English only if there's a guide and demand, meet in front of City Hall at Place de la Palud, call TI to confirm time and language).

If you're here between mid-June and late September—prime time for cultural events—pick up the TI's *Lausanne Estivale* program. At any time of year, ask about organ concerts at the cathedral.

Arrival in Lausanne

By Train: The train station is midway between the old town and the lakefront. This sounds inconvenient, but the Métro takes you either up to the old town or down to the lake in about two minutes, with constant departures. For most recommended hotels, take the Métro to the Lausanne-Flon stop (details listed under "Sleeping in Lausanne," later). It seems confusing only until you do it. A **taxi** from the train station to your hotel runs about 15 SF.

By Car: Driving is tricky in this nearly vertical city—especially in the twisty old town. Consider avoiding the headaches by leaving your car at a park-and-ride; two of these flank the city and are well-connected by Métro to the old town. If you're coming on the freeway from the north (such as from Bern), get off at the Vennes exit. Either park at the park-and-ride here (*P+R*, 10 SF/day, Vennes Métro stop), or—if you want to head into the city center to find a pricier garage—follow *Centre* signs. Alternatively, you can stay on the freeway as it loops around and down to *Lausanne Sud,* ending at the lakefront Ouchy district, with another handy park-and-ride (Pêcheurs, near the base station of the Métro). If you're coming on the lakeside road from the east (such as from Montreux), follow blue signs along the lakeshore directly into Lausanne.

By Plane: For arrival at the nearby Geneva Airport, see page 244.

Helpful Hints

Market Days: On Wednesday and Saturday mornings, produce stands fill the pedestrian streets of the old town. Saturday is flea market day on Place de la Riponne.

Internet Access: Get online at **Quanta** (daily 9:00–24:00, plenty of terminals surrounded by a noisy arcade, across street from train station and above McDonald's at Place de la Gare 4) or **Shiva Cyber-Bar** (daily 7:30–24:00, in the old town, just over pedestrian walkway at Rue du Grand-Pont 10).

Laundry: Quick-Wash is well-run and handy to the train station (Mon–Fri 8:00–21:30, Sat–Sun 9:00–21:30, self-service only, good English instructions, below train station at Boulevard de Grancy 44, tel. 079-449-3761). Exit behind the train station (down the stairs past track 9), turn right, then head left down Passage de Montriond to the corner.

Bike Rental: A bike is pretty worthless in this steep city, but it's great for exploring the lakefront, vineyards, and nearby villages. It's a three-hour waterfront pedal to Montreux. Unfortunately, there's no handy bike rental in lakefront Ouchy, which would be a great starting point for a bike ride.

Near the old town, the city offers free loaner bikes through **Lausanne Roule,** tucked under the arches in front of the Lausanne-Flon Métro stop (at the right end of Place de l'Europe as you exit the Métro). Flash your ID, give them a 20-SF deposit, and the bike is yours until 20:00; if you return it after that, you'll pay a prorated price (April–Oct daily 8:00–21:00, closed Nov–March, Place de l'Europe 1, tel. 021-533-0115, www.lausanneroule.ch).

You can rent a bike at Lausanne's **train-station** baggage office (25 SF/half-day, 33 SF/day, 5 SF less with Eurailpass or Swiss Pass, daily 8:30–19:00 except closed Sat–Sun 12:00–13:00, tel. 051-224-2162, www.rentabike.ch). It's possible to reserve ahead on popular weekends (at least 48 hours ahead, online only). Ask about dropping off the bike at a different train station (7 SF extra, limited to a few stations).

Late-Night Grocery: The train station has an **Aperto** grocery store open long hours (daily 6:00–24:00).

Getting Around Lausanne

Lausanne is steeper than it is big, and the nifty Métro and bus network make it easy to get around. While the Métro has two lines (converging at the Lausanne-Flon stop), only line #2 is useful for travelers. This mostly vertical, 14-stop Métro line climbs up from the lakefront to the old town, then all the way up to the freeway. The key stops are **Ouchy** (at the lakefront); **Lausanne-Gare** (at the train station); **Lausanne-Flon** (at the bottom end of the old town—exit into Place de l'Europe, ride the elevator up to the pedestrian bridge, and stroll straight into the town center); and **Riponne-M. Béjart** (at the top end of the old town, on Place de la Riponne). When boarding the Métro, watch the direction: Croisettes will take you up, Ouchy will take you down. You're unlikely to need the bus, except to reach the l'Art Brut museum (described later, under "Sights in Lausanne").

If you're sleeping in Lausanne, ask your hotel for a Mobilis Card, which covers local transit and is included in your hotel tax. Otherwise, you'll need to buy tickets, even if you have a Swiss Pass. The city center is covered by one zone (zone 11); if you're headed a bit farther (such as to Lutry or the Vennes park-and-ride), you might cross into zone 12. Tickets are valid on both Métro and buses. A short-ride ticket, valid for 30 minutes and up to three stops, costs 1.90 SF. If you're staying within one zone, a single ticket of up to an hour costs 2.60 SF, and an all-day ticket (valid 6:00–24:00) costs 7.60 SF. Adding a second zone costs a bit more. Before boarding, buy bus tickets from the TI, ticket windows, or user-friendly ticket machines (with English instructions). Your railpass is not good on public transportation in Lausanne (except lake boats—see above).

Taxis are pricey—figure 15 SF for a short ride.

Self-Guided Walk

A Stroll Through Old Lausanne

There's no way to see this town without lots of climbing. Locals are used to it (enjoy the firm legs). This self-guided stroll introduces you to both parts of Lausanne's charming old town (*vieille ville*, then *centre-ville*). It's a big counterclockwise circle, taking you from the Church of St. Francis up to the cathedral (and castle just beyond), then more or less back to the starting point. You can begin this walk at the Church of St. Francis (skip down to the "Place St-François" section), but I've started it at the Lausanne-Flon Métro station, where you're most likely to arrive in town.

Rue du Grand-Pont: From the Lausanne-Flon Métro stop, ride the elevator up to the high pedestrian bridge. This leads to the

main thoroughfare through the city, Rue du Grand-Pont. Orient yourself from midway across the pedestrian bridge (Passerelle du Flon). Below you stretches Flon—until recently, a down-and-dirty industrial zone. Now, the old warehouses are renovated and throb at night with

trendy bars, restaurants, theaters, and discos. The recommended Vinothèque Nomade is immediately below. The only reminder of the mills that once churned here is the name of the hottest dance club in town: MàD (stands for "Moulin à Danse," or "Dance at the Mill," Rue de Genève 23).

Old Lausanne Stroll

Hotels, Eateries & Services
- 🔟 Hôtel Régina
- 1️⃣1️⃣ Hôtel des Voyageurs
- 1️⃣2️⃣ Hôtel du Marché
- 1️⃣3️⃣ Hôtel Elite
- 1️⃣4️⃣ To Lausanne Guest-House & Backpacker
- 1️⃣5️⃣ Café Romand
- 1️⃣6️⃣ Café du Grütli
- 1️⃣7️⃣ Restaurant Manora
- 1️⃣8️⃣ Le Bleu Lézard
- 1️⃣9️⃣ Vinothèque Nomade
- 2️⃣0️⃣ Le Lyrique
- 2️⃣1️⃣ Traiteur Bosphore
- 2️⃣2️⃣ Launderette
- 2️⃣3️⃣ Bike Rentals (2)
- 2️⃣4️⃣ Internet Access (2)
- 2️⃣5️⃣ Bus #2 to l'Art Brut (2)

Self-Guided Walk
- ① Start of Old Town Walk
- ② Rue du Grand-Pont
- ③ Place St-François
- ④ Castle
- ⑤ Cantonal High School
- ⑥ Cathedral
- ⑦ Esplanade de la Cathédrale
- ⑧ Place de la Palud
- ⑨ Place de la Riponne

• *Walk to where the pedestrian bridge hits the busy street. Head for the green copper spire of the Church of St. Francis (to the right). As you walk along Rue du Grand-Pont, enjoy lovely views of the cathedral on your left. You'll soon reach...*

Place St-François: The Church of St. Francis marks the town's center and transportation hub, with the grand post office and banks on the right. The church is Gothic, founded by Franciscans in the 13th century. But in 1536, it went Protestant—and was gutted of decorations. Later, a grand Baroque organ was installed. (Note that bus #2 goes from the street alongside the church to the Collection de l'Art Brut.)

• *Head uphill (passing to the left of the church) up Lausanne's pedestrianized "Fifth Avenue," Rue de Bourg—home to the finest shops. When the street ends, turn left, continuing uphill and over the* **bridge** *toward the cathedral.*

The railing on the bridge is designed to discourage suicidal people from leaping. While Switzerland seems to have it all, its mind-set can be conservative, the orderliness can be stifling, and life here can be stressful—or even depressing (the country has one of the highest suicide rates in Western Europe). Here in Lausanne, between Christmas and New Year's, social workers are stationed on this bridge with soup and coffee to counsel and comfort the distraught people who congregate here, contemplating ending it all.

Walking toward the cathedral, you'll notice that Lausanne's old town—filled with administration buildings, offices, schools, and apartments—is subdued compared to most other European old towns, which are lively with lots of eateries.

• *Climb up past the Design Museum, then around the right end of the cathedral (we'll come back later). Continue up the cobbled Rue Cité-Derrière (under the two stone arches) and hike a few short blocks to the summit of the old town, where you'll find the...*

Castle: Lausanne's castle is closed to the public, but the views from the terrace behind it are free. The statue celebrates Major Abraham Davel, a local William Tell–like hero. In 1536, the German-speaking Bernese swept into this region (the canton of Vaud) and took over, converting it to Protestantism and ruling it for two centuries. In 1723, Davel's heroic attempt to free Lausanne ended in his decapitation. It wasn't until 1798 that the local population, inspired by the French Revolution, invited French troops to the region, and with their help, drove the Bernese out. In 1803, the region entered the Swiss Confederation.

Walk downhill on Rue Cité-Devant, toward the big, blocky cathedral tower. Halfway down on your right, you can't miss the **cantonal high school** *(gymnases cantonaux).* One of two great buildings from the Bernese period, this was built as a school to train a new kind of Christian leader after the Reformation. This was the first French-speaking Protestant school (c. 1590)—predating similar schools in Geneva (which, under the leadership of John Calvin, was the center of the Swiss Reformation).

• *Continue to the...*

Cathedral: This is the biggest church in Switzerland, at more than 300 feet long. Go inside (free, April–Aug Mon–Fri 7:00–19:00, Sat–Sun 8:00–19:00, Sept–March daily until 17:30).

This is an Evangelical Reform Church, meaning that it belongs to the tradition of early Protestant reformer John Calvin—and,

like its founder, it remains very strict (members aren't allowed to dance, or even to have buckles on their shoes). Iconoclasm, the removal of religious symbols, suited the Calvinists well. The once-ornate cathedral, originally dedicated to Mary, was cleared of all its statues and decorations. Its frescoes were plastered over, and its colorful windows were trashed and replaced by plain ones (the colored windows were added in the 20th century).

The **pipe organ** above the main door is American-made by Fisk, a Boston company that won the commission and installed it in 2003. Locals love their organ and figure its cost (four million SF) was money well spent. They hold free concerts here, generally on Friday evenings (about 12 times per year—ask about schedule in cathedral welcome center or TI). Look back at its 6,700 pipes: The "stiletto in Oz" design represents the wings of angels. (The old pipes now toot in a church in Gdańsk, Poland.)

The **rose window** in the south (right) transept has the church's only surviving 13th-century glass. The rest of the glass dates from the early 1900s. The north (left) transept has some dreamy blue Art Nouveau scenes. Below the rose window (and just to the left) is the Mary Chapel—once the most elaborate in the church. In 1536, it was scraped clean of anything fancy or hinting of the Virgin Mary. Look at the bits of surviving original paint, and imagine the church in its colorful glory six centuries ago.

The **painted portal** (on the right side of the nave, as you face the altar) was the church's main entrance in the Middle Ages, but is now glassed in to protect its remarkable painted Gothic statuary: Jesus overseeing the coronation of Mary. The panels beneath Jesus illustrate Mary's death and Assumption.

In the back-right corner of the church, you'll find a **welcome center** and gift shop (April–Aug Mon–Sat 8:30–11:45 & 13:30–18:00, Sun 14:00–17:30, Sept–March daily until 17:00). Here you can buy a ticket to climb the 224-step **tower,** which offers a grand view of nearly the entire lake—and lots of Alps (2 SF, last entry 30 min before welcome center closes).

As the city was originally built of wood, it burned down several times. Since the Middle Ages, a **watchman** has lived in the church's tower. His job: to watch for fires and to call out the hours. The city is made of stone today—so there's little danger of fire—and people now sport watches of their own. Nevertheless, Lausanne's night watchman, the last one of his kind in Switzerland, still calls out the hours. Every night on the hour, from 22:00 to 2:00 in the morning, he steps onto his balcony and hollers. His first announcement: "I am the watchman. I am the watchman. We just had 10 o'clock. We just had 10 o'clock."

• *Back outside, belly up to the fine viewpoint immediately in front of the cathedral.*

Esplanade de la Cathédrale: On a clear day, look beyond the spire of the Church of St. Francis to see the French Alps (Chamonix and Mont Blanc, over there somewhere, are just out of sight). Evian-les-Bains, the famous French spa town, is immediately opposite Lausanne. On the right, the soft, rolling Jura Mountains, which mark the border of France and Switzerland, stretch all the way from Lake Geneva to Germany.

• *Notice that the City History Museum is across the square from the cathedral (described later, under "Sights in Lausanne"). Now's a good time to visit. Then go from the cathedral to...*

Place de la Palud and Place de la Riponne: A covered wooden staircase (Escaliers du Marché) leads down from the cathedral's front door. At the top of the stairs, look for the stylized seashell sign marked *Chemin de St. Jacques.* This is a stop on one of the many pilgrimage routes across Europe that funnel hikers to the Camino de Santiago across northern Spain. Head through the tunnel under the busy road. You'll pass Le Barbare ("The Barbarian"), a pub famous for its fine hot chocolate, and the recommended Café du Grütli.

Place de la Palud (pictured on page 228) is marked by its colorful Fountain of Justice (with the blindfolded figure of Justice holding her sword and scales...commanding fairness as she stands triumphantly over kings and bishops). Imagine the neighborhood moms sending kids here to fetch water in the days before plumbing. Behind the fountain is a mechanical clock whose animated figures perform with recorded French narration every hour, on the hour (9:00–19:00). The City Hall at the bottom of the square, dating from 1685, is, along with the cantonal high school we saw earlier, the other fine Bernese building in town.

Uphill from City Hall, Rue de la Madeleine leads to the vast and modern **Place de la Riponne.** The Palais du Rumine (former university), overlooking the square, now houses a collection of museums (all of which are skippable).

• *Your tour is over. Now enjoy some of Lausanne's fine museums. To reach the Collection de l'Art Brut, you can walk about 10 minutes, or catch bus #2 from Rue Neuve (a block west of Place de la Riponne, across the street from the blocky church). To head down to the lakefront Ouchy district—with its lake cruises and excellent Olympics Museum—ride the Métro from the Riponne-M. Béjart stop down to Ouchy. Or simply enjoy poking around more of the old town's twisty lanes.*

Sights in Lausanne

In and near the Old Town

▲**City History Museum (Musée Historique de Lausanne)**— Facing the cathedral, this museum traces life in Lausanne from

Roman times to the present with many fascinating displays. You'll begin downstairs, following the one-way route of "Lausanne Through the Ages." Look for the English fliers in each room. The highlight for many is the 1:200-scale model of Lausanne in the 17th century (based on an engraving from 1638—see copy on wall). You're viewing the town from the perspective of the lakefront district of Ouchy, with the Church of St. Francis in the foreground. You can see river valleys that have since been obliterated by the modern city. The little water mills mark the birthplace of industrial Flon. Though the city's walls are long gone, its vineyards survive. (When you enter the museum, request to hear the 18-minute recorded English commentary on the model, and they'll book you a time.) Adjacent rooms show the construction of the Grand-Pont and an interesting collection of historic photos. Rounding out the collection are several rooms upstairs dedicated to the Bernese epoch (Protestant, 1536–1798), Lausanne silver from the 18th century, a collection of musical instruments, an exhibit about the beginnings of the modern era, and several temporary exhibits (8 SF, covered by Swiss Pass, Tue–Thu 11:00–18:00, Fri–Sun 11:00–17:00, closed Mon except July–Aug, Place de la Cathédrale 4, tel. 021-315-4101, www.lausanne.ch/mhl).

▲▲**Collection de l'Art Brut**—This well-displayed, thought-provoking collection shows art produced by untrained artists,

many labeled (and even locked up) by society as "criminal" or "insane." The works are displayed (perhaps fittingly) without much rhyme or reason on four floors. Read thumbnail biographies of these outsiders (posted next to their works), and then enjoy their unbridled creativity.

In 1945, artist Jean Dubuffet began collecting art he called "Brut"—untrained, ignoring rules, highly original, produced by people "free from artistic culture and free from fashion tendencies." In the 1970s, he donated his huge collection to Lausanne, which now displays 35,000 works by 500 artists—loners, mavericks, fringe people, prisoners, and mental-ward patients. Dubuffet said, "The art does not lie in beds ready-made for it. It runs away when its name is called. It wants to be incognito." As you tour the thought-provoking collection and learn about the artists, ponder the fine line that separates sanity and insanity when it comes to creative output (10 SF, covered by Swiss Pass, Tue–Sun 11:00–18:00, closed Mon except July–Aug, Avenue des Bergières 11, tel. 021-315-2570, www.artbrut.ch).

Getting There: The museum is an easy 10-minute walk from the old town (west from Place de la Riponne). Or you can reach it by bus: Bus #2 (direction: Désert, stop: Jomini) makes several convenient stops in the old town, including at Place St-François and at Rue Neuve near Place de la Riponne. From the train station, take bus #3 or #21 (direction: Bellevaux, stop: Beaulieu).

In Ouchy, Lausanne's Waterfront

The lazy resort charm of Lausanne lies on its lakefront. The handy Métro connects Ouchy with the train station and the old town every few minutes. Within 100 yards of the Ouchy Métro stop, you'll find plenty of handy services: TI, boat dock, paddleboat rental, the start of the lakeside promenade, and a park. The place is lively from Easter through October, and dead otherwise.

From the Métro, walk straight out to the water. A big C-shaped **weathervane** stands on the breakwater. Identify which of the four winds is blowing by lining the "C" up with semicircle cutouts in the four granite pillars (crouch). By matching the "C" with the pillar that creates a perfect "O," you learn the prevailing wind. Nearby, notice the solar-powered **Aquarel tour boats,** which run quietly, smoothly, slowly, and greenly (8 SF, 40-min tours, www.lausanne.ch/aquarel). Lausanne's current mayor, from the Green Party, is making environmentalism popular. Speaking of green, this city has more green space per inhabitant (300 square feet) than nearly any city in Europe.

Lake Geneva **cruise boats** leave from the piers just to the left (described under "Getting Around Lake Geneva" on page 227). Beyond those, you'll find Ouchy's main attraction...

▲▲**Olympic Museum and Park**—This high-tech museum and beautiful park celebrate the colorful history of the Olympic Games.

The expensive but excellent museum is a thrill for Olympics buffs—and plenty of fun for those of us who just watch every two years. Given the informative English descriptions and many thrilling video clips to see, plan on spending two hours here (15 SF, family-35 SF, covered by Swiss Pass, May–Sept daily 9:00–18:00, Oct–April closed Mon; from Ouchy Métro stop, turn left and walk 5 min to Quai d'Ouchy 1, then ride up the outdoor escalator; tel. 021-621-6511, www.olympic.org). As you enter, note the time of the next six-minute introductory video—it's worth watching. While everything is nicely explained in English, the 3-SF iPod audioguide provides an engaging 24-stop tour.

The museum celebrates Pierre de Coubertin, who in 1894 founded the International Olympic Committee and restarted the games after a 1,500-year lapse. The Olympic spirit is one of peace. Coubertin acknowledged that to ask nations to love one another was naive, but to ask them to respect one another was a realistic and worthy goal.

The ground floor traces the history of the Games, from ancient Greek artifacts to a century's worth of ceremonial torches. Upstairs are medals and highlights from each Olympiad and historic, well-described equipment used for various Olympic events (look for Jesse Owens' spiky jumping shoe from 1936, given to him by Adi Dassler, the founder of Adidas; Carl Lewis' shoes from L.A. in 1984; the Michael Jordan–signed basketball from the 1992 Barcelona "Dream Team"; and Cathy Freeman's shoes from the 2000 Sydney games). At the top of the museum, you'll find a lakeview terrace and swanky restaurant (healthy *plat du jour* for 19 SF).

In the basement is a 3-D theater (called "Salle Nagano")

showing various 15- to 30-minute films, which generally start at :30 past the hour—note the posted movie times as you buy your ticket, and plan accordingly. Nearby is an extensive film archive of suspenseful moments in the history of the Games (roughly 5 min each, 450 to choose from). Your ticket includes two of these mini-documentaries—if enthralled, you can buy three more for 5 SF.

Budget Tip: Pauper athletes can enjoy much of the complex for free. Walk through the spiraling core of the complex for a sense of the action (tickets are only necessary to enter the exhibit halls themselves). At the top of the atrium, you can sit and watch Olympic highlights on the giant screens. Then enjoy the park's Olympic flame in front of the museum, athletic monuments, and lake views (take escalator to top, ask in museum for free brochure explaining sculptures, and wander back down to lake; avoid the pricey café in the park).

Near Lausanne: Lakeside and Vineyard Excursions on Foot or Bike

A delightful promenade stretches in both directions from the Ouchy Métro stop. The best easy **walk** is east (left as you face the lake, 75 min to Lutry). From Lutry you can catch the train back to Lausanne (2/hr, 8 min). If you hike, bring the TI's *Discover the Terraces of Lavaux* flier (describes several hikes, including this one). The trail is marked with blue plaques explaining in English the flora, fauna, and culture you're enjoying.

Picturesque **vineyards** abound along the lake near Lausanne. My favorite plan: a 5- to 10-minute train ride to Chexbres or Grandvaux, then a walk through the villages—following the yellow signs—toward Lutry for stunning views of Lake Geneva. From Lutry, hop the train back to Lausanne (2/hr, 8 min). For tips on seeing this area by car, see page 245.

The best **bike path** goes west (after sharing with cars for half a mile, the trail leaves the road and hugs the shoreline all the way to Morges). You'll pass Vidy (with its Roman ruins—just foundations, free), the headquarters of the International Olympic Committee (not open to the public), lots of sports facilities, and finally just peaceful lakefront parkland stretching to Morges (about 6 miles away, easy return by boat or train).

Sleeping in Lausanne

Lausanne hotels are expensive. The only cheap doubles are at the Lausanne GuestHouse. Lausanne charges a tourist tax of 2.50 SF per person per night (which is generally not included in the rates listed below). This buys you a Mobilis Card, which gives you free access to the city's public transportation for the duration of your

Sleep Code

(1 SF = about $1, country code: 41)

S = Single, **D** = Double/Twin, **T** = Triple, **Q** = Quad, **b** = bathroom, **s** = shower only. Unless otherwise noted, credit cards are accepted, English is spoken, and breakfast is included.

To help you sort easily through these listings, I've divided the rooms into three categories, based on the price for a standard double room with bath:

$$$ Higher Priced—Most rooms 170 SF or more.
  $$ Moderately Priced—Most rooms between 100–170 SF.
    $ Lower Priced—Most rooms 100 SF or less.

stay (potentially worth far more than the tax). Ask for yours when you check in.

In the Old Town

To find the Régina and Voyageurs, take the Métro to the Lausanne-Flon stop, ride the elevator up to the pedestrian bridge, cross Rue du Grand-Pont, walk up Rue Pichard, and take the first right. For the Marché, continue one more stop up on the Métro to Riponne-M. Béjart, then walk five minutes up Rue Pré-du-Marché. Because the Régina and Voyageurs are buried in Lausanne's old town, they can be challenging for drivers. You are allowed to drive through the pedestrian zone to your hotel to drop off your things, but you'll have to park the car at a nearby garage. Get careful instructions, or leave your car at a park-and-ride and arrive by Métro.

$$$ Hôtel Régina, on a steep pedestrian street immersed in old-town charm, is a find: 36 comfy, remodeled rooms, hospitable hosts (Michel and Dora), and a great location (Sb-138 SF, Db-178 SF, Tb-208 SF, suites-165–325 SF depending on number of people, 10 percent less Fri–Sun for stays of at least 2 nights, email the hotel directly to get these special prices for Rick Steves readers, non-smoking, elevator, free Internet access and Wi-Fi, Rue Grand Saint-Jean 18, tel. 021-320-2441, fax 021-320-2529, www.hotel -regina.ch, info@hotel-regina.ch).

$$$ Hôtel des Voyageurs has 33 predictable rooms across the street from Hôtel Régina. It lacks Régina's charm, but it's in an equally good location (Sb-140 SF, Db-185 SF, Tb-205 SF, about 10 percent cheaper July–Aug and on weekends, non-smoking rooms, elevator, pay Internet access, free Wi-Fi, parking-15 SF/day, Rue Grand Saint-Jean 19, tel. 021-319-9111, fax 021-319-9112, www .voyageurs.ch, hotel@voyageurs.ch).

$$ Hôtel du Marché has older public spaces, but most of its 26 rooms are nicely renovated. It's a five-minute walk from Place de la Riponne in the old town, on the way to the l'Art Brut museum (S-80 SF, Sb-110 SF, D-115 SF, Db-135 SF, Tb-155 SF, breakfast-12 SF, non-smoking, elevator, free Internet access and Wi-Fi, Rue Pré-du-Marché 42, tel. 021-647-9900, fax 021-646-4723, www.hoteldumarche-lausanne.ch, info@hoteldumarche-lausanne.ch).

Near the Train Station

These accommodations are easier for drivers.

$$$ Hôtel Elite, run by the Zufferey family, is on a quiet, leafy, residential street just above the train station. Its 33 rooms are businesslike and modern (Sb-140 SF, Db-180–260 SF depending on size and view, Tb-210–265 SF, non-smoking, elevator, pay Internet access, free Wi-Fi; from station, cross the street and go uphill around McDonald's, take first right to Avenue Sainte-Luce 1; tel. 021-320-2361, fax 021-320-3963, www.elite-lausanne.ch, info@elite-lausanne.ch).

$ Lausanne GuestHouse & Backpacker has to be one of Switzerland's best hostels. This elegant, century-old house, which offers dorm beds and private rooms, turns its back on the train tracks. All of its rooms overlook the lake on the quiet side, and all of the bathrooms face the tracks—which means that even if you have a "private" bathroom, you'll have to cross the hall to reach it (bunk in 4-bed dorm-38 SF, S-85 SF, Sb-94 SF, D-95 SF, Db-115 SF, includes sheets and tax, no breakfast, no smoking, no curfew, reception open 7:30–12:00 & 15:00–22:00, elevator, pay Internet access and Wi-Fi, lockers, laundry, kitchen, garden, reserve ahead for parking; 5-min walk from train station: Leave out the back by track 9, go down the stairs, and turn right to Epinettes 4; tel. 021-601-8000, www.lausanne-guesthouse.ch, info@lausanne-guesthouse.ch).

Eating in Lausanne

In Ouchy

The lakeside Ouchy district is *the* place to relax. Immediately in front of the Métro stop is a fun zone with fountains, parks, playgrounds, promenades, and restaurants. The only good, budget eating option is a picnic with the local office gang on any of the many inviting benches or scenic lakeside perches. **Aux Bonnes Choses** is a small bakery with a heart for picnickers, offering good sandwiches, salads, pastries, and drinks to go. This is infinitely better than the lousy kiosk options in the waterfront park (5-SF salads, daily 6:30–19:00, left as you exit Métro, Place de la Navigation 2, tel. 021-617-8857). Another good spot to shop for your picnic is the

Migros grocery store on Avenue de Rhodanie (daily 8:00–21:45, to the right as you exit the Métro).

Café du Vieil-Ouchy, charming and reasonably priced, seems a bit out of place among all the fancy, expensive restaurants. It offers traditional Swiss cuisine, including cheese fondue and hash brown–like *Rösti* (17–27-SF entrées, Thu–Mon 11:30–14:30 & 17:30–22:00, closed Tue–Wed, Place du Port 3, tel. 021-616-2194).

In the Old Town

Café Romand is a classic Swiss brasserie filled with natives enjoying hearty French Swiss home cooking. Local students, pensioners, and professionals sit under old-time photos in this characteristic yet simple eatery like they own the place (18–27-SF plates, Swiss white wines by the glass and carafe—see list of what bottles are open above the bar, daily specials, Mon–Sat 9:00–1:00 in the morning, closed Sun, Place St-François 2, tel. 021-312-6375).

Café du Grütli, named for the meadow where Switzerland was born, offers typical French Swiss cuisine near Place de la Palud. Choose from three tempting areas to eat: outside on a cozy cobbled lane; ground-floor, circa-1850, Parisian-bistro style; or upstairs, with antlers and the ambience of a 13th-century castle (often closed for special events). The Prutsch family is into hunting, so you'll find game on the menu (27–40-SF plates, Mon–Fri 9:00–14:30 & 18:00–23:00, Sat 8:30–15:30 & 18:00–23:30, closed Sun, Rue de la Mercerie 4, tel. 021-312-9493).

Restaurant Manora is part of a modern, self-service chain offering a quick and healthy series of buffet lines where you grab what looks good: hot meals, salads (4.90-SF, 8.30-SF, and 11.50-SF plates), fancy fruit juices, desserts, and so on (Mon–Sat 6:45–22:00, Sun 7:45–22:00, where Rue du Grand-Pont hits Place St-François).

Le Bleu Lézard has great French cuisine, a typical French atmosphere, and a trendy clientele that appreciates its candlelit, bohemian interior and fun outdoor patio (22-SF salads, good 21-SF veggie options, 25–30-SF meat dishes, daily 7:00–24:00, open later on weekends, La Cave music club downstairs, Rue Enning 10, tel. 021-321-3830).

Vinothèque Nomade is primarily a wine bar, where you can choose from 40 different wines available by the glass (generally 7–10 SF; many more by the bottle). To order appetizers, see their short "tapas" menu (8–13 SF). For a full meal, browse among the many bottles and take your favorite into the restaurant, where they serve tasty and beautifully presented Mediterranean dishes (25–45-SF plates, 19-SF daily specials, strong on vegetables). Locals sip their wine and hang out on the big, modern sun terrace (daily 9:00–24:00, later on weekends, below the pedestrian bridge and across from Lausanne-Flon Métro stop at Place de l'Europe 9, tel. 021-320-1313).

Le Lyrique is a neighborhood restaurant filled with locals enjoying their *souvlaki, keftedes,* and calamari in a warm, candlelit interior. The traditionally Greek dishes include vegetarian options, and the wine selection is good (18–35-SF main dishes, Mon–Sat 12:00–14:00 & 18:00–22:30, closed Sun, no English menu, Rue Beau-Séjour 29, tel. 021-312-8887).

Traiteur Bosphore is a good option for a quick and inexpensive take-away lunch or early dinner. Popular with locals who enjoy the better-than-average *döner kebabs* (8 SF), the place has no seating—stand at back counter or walk to the nearby Place de la Louve and find a seat with the other budget eaters (Mon–Fri 9:30–19:00, Sat 8:30–1:00 in the morning, closed Sun, Rue de la Louve 7, across from Manor department store, tel. 021-311-0770).

Lausanne Connections

From Lausanne by Train to: Montreux (4/hr, 25 min), **Château de Chillon** (2/hr, 35 min on REV train), **Geneva** (5/hr, 40 min), **Geneva Airport** (4/hr, 45–55 min), **Bern** (2/hr, 70 min), **Murten** (hourly, 1.5 hrs, change in Fribourg, Neuchâtel, or Payerne), **Interlaken** (2/hr, 2.25 hrs, transfer in Bern; or go by Golden Pass scenic route, with transfers in Montreux and Zweisimmen—see the Scenic Rail Journeys chapter), **Luzern** (hourly, 2.25 hrs direct; more frequent with transfer in Olten and/or Bern; or go by Golden Pass route—see the Scenic Rail Journeys chapter), **Zürich** (2/hr, 2.25 hrs), **Zermatt** (1–2/hr, 3 hrs, change in Visp—not Brig, unless connecting to Glacier Express), **Lyon** (almost hourly, 2.75–3.25 hrs, transfer in Geneva), **Chamonix** (every 2 hrs, 2.5–3 hrs, change in Martigny and/or Le Châtelard-Frontière), **Paris** (6/day, 4 hrs). Train info: toll tel. 0900-300-300 or www.rail.ch.

By Boat: For boat connections from Lausanne, see "Getting Around Lake Geneva" near the beginning of this chapter.

By Plane: Lausanne and the Lake Geneva area are served by the airport in the city of **Geneva,** at the lake's southwest corner. The airport sits on the western edge of Geneva, straddling the French border—it's straightforward and easy to manage. Exiting from the baggage claim area, you're met by various local tourist information desks. To the left is a bank of ATMs and, beyond that, the airport's train station, with handy connections all over Switzerland. Geneva's city-center train station is the first stop on any train departing from the airport; you can get a free ticket for this short hop in the baggage-claim area (before customs—look for machines). Trains leave for Lausanne about four times each hour (25 SF, 45–55 min).

Route Tips for Drivers

If connecting the Lake Geneva sights by car, note the various routes. The expressway high above the lake zips you quickly between Lausanne and Montreux; although slower, the lakeside road provides great lake-and-vineyards views for about half of the drive (but also passes through several congested towns along the way).

For an even slower but more scenic approach, consider detouring to the **Corniche de Lavaux**. This rugged, sometimes frightening Swiss Wine Road swerves through picturesque towns and the stingy vineyards that produce Lake Geneva's tasty but expensive wine. It lies roughly between Lausanne and Montreux; to get a taste, detour from the lakeside road between Cully (near Lausanne) and Vevey (near Montreux). Going in either direction, follow signs for Chexbres to find the wine road. The "Route de la Corniche" between Chexbres and Cully is particularly well-known. Note that this isn't a tidy, straightforward route; expect lots of exploring on twisty vineyard roads. Getting lost is the point.

Château de Chillon

This medieval castle, set wistfully at the edge of Lake Geneva on the outskirts of Montreux, is a ▲▲▲ joy. Because it's built on a

rocky island, it has a uniquely higgledy-piggledy shape that combines both a stout fortress (on the land side) and a residence (on the lake side). Remarkably well-preserved, Château de Chillon (shee-yohn) has never been damaged or destroyed—always inhabited, always maintained. Today it's Switzerland's best castle experience. Enjoy the château's tingly views, dank prison, battle-scarred weapons, simple Swiss-style mobile furniture, and 700-year-old toilets. Stroll the patrol ramparts, then curl up on a windowsill to enjoy the lake.

Getting to Château de Chillon

The castle sits at the eastern tip of Lake Geneva, about 20 miles east of Lausanne, and about two miles east of Montreux. From Lausanne you can connect to the castle using a combination of various methods: train, bus, boat, and hike. For a memorable outing, consider mixing and matching these various options.

The twice-hourly **REV train** (direction: Villeneuve, 35 min,

10.80 SF) takes you directly to the station at Veytaux-Chillon, a 10-minute walk along the lake (ideal for picnicking) from the castle.

The faster, more frequent **Direct train** whisks you to Montreux (4/hr, 20 min, 10.20 SF), where you transfer to a bus. From the Montreux station, cross Avenue des Alpes and go down the stairs. Cross the street and find the blue bus stop on your right, where you can hop **bus #1** to Château de Chillon (3.20 SF, direction: Villeneuve, stop: Chillon; buy tickets from machine, select fare: Adult, zone 77). You can also **hike** the two miles from Montreux to Château de Chillon (figure about 45 minutes one-way).

To return to Lausanne, simply reverse the directions (catch the train from the Veytaux-Chillon station back to Lausanne—trains leave hourly at :26 past the hour—or hop the bus from Château de Chillon to Montreux, direction: Vevey, stop: Escaliers de la Gare, take handy escalator up to the station and catch the train the rest of the way to Lausanne).

A slower but more scenic route to Château de Chillon is by **boat;** you can cruise between the château and Montreux (20 min), Vevey (30 min), or even Lausanne (1.5 hours). For details, see "Getting Around Lake Geneva" on page 227.

Orientation to Château de Chillon

Cost and Hours: 12 SF, 6 SF with Riviera Card (see "Sleeping in Montreux"), free with Swiss Pass, 28-SF family ticket, daily April–Sept 9:00–19:00, March and Oct 9:30–18:00, Nov–Feb 10:00–17:00, last entry one hour before closing, free and easy parking along road above the castle, then walk down to entrance, tel. 021-966-8910, www.chillon.ch.

Audioguide: The excellent 6-SF iPod audioguide is worth the investment if you want a thorough tour of the complex; bring a splitter and extra headphones to share one with your travel partner (1.5 hours, leave ID as deposit). My self-guided tour hits the highlights.

Eating: Food available at the castle is expensive, whether from the vending machines inside or the basic garden café outside. This is an ideal place to bring your own picnic.

Background

The aristocratic Savoy family (their seal is the skinny red cross on the towers) enlarged Château de Chillon to its current state in the 13th century, when this was a prime location—at a crossroads of a major trade route from England and France to Rome. This was the Savoys' fortress and residence, with four big halls (a major status symbol) and impractically large lakeview windows (because their powerful navy could defend against possible attack from the water). But when the Bernese invaded in 1536, the castle was conquered in just two days, and the new governor made Château de Chillon his residence (and a Counter-Reformation prison). With the help of French troops, the French-speaking Swiss on Lake Geneva finally kicked out their German-speaking Bernese oppressors in 1798. The castle became—and remains—the property of the canton of Vaud. It's been used as an armory, a warehouse, a prison, a hospital, and a tourist attraction. Jean-Jacques Rousseau's writings first drew attention to the castle, inspiring visits by Romantics such as Lord Byron and Victor Hugo, plus other notables, including Dickens, Goethe, and Hemingway.

Self-Guided Tour

Conquering Château de Chillon

When you buy your ticket, ask for the free self-guided English brochure and map. The numbers below correspond to those in the brochure, on the audioguide, and posted at the site.

You'll cross a natural moat (since the château is built on an island) and enter the **first courtyard** (#3). In the room marked #4, you can pick up an audioguide and get oriented with a good model of the castle.

Head down the stairs marked *5/9* to a series of cellars. You can see how the castle was built upon a foundation of jagged natural stone. At the far end is Room #9, **Bonivard's Prison,** named for a renegade Savoyard who was tortured here for five years (lashed to the fifth column from the entrance). When the Romantic poet Lord Byron came to visit, Bonivard's story inspired him to write *The Prisoner of Chillon,* which vividly recounts a prisoner's dark and solitary life ("And mine has been the fate of those/To whom the goodly earth and air/Are bann'd, and barr'd—forbidden fare"; full text available in the gift shop). You can still see where Byron scratched his name in a column (third from entrance, covered by glass).

Head back out into the daylight and turn left through the big gate into the **second courtyard** (#12), which is dominated by the towering keep (more on that later). Just before the keep on the left, go into the **constable's dining room** (#13), one of the château's finest halls. The gigantic fireplace was used to roast large animals (including bears and boars) for feasts. The opposite wall has the first of many grand lakeview windows you'll see in the castle. Look up to the six-centuries-old wooden ceiling.

Climb up the spiral staircase to the *aula nova* (#14), with a striking barrel-vaulted ceiling that was restored in the 1920s. The collection of mobile furniture recalls a time when nobility traveled throughout their realm (and took their belongings with them) to keep an eye on things and collect taxes. In fact, in many European languages, the word for "furniture" implies that it's mobile—German *Möbel*, French *mobilier*, and so on. Enjoy the ornate decorations on each traveling chest.

Continue up to the **private quarters** (#15–17). The **bedroom** (#16) has a short bed—only about five and a half feet long. Not only were people shorter back then, but they slept propped up. The **coat-of-arms hall** (#18) is usually filled with temporary exhibits. The walls are lined with the family crests of some 50 "bailiffs" who governed this territory during Bernese rule. Capping this hall is another great wooden ceiling.

Exit at the far end of the hall, and turn right into the *camera domini* (#19), the bedroom of the master of the house. This location—at the farthest end of the castle from the entrance—was particularly secure. In the corner, notice the spiral stairs (closed to the public) that the lord could use to scamper down to Mass in his private chapel, or up to the ramparts. Under a sumptuous red fleur-de-lis ceiling, wall paintings (imitating tapestries) illustrate various animals, including the trademark Bernese bear.

Leave the room and turn right (following the *20/24* sign), and pass through a few more rooms—making sure not to miss the **medieval latrines** (#21, on the left), a feature that aims to please a certain class of traveler. You'll end up in a **small courtyard** (#23), which leads to that **private chapel** (#24) where the lord's staircase ended up.

Leave this room following the signs for *26,* and you'll wind up in the **third courtyard** (#25). Notice that the courtyard's irregular shape causes the angled walkways to focus your attention on the grand window of the master's bedroom—the *camera domini* we visited earlier. There's no question who was the king of this castle.

Go in the door marked *26/33.* The *aula magna* (#26) is yet another grand hall— this one for banquets—with spectacular lakeview windows. Proceed through a few more rooms (including more latrines, #29) to the *domus clericorum* (#31). In this "house of the clerks," the castle bean-counters kept meticulous records of all money and goods that passed through here, creating an invaluable historical record. In Room #32 you'll find a series of **models and illustrations** that explain the gradual construction of the château over time.

Climb back up into the third courtyard again, then pass through to the **fourth courtyard** (#34). Remember the grand views from the lakeside windows? Notice the small slits facing the road on the landside, which are more practical for defense.

Now's the time to scramble along the **sentry walk**—perhaps pretending that you're defending the château from invaders—as you pass through various indoor rooms and outdoor galleries (marked *38/46*). Enjoy the castle courtyard and lake views.

You'll circle all the way around to the **keep** (#42), which was

the last line of defense and final refuge in the event of a siege. To climb to the top of the eight-story tower, you can scale 76 claustrophobic steps for views over the castle, lake, and surrounding mountains. From here you can see France (across the lake) as well as three different Swiss cantons.

Our tour is over. You may scramble the ramparts, enjoy the lake views, and play king of the castle at will.

Montreux

This expensive resort is famous for its jazz festival each July. The lakeside promenade takes you along parks, palm trees, *crêperies,* ice-cream stands, modern sculptures, and the Friday produce market. In the center, meet the statue of Freddie Mercury, who had strong bonds with Montreux. His band, Queen, bought the local Mountain Recording Studios in 1978.

The wonderful Montreux **TI** has tons of brochures and extensive information about the region, excursions, and a list of moderately priced rooms in the center (mid-May–mid-Sept Mon–Fri 9:00–18:00, Sat–Sun 9:30–17:00; off-season Mon–Fri 9:00–12:00 & 13:00–17:30, Sat–Sun 10:00–14:00; tel. 084-886-8484, www.montreuxriviera.com). In summer you can take a two-hour **walking tour** of the city (10 SF, April–Sept Wed–Sat at 10:00, no tours Sun–Tue or Oct–March, meet in front of TI, call TI to confirm).

For an easy way to see several sights in the French Swiss countryside, including the town of Gruyères and the chocolate factory in Broc, take a ride from Montreux on the **Chocolate Train** (described on the next page).

The **boat** connecting Montreux to Lausanne, Château de Chillon, and several other Lake Geneva destinations departs from the big park next to the TI (see page 227).

Sleeping in Montreux

(1 SF = about $1, country code: 41)

Accommodations in Montreux levy a tourist tax of 3.50 SF per person per night (generally not included in the rates listed below). This buys you a Riviera Card, giving you free use of local buses and discounts on sights (including half off at Château de Chillon), trains, and boats.

$$$ Hôtel Splendid claims to be the second-oldest hotel in town, with faded public spaces and 28 refurbished rooms. The front rooms are bigger and more expensive, with lake views worth the extra cost (Sb-115–160 SF, Db-190–230 SF, Tb-255–280 SF, non-smoking, elevator, free Internet access and Wi-Fi, 5-min walk from train station, across the street from TI, above Mayfair Café at Grand-Rue 52, tel. 021-966-7979, fax 021-966-7977, www.hotel-splendid.ch, info@hotel-splendid.ch, David).

$$ Hôtel Parc et Lac, just a few doors down from Hôtel Splendid, has seen better days, but its 30 creaky rooms—with worn carpets and old furnishings—have a certain charm. It also has about the cheapest beds you'll find in the town center. Rooms in front are more expensive and come with a nice view of the lake (most with small balconies), but also some street noise (Sb-100–120 SF, Db-150–160 SF, elevator, free Wi-Fi, 5-min walk from train station, Grand-Rue 38, tel. 021-963-3738, fax 021-963-2317, parcetlac@bluewin.ch).

$ Montreux Youth Hostel is on the lake in the village of Territet, actually closer to Château de Chillon than to Montreux (bunk in 6-bed dorm-34 SF, bunk in 4-bed dorm-38 SF, D-96 SF, includes breakfast and sheets, nonmembers pay 6 SF extra, 15-SF meals available, check-in 17:00–22:00, Passage de l'Auberge 8, tel. 021-963-4934, fax 021-963-2729, www.youthhostel.ch/montreux, montreux@youthhostel.ch).

$ Backpackers Riviera Lodge, centrally located on the main square in nearby Vevey, offers "chic and cheap" beds in a 19th-century townhouse on the lake (July–mid-Sept: dorm bed-32 SF, D-98 SF; mid-March–June and mid-Sept–Oct: dorm bed-30 SF, D-90 SF; cheaper Nov–mid-March, sheets included in doubles or 5 SF extra in dorms, breakfast-8 SF, Internet access and Wi-Fi, kitchen, laundry facilities, reception open 8:00–12:00 & 16:00–20:00, 3-min walk from station, Place du Marché 5, tel. 021-923-8040, www.rivieralodge.ch, info@rivieralodge.ch).

Montreux Connections

From Montreux by Train to: Lausanne (4/hr, 25 min), **Bern** (2/hr, 1.5 hrs, transfer in Lausanne), **Geneva** (2/hr, 1–1.25 hr).

French Swiss Countryside

The sublime French Swiss countryside is sprinkled with crystal-clear lakes, tasty chocolates, fragrant cheese, and sleepy cows. If

you're passing through this enticing region, take time to sample a few of its sights, tastes, and smells.

I've divided these attractions into two groups: in and around Gruyères (easy to reach by car or train), and in the mountains southeast of Lake Geneva (out of the way and worthwhile only with a car).

Around the famous and touristy cheesemaking town of Gruyères, just north of Lake Geneva, you'll find two very different cheesemakers, a tourable chocolate factory, and a workaday town with a fine folk museum. This area is particularly handy if you're traveling between Lake Geneva and points north (e.g., Bern, Murten, or the Berner Oberland). In the mountainous area southeast of the lake, you'll find a remote, time-passed cow-herding village and a lift to a mountaintop glacier.

Getting Around the French Swiss Countryside

The Gruyères region is ideal by car. By public transportation, it's a bit more challenging, but workable. The city of Fribourg and the large town of Bulle are the area's transit hubs. Major trains go through Fribourg, from which you can take the bus to Bulle (2/hr, 30 min). From Bulle, trains connect easily to Gruyères (hourly, 7 min) and to Broc (hourly, 10 min). Buses are less useful, but a few routes are worth knowing about, including Bulle–Gruyères–Moléson (5/day, 15 min from Bulle to Gruyères, then 15–20 min more to Moléson).

For an easy all-day side-trip from Lake Geneva, consider hopping on the **Chocolate Train** in Montreux. The train carries

French Switzerland

To Fribourg & Bern

A12 · N12

FRANCE

To Paris

Vallorbe

To Yverdon

To Avenches & Murten

Romont

Lake Gruyère

A1 · E23

N1

Bulle

(CHOCOLATE FACTORY)

Broc

E27

Le Pâquier

Gruyères

To Spiez & Interlaken

Lausanne

Pal.

N12

Moléson

CHOCOLATE TRAIN

To Geneva

A1 · E62

Cully

A9

CORNICHE DE LAVAUX

Mont-bovon

Ouchy

Chexbres

Nyon

Vevey

Gstaad

Lake Geneva

Montreux

Château de Chillon

GOLDEN PASS TRAIN

Evian-les-Bains

Ville-Neuve

Les Diablerets

Gsteig

To Yvoire

COL DU PILLON

To Geneva

N11

COL DE LA CROIX

GLACIER DES DIABLERETS

FRANCE

Aigle

Ollon

Taveyanne

Villars-sur-Ollon

To Geneva

Bex

Barboleusaz

A9

A9 · N9

To Zermatt & Milan

SWITZ.

10 Miles

10 Kilometers

To Chamonix

Martigny

either panoramic or old-time belle époque coaches. It leaves from Montreux at 9:25 and begins by following the same route as the Golden Pass (described in the Scenic Rail Journeys chapter). You'll be served coffee and a croissant while enjoying the scenic ride. At 10:45, the train lets you off for a visit to the Gruyères cheese factory. From there, a bus takes you up to the picturesque old town of Gruyères for a visit to the castle (included) and some time for lunch (on your own). Then the journey continues to the town of Broc, where you'll tour the Cailler Chocolate Factory (including a film and chocolate tasting). The train returns to Montreux at 18:10 (89 SF, first class only, 39 SF reservation fee with first-class Swiss Pass, or 49 SF fee with second-class Swiss Pass, July–Aug daily; May–June and Sept–Oct Mon, Wed, and Thu only; toll tel. 0900-245-245, from European countries outside Switzerland call 00-41-840-245-245, from the US call 011-41-840-245-245, www goldenpass.ch/goldenpass_chocolate_train).

The sights to the southeast of Lake Geneva (Taveyanne and the Glacier des Diablerets), though beautiful, aren't worth trying to do on public transit—without a car, I'd skip them.

Gruyères

This ultratouristy town, famous for its cheese, fills its fortified hilltop like a bouquet. Its ramparts are a park, and the ancient buildings serve tourists. Everything is expensive, from the museums to the food, but the town's magical ambience makes it worth a visit.

Orientation to Gruyères

The helpful **TI** is at the town entrance (daily 9:30–12:00 & 13:00–17:30, no lunch break July–Aug, shorter hours off-season, tel. 0848-424-424, www.la-gruyere.ch). The ATM, with its conspicuous location just in front of the TI, strikes a delicate balance between convenient and greedy.

Arrival in Gruyères: The town's train station is at the foot of the hill, a steep 15-minute hike up to the village itself. If you're driving, note the three parking lots on the way up to the town—to reduce walking, drive as high up as you can find space.

Sights in and near Gruyères

In Gruyères

Gruyères' main attraction is the charming town itself. Wander

around the manicured main square, which feels like a movie set. You'll see the town symbol—the crane (*grue* in French)—everywhere. If you have time to kill and/or a special interest, consider dipping into one of these three museums.

Castle—Gruyères' castle has a fine setting and a ho-hum interior. While tidy and nicely restored, the place feels empty and could use a lively audioguide—it's not quite worth the cost of entry, but it merits a short stop if you have a Swiss Pass. Admission includes a dull 18-minute audiovisual show about the town's history, heavy on myths and legends (you'll be assigned an entry time when you buy your ticket). Then, with the help of the English brochure, you can explore the various halls and rooms of the castle itself. Spend some time poking around the grounds, including the view terrace and the manicured garden (9.50 SF, 17-SF combo-ticket includes Giger Museum, covered by Swiss Pass, daily April–Oct 9:00–18:00, Nov–March 10:00–16:30, last entry 30 min before closing, tel. 026-921-2102, www.chateau-gruyeres.ch).

H. R. Giger Museum—This museum—a spooky, offbeat contrast to idyllic Gruyères—is dedicated to the Swiss artist who designed the monsters in the *Alien* movies. Not for the faint of heart, this museum shares those movies' dark aesthetic. It also displays temporary exhibits by other out-there artists (12.50 SF, 17-SF combo-ticket includes castle, covered by Swiss Pass, April–Oct daily 10:00–18:00; Nov–March Tue–Fri 13:00–17:00, Sat–Sun 10:00–18:00, closed Mon; below the castle in the Château St. Germain, tel. 026-921-2200, www.hrgigermuseum.com).

Tibet Museum—Rounding out Gruyères' oddball attractions is this offbeat but genuinely interesting collection of art and artifacts—statues, paintings, and other objects—from the top of the world. These prized Tibetan possessions of a Swiss collector are thoughtfully displayed inside a former church, making it feel as though the Tibetan deities are squatting in Jesus' old house. Dim lighting and mood music add to the mellow ambience. It's very small—especially considering its high price—but might interest anyone who enjoys Tibetan culture (12 SF, covered by Swiss Pass; April–Oct daily 11:00–18:00; Nov–March Mon–Fri 13:00–17:00, Sat–Sun 11:00–18:00, closed Mon; 4 Rue de Château, tel. 026-921-3010, www.tibetmuseum.ch).

▲▲Fromageries near Gruyères

Gruyères is justifiably famous for its Gruyère cheese (no "s" at the end when it comes to the cheese itself). In fact, since 2001 the cheese has been an A.O.C. product, meaning that to be called Gruyère, it must be made right here, according to exacting standards. In addition to the cheese you'll find on menus, the breakfast table, and everywhere else, you can actually watch cheese being made. Choose your cheese-production setting: an old farm in the hills outside town, or in a new facility handy to the town. If you have time and interest, consider visiting both.

Ye Olde Cheesemaker: Moléson Fromagerie d'Alpage—Five miles above Gruyères, a dark and smoky 17th-century farmhouse in the village of Moléson gives you a fun look at the traditional, smelly way of crafting cheese in a huge cauldron over an open fire. There's no point venturing here unless you actually get to watch them make the cheese (May–Sept daily at 10:00, June–Aug also at 14:30). Since space is limited, it's wise to reserve a slot the day before (the staff speaks only French—consider asking your hotelier or the Moléson TI to reserve for you; TI tel. 026-921-8500). You'll see a slow-moving video that traces the entire process (with some English titles), then you'll watch them do it all again in the flesh: First the milk is brought to the proper temperature and consistency. Then the cheesemaker skims out the curds with a cloth and packs it into a frame to drain and compress. Finally he chops it into blocks and separates it into smaller circular frames that will turn it into wheels of cheese. They dispense cups of the cheesemaking leftovers (milk minus curds, a.k.a. whey) for visitors to taste—it's like sweet skim milk. Then the cheesemaker takes buckets of the whey out to feed to the pigs. Unfortunately, there's not a word of English during the presentation, but even for non-Francophones, it's still fascinating (5 SF, or 4 SF without the presentation—pointless as it's otherwise just a rustic barn with a cheese shop, mid-May–Sept daily 9:00–19:00, closed off-season, Place de l'Aigle 12, tel. 026-921-1044, www.fromagerie-alpage.ch).

Getting There: From Gruyères, it's about a 10-minute drive (follow signs to *Moléson*). Park in the giant lot at the entrance to the village, then hike about five minutes up to the *fromagerie*—just follow the cartoon cows. Buses connect Gruyères and Moléson, but service is sparse (best in the morning).

Moléson: Aside from the cheesemaker, the sleepy village of Moléson has a few other high-mountain attractions, as well as a very helpful **TI** (Mon–Sat 8:00–12:00 & 13:30–18:00, closed Sun, tel. 026-921-8500, www.moleson.ch). There's a **luge ride** on the hillside adjacent to the *fromagerie* (6 SF, July–Aug daily 10:00–18:00, June and Sept–Oct Sat–Sun only). From the parking lot, a **lift** carries you in two stages (funicular, then cable car) to a mountaintop perch, offering you a lovely view over the Gruyères countryside (27 SF round-trip, departs every 20 min, May–Oct daily 9:00–18:00).

Cheese Factory: La Maison du Gruyère—This modern cheese-production center at the foot of Gruyères opens its doors to tourists, sharing such facts as these: A cow consumes 100 kilograms of grass and 85 liters of water each day to produce 25 liters of milk; and 400 liters of milk goes into making one 35-kilogram wheel of cheese. Admission includes a sample of three varieties of Gruyère cheese (aged different lengths of time), plus an audioguide narrated by an English-speaking cow named Cherry, essential for understanding the otherwise sparse exhibits. Punch in the number listed next to each display to learn about the whole process. You'll be able to smell various alpine flowers and plants (which imbue the cheese with subtle flavors) and touch various cheesemaking tools. Then you'll look through big windows down to the production floor, where cheese is being made. It's most interesting when the cheese production is going on (9:00–11:00 & 12:30–14:30); the action peaks at the end, when the curds are pulled from the vats (around 10:30 and 14:00). Even if cheesemakers aren't working during your visit, video screens show the process. The finale is the cellar (near the ticket desk), where long rows of cheese wheels age. You can watch a robot cheesemaker move up and down the aisles, lovingly flipping and rubbing each wheel just right (7 SF, 12-SF family ticket, daily 9:00–19:00, until 18:00 Oct–May, restaurant, well-stocked gift shop, straight ahead as you come down the road from Gruyères' hilltop, tel. 026-921-8400, www.lamaisondu gruyere.ch).

More Sights near Gruyères

The following worthwhile sights—a folk museum and a chocolate factory—are just a short hop north of Gruyères.

Bulle

The biggest town in the region is Bulle (pronounced "bool"), which has a charming, distinctly French ambience and proudly flies banners with its mascot and namesake bull. Unlike the many cutesy time-passed villages in this region, Bulle feels like a real town. On Tuesdays the weekly produce-and-craft market fills the center of town. The market gets bigger and more colorful in summer, when many vendors wear their traditional costumes and sell handmade crafts. The castle that dominates the main square, while impressive from the outside, is closed to the public (it houses municipal offices).

The **TI**, which covers the entire region, is located between the castle and the train station (Mon–Fri 9:00–12:00 & 14:00–18:00, Sat 9:00–12:00, closed Sun, Place des Alpes 26, tel. 0848-424-424, www.la-gruyere.ch).

▲**Musée Gruèrien**—Somehow the unassuming little town of Bulle built a refreshing, cheery folk museum that manages to teach you all about life in these parts and leave you feeling good. A two-minute walk behind the castle (through the grounds and garden), the museum is located in the basement of the local library, with thoughtfully selected pieces well-displayed in one large room. The self-guided English tour guidebooklet you'll pick up at the entry helps bring the exhibits to life. In this cheese-crazy region, cows are key—notice the many cowbells displayed and the panels from barns painted with murals of the cows' twice-yearly procession up and down the Alps (8 SF, Tue–Sat 10:00–12:00 & 14:00–17:00, Sun 14:00–17:00, closed Mon, tel. 026-916-1010, www.musee-gruerien.ch). When the tour is over, the guidebooklet beseeches you, "Don't you think that the Musée Gruèrien offers sufficient material to justify an additional visit? The Golden Book of Visitors awaits your signature and your comments. Thank you for your visit!"

Cailler Chocolate Factory

To fight their image of being a boring "old grannies'" chocolate, Cailler invited famous designers to reinvent the brand. Wonderful new chocolate creations resulted. The winner of the competition was Parisian Jean Nouvel (the architect responsible for Luzern's Culture and Conference Center). Nouvel also designed imaginative displays for the factory, and a revamped "Maison Callier" visitors center opened in April 2010 with a new tour: Chocolate-dark corridors lead to exhibits about the production and shipment of chocolate, a collection of old chocolate molds, vintage films about chocolate production, and an opportunity to taste almonds and hazelnuts, crumble a cocoa bean in the palm of your hand, and touch a block of cocoa butter. In the tasting room, friendly employees are happy to answer questions as visitors sample creations from elegant trays. Peek into the actual working factory, as video screens explain the process, before concluding in the chock-full-of-chocolate gift shop (likely April–Oct Mon–Fri 9:30–16:00, closed Sat–Sun and Nov–March, groups of 4 or more should call a day in advance to reserve, located in sweet-smelling town of Broc, follow signs to *Nestlé* and *Broc Fabrique*, tel. 026-921-5151, http://main.cailler.ch).

Sleeping in and near Gruyères

Hotels in Gruyères are expensive. If you'd like to pay a premium to sleep right on Gruyères' main square, you can do it at **$$$ Hostellerie Saint-Georges,** which has 14 small, old-fashioned rooms above a restaurant (Sb-130 SF, Db-180 SF, 20 SF more for view, 40 SF more for large view room, free Wi-Fi, tel. 026-921-8300, www.hostellerie-saint-georges.com, hostellerie-st-georges@swiss online.ch).

For something more affordable, I prefer **$$ B&B Lepatchi,** at the main intersection of the nearby town of Le Pâquier, a five-minute drive or easy train ride from Gruyères (toward Bulle). At this B&B, André and Hedwige rent three pleasantly appointed rooms with kitchenettes (Db-120 SF, or 110 SF mid-Sept–mid-June, 2-night stays preferred, free Wi-Fi, Rue de la Gare 10, tel. 026-912-2025, mobile 079-774-4990, www.lepatchi.ch, contact @lepatchi.ch).

Eating in Gruyères

The main square of Gruyères is surrounded by eateries with indoor and outdoor seating, serving (guess what?) all manner of Gruyère cheese dishes. These places are more or less interchangeable; pick the place that looks best to you. **Chalet de Gruyères** looks like a giant cuckoo clock perched atop the square (on the way to the castle). With stuffy indoor seating or a fine terrace, this restaurant has a good reputation and serves up huge portions (20–40-SF meals, open daily, tel. 026-921-2154).

Countryside Sights Southeast of Lake Geneva

Tucked in the slow-going mountainous countryside just southeast of Lake Geneva, these two places are less convenient than the ones listed above, as they're not in the immediate direction of other recommended destinations. They do, however, give you a French-flavored taste of high-altitude life in *les Alpes suisse.*

▲▲Taveyanne

This remote hamlet is a huddle of log cabins used by cowherds in the summer. Actually part of a nature reserve, Taveyanne is two miles off the main road between Col de la Croix and Villars (a small sign points down a tiny road to a jumble of huts and snoozing cows stranded at 5,000 feet). The hamlet's old bar is a restaurant, serving a tiny community of vacationers and hikers.

The town's inn is **$ Refuge de Taveyanne** (from 1882), where the Seibenthal family serves meals in a rustic setting with no electricity, low ceilings, and a huge, charred fireplace. Consider sleeping in their primitive five-mattress loft (15 SF, D-30 SF, cash only, access by a ladder outside, bathroom outside, closed Mon–Tue except July–Aug, closed Nov–April, tel. 024-498-1947). It's a great opportunity to really get to know prizewinning cows...you'll see, hear, and smell them all around.

Getting There: Taveyanne is perched in the middle of nowhere, on a backcountry, summer-only road that twists from Villars to Col de la Croix. From Lake Geneva (Lausanne or Montreux), head south on expressway 9. From here there are various ways to reach Villars (a.k.a. Villars-sur-Ollon). From Villars, proceed toward Col de la Croix; along this road, watch for the Taveyanne turnoff. Or, for a less straightforward but particularly scenic approach, stay on expressway 9 to the Bex exit. Drive through Bex, then follow signs to Gryon and Villars. You'll twist up through tidy vineyards and villages to the pleasant town of Gryon. Shortly after Gryon (but before Villars), in the town of Barboleusaz, keep an eye out for *Taveyanne* signs, which you'll carefully track on very narrow mountain roads. After visiting Taveyanne, you can go more directly to the main Villars–Col de la Coix. Note that these roads are extremely narrow and winding, through meadows, woods, and along cliffs; Taveyanne is not for fainthearted drivers.

Glacier des Diablerets

For a grand alpine trip to the tip of a 10,000-foot peak, ascend

to the Glacier des Diablerets, which does its icy thing high above the charming town of Les Diablerets. Up top you'll not only have views of peaks all around and a vast glacier slowly oozing down below you, but also have access to fun attractions (such as a mountaintop luge trip, chairlift ride, and chance to ride across the glacier on a "snow bus"). While similar lifts in the Berner Oberland and Zermatt area are more thrilling, this is French Switzerland's answer to high-altitude fun. Allow about an hour and a half total to get your money's worth.

The handiest approach is from **Col du Pillon,** a 10-minute drive east of Les Diablerets (on the smaller road toward Gstaad). Here you'll load into the cable car, ride five minutes up, switch to another car (follow *Glacier* signs), then ride another five minutes to the summit. In just 15 minutes total, you're standing on a perch overlooking a glacier, with alpine panoramas all around, and plenty of activities to keep you entertained.

The top of the lift is called **Scex Rouge**. The boxy gray tower adjacent to the cable car has an elevator zipping you to various services (shop, view terrace, self-service cafeteria, and a sit-down restaurant). Ride the elevator to floor 3 and use the walkway to reach the staircase up to the summit viewpoint, where orientation panels identify the mountain ranges all around you. You can see the Matterhorn and a bit of Mont Blanc, the Alps' highest peak. At your feet sprawls a glacier filled with skiers in cold weather (Oct–May), gray and gloomy in summer.

Just outside the main building are several other options. The most exciting is the **"alpine coaster"**—actually the world's highest luge course, perched on a rocky bluff (6 SF per ride). You'll sit on a plastic sled and shoot down a 1,000-meter-long metal rail, with twists and turns that feel like they're about to send you over the edge (pull back on your handles to brake as needed). At the end, you and your cart are pulled safely back up to the top. A **chairlift** (included in your lift ticket) takes you down to the glacier itself, where you can pay 15 SF to ride a **"snow bus"** across its surface.

Cost and Hours: 58 SF round-trip, departs every 20 min, daily early May–mid-Sept 9:00–16:50, Oct–early May 9:00–16:30, closed for maintenance in late Sept, these are last ascent times, tel. 024-492-0923, www.glacier3000.ch.

Getting There: It's easiest for drivers, who will find the base of the Col du Pillon lift about 10 minutes west of Les Diablerets. (If you'd like a scenic drive through the mountains on smaller roads, this combines well with a visit to Taveyanne.) It's doable by public transportation: Take the train to Les Diablerets, where there are eight buses per day to Col du Pillon.

LUGANO

Lugano, the leading city of the Italian-speaking Swiss canton of Ticino, gives you Switzerland with an Italian accent. The town (population 53,000) sprawls luxuriously along the shores of Lake Lugano. Just a short, scenic train ride over the Alps from the German and French regions of Switzerland, Lugano has a splashy, zesty, Mediterranean ambience. It attracts vacationers from the rainy north with its sunshine, lush vegetation, inviting lake, and shopping. While many travelers come here for the fancy boutiques, others make this a base for hiking, cruising the lake, and passing lazy afternoons in its many gardens. Its mountains aren't mighty, its beaches are lousy, the cityscape is nothing thrilling, and it can all feel a little geriatric, but Lugano has a unique charm that merits at least a short visit.

Planning Your Time

Lugano lies conveniently at the intersection of the William Tell Express and the Bernina Express—two of Switzerland's more scenic train rides. Blitz sightseers arrive on the William Tell one day and take off on the Bernina Express the next.

If relaxing is on your itinerary, spend two nights and a full day here, arriving and departing on the scenic trains. With a day, spend the morning exploring the old town with my self-guided walk, then do a boat cruise and ascend a mountain lift in the afternoon. Extra time (and you'll have some) can be spent relaxing in gardens and along the lakefront.

Orientation to Lugano

The old town is on Lake Lugano, which is bordered by promenades and parks. A funicular connects the old town with the train station above. Nearly everything in this chapter (with the exception of the mountain lifts) is within a five-minute walk of the base of the funicular. The town of Lugano fades into other, smaller waterfront communities all around the lake.

Note that most people in Lugano speak Italian; you're surrounded on three sides by Italy (see "Italian Survival Phrases" in the appendix). In this corner of Switzerland, a *Strasse* (street) becomes a *Via*, and a *Platz* (square) becomes a *Piazza*.

Tourist Information

Lugano's TI faces the boat dock a couple of blocks below the funicular (Easter–mid-Oct Mon–Fri 9:00–19:00, Sat 9:00–18:00, Sun 10:00–18:00; off-season Mon–Fri 9:00–12:00 & 14:00–17:30, Sat 10:00–12:30 & 13:30–17:00, closed Sun; Palazzo Civico, Riva Albertolli, tel. 091-913-3232, fax 091-922-7653, www.lugano -tourism.ch).

The TI offers free **walking tours** in English four days a week, with a different theme each day (Mon at 9:30—classic tour; Thu at 9:30—history through architecture; Fri at 14:30—to the top of Monte Brè; Sun at 10:00—parks and gardens; all tours 2.5 hours except Monte Brè, which is 4 hours; details at TI).

Arrival in Lugano

The train station has lockers (in the underground passage and out front, small locker-5 SF, big locker-8 SF, always accessible), a less convenient and pricier baggage-storage counter (10 SF, short hours), ATMs, a convenient grocery (Piccobello, daily 6:00–22:00), a surprisingly genteel restaurant, and a room-finding service—but no real TI. The easiest way to get to the town below is by funicular (look for *funicolare per il centro* sign in the middle of the station, every 5 min, daily 5:20–23:50, 1.10 SF, free with Swiss Pass). The funicular deposits you right in the heart of the old town, at Piazza Cioccaro, a short walk from my recommended accommodations (and at the start of my self-guided walk).

Helpful Hints

Internet Access: Mondialpay is the only real Internet café in town (8 SF/hr, Mon–Fri 9:00–18:30, Sat 10:00–17:00, closed Sun, Via Canova 9).

Local Guide: Christa Branchi teaches enthusiastically about her hometown (180 SF/1–3 hrs, 220 SF/half-day, 330 SF/day, tel. 091-606-3302, christabranchi@hotmail.com).

Self-Guided Walk

Welcome to Lugano

While many might think a guided walk of resort Lugano is absurd, there's actually some interesting history hiding here. This short stroll gets you well-oriented and covers the essentials. Start on Piazza Cioccaro, at the base of the funicular that connects the train station with the town center.

• *With your back to the funicular, go down the narrow street to the right of the building at the bottom of the square.*

Via Pessina: In this tangled, colorful little corner are several small shops run by Signor Gabbani. Enter the wine shop (marked *Bottega del Vino*). Its ceiling is mossy with *boccalini* hung from hooks. These traditional quarter-liter wine carafes are typical of the rustic grottos of Ticino.

• *Farther down, at Via Pessina 3, is...*

Lugano Center

1. To Hotel International au Lac
2. Hotel San Carlo
3. Hotel/Restaurant Pestalozzi
4. Art Hotel Stella
5. Hotel & Backpackers Montarina
6. La Tinera
7. Manora Cafeteria
8. Bottegone del Vino
9. Co-op Cafeteria
10. Pizzeria Tango
11. Sass Café
12. Olympia Restaurant
13. Vanini Café
14. To Gandria Eateries
15. Gelateria
16. Internet Café
17. Paddleboat Rentals (2)
18. To Star Bus Stop
19. Giosy Tours Bus Stop

Grand Café al Porto: This venerable institution is both Lugano's best spot for cakes and coffee and the most historic café in town (Mon–Sat 8:00–18:30, closed Sun). The *1803* above the fireplace is the date it opened—and also when Ticino joined the Swiss Federation. Once a convent (notice the fine *sgraffito* facade), the café evokes the 19th-century days when Giuseppe Mazzini and fellow Italian patriots would huddle here—safely over the border—planning their next move to unify Italy. Much later, as World War II wound down, US dignitary Allen Welsh Dulles met right here with Nazi and Italian representatives to organize a graceful end to the war and prevent the Germans from ruining Italy with a scorched-earth retreat. And in more carefree times, this is where Clark Gable and Sofia Loren dipped cookies in their coffee.

• *Just past Grand Café al Porto, take a left at the fountain into...*

Piazza della Riforma: This square is Lugano's living room. The city is proudly liberal, as the name of its main square implies. Its progressive spirit from the days of

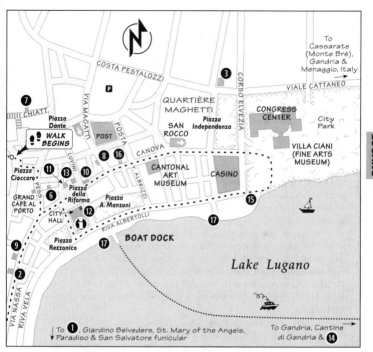

the Risorgimento (Italian unification) survives today, as Lugano remains one of the most liberal-voting cities in Switzerland. This square—with geraniums cascading on all sides—hosts an open-air cinema, markets (Tue and Fri), and local festivals.

• *Facing the giant, yellow City Hall, go left (past the* farmacia*) down...*

Via Canova: This street leads directly to the city park. Follow it for a few blocks, watching for the elegant gallery that burrows through a block (on your left). Just after that, on your right, you'll pass the **Cantonal Art Museum** (Museo Cantonale d'Arte), which displays ever-changing art exhibits (main collection-7 SF, with special exhibits-10 SF, Wed–Sun 10:00–17:00, Tue 14:00–17:00, closed Mon, Via Canova 10, tel. 091-910-4780).

Next you'll reach the creamy little **Church of San Rocco.** Its rich frescoes celebrate the saint responsible for protecting the city against the plague. Behind that is the **Quartière Maghetti,** an entire city block turned into a popular mall with colorful mosaics. Here you'll find lots of shops and fun eateries by day and a lively, youthful bar scene by night.

Beyond the Church of San Rocco, you'll reach the park-like **Piazza Indipendenza.** The giant head on its side is the work of Polish sculptor Igor Mitoraj, who is decorating squares all over

The Story of Lugano

Lugano's history is tied to its strategic position: where the Italian world is pressed up against the Alps, and just below the most convenient alpine passes. The Celts crossed the Alps here and left their mark. The ancient Romans were here, too—the oldest sacred building in Switzerland is an early Christian baptistery on this lake.

In 1220, when the first road over the Gotthard Pass was built, the Swiss took an interest in acquiring the Italian-speaking region of Ticino, leading to a battle for control. The nearby town of Bellinzona is named not for the Italian *bella* ("beautiful"), but for the Latin *bellum* ("war"), and this truly was a medieval war zone. Several castles in Bellinzona recall a pivotal Swiss victory in 1513. With this success, the Swiss gained a toehold in Ticino.

But the feisty region maintained its independence. In 1798, Ticino even stood up to Napoleon by creating an independent Republic of Ticino. However, the people of Ticino were unable to rule themselves peacefully, and five years later (in 1803) they decided to join the Swiss Federation. With that event, the present-day borders of Switzerland were finally established.

In the 19th century, Lugano—Italian-speaking, just a short trip from Milan, yet safely over the border in Switzerland—provided a refuge and staging ground for intellectual Italian revolutionaries. They'd meet here to plan the Risorgimento, the struggle for Italian unification (c. 1840-1869). Later in the 19th century, tourism arrived and the grand lakefront hotels were built.

Today, Lugano is second among Swiss cities only to Zürich in its number of banks. It's easy for Italians and others with suitcases of hard cash—black money—to swing by and take advantage of the secret bank accounts. (Locals claim George H. W. Bush stops in annually.) But the mentality here remains Italian. Rather than the Zürich model ("live to work"), the people of Lugano brag that they work to live.

Europe with similar sculptures. On your right is the vast, sterile **casino** building. Though its blocky, modern style doesn't quite fit the otherwise elegant architecture of this area, it does have an elevator leading up to a fine lake view (lake side of building—we'll pass there later on this walk).

• *Continuing straight across the street from Piazza Indipendenza, pass through the gate to come face-to-face with the pink palace in the...*

City Park (Parco Civico Villa Ciani): The park's centerpiece, the Villa Ciani, houses a fine-arts museum. Sprawling from here along the lake is a lush park filled

with modern art and exotic trees from around the world. Its water gate evokes the 19th century, when this was the private domain of aristocrats. The flower beds are organized to show off maximum color all year long. If the weather's nice, stow your guidebook and remember you're on vacation as you explore this ingeniously landscaped, people-friendly space. It's lit at night and particularly good for a late, romantic stroll (open daily 6:00–23:00, until 21:00 in winter).

• *From the city park, walk back to the town center along the...*

Waterfront: As you exit the park along the water, you'll spot the source of all those ice-cream cones you've been seeing—a popular *gelateria*. Walking along the lakefront, you'll find several places to rent paddleboats (8 SF/30 min). Out on the lake, these colorful squat vessels jostle for space with sailboats, big lake-cruise boats, and adventurous swimmers.

On the right, the casino's top-floor restaurant overlooks the lake. If it's open, ride the glass *elevatore* up and down for a fun and free view (Mon–Fri 12:00–15:00 & 19:00–2:00 in the morning, Sat–Sun 19:00–2:00 in the morning). Then continue strolling through the arcade or under the mulberry trees (a favorite of silk worms, dating from the time when silk was a local industry) until you reach the **boat dock** (for information on lake cruises, see page 270) and the **TI**.

• *Now cross the busy road (notice the handy pedestrian underpass nearby). A block inland from the TI is Piazza della Riforma again. The first left is...*

Via Nassa: This is one of Lugano's main shopping streets. Slow your pace and just enjoy the wandering, window-shopping, and people-watching for several blocks. It's fun to imagine that half the briefcases you pass are filled with cash. Along this gauntlet of boutiques and jewelry shops under typical Lombardi arcades, notice all the clocks. If you're trying to get away from time...this is a nightmare. On the right, at #22, the Co-op department store (closed Sun) has a good selection of Swiss chocolates (just inside the door on the left) and a handy, recommended top-floor cafeteria (lunch only, great views).

• *Follow Via Nassa until it dead-ends at the small but historic…*

Church of St. Mary of the Angels (Chiesa Santa Maria degli Angioli): This unpretentious lakefront church, which dates from 1499, was part of a monastery (next door). Inside the church you'll find the city's best frescoes. Bernardino Luini (from Milan) painted *The Passion and Crucifixion of Christ* and *The Last Supper* in 1529. After enjoying the gentle expressions and calm beauty of his art, you'll understand why Luini is nicknamed the "Raphael of the North."

The Passion and Crucifixion of Christ, the artistic highlight of all Ticino and the finest Renaissance fresco in Switzerland, is on the wall that separates the nave from the altar area. Follow the action as the scenes from Christ's passion are played out, from Jesus being crowned with thorns (left) to the doubting apostle Thomas touching Jesus' wound after his Resurrection (right). The central dominating theme is the Crucifixion. The work is riddled with symbolism. For instance, at the base of the cross, notice the skull and femur of Adam, as well as his rib (from which Eve was created). Worshippers saw this and remembered that without Adam and Eve's first sin, none of the terrible action in the rest of the fresco would have been necessary. Luini spent a decade working on this. Take an extremely close-up look at the fresco technique.

Facing the giant fresco, look to your left to find the three smaller frames. This is Luini's *Last Supper,* which was sliced off a wall of the monks' dining hall and put on canvas to be hung here.

Finally, wander up to the front of the church. The altar is rich and unusual with its wooden inlay work.

• *Along the lakefront across from the church begins the…*

Giardino Belvedere: This delightful little garden park is an open-air modern-art museum. The building facing it was once a monastery, then the Grand Hotel Palace. This first grand hotel on the lake was radical in that it actually faced the lake. From here, survey the scene. Paradiso, the big hotel zone with its 80-foot-high fountain, is a 15-minute walk along the lakeside. From there, the San Salvatore lift zips sightseers to the summit (described next). The ridge across the lake marks the border of Italy.

• *Our walk is finished. If you've got energy left, continue along the lakefront on the pleasant path to Paradiso; there you can summit San Salvatore, hop on a lake cruise, or do both.*

Sights near Lugano

Mountain Lifts

Lugano is a base from which several relatively small peaks can be conquered, sweat-free, by lifts. At about 3,000 feet, Lake Lugano's mountains are unimpressive compared with the mightier Alps farther north; if you've done some of the higher lifts in the Berner Oberland or Zermatt regions, nothing here will thrill you. Still, if you want the complete Lugano experience, you need to enjoy commanding mountaintop views over the lake. Doing more than one is overkill; San Salvatore is best and relatively handy to Lugano town.

▲**San Salvatore**—The easiest and most rewarding peak on the lake, thanks to its fine panoramic views, San Salvatore (2,990 feet)

rockets up from the Lugano suburb of Paradiso. First head to Paradiso (a 20-min walk from Lugano's old town, or take bus #1 from the Piazza Rezzonico stop next to the TI). From Paradiso, a funicular slides you up and up (26 SF round-trip, 19 SF one-way, half-price with Swiss Pass, 12-min ride, transfer to another funicular midway up, 2/hr—departs on the hour and the half-hour, daily June–Sept 8:30–22:30, April–May 9:00–18:00, late March and Oct–mid-Nov 9:00–17:00, closed mid-Nov–mid-March, these are last ascent times—last descent generally 30 min later, tel. 091-985-2828, www.montesansalvatore.ch).

At the top you'll find good viewpoints, as well as a playground, a self-serve cafeteria (13–16-SF meals, closes at 18:00), and an overpriced restaurant (10–20-SF pastas, 30–35-SF main dishes, food served 11:00–15:00 & 19:00–23:00, after dark you have no views). From the lift, be sure to climb five more minutes to the actual summit. On the way up, pop into the Salvatore Museum, with its small collection of religious art and exhibits on local geology (included in funicular ticket, Wed–Sun 10:00–12:00 & 13:00–15:00, closed Mon–Tue). At the top of the mountain, there's a small church surrounded by a view terrace. For the best panorama, climb to the rooftop of the church (entrance around the right side) for a sweeping, nearly 360-degree view. Unfortunately, the bay directly in front of Lugano is just about the only thing you can't see from up here.

Monte Brè—Departing from the other end of Lugano, in the sub-urb of Cassarate, this funicular takes you to arguably the best view down on the lagoon of Lugano itself (3,005 feet). From Lugano's old town you can take bus #1 to the Cassarate/Monte Brè stop, then ride up (14 SF one-way, 20 SF round-trip, 2/hr, June–Oct daily 9:00–19:00, Nov–May until 17:00, 20-min trip, tel. 091-971-3171, www.montebre.ch).

Monte Generoso—The tallest but farthest from Lugano, Monte Generoso (5,590 feet) is high enough that you can see some of the more distant cut-glass peaks. You'll take the train (15 min) or a much slower boat to Capolago, then ride 35 minutes on a cogwheel train up to Generoso Vetta, the summit; from the Lugano train station, you can reach the top in less than an hour (29 SF one-way, 39 SF round-trip, April–Oct departs from Capolago train station at :15 past the hour 9:15–15:15, plus 16:15 mid-May–mid-Sept, few or no trains Nov–March, tel. 091-630-5111, www.monte generoso.ch).

Cruising Lake Lugano with a Stop in Gandria

Lake Lugano is made to order for a boat trip. Along with paddle-boats and simple cruises from village to village, you have a dizzying array of more elaborate excursions to choose from (a lunch trip, a grand tour, a shopping excursion into Italy, and an evening dinner cruise). Pick up the boat schedule *(orario)* listing your options, and ask the TI or at one of the boat docks for details.

One-Hour Loop Trip: The best basic trip is the one-hour circle from Lugano. This cruise stops at a few desolate restaurants and hamlets along the far side of the lake, visits Gandria (a peaceful and picturesque little fish-ing town with several romantic view restaurants), then returns to Lugano (22.60 SF round-trip including stopovers, or 13.60 SF for one segment, free with Swiss Pass). You can get off and hike. The far side of the lake has a trail lacing together several little grottos and hamlets (each with a boat stop) with hiking times and direc-tions clearly marked. For information on the hike, ask the TI, your hotel, or even the guys on the boat. Note that if you're hopping on and off the boat, you'll actually cobble together the trip from various longer cruises, each with different itineraries. Some circle the lake clockwise, others counterclockwise, and not every boat makes every stop. Study the boat schedule, carefully noting when the next boat comes by and exactly where it stops (as this can be confusing).

Cantine di Gandria has two characteristic trattorias and wine grottos—great for a rustic meal or just a snack and a drink (note they close on different days, so at least one is sure to be open on any given day). A five-minute walk from Cantine di Gandria takes you to the **Customs Museum** (Museo Doganale) with underwhelming exhibits on customs and smuggling (free, no English but worth a 10-min visit, April–Oct daily 13:30–17:30, closed Nov–March). Boats stop alternately at Cantine di Gandria and Museo Doganale.

Gandria, around the headland on the Lugano side of the lake, is the most intriguing stop. This dense cluster of fishing

houses hangs over the lake with a few lazy, romantic hotels and several inviting restaurants. Of the various waterfront options, **Restaurant Miralago Gandria** is immediately above the ferry dock, with an extremely romantic setting (mediocre food, fair prices, 18–20-SF pastas, 30-SF main dishes, open daily, tel. 091-971-4361). You can lob bits of bread to the hungry birds, rewarding the ones who fly high circles by your lakeside table. **Locanda Gandriesi** has better cooking and a smaller, quieter terrace, but is farther from the boat dock and birds (go left from the dock—it's about a five-minute walk, just below the church; 18–20-SF pasta and polenta dishes, 26–36-SF main dishes, open daily, tel. 091-971-4181).

If stopping in Gandria, you can walk back to Lugano (great 45-min lakeside path before hitting the Castagnola suburb of Lugano and a boring 30-min walk along streets into town). To enjoy only the more interesting part of the walk, catch bus #1 from the Castagnola post office back into Lugano.

Note that the last boat of the day from Gandria back to Lugano leaves at 18:15 (or 19:20 in July–Aug); a bus runs after that (bus #490, departing Gandria at 18:25), except on Sundays. If you stay longer and miss the boat and bus, you'll have to walk or fork over 40–50 SF for a taxi.

Half-Day Plan: Here's a pleasant way to spend a late afternoon and evening (schedules are subject to change—confirm boat times before departing): 15:45–Walk from Lugano to Paradiso (20-min walk, plus time to stroll and snap photos), 16:13–Catch the boat from Paradiso to Gandria and have a drink and appetizer, or an early dinner in Gandria (at Miralago Gandria—early diners always get lakeside tables), 18:15 (or 19:20 in July–Aug)–Catch the last boat to Paradiso. Once at Paradiso, walk to the San Salvatore lift, ride the lift to the summit of the mountain (beautiful at twilight but disappointing after dark), ride back down, and walk along the lake from Paradiso back to Lugano.

Sleeping in Lugano

In Lugano's Old Town

$$$ **Hotel International au Lac** is a classic, pricey old hotel with 80 rooms with slightly faded furnishings and some Lake Lugano views. It's conveniently and scenically located where pedestrian-only Via Nassa hits the lake. Four generations of Schmids have maintained the early-20th-century ambience since 1906, with old photos, inviting lounges, antique furniture, and, it seems, many of their original guests (Sb-120–185 SF, Db-206–310 SF, price depends on size and view, extra adult-40 SF, extra child-20 SF, family-friendly, air-con, elevator, free Internet access, free Wi-Fi in lobby, terrace restaurant, fun view seats on balcony of bar, swimming pool, parking-20 SF/day, Via Nassa 68, tel. 091-922-7541, fax 091-922-7544, www.hotel-international.ch, info@hotel-international.ch).

$$ **Hotel San Carlo,** also on the pedestrian-only shopping street, but closer to the center, rents 22 small but cheerful rooms. This welcoming place is run by Anna Martina and Beppe. The flamboyant Italian-mod design within its old walls is fun and refreshing (Ss-95 SF, Sb-130 SF, Ds-145 SF, Db-170 SF, cheaper off-season, non-smoking rooms, elevator, no air-con but fans, pay Internet access, Via Nassa 28, tel. 091-922-7107, fax 091-922-8022, sancarlo@ticino.com).

$$ **Hotel Pestalozzi,** near the city park, is plain and vaguely institutional. It offers 54 fresh, modern, somewhat sterile rooms with a woody Nordic touch and some lake views. Though it's a bit longer walk from the train station funicular, this hotel is a particularly good value (S-66 SF, Sb-102–108 SF, D-112 SF, Db-172–192 SF—pricier rooms have lake view and/or air-con, elevator, pay Internet access and Wi-Fi, recommended and affordable restaurant, Piazza Indipendenza 9, tel. 091-921-4646, fax 091-922-2045, www.pestalozzi-lugano.ch, pestalo@bluewin.ch).

Near the Train Station

$$ **Art Hotel Stella,** a wonderful little oasis, offers 14 rooms between slick office buildings just behind the train station. Owner Antoinette Burkhard's love of modern art is evident, with statues on the patio and fun paintings throughout. Enjoy the garden and the tiny swimming pool (Sb-110 SF, Db-170 SF, 5 percent discount with this book, some rooms have terraces, most have air-con, free Internet access and Wi-Fi, Via F. Borromini 5, tel. 091-966-3370, fax 091-966-6755, www.arthotelstella.ch, info@arthotelstella.ch).

LUGANO

Sleep Code

(1 SF = about $1, country code: 41)
S = Single, **D** = Double/Twin, **T** = Triple, **Q** = Quad, **b** = bathroom,
s = shower only. Unless otherwise noted, credit cards are
accepted, English is spoken, and breakfast is included.

    To help you sort easily through these listings, I've divided
the rooms into three categories, based on the price for a
standard double room with bath:

  $$$ Higher Priced—Most rooms 200 SF or more.
  $$ Moderately Priced—Most rooms between 120–200 SF.
    $ Lower Priced—Most rooms 120 SF or less.

Exit the station to the rear, turn right and follow the tracks for 50
yards, take the first left uphill, then turn left up Via Borromini.

    $$ Hotel & Backpackers Montarina, a creaky old man-
sion in a palm garden overlooking the lake, has to be one of
Switzerland's most appealing hostels. It has 140 dorm beds (30

SF, includes sheets, 5–16 bunks
per dorm), as well as 24 private
rooms; half of these are antique
rooms with classic furniture
and shared bathrooms (S-75 SF,
D-105 SF), and the other half
are modern "comfort" rooms,
with private bathrooms (Sb-85
SF, Db-125 SF). Surrounded by
lush gardens and an extremely
inviting swimming pool, and with a helpful staff, this place is well
worth considering even for non-hostelers (breakfast buffet-12 SF,
reception open 7:30–23:00, lockers, small kitchen, self-service
laundry, pay Internet access, free Wi-Fi in lobby, free parking,
Via Montarina 1, tel. 091-966-7272, fax 091-966-0017, www
.montarina.ch, info@montarina.ch). As you exit the train station
at the rear, walk left along the tracks, then take the sharp uphill
turn to the right; halfway up the hill, go left through the gate
marked *#1*.

Eating in Lugano

My recommended restaurants are all in the old town. I've empha-
sized some more affordable options, with a few splurges (you'll pay
a premium to dine on Piazza della Riforma, but many find it worth
the expense). Lugano is not the best place for lakeside dining.

For better value, cross the lake to the remote little grotto restaurants, or visit the town of Gandria (both options described on page 270). Good news for the wine-curious: You'll pay the same per liter for the little one-deciliter (about 3.5 oz) glasses as you do for the big half-liter (about 17 oz) carafes—so go with the small glasses and try several different wines. Experiment. The Ticino merlot is great.

La Tinera, beloved by locals, serves affordable, traditional Ticinese cuisine. It's tucked away in an old wine cellar, with heavy wooden furniture and decorated with wine bottles and antique copper cookware (often closed mid-July–mid-Aug, 20-SF daily specials, 20–30-SF meat dishes, 14–20-SF smaller dishes, Tue–Sat 8:30–15:00 & 17:30–23:00, closed Sun–Mon, Via dei Gorini, just a block behind Piazza della Riforma, tel. 091-923-5219, Antonio).

Manora is an easy self-service restaurant offering affordable, healthy food. Choose to sit inside or out on the covered terrace (with a playground). It's in the Manor supermarket on Piazza Dante Alighieri (100 yards from bottom of train station funicular; 10–16-SF main dishes, salad bar, pasta bar, lots more, Mon–Sat 7:30–22:00, Sun 10:00–22:00).

Bottegone del Vino is an expensive little eatery appreciated for its fine wine. The menu is small and rustic, the wine is excellent, and the indoor or outdoor ambience is of a quality wine bar. Sitting here, you feel in the know—but order carefully, as prices really add up (20–30-SF dishes, Mon–Sat 11:30–24:00, closed Sun, a block off Piazza della Riforma at Via Magatti 3, tel. 091-922-7689).

Restaurante Pestalozzi, close to the city park, serves reasonably priced, crank-'em-out meals in an alcohol-free setting (15–20-SF daily specials, open daily 11:00–14:00 & 18:00–21:30, Piazza Indipendenza 9, tel. 091-921-4646).

Co-op Cafeteria, midway along the Via Nassa pedestrian mall, has an elegant-as-cafeterias-go dining area on its top floor, with a pretty rooftop terrace (Mon–Sat 11:30–14:30, closed Sun, Via Nassa 22).

Around Piazza della Riforma: Various restaurants offer decent food and great people-watching from outdoor tables on Lugano's

main piazza. The ambience here is magical at twilight. I like **Pizzeria Tango,** where a helpful waitstaff serves Italian cuisine with a Ticino influence. While many of its tables face the busy main piazza, its interior and the tables facing a quiet little square on the back may be more inviting (14–18-SF pizzas, 20–25-SF pastas, 35–40-SF meat dishes, daily 8:00–1:00 in the morning, Piazza della Riforma, tel. 091-922-2701). Also consider **Sass Café** (classy wine bar with 20–30-SF daily specials, 22–26-SF pastas, and 50-SF à la carte items), **Olympia** (the mayor's fave, below City Hall, 12–18-SF pizzas, 20–24-SF pastas, 30–50-SF main dishes), and **Vanini Café** (tops for coffee and desserts; try the *marron glace*—candied chestnuts).

Lugano Connections

Lugano is a long detour from virtually anywhere else in Switzerland. It's best connected to other Swiss destinations by scenic trains—the **William Tell Express** (train-and-boat combination to Luzern) or the **Bernina Express** (bus-and-train combination to eastern Switzerland). The Bernina Express bus leaves for Tirano near Lugano's train station (200 yards to the left as you leave the station, see chart at station). More details about these trips are in the Scenic Rail Journeys chapter. Train info: toll tel. 0900-300-300 or www.rail.ch.

From Lugano by Train to: Luzern (hourly, 2.5 hrs, half with easy change in Arth-Goldau), **Zürich** (hourly, 2.75 hrs, half with easy change in Arth-Goldau), **Interlaken** (hourly, 4.75 hrs, transfer in Luzern, Zürich, or Olten), **Bern** (hourly, 3.75 hrs, transfer in Luzern or Zürich), **Milan** (hourly, 1.5 hrs).

From Lugano by Bus to St. Moritz: The "Palm Express" bus to St. Moritz leaves only once a day in peak season and just on weekends off-season, but it's handy if you're headed to Italy's Lake Como, because it stops in lakeside Menaggio en route (departs Lugano's train station usually at 11:40 but confirm time in advance; 50 min to Menaggio, 4 hrs to St. Moritz; daily mid-June–mid-Oct, mid-Oct–mid-June runs Sat–Mon only).

From Lugano by Bus to Italy's Lake Como: In addition to the handy Palm Express described above, an Italian-run bus (#C12) goes from Cassarate (a suburb just east of Lugano, served by local bus #1 from Lugano's old town) to Menaggio on Lake Como (departs about every 2 hours, 1 hr).

From Lugano to Milan's Airports: The closest major airports to Lugano are actually in Italy, near the city of Milan: Malpensa Airport and Linate Airport (www.sea-aeroportimilano .it). The handiest way to reach either is to use the direct shuttle service, operated by two different companies: **Star Bus** (15/day to Malpensa, 1.5 hrs, 30 SF, 20 SF extra early and late; 8/day to Linate, 1.5–2 hrs, 60 SF, 20 SF extra early and late; departs from garage a 5-min walk north of train station, tel. 091-994-8878, www.starstation.ch) and **Giosy Tours** (10/day, 1.5 hrs, 30 SF,

departs from in front of train station, tel. 091-858-2323, www
.giosytours.ch). Check the websites to see which company's schedule suits yours, then reserve ahead.

Alternatively, you can take the 1.5-hour train to Milan's
Central Station, where cheap and easy shuttle buses leave about
every 15 minutes for both Malpensa and Linate.

LUGANO

PONTRESINA, SAMEDAN, and ST. MORITZ

The Romansh Resorts of the Upper Engadine

Pontresina, Samedan, and St. Moritz are a trio of towns that anchor the Upper Engadine region, tucked away in an intriguing and scenic fringe of Switzerland. Here you'll ride a lift to a thrilling mountain-capping hike, stroll with the high rollers in a ritzy resort, explore the unique townscapes of an exotically remote mountain valley, and hear enticing snippets of the obscure Romansh language.

Nestled in the southeast corner of the country, the time-passed Upper Engadine (Engiadin Ota in Romansh, Oberengadin in German) is arguably less thrilling—and certainly more difficult to reach—than the mountain resorts of the Berner Oberland and Zermatt. But this region—wedged in the Alps between Italy and Austria, in the canton of Graubünden—offers rough-around-the-edges mountain culture that feels far from Germanic influence, and closer to the Latin roots that run deep beneath this part of Switzerland. And for tourists riding the scenic Bernina Express or Glacier Express, this area is an easy stopover.

On first glance, there may not seem to be much history here—but the trained eye sees it everywhere. Celtic people inhabited this region centuries before Christ. The hillsides are still terraced, recalling the hard work that came with farming up here in ancient times. History is in the region's unique language, too: Romansh is a vulgar form of Latin that arrived with the Etruscans, who were chased here as Rome expanded. Town names date back to various invaders. For instance, "Pontresina" comes from "Bridge of the Saracens."

Two valleys meet here, carving out a picturesque region dominated by three very different towns. The most famous is the swanky ski resort of St. Moritz, which, like a too-sweet dessert, is enjoyable only until its glitz makes you sick. Pontresina is a lower-key but still upper-crust resort town with even better access to high-mountain lifts, making it an ideal base for hikers. And humble little Samedan feels more like a real town, with just enough hotels to make it cozy. If you can set aside the jet set comparing tans in St. Moritz, the Upper Engadine feels like a place where workaday Swiss people go to find some high-altitude fun. English-language newspapers are in short supply, an indication that while there are many visitors, most are local.

Planning Your Time

Unless you're passing through on a scenic rail journey, the Upper Engadine is probably too time-consuming to reach to be worth cramming into a busy itinerary—head for the Berner Oberland instead. But with plenty of time to enjoy Switzerland—and a healthy curiosity about its overlooked Romansh corner, not to mention this area's famous resorts—it's worth a visit. Conveniently, the Upper Engadine happens to link two scenic rail trips: the Bernina Express and the Glacier Express (see the Scenic Rail Journeys chapter). Hop off the train here, set up a home base, explore—then continue on your way.

The three towns in this chapter—Pontresina, Samedan, and St. Moritz—form a convenient little triangle, each about 10 minutes apart by train. With a full day here and some good planning, you can sample all three and throw in a hike to boot.

Like other resort areas, this region has two distinct tourist seasons: summer (June–Oct) and winter (Dec–March). Outside of these seasons, many places are closed and the area can feel dead.

Getting Around the Upper Engadine

There's no need for a car in this region. Pontresina, Samedan, St. Moritz, and Punt Muragl (the base of the funicular to Muottas Muragl) are all well-connected by train and bus.

Trains connect each of the three towns about hourly (about 10 min between towns, 5 SF).

The local **bus** system is good, but a bit confusing. Pick up the bus schedule *(Fahrplan/Urari)* at a local TI, and study its table of contents to familiarize yourself with your options. Pay attention to which stop you want to use in a given town. For example, Pontresina Bahnhof is at the bottom of town, while two other stops are up in the town center: Pontresina Post, near my recommended hotels; and Pontresina Rondo, near the TI. St. Moritz has several stops, including Dorf (charming town center), Bahnhof (train station), and Bad (dull lakeside spa zone). Rides between towns cost

Pontresina, Samedan & St. Moritz

PONTRESINA

5 SF; rides within a town (such as between St. Moritz Bad and St. Moritz Dorf) cost 3 SF.

Bus #1 is particularly confusing, as two different routes operate using this same number. One bus #1 goes from Pontresina to Punt Muragl, then on to Samedan (1–2/hr, 15 min). A different bus #1 goes from Pontresina to Punt Muragl, then to St. Moritz Bahnhof and St. Moritz Bad (but skips Samedan; figure 15–20 min from Pontresina to St. Moritz). Carefully check the schedule and the destination posted on the bus before boarding.

Other buses are more predictable:

Bus #2 links Pontresina–Punt Muragl–St. Moritz Dorf (2/hr);

Bus #3 connects St. Moritz Bahnhof with St. Moritz Dorf (4/hr); and

Buses #5 and **#6** connect Samedan with St. Moritz Dorf (2/hr).

Helpful Hints

Guest Card: If you're staying at least two nights in the Upper Engadine region in the summer, your hotel may give you a free "Mountain Railways Inclusive" card that can save you plenty. Sometimes this card covers local public transportation (including trains and buses), sometimes it covers mountain lifts, but usually it covers both (as well as guided hikes). Hoteliers can choose to opt in or out of the various versions—ask when you reserve.

Winter Activities: If you're here in winter and want to ski some of the most famous slopes in the world, head for Corviglia, the largest ski area in the region, which offers varied terrain, mostly intermediate runs, and good snowboarding (convenient from St. Moritz, or a bus ride from Pontresina). Other areas to consider are Corvatsch–Furtschellas (great views) and Diavolezza–Lagalb (smaller, less crowded, mostly intermediate and expert runs, great for non-skiers who want views). Both cater mainly to intermediate and expert skiers. See www.bergbahnenengadin.ch for more information and to buy lift tickets in advance. Winter isn't just about hitting the slopes, though—the area has more than 100 miles of cross-country skiing trails, great sledding, Nordic walking, and spectator sports such as polo in the snow (horses and all). Ask at any TI for information; for more tips, see the Switzerland in Winter chapter.

Pontresina

Pontresina—a popular winter and summer mountain resort with about 2,000 residents—makes a good Upper Engadine home base. At 6,000 feet above sea level on a wind-protected terrace overlooking the Bernina Valley, Pontresina faces southwest and enjoys plenty of sunshine. Popular trails through its larch forests offer spectacular views of the 13,000-foot Piz Bernina peak and the immense Morteratsch glacier.

Pontresina's first tourists, mostly German and British, arrived in the 1850s. For a while, it was a summer-only destination. But by the early 1900s, the Muottas Muragl railway was inaugurated, the first grand hotels were built, and tourists began showing up in winter, too. While it's a bit sterile and resorty—with not quite enough local charm or character—it's handier than Samedan and not as glitzy as St. Moritz, making it the best compromise home base in this region.

Orientation to Pontresina

Pontresina sits on a ledge overlooking a valley where the Bernina and Roseg rivers meet, forming the Flazbach river. Virtually everything of interest is along Via Maistra (may-strah), which means "Main Street" in Romansh. The post office and my recommended hotels are at the top end of Via Maistra, and the TI is near the bottom end. The train station sits in the valley floor just below.

PONTRESINA

Tourist Information

The TI is in the heart of town in the slick Rondo Culture and Congress Center, right on Via Maistra. Pick up a pile of handy, free brochures: town map, local bus schedule (Fahrplan/Urari), Panorama map showing the lifts and hiking trails, and bi-weekly Information for Visitors guide. The TI is happy to suggest tips for hikes and mountain lifts around the region (late June–mid-Oct and mid-Dec–mid-April Mon–Fri 8:30–18:00, Sat 8:30–12:00 & 15:00–18:00, Sun 16:00–18:00; mid-April–late June and mid-Oct–mid-Dec Mon–Fri 8:30–12:00 & 14:00–18:00, Sat 8:30–12:00, closed Sun; tel. 081-838-8300, www.pontresina.ch).

Arrival in Pontresina

The train station lies at the foot of the town. You can hike about 10 minutes steeply uphill to the town center, following the white signs to Pontresina. Or, easier, take bus #2 to Pontresina Post (near my recommended hotels) or Pontresina Rondo (near the TI; 2/hr, 3 SF, free with Swiss Pass, buy ticket at counter inside train station or on board bus). Walking the 10 minutes from Pontresina back down to the train station on Via da Mulin offers spectacular gorge views along the way.

Helpful Hints

Internet Access: Most hotels offer Internet access to their guests (generally for a fee). You'll find public Internet terminals in the lobby of **Hotel Post** (8 SF/30 min, daily 8:00–21:00,

Allegra (Welcome) to Graubünden

Pontresina, Samedan, St. Moritz, and the rest of the Upper Engadine belong to Switzerland's biggest canton, Graubünden. Isolated by high mountain ranges, this canton is also one of the country's most conservative. The name Graubünden goes back to 1395, when a group of farmers wearing gray clothes organized themselves in the "Gray League" to fight for their autonomy. This fiercely independent region didn't join the Swiss Confederation until 1803.

People in Graubünden believe the best way to control nature is to obey it. Passionate about their environment, they purify all dirty water before returning it to the rivers. Locals are currently going through the expensive process of removing canals (built to direct streams and rivers) and allowing the water to choose its own course once again. The natives love their beautiful countryside and cherish their customs—predictably voting against EU membership and other issues that might compromise Swiss neutrality and self-determination.

Graubünden cuisine is hearty. Try *Pizokel,* a *Spätzle*-like creation of cheesy flour dumplings. In fall you might find *Pizokel* made from chestnut flour and served with wild mushroom stew. The Graubünden's air-dried beef, *Bündnerfleisch*—very expensive and sliced paper-thin—is popular throughout Switzerland. *Capuns* are cabbage leaves stuffed with a mix of dough, leeks, bacon, onion, and air-dried beef. *Bündner Gerstensuppe* is a creamy barley and vegetable soup. For a Graubünden dessert, it's got to be *Nusstorte,* a rich walnut cake.

Graubünden has three official languages: German, Italian, and Romansh (an ancient dialect that comes directly from Latin). You'll overhear conversations where one person speaks Italian, the other replies in German, a third butts in with Romansh...and everybody understands each other. On the trains, the announcements are in German and Romansh (which sounds a bit like Italian).

Most tourists here speak German (others Italian, others English), but if you'd like to please your Romansh hosts, try these phrases:

Welcome.	*Allegra.*	ah-LEY-grah
Hello (Good day).	*Bun di.*	boon dee
Good evening. (after 17:00)	*Buna saira.*	BOO-nah SIGH-rah
Please.	*Per plaschair.*	pehr plah-ZHAIR
Thank you (very much).	*Grazcha (fich).*	GRAHTS-chah (feech)
Goodbye.	*Arevair.*	ah-reh-VAIR

closed in May, Via Maistra 160) and at the **Bellavita** pool and spa complex (5 SF/hr, described later).

Ski Rental: Try **Gruber Sport** (at Via Maistra 190, across from Hotel Schweizerhof, tel. 081-842-6236) or **Engadina Sport** (also on the main drag at Via Maistra 41, tel. 081-842-6262).

Sights in Pontresina

Church of St. Mary—Above town, just beyond the five-sided, 13th-century Spaniola Tower, stands this remarkable little church. Inside, the wooden ceiling is entirely original. Faded 13th-century,

Byzantine-inspired frescoes survive on the west wall. The other walls and ceiling were richly decorated by an Italian workshop (1497). The frescoes depict the legend of Mary Magdalene and (above) the story of Lazarus' resurrection. Imagine this church packed with illiterate villagers five centuries ago (free entry, but limited hours: generally July–mid-Oct Mon–Fri 15:30–17:30; late Dec–mid-April Mon–Tue and Fri 15:00–17:30; most of June Mon, Wed, and Fri 15:30–17:30; closed mid-Oct–late Dec and mid-April–early June).

Alpine Museum—This little museum is worth a quick visit. Situated on three floors of an old Engadine town house, it offers exhibits on the development of alpine mountain climbing and skiing, the regional mining industry (with plenty of mineral samples), hunting, local animals, and replicas of traditional rooms (bedroom, kitchen, living room). About 130 of the 250 different bird species found in the Upper Engadine are shown here. Listen to the recorded songs of 60 different birds on the primitive aviary jukebox. The 20-minute slideshow is in German and makes you feel like a wimp. Still, it's interesting for its images of "the mountain experience." Rounding out the space are temporary exhibits. Be sure to pick up the brief English descriptions when you enter (6 SF, June–Oct and late Dec–mid-April Mon–Sat 16:00–18:00—or from 15:00 in bad weather, closed Sun, closed mid-April–May and Nov–late Dec, Via Maistra).

Biking—Several sports stores rent bicycles, inline skates, tennis rackets, and other gear. Riding the train to the Bernina Pass and biking nine miles back into town is just one of many fun biking options. In the town center, **Fähndrich Sport** rents good mountain bikes with various suspensions (22–25 SF/half-day, 35–40 SF/day, helmets-7 SF/half-day or 10 SF/day, Mon–Fri 8:00–12:00 & 14:00–18:30, Sat until 17:00, closed Sun except July–Aug, at Hotel

Pontresina

200 Meters
200 Yards

To Samedan & St. Moritz

Bernina River

To Alp Languard & Trail to Muottas Muragl

ALP LANGUARD CHAIRLIFT

ST. MARY

BELLAVITA POOL & SPA

ALPINE MUSEUM

SPANIOLA TOWER

PONTRESINA TRAIN STATION

Tais Forest

Roseg River

To Roseg Valley

CONCERTS

SUROVAS TRAIN STATION

To Bernina Pass

PONTRESINA

❶ Hotel Bernina
❷ Chesa Mulin Hotel Garni
❸ Hotel Engadinerhof
❹ Youth Hostel Tolais & Flying Cycles
❺ Café Puntschella
❻ Colani Stübli
❼ Bündnerstübli
❽ Stüva-Bella Restaurant
❾ Kronenstübli
❿ To Alp Languard Chalet
⓫ Co-op Grocery
⓬ Rominger Möbel Furniture Shop
⓭ Internet Café (Hotel Post)
⓮ Bellavita Pool & Spa
⓯ Gruber Sport
⓰ Fähndrich Sport
⓱ To Engadina Sport

Allegra on Via Maistra, tel. 081-842-7155, www.faehndrich-sport .ch). There are two bike-rental outlets near the train station. In the train station itself, you can rent bikes at the **luggage counter** (25 SF/half-day, 33 SF/day, daily 8:00–18:00). Across the street, in the lower level of the big youth hostel building, **Flying Cycles** rents a huge selection of mountain bikes and fun, easy-to-learn electric-powered bikes (35 SF/day for a mountain bike, 45 SF/day for an electric bike, helmets-5 SF, mid-June–mid-Oct Mon–Fri 8:30–12:00 & 13:30–18:30, Sat 8:30–17:00, closed Sun, shorter hours in shoulder season, closed in winter, tel. 081-834-5750).

Music—Free summer classical music concerts are offered in the Tais Forest across the river, and (on rainy days) in the Rondo Center or in the church next door (daily at 11:00, mid-June–mid-Sept, confirm and get details at TI).

Bellavita Pool and Spa—This delightful, newly renovated pool complex is an ideal place to relax in any weather. The fun indoor-outdoor swimming-pool complex includes an enclosed 250-foot-long spiral waterslide and an outdoor pool that stays at 93 degrees Fahrenheit year-round. There's also an indoor water playground for kids and a spa with a series of saunas, steam baths, and more. (The spa is usually mixed-gender and clothing-optional, but women-only Mon 14:00–17:00 and Thu after 17:00.) You can rent a swim-suit for 10 SF, or buy one in the shop. The complex is smack-dab in the middle of Via Maistra (pool only-10 SF, pool and spa-24 SF; pool open Mon–Fri 10:00–21:30, Sat–Sun 10:00–20:30; spa open Mon 14:00–22:00, Tue–Fri 10:00–22:00, Sat–Sun 10:00–21:00; public pay Internet terminal in lobby, tel. 081-837-0037, www .pontresina-bellavita.ch).

Hiking

Pontresina is a hiker's paradise. The town boasts one of Switzerland's largest mountaineering schools and has a good reputation for adventure sports. Shops lining Via Maistra rent and sell all kinds of sports gear. The TI knows your options and will help you find the right hike for you. Their great, free fold-out *Panorama* map is marked with hiking trails and lists details for the various hikes in the region. They also hand out a *Hiking Suggestions in Pontresina* leaflet describing a few popular routes. (Most hikers agree that the Muottas Muragl-Alp Languard hike is tops.)

Upper Engadine trails come with high altitudes. Hikers should bring the appropriate gear (solid shoes, sun protection, windbreaker, hat, and water). Even in summer, with cold winds blowing down from the snow-capped mountains, it can get cold—especially on chairlifts. The sun is strong and the air is thin, so use sunscreen. Hiking trails are marked according to their difficulty. Yellow signs indicate easy hikes and walks. White-and-red signs indicate more demanding hikes, where real hiking boots are in order. Blue signs indicate alpine routes that require serious gear (these dangerous trails include rock climbing and glacier crossings).

Some flowers in the Alps are protected; pick one, and you may be fined. Some meadows are also protected for haymaking. Signs ask you to stick to the trails, as trampled grass is hard to cut.

Pontresina to Muottas Muragl to Alp Languard—For maximum alpine thrills per calorie burned, consider this three-hour hike. It comes with grand views and takes you gradually down 1,000 feet in altitude. From Pontresina (6,000 feet), catch bus #1 or #2 (2/hr, 3 SF) to Pont Muragl, where you can catch the Muottas Muragl funicular (21 SF one-way, 30 SF round-trip—you can return either on this funicular or on the Alp Languard lift, explained below).

The funicular lifts you to a lofty restaurant (8,105 feet), from where you hike over to Alp Languard (7,710 feet). Midway, there's a great soup or coffee-and-cakes stop (ask for the WC key for a fun

alpine memory). Keep your eyes
open for ibex, bighorn stags, and
marmots. For extra credit, notice
that a more challenging upper
trail climbs the mountainside
above the main one. Each year a
different appreciation-of-nature
theme is displayed along this trail.
If you're up for this more serious
hike, ask for details at the TI.

At Alp Languard, a chalet serves reasonably priced traditional meals (see page 289). From Alp Languard, hike or ride the
lift down to Pontresina (15 SF one-way, 22 SF round-trip, also
covered by 30-SF Muottas Muragl round-trip ticket, runs daily
8:30–17:30).

Other Hikes—A fun way to explore the nearby Roseg Valley and
marvel at its glacier (from a distance) is to hike two hours up the
valley and take the **horse-drawn "omnibus"** back to Pontresina
(reservations required, June–Oct departures at fixed hours, 16 SF
one-way, 26 SF round-trip, tel. 081-842-6057, Luigi Costa). You can
also rent a private carriage (100 SF one-way, 150 SF round-trip).

Consider taking the train up to the **Bernina Pass** (7,000 feet),
hike around for a couple of hours, then take the train back—or,
to get even higher, ride the cable car from the Bernina Pass up to
Diavolezza (9,930 feet, 24 SF one-way, 33 SF round-trip, 2/hr,
daily 8:30–17:00, until 17:30 in July–Aug).

The TI offers various guided hikes with themes, such as
"Experiencing Wilderness with Marmots and Ibex" (free, cable-
car ride costs 15 SF one-way, 22 SF round-trip, 3–4 hikes per week,
reservations required). The hikes are guided in German, but some
mountaineers speak English and can be hired privately through
the TI.

Near Pontresina: Muottas Muragl

This impressive alpine perch (8,105 feet) overlooking Samedan
and the valley is accessible by foot (from Pontresina) or by funicular. To reach the funicular, you can either take bus #1 or #2 from
Pontresina, or you can catch the train between Pontresina and
Samedan and get off at Punt Muragl (it's a request-only stop—
press the green button, or it won't stop). The funicular dates from
1907 (21 SF one-way, 30 SF round-trip—lets you return either on
this funicular or on the Alp Languard lift, 15 SF round-trip after
18:00, 2/hr, early June–mid-Oct daily 8:00–23:00).

Once up top on Muottas Muragl, you can hike, rent a deck
chair to lounge around on, have a meal (self-service or pricey but
good restaurant), or even spend the night if the hotel is open.

PONTRESINA

Keep an eye out for alpine animals.

Sleeping at Muottas Muragl: **Alpine Hotel Muottas Muragl** offers a secluded overnight high in the Alps. When the lift takes the last tourist down, things become as peaceful as the Alps can be. However, the hotel is closed for renovation for most of 2010 (otherwise open June–Oct only, call or check online for status and prices, tel. 081-842-8232, fax 081-842-8290, www.muottasmuragl .ch, info@muottasmuragl.ch).

Shopping in Pontresina

Many sports and souvenir shops line Via Maistra. A typical product from the Upper Engadine is furniture carved from Arven pine (a.k.a. Scotch pine). The pine, special to this region, starts out light, darkens with time, and has spots where the branches used to be. Look for the tree's characteristic five-needle clusters when hiking.

Rominger Möbel, a local furniture store, makes the Arven pine furniture it sells. Its upstairs showroom is like a modern Engadine home show—walking among hand-carved beds, tables, and dressers gives you a sense of good living high in this remote corner of Switzerland (Mon–Fri 9:00–12:00 & 14:00–18:30, Sat 8:30–12:00 & 14:00–17:00, closed Sun, 5-min walk from town center on Via Maistra in the direction of Bernina Pass, tel. 081-842-6263, www.rominger.ch).

Sleeping in Pontresina

$$$ Hotel Bernina, a well-run and woody three-star place, feels high-quality, from the free and friendly pick-up at the station (let them know what time you'll arrive) to the traditionally clad waitresses who serve your breakfast coffee. Its 41 traditional and neat rooms are a fine value for this area (Sb-110–135 SF, Db-210–260 SF, price depends on room and season, elevator, sauna, free Internet access, free Wi-Fi in some parts of hotel, good restaurant serving Engadine specialties, Via Maistra 207, tel. 081-838-8686, fax 081-838-8687, www.hotelbernina.ch, info@hotelbernina.ch).

$$$ Chesa Mulin Hotel Garni, below the main street, offers 30 modern, bright, and comfortable rooms, each with a painting depicting a local legend, and almost all with new bathrooms. The inviting sitting area with open fireplace and library makes bad weather tolerable. The friendly Isepponi-Schmid family takes good care of their guests (Sb-115 SF, Db-200 SF, elevator, sauna, sundeck, free access to Bellavita pool and spa with 2-night stay, pay cable Internet in rooms, Via da Mulin 15, tel. 081-838-8200, fax 081-838-8230, www.chesa-mulin.ch, info@chesa-mulin.ch).

Sleep Code

(1 SF = about $1, country code: 41)
S = Single, **D** = Double/Twin, **T** = Triple, **Q** = Quad, **b** = bathroom, **s** = shower only. Unless otherwise noted, credit cards are accepted, English is spoken, and breakfast is included.

To help you sort easily through these listings, I've divided the rooms into three categories, based on the price for a standard double room with bath:

$$$ Higher Priced—Most rooms 180 SF or more.
$$ Moderately Priced—Most rooms between 130–180 SF.
$ Lower Priced—Most rooms 130 SF or less.

Most hotels in this region have a strict cancellation policy (30 days in advance with no penalty, but, thereafter, you'll generally have to pay for the entire period you reserved).

$$ Hotel Engadinerhof, while less cozy, can be a good value. Its 80 rooms gather around a sprawling and classic Old World lounge. The cheaper sink-only rooms ("Category A") are clean and have well-preserved furniture from the 1930s (S-70 SF, D-125 SF). "Category B" offers the same old-fashioned rooms, plus antique bathrooms (Sb-90 SF, Db-170 SF). "Category C" gets you modern rooms (Sb-100 SF, Db-190 SF; elevator, free Internet access, Via Maistra 203, tel. 081-839-3100, fax 081-839-3200, www.engadiner hof.com, info@engadinerhof.com).

$ Youth Hostel Tolais, across the street from the train station, rents 120 beds. There's no curfew, and guests have 24-hour access (though check-in is limited to 16:00–18:30 & 19:30–21:00 and checkout is 7:30–10:00; dorm bed–49–67 SF depending on season and number of beds in room, S-97 SF, D-151 SF; price includes sheets, breakfast, and three-course dinner; 7 SF less for breakfast only, nonmembers pay 6 SF more per day, self-serve restaurant, game and TV room, tel. 081-842-7223, fax 081-842-7031, www .youthhostel.ch/pontresina, pontresina@youthhostel.ch).

Eating in Pontresina

Virtually all restaurants in Pontresina are part of a hotel, apart from a few bakeries that serve reasonably priced meals. Picnickers will seek out the **Co-op** grocery, just below Via Maistra on Via da Mulin (Mon–Fri 8:00–12:15 & 14:00–18:30, Sat 8:00–17:00, closed Sun).

Café Puntschella is the local favorite for good, healthy, reasonably priced, local-style dishes and great desserts (they also have a bakery for take-away). With a no-frills diner ambience, it offers indoor and outdoor seating and an entertaining menu (20–27-SF Engadine specialties, 18-SF pastas, 10–24-SF salads, daily 7:30–19:00, Via da Mulin, tel. 081-838-8030).

Colani Stübli, a cozy eatery, serves regional and seasonal specialties (17–21-SF local dishes such as *Krautpizokel* and *Capuns*, 30–40-SF entrées, 46–58-SF fixed-price meals, daily 11:30–14:00 & 18:00–21:00, smaller dishes available in the afternoon and after 21:00, at Hotel Steinbock, Via Maistra 219, tel. 081-839-3626).

Bündnerstübli dishes up hearty, traditional meals with fish and game in a woody, Old World setting. Many dishes are available in a cheaper "starter" size for a light meal. Consider being adventurous with the traditional appetizers, which work as main plates (29–46-SF fish and game, 16–20-SF vegetarian dishes, 28-SF *Fitnessteller*, daily 18:00–21:30, at Hotel Rosatsch, Via Maistra 71, tel. 081-838-9800).

Elegant Five-Star Hotel Dining Rooms: Pontresina's two top hotels each have wonderful restaurants in sumptuous dining rooms. **Stüva-Bella Restaurant,** in the cellar of the fanciful faux-castle Hotel Walther at the top end of town, is expensive and exclusive, with a flair for serving inventive and light regional and international cuisine. Their five-course fixed-price meal for 85–100-SF is a good splurge, but you'll be amazed at how well you can eat with only their 10-SF salad bar and a cheese plate (30–50-SF entrées, June–Sept and Jan–Easter daily 19:00–22:30—kitchen closes at 21:30, closed Easter–May and Oct–Dec, Via Maistra 215, tel. 081-839-3636). **Kronenstübli** is in the Grand Hotel Kronenhof, which dominates the bottom end of town and has public rooms fit for a Vienna palace. It's less accommodating to anyone concerned about price, but if you've got francs to burn, its five-course fixed-price meal for 150 SF is a memorable splurge (100-SF three-course-meal, 45–60-SF main dishes, closed Sun–Mon, Via Maistra, tel. 081-830-3030, www.kronenhof.com).

Eating Above Pontresina: **Alp Languard Chalet,** at the top of the lift (7,710 feet up—see page 285), serves affordable meals with unbeatable views (18-SF daily special, mid-June–mid-Oct daily 8:30–17:00, tel. 079-719-7810).

Samedan

Little Samedan (sah-MAY-den) offers a convenient peek at Upper Engadine village culture and buildings. This town, which has the most traditional Engadine architecture of the three destinations in this chapter, is the historic capital of the valley. Romansh remains its first language. Though charming, Samedan is also humble and a bit rough around the edges—it feels like the backwater cousin of ritzy St. Moritz and Pontresina.

Orientation to Samedan

Samedan is gently spread over a hill that rises up from the Inn River. It's steeper than it is big. The train station is at the bottom of town; the town center clusters just above. The characteristic cobbled street called Via Plazzet runs through the middle of town, parallel to the river. All of the streets seem to converge at the Protestant church on the square called Plaz.

Tourist Information: Samedan's TI is at Via Plazzet 21, across from the giant, pink Hotel Bernina (Mon–Fri 8:45–12:00 & 13:30–18:00, Sat until 17:30, closed Sun, also closed Sat off-season, tel. 081-851-0060, www.samedan.ch).

Arrival in Samedan: Whether you come by bus or train, you'll wind up at the train station (though some buses do go up into the town itself—ask). From here, just hike up the hill, bearing left (on Via Mulin) to reach the main square, or right (on Via Retica) to reach the TI.

Self-Guided Walk

Samedan Town Stroll

There's little to do in Samedan other than relax and enjoy a pleasant walk with nice views. The route described here takes you steeply up through town to a perch overlooking Samedan's magnificent setting.

Begin at the **main square (Plaz),** where all of Samedan's cobbled streets meet. Just downhill, the blocky, modern building with the colorful window frames is Samedan's new "vertical spa," with several levels of pools (www.mineralbad-samedan.ch). As you face the church, a left on the main drag, Via Plazzet, would take you to the Chesa Planta mansion, the TI, and the recommended

Traditional Engadine Architecture

Samedan and Pontresina both have fine old traditional houses. A short stroll in either town shows plenty of traditional elements and medieval ingenuity intended to keep inhabitants warm in the harsh mountain weather. Walls are thick—typically two feet—for insulation. Notice how windows are like the narrow end of a funnel—originally covered with animal skin rather than glass. Bay windows gathered maximum precious light and came with built-in seats where women would sit to do handwork.

Even though they're thoroughly modernized, the structural essence of these grand farmhouses survives. You can still see the big lower door for animals and the big upper door for hay and the carriage—with a smaller door built into it for people to get in and out while minimizing heat loss. People had the animals sleep below in the hope their rising body heat would warm the living space above. Proud noble family coats of arms still decorate buildings; many local families can trace their heritage to the Middle Ages.

Look for the traditional Engadine *sgraffito* ornamentation on exterior walls. To make *sgraffito*, facades are covered with a layer of dark plaster, which is then covered with white or colored plaster. Decorations, which are much more durable than painted facades, are scratched within three hours through the wet white layer, so that the dark background appears. These rustic and crude decorations look modern, but have a long history.

Hotel/Restaurant da la Posta (all described later).

But to begin our hike, let's walk uphill on Surtuor, following the white sign for *Kath. Kirch*. After a few blocks, on the right, the 13th-century, castle-like **stone tower** was the private tower of a noble family. From its wooden balcony, they'd oversee festivities in their little domain.

The next house up, at **#12,** dates from 1656. This X-shaped house is in the form of a St. Andrew's cross, made of extended roof beams. This was a popular way to bless homes here. Notice the sturdy beam ends—roofs were built to support heavy stones and snow. Houses come with Romansh names—for example, you'll see houses marked *Chesa Juzi* (Juzi's House) and *Chesa dals 3 Frers* (House of the Three Brothers).

The **Catholic Church** (Neo-Romanesque from 1910, with a bell dating back to 1505) stands at the top of the town. From here, survey the surrounding slopes. Notice the ancient terracing from Celtic peoples.

Continue uphill, passing the ski lift. Where the road swings right, pause at the yellow bench for the gorgeous **view.** Samedan lies at the point where the two valleys of the Inn and Flazbach rivers merge. From here, the Inn River continues through Innsbruck before joining the Danube.

Huff and puff the thin air (you're at 6,000 feet) to the dramatically situated Protestant **Church of St. Peter.** The Romanesque bell tower (c. 1100) predates today's late Gothic church (c. 1480; now a burial church, generally closed to tourists). Benches line the cemetery walls and offer sunny, wind-protected picnic spots. Beneath you stretches the highest-altitude airport in Europe, a favorite among gliders (launched by a yellow truck with a huge winch, rather than an airplane). When you've had your fill of the views, head back down into town.

Sights in Samedan

Chesa Planta—This interesting old mansion, just a block from the main square, shows off upper-crust lifestyles of the 18th and 19th centuries. This former residence of the wealthy local Planta family is preserved as it was when they lived here. It can only be visited with a 1.5-hour German tour (with an English handout), but the fascinating interior makes it worth considering if you happen to be here at the right time (10 SF; Tue, Wed, and Thu at 16:30; tel. 081-852-5624, www.chesaplanta.ch).

You'll see some gorgeous wood-carved rooms, a beautifully painted dining room, original granite slab floors, and fancy ceramic stoves. Upstairs, the same building houses the Romansh library *(biblioteca rumauntscha),* where scholars collect Romansh literature. A copy of any new book published in the Romansh language is sent to this library.

Sleeping and Eating in Samedan

(1 SF = about $1, country code: 41)

While Pontresina has more eating and sleeping options, Samedan hoards the lion's share of this valley's Graubünden quaintness.

$$$ Hotel Palazzo Mÿsanus is a nicely renovated historic hotel just a block below the main square. The building also houses the "smallest whisky bar on Earth." Of the 16 rooms, the cheaper "comfort" rooms come in two types: cozy pine-wood rustic or modern, all with tiny bathrooms (Sb-90 SF, Db-180 SF). The pricier "superior" rooms are all modern (Sb-115 SF, Db-230 SF; all rooms 15 SF more per person in mid-July–late Aug, 15 SF more per person for stays less than 3 nights; free Wi-Fi, Crappun 26, tel. 081-852-1080, www.palazzomysanus.ch, info@palazzomysanus).

$$ Hotel da la Posta dates back to the days when people stopped here to warm up and change horses rather than to play golf and ski. It rents nine comfy, woody rooms (Sb-80 SF, Db-160 SF, good restaurant, Via Plazzet 16, tel. 081-852-5354, fax 081-852-4692, ursula.baumann2@bluewin.ch, Ursula and Renzo).

$$ Gasthaus zum Weissen Kreuz/Croce Bianca is your budget option, with 20 tight, basic, old-fashioned rooms with new bathrooms above a restaurant just downhill from the main square (S-70 SF, Sb-90 SF, D-120 SF, Db-140 SF, cash only, tel. 081-852-5353, www.crocesamedan.ch, info@crocesamedan.ch).

Eating: **Restaurant da la Posta,** in the recommended Hotel da la Posta, is a characteristic old eatery run with a passion for the local culture (15–20-SF pastas, 14–31-SF main dishes, 15-SF lunch special, closed Sun). The **Bernina Pizzeria,** next door in the grand Hotel Bernina, is also a good value (closed Tue).

St. Moritz

The oldest and perhaps best-known winter resort in the world, St. Moritz has long been the winter haunt of Europe's rich and famous. Its sister city says it all: Vail.

It's said that in 1864, St. Moritz hotel pioneer Johannes Badrutt invented winter tourism in the Alps. To allay his British guests' skepticism, he offered them free accommodations if the winter weather was bad. They came and enjoyed fine weather. He liquored them up, they had fun...and they brought their friends along the next year. St. Moritz hosted the Winter Olympics in 1928 and 1948.

Although St. Moritz might have once been a real town, today it's little more than a cluster of luxury hotels and designer boutiques. (Think of it as the anti-Gimmelwald.) But it's still fun to spend a couple of hours exploring its highly manicured cobbles, and nightlife-seekers find St. Moritz livelier than the surrounding towns. For the jet set, winter is prime time in St. Moritz. Summer is quieter and popular with sporty types and nature lovers. While celebrity-spotting drops way, way off in the summer, prices are more reasonable. It's also a great time for hiking and adventure sports. Visitors enjoy inline skating, polo, golf, paragliding, horseback riding, strolling around the lake, and evening concerts. Cable cars zip you to some great mountaintops.

Orientation to St. Moritz

St. Moritz has two centers: the town *(Dorf)* and the spa *(Bad)*.

St. Moritz Dorf is on a steep slope, with the train station *(Bahnhof)* at its base. St. Moritz Bad sprawls on a level plain along the lake; it has some sport facilities (covered pool, tennis courts, ice-skating hall, horseback riding, and so on), but it's mostly a characterless concrete town. Most visitors spend their time in St. Moritz Dorf...and should. Aside from the chance to walk around the lake, St. Moritz Bad is pretty, well, bad.

Connecting the two zones is easy: Convenient bus #3 does a loop between the train station *(Bahnhof)*, St. Moritz Dorf, and St. Moritz Bad (4/hr, 3 SF).

Tourist Information

The slick TI is in the center of St. Moritz Dorf, just a block off of the main square (July–mid-Oct Mon–Fri 9:00–18:30, Sat 9:00–12:30 & 13:30–18:00, Sun 16:00–18:00; off-season Mon–Fri 9:00–12:00 & 14:00–18:00, Sat 9:00–12:00, closed Sun; Plaza Mauritius, tel. 081-837-3333, www.engadin.stmoritz.ch).

Arrival in St. Moritz

St. Moritz's train station is near the lake, just below the Dorf. The station has lockers and WCs, but no TI or bike rental. Pick up a free map at the train information counter. The train station café is a rare budget option in this pricey town (10–17 SF dishes, Mon–Sat 6:00–20:00, Sun 6:30–20:00).

To reach the Dorf, it's about a 15-minute steep uphill hike, or you can hop on bus #3 (4/hr, 3 SF). If walking, to save some sweat, exit the station to the left and walk to the Serletta parking garage. Inside the garage, find the art-lined escalator (Switzerland's longest) that zips you up next to the Palace Hotel. From there it's a relatively quick walk up to the center of St. Moritz Dorf.

Helpful Hints

Altitude Alert: Don't forget that St. Moritz is at a high elevation (6,090 feet); you might feel dizzy and tired, and your body needs time to adapt. Top athletes from all over the world come here for altitude training before the Olympics.

Shopping: You'll find two **Co-op** stores in St. Moritz. In St. Moritz Dorf, the basic Co-op grocery right on the main square (Plaza da Scoula) is the only budget eating option I've found in this part of town. A giant Co-op supermarket/department store is on Via dal Bagn, at the entrance to St. Moritz Bad (both open Mon–Fri 8:00–18:30, Sat 8:00–17:00, closed Sun).

Ski Rental: In St. Moritz Dorf, **Ender Sport** is one of many rental shops (just uphill from TI and recommended hotels at Via Maistra 26, tel. 081-833-3536). In St. Moritz Bad, **Boom Sport** has a knowledgeable staff, good selection, and handy location (closed Sun and for lunch 12:15–14:00, Via Tegiatscha 5, tel. 081-832-2222).

Sights in St. Moritz

▲▲**Segantini Museum**—This museum is dedicated to the ultimate painter of alpine life. Giovanni Segantini (1858–1899) came here to get away from the misty air of Milan. The crisp alpine atmosphere was great for capturing the bright, sharp, crystal-clear mountain light. Painting in the open air with brushstrokes that invigorated his fascinating scenes, Segantini created works reminiscent of the French Impressionists. The tiny museum, which looks like a Neo-Byzantine church, is actually based on Segantini's design of the Swiss Pavilion for the 1900 World's Fair in Paris—but made of local stone, rather than the originally intended

_marginal:_ ST. MORITZ

steel. Segantini died young (at age 41, in 1899), and money ran out before this grandiose pavilion could be built. Segantini's masterpiece, the *Alpine Triptych*, was painted for the World's Fair, but also never completed. Segantini's ill-fated vision—both his pavilion and his life's major work—is now here, near where he settled in his thirties.

The paintings are exhibited on two floors. The worthwhile 3-SF audioguide includes about 30 minutes of commentary that brings meaning to your visit. Begin by climbing the stairs up to the round room on the top floor, where you can view the haunting *Alpine Triptych:* three paintings representing (left to right) life, nature, and death. Notice how, even in the death scene—as the body of a newly deceased loved one is brought out to a horse cart while mourning women look on—there's a glimmer of hope and faith in the swirling clouds above. Segantini even designed the *Triptych*'s frames, ornamented with the local five-needled Arven pine.

Then head to back to the entry level, and spend some time with the many smaller canvases here. Particularly notable is *Ave Maria at the Crossing,* as a man rowing a simple boat—laden with a flock of sheep and a mother and baby—pauses to pray at sunset as the church bells toll.

Cost and Hours: 10 SF, audioguide-3 SF, late May–late Oct and mid-Dec–late April Tue–Sun 10:00–12:00 & 14:00–18:00, closed Mon, closed late Oct–mid-Dec and late April–late May, Via Somplaz 30, tel. 081-833-4454, www.segantini-museum.ch.

Getting There: The museum is perched on the road above the lake about a 15-minute walk southwest of St. Moritz (well-marked from the central roundabout). Rather than walking on the road itself, look for the "Segantiniweg" path that cuts through the woods just above the road. Or you can take bus #2 or #5 to the Segantini Museum stop. Drivers will find metered roadside parking just before the museum.

Engadiner Museum—The historic, domestic, and social cultures of the Engadine region are displayed in this museum. The building (from 1905) houses interiors and furniture from throughout the Engadine (such as a patrician living room, a smoky farm kitchen, and a four-poster bed), as well as an exhibit on the discovery of the spa water that put St. Moritz on the vacation map (8 SF, Sun–Fri 10:00–12:00 & 14:00–17:00, closed Sat, closed May and Nov, Via dal Bagn 39, take bus #3 to Via Aruons, tel. 081-833-4333, www.engadiner-museum.ch).

Berry Museum—Dedicated not to delicious little fruits, but to local painter Peter Robert Berry (1864–1942), this museum introduces visitors to another talented alpine artist. While Berry enjoyed neither the talent nor the fame of Segantini, and the entry price is steep, this is a suitable rainy-day activity for art lovers (15 SF, includes audioguide, Wed–Mon 10:00–13:00 & 16:00–19:00, closed Tue, just below the center of St. Moritz Dorf at Via Arona 32, tel. 081-833-3018, www.berrymuseum.com).

Walk Around the Lake—The charming lake below St. Moritz is a delightful place for a stroll—especially on sunny summer days, when it's filled with sailboats. It takes about an hour to walk all the way around.

Sleeping in St. Moritz

(1 SF = about $1, country code: 41)

I prefer sleeping in Pontresina or Samedan, but St. Moritz has a certain allure. I've ignored the giant, overpriced hotels in favor of these smaller, cozier options, which have more character. The first two hotels are in St. Moritz Dorf, just uphill from the TI. The youth hostel is down below and across the lake, at the far end of St. Moritz Bad.

$$$ Hotel Eden is a classy-feeling small hotel renting 34 rooms. The public spaces are a mix of old-style and modern. This place seems to offer all the little extras, such as free afternoon tea in a grand lounge (Sb-132–152 SF, Db-208–260 SF; bigger "superior" rooms with views: Sb-143–165 SF, Db-244–332 SF; higher prices are mid-July–Aug, elevator, free Wi-Fi, free parking, Via Veglia 12, tel. 081-830-8100, www.edenstmoritz.ch, info @edenstmoritz.ch).

$$$ Hotel Languard, next door, is a bit cozier and friendlier, with 22 pine-wood rooms (Sb-90–110 SF, Db-180–195 SF; "superior" rooms with views: Sb-110–140 SF, Db-195–295 SF; higher prices are for early July–late Aug, 10 percent more for stays of 1 or 2 nights, elevator, free Wi-Fi, free parking, Via Veglia 14, tel. 081-833-3137, fax 081-833-4546, www.languard-stmoritz.ch, hotel@languard-stmoritz.ch).

$$ Youth Hostel Stille is at the boring, residential eastern end of St. Moritz Bad—one of the last buildings before the woods. Despite its inconvenient location, it offers 190 beds and all the services, activities, games, and lavish extras a top-end hostel can have (dorm beds-51 SF, D-130 SF, Db-152 SF, price includes breakfast and four-course dinner, prices about 10 SF per person higher in winter, nonmembers pay 6 SF more, reception open 7:00–10:00 & 16:00–22:00, 10-min walk from bus stop on Via Sela, Via Surpunt 60, tel. 081-836-6111, fax 081-836-6112, www.youthhostel.ch /st.moritz, st.moritz@youthhostel.ch).

Eating in St. Moritz

Similar to Pontresina, most of St. Moritz's restaurants are in hotels. An exception is **Restaurant Engiadina,** well-regarded for its raclette and fondues (lunches around 20 SF, 17-SF pizzas, 30–50-SF main dishes, Mon–Sat 11:30–14:00 & 18:15–21:30, closed Sun, dead-center in St. Moritz Dorf at Plaza da Scuola 2, tel. 081-833-3265).

Restaurant Hauser is the standard stop for local workers who know where to find the best-value meal in town. Centrally located in St. Moritz Dorf, this place has everything: restaurant, café, pastry shop, indoor and outdoor seating, and a vast menu (most meals 17–27 SF, weekday lunch specials under 20 SF, daily 8:00–23:00, below Hotel Hauser at Via Traunter Plazzas 7, tel. 081-837-5050).

In St. Moritz Bad: **Veltlinerkeller,** decorated with a huge stuffed moose head, is a casual-feeling eatery that serves a variety of grilled meats and Italian specialties (20–25-SF pastas, 25–40-SF main dishes, daily 9:00–14:00 & 17:00–23:00, in St. Moritz Bad at Via dal Bagn 11, tel. 081-833-4009).

Upper Engadine Connections

By Train: St. Moritz, Pontresina, and **Samedan** are all connected to each other by train (hourly, 10 min, 5 SF). From these towns, trains go to **Chur** (hourly, 2 hrs), **Tirano** (hourly, 2.5 hrs), and **Zürich** (hourly, 3.75 hrs, transfer in Chur). From Pontresina, you may have to change in Samedan. For details on the Bernina Express and Glacier Express, see the Scenic Rail Journeys chapter. Train info: toll tel. 0900-300-300 or www.rail.ch.

By Bus: For details on getting around the region by bus, see page 278. If connecting to **Lugano** in the Italian–Swiss canton of Ticino, consider the "Palm Express" bus (departs St. Moritz train station at 12:20, stops at Menaggio on Italy's Lake Como en route, arrives at Lugano's train station at 16:10; daily mid-June–mid-Oct, Sat–Mon only mid-Oct–mid-June).

SCENIC RAIL JOURNEYS

Golden Pass • William Tell Express • Bernina Express •
Glacier Express • Chur

Switzerland has one of the world's best rail networks, and many of its tracks run through some of the world's best scenery. While just about any train ride in Switzerland is photogenic, four are aggressively marketed as the most spectacular: the Golden Pass, the William Tell Express, the Bernina Express, and the Glacier Express. If you're looking for a scenic day enjoying the Alps from the window of your train, and would like to do it in one of Switzerland's unique "panoramic cars" (offering huge windows that sweep halfway across the ceiling), these journeys can be great experiences. Though they aren't quite as "fantastic with countless highlights" as they're advertised to be (the high lifts in ski areas like the Berner Oberland are much higher and more breathtaking), the trains are a fun way to do some sightseeing while getting from point A to point B.

This chapter provides you with all the logistical, nuts-and-bolts information you'll need to splice each journey into your itinerary. I've also written a commentary on each route, describing the highlights in the direction that most travelers are likely to go. If you travel in the opposite direction, the same information still applies—just hold the book upside-down.

This chapter also includes information about Chur, a town that's not really worth a visit, except that it lies at the intersection of the Bernina Express and Glacier Express routes. Chur makes for a handy pit stop or overnight if connecting these trips.

Tickets

Schedules Can Change: In this chapter, I've listed specific departure and arrival times, but these schedules are always subject to change, so it's essential to confirm the times before you travel. Timetables for most of these trains appear on the Swiss Rail website: www.rail.ch. (Also try Germany's all-Europe rail site, http://bahn.hafas.de/bin/query.exe/en; or call the Swiss Rail info line at 0900-300-300, 1.20 SF/min.) Any train station in Switzerland can provide you with free schedules. Each scenic rail line also operates its own website, with even more details (listed in each section, below).

Buying Tickets: Tickets and reservations for all of these scenic rail lines can be purchased at any train station in Switzerland. In the US, you'll pay more (about $20 per order) to get tickets and reservations through your travel agent or at www.raileurope.com. Getting your reservations before you go also limits your flexibility, as reservations made through US agents are nonchangeable and nonrefundable—unlike reservations made at train stations in Europe.

Reservations: You can book these journeys as early as three months ahead, or as late as the day before, at any Swiss train station or on the various websites (but be warned that many sell out several days ahead in high season). The Glacier Express requires reservations. If you want to take the official tourist package for the William Tell Express or the Bernina Express, reservations are also required. Reserve the Golden Pass only if you want a front-row VIP seat. To save money and maximize your flexibility, you can take standard regional trains (without panoramic cars) on all scenic routes without a reservation (though the bus segment of the Bernina Express requires a reservation, it's easy to purchase from the driver on the bus). These alternatives are explained in each section below.

Eurailpass and Swiss Pass: Two major types of railpasses can be useful in Switzerland: A Eurailpass (Global Pass or Selectpass that includes Switzerland) and a Swiss Pass. These railpasses cover most of your travel on the scenic rail journeys. But seat reservations always cost extra, and some trips aren't fully covered by a railpass: Even if you have a first-class Eurailpass or Swiss Pass, you'll pay 39 SF extra for the William Tell Express package trip (or 86 SF extra with a second-class pass). However, traveling the same route on standard regional trains, rather than on the designated tourist trains, is fully covered by a railpass. And on the Glacier Express, two different segments of the trip are free with a Swiss Pass, but not covered by a Eurailpass (with a Eurailpass, Disentis to Brig costs 46 SF second-class; Brig to Zermatt costs 34 SF).

When buying your ticket or making reservations, be sure the ticket agent understands what type of pass you have (if any) and exactly what trip you're taking. Confirm that you've gotten all the reservations and other tickets you need to complete your trip.

Scenic Swiss Rail Routes

GERMANY

FRANCE

AUSTRIA

ITALY

Zürich

Luzern

BOAT

Flüelen

Wassen

Landquart

Chur

Davos

Inter-
laken

Spiez

Zweisimmen

Andermatt

Disentis

Filisur

St. Moritz

Lausanne

Gstaad

Airolo

Montreux

Brig

Pontresina

Visp

Poschiavo

Geneva

Locarno

Bellinzona

Tirano

Zermatt

Lugano

Sorico
Menaggio

BUS

- - - - - - - - **Golden Pass**   ———— **William Tell Express**
- - - - - - - - **Glacier Express**   ———— **Bernina Express**

While rail agents generally know what railpasses cover, sometimes they don't, which leads to frustrating run-ins with conductors who insist that you've only paid for part of your trip.

Train Types

Various types of trains, with various types of cars, run these routes. Here are the key distinctions to look for:

Classes: Most trains have both first- and second-class cars. The difference between the first- and second-class cars is generally the same on tourist trains as on standard trains (first class has somewhat wider seats, a little more legroom, and fewer passengers; second-class cars offer the same scenery, go just as fast, and usually still have plenty of room). On some of the tourist trains (such as portions of the Golden Pass), panoramic cars are only available in first class. If you have a second-class railpass, you can always pay extra to sit in first on any given train. In bigger train stations, a digital panel on the tracks indicates departure time, destination, and composition of the train (that is, at which part of the platform you'll find the first- or second-class cars).

Standard vs. Tourist Trains: In many cases, standard trains operated by Swiss Rail run these same routes—more frequently, and usually less expensively (though you'll sacrifice things such as fancy dining cars and souvenir key chains). Because standard trains are used by local commuters, they may stop at more stations along the route than the designed-for-tourists panoramic trains. Many travelers enjoy the flexibility of following the scenic route on standard trains, enabling them to hop off and explore a village, then hop on the next standard train that comes through—without the headache of reservations

(which are rarely necessary on standard trains).

Panoramic vs. Standard Cars: All of the tourist trains on the routes in this chapter offer special panoramic cars, usually in both first and second class, so there's no need to splurge for first class.

Panoramic cars have huge wrap-around windows, allowing you to see through part of the ceiling and most of the walls. The

Golden Pass trains go one better: The driver sits in a little bubble upstairs, leaving the very front of the train open for VIP seating with completely unobstructed views of what's coming up. The windows in the panoramic cars generally can't open, meaning that photographs often suffer from glare, and the interior (even with air-conditioning) can heat up on sunny days.

Since nonpanoramic cars have a smaller field of vision than the panoramic cars, these require a little more bobbing and weaving to enjoy the views. Aside from being cheaper, the chief advantage of the standard cars is that the windows generally can be opened, for cool air and photos without reflections. Passengers in panoramic cars are free to walk to the standard cars to open a window and snap a photo.

Golden Pass

The exceptionally picturesque Golden Pass train route cuts a swath diagonally across the pristine center of Switzerland, connecting Luzern with Lake Geneva. Of all the rail journeys in this chapter, its central location—lacing together many of Switzerland's top sights—makes the Golden Pass the one you're most likely to take.

Orientation to the Golden Pass

The Route

The Golden Pass officially runs between Luzern and Lake Geneva's Montreux, though you could easily connect onward to Zürich or Geneva with standard trains. With less time, you could hone in even more on the very best stretch, from Interlaken to Montreux.

Because the tracks change from narrow to standard gauge to narrow again, two train changes are required (at Interlaken Ost and Zweisimmen). On each stretch, you can choose between the official Golden Pass tourist train with panoramic cars (on the last stretch, you can also opt for a Golden Pass train with vintage rail cars) and more frequent standard trains without panoramic cars. Here's the breakdown.

Luzern to Interlaken Ost (East): Tourist trains (3/day, 2 hrs); standard trains (hourly, 2–2.5 hrs).

Interlaken Ost to Zweisimmen: Direct tourist trains (3/day, 1.25 hr); standard trains (at least hourly, 1.25–1.5 hrs).

Zweisimmen to Montreux: Tourist trains (3/day, 1.75 hrs); "classic" Golden Pass trains with vintage rail cars (2/day, 1.75 hrs); standard trains (almost hourly, 1.75–2 hrs). This is the stretch most likely to fill up, so consider reserving ahead for either of the two tourist-train options.

Planning Your Time: Because it connects so many knockout Swiss destinations (Luzern, Interlaken, and Lake Geneva), and because it goes in both directions, the Golden Pass can be spliced into your itinerary in many different ways. I'd focus on the best stretch, using it to connect Interlaken and Lake Geneva (3 hrs total, including the lovely 2-hr segment from Zweisimmen to Montreux).

However you use it, check schedules along the way and plan your layovers strategically to maximize time on the panoramic cars. For example, if traveling from Luzern to Lake Geneva, consider taking the 8:55 panoramic train from Luzern to Interlaken Ost (arriving at 10:55), then wander Interlaken and have lunch before catching the 13:08 panoramic train to Montreux (change trains in Zweisimmen at 14:19, arrive Montreux at 16:13).

Cost and Schedule

The Golden Pass trip from Luzern to Montreux costs 69 SF second class; the "best of" segment from Interlaken to Montreux is 48 SF. The entire ride is covered by a Eurailpass or Swiss Pass. Reservations, while not required, are recommended for summer midmorning departures and the super-scenic front seats (15 SF for front-row VIP seats, 5–10 SF for other seats in panoramic cars; more details under "Seating," below).

Special Golden Pass trains—all with panoramic cars and some with front-row VIP seating—depart several times each day. Standard trains run from Spiez to Montreux every hour (2-hr trip, change trains in Zweisimmen). These regular regional trains show you the same scenery without the big windows.

Information: Most of the route is part of the Swiss Rail network. Golden Pass panoramic trains on the section between Zweisimmen and Montreux are operated by MOB (toll tel. 0900-245-245 within Switzerland, 1 SF/min, from elsewhere in Europe dial 00-41-840-245-245, from the US call 011-41-840-245-245, www.goldenpass.ch). BLS runs some panoramic trains between Interlaken and Zweisimmen (tel. 313-327-2727, www.bls.ch). An English-language guidebook describing the route is sold on the train (12 SF).

Seating: Both tourist and standard trains run the entire Luzern–Montreux route. Again, for the lovely stretch from Zweisimmen to Montreux, you have three options: standard trains (almost hourly); trains with panoramic cars (3/day); and trains with "classic" vintage cars (2/day).

Some panoramic cars have special VIP seats (up to 3/day May–Nov, 1/day Dec–April). On these cars, the conductor drives the train from a little domed area upstairs—leaving both the front and back of the train open for passengers. The first two rows, offering VIP seats with an unobstructed view of the pristine alpine scenery coming right at you, require a supplement of 15 SF (reserve in advance, or just grab one if available and pay the conductor on the spot).

The nonsupplement seats just behind the VIP seats give you a bit of the grand front view (and cheapskates have been known to grab a few free minutes up front). The panoramic cars have first- and second-class seating (with panoramic ceilings in both—no need to spring for first class, unless you want VIP seats).

Note that on the Luzern–Interlaken section, you'll need to

choose between panoramic (first class) and nonpanoramic (second class) cars.

Eating on the Golden Pass: The Luzern–Interlaken stretch is the only section with a restaurant car, but it may be closed on trains running early or late in the day. Snacks and bar service may be available on other sections of the trip, but the menu is limited and pricey. Save your money and eat fresh by packing a picnic.

Self-Guided Tour

The Golden Pass

I've described only the best and most visually exciting portion of the Golden Pass journey, the five-hour stretch from Luzern to Lake Geneva, focusing on the *crème de la crème*—the two hours between Zweisimmen and Montreux (described from north to south).

As you leave Luzern (sit on the right side), you'll go along the lake to Alpnachstad, the starting point for the cogwheel train that climbs to the top of Mount Pilatus (the massive bulk on the right, see page 88). Then the train follows the Sarner Aa river through farmland, passing through the town of Sarnen. Lake Sarnen comes into view, and the tracks run alongside it. Beyond the end of the lake is the town of Giswil, where the train begins its gradual ascent to **Brünig Pass.** Eventually the train runs above the beautiful turquoise waters of the Lungernsee reservoir. After passing the resort of Lungern, the train climbs gradually through the forest to the summit station of Brunig-Hasliberg (keep an eye out for fake animal cutouts—lynx, ibex, deer—placed whimsically in the woods at eye-level). After cresting the pass, the train descends to the Aare river valley, with its sheer cliffs and waterfalls. The arrow-straight river channel, straightened by the ever-efficient Swiss, slices through the broad valley. Sir Arthur Conan Doyle chose the town of Meiringen and nearby Reichenbach Falls as the setting for the death of Sherlock Holmes. The train then follows the river to beautiful **Lake Brienz** (Brienzersee). From the town of Brienz, a bus runs to the remarkable open-air museum at Ballenberg (see page 142). Beyond Brienz, the train follows the lakeshore to Interlaken.

As the train pulls out of Interlaken, you cruise along the south bank of **Lake Thun** (Thunersee). Interlaken ("between the lakes") is situated between the big lakes of Thun and Brienz. Before long, at the town of Spiez, you'll split off and head southwest to Zweisimmen.

Leaving Zweisimmen, you'll roll through **Simmental** valley, famous among American farmers for its top-end cows. Big farmhouses lie scattered in the lush meadows—an indication that the farmland is good here. The large wooden buildings are typical of Bernese farm architecture: housing the barn, sheltering the crops, and storing agricultural machines, all under one huge roof. Farming is heavily subsidized in Switzerland, and farmers form the strongest economic lobby. Trying to increase their modest income, many farmers have switched to exotic crops (like melons) or animals. Ostriches, yaks, bison, and highland cattle have become a common sight in the Swiss Alps lately.

Between Saanenmoser and Schonried, the train reaches its highest point (about 4,000 feet) and stops at the famous resort town of **Gstaad.** Although known as a favorite hangout for famous "backpackers" such as Monaco's Princess Caroline, Liz Taylor, Roger Moore, and Roman Polanski, the town does not offer many exciting sights. In winter, the modest ski slopes are not as crowded as the flashy nightspots, as most of the skiers are more into *après*-ski activities. Sipping their cocktails, they eye each other and discuss the latest trends in ski gear fashion. In summer, Gstaad hosts the Swiss Open tennis, polo, and golf tournaments, as well as music festivals. Violin virtuoso Yehudi Menuhin founded the Menuhin Festival here. While it started as an opportunity for young classical musicians to show their talent, today it's known for high-quality classical concerts.

Just south of Gstaad, you say *auf Wiedersehen* to the German-speaking part of Switzerland and *bonjour* to **French Switzerland.** The mountains are jagged. In fact, many are called *dents,* the French word for "teeth." With the change in language comes a change in culture and architecture. French-style gray stone houses are replacing half-timbered, woody, German-style chalets. The mountain airstrips—generally made for the Swiss Air Force during World War II—are used today for sightseeing flights around the Alps. The cute village of Rougemont, with its traditional chalets, is famous among the Swiss as the place where the wealthy send their girls to boarding school.

Happy **cows** spend their summers on the Alps, wandering freely and munching the fragrant herbs of these lush alpine meadows. The resulting milk is the secret ingredient for tasty Gruyère cheese. On steep hillsides here, the grass is still cut by hand. It dries in the summer sun, then is collected and stored in the barns to serve as cow salads through the winter (see "Swiss Cow Culture" sidebar on page 158).

You might consider interrupting your journey in **Château d'Oex,** known for its Hot-Air Ballooning Week (last week of January). Bertrand Piccard and Brian Jones took off from here on March 1, 1999, and sailed their balloon all the way around the world. Below the train station, Le Chalet restaurant gives insight on Gruyère cheese production.

SCENIC RAIL JOURNEYS

South of Château d'Oex, the valley narrows to a deep gorge. Up on the hillsides, the damage of the devastating 1999 winter storm "**Lothar**" can still be seen. Entire forests were leveled, aggravating the already precarious avalanche situation. The trees on the steep slopes stop the snow from sliding down and burying the villages. Once the trees are gone, they don't grow back. Artificial avalanche barriers need to be erected. Landslides and floods have been relatively common in recent years—an unfortunate consequence of uncontrolled deforestation and construction of vacation homes in areas that traditionally served as pastures and forestlands.

The small **lake** is dammed and used for hydroelectric power. Switzerland makes good use of its Alps for production of electricity. Although it has some nuclear power plants, 60 percent of Switzerland's energy is hydroelectric. The country exports its electricity to France and Italy.

Montbovon is the place to change trains if you're going to Bulle or Gruyères (see "French Swiss Countryside" on page 251). After the first tunnel, an inscription on the barn to the right welcomes you to the Gruyère region: *La Gruyère vous salue.*

The train winds its way uphill with more curves and tunnels than before. Passing through the **Jaman Tunnel,** you're engulfed in nearly two miles of darkness. When you emerge, you're in another world—you've left the feudal Middle Ages and entered the 19th-century belle époque. At the village of Les Avants, one of Switzerland's oldest winter resorts, you catch the first glimpses of Lake Geneva sprawling deep underneath you and begin a steep descent. A series of sharp bends in tunnels takes you out of the mountains and down to lake level.

The architecture has even more of a French flair now that you've entered the **"Swiss Riviera."** Palm trees, vines, and many sanatoriums indicate that this is a warmer climate. You're surrounded by the vineyards of the Lavaux region, famous for its white wine. The view broadens to include the French Alps of Savoy across the lake, the lakeshore of the Swiss Riviera to the west, and the broad Rhône Valley to the east. As you approach Montreux—with its grand hotels—the train meanders its way intimately through private gardens.

Montreux has the only train station in Europe with three different rail gauges: regular, narrow (which you're on), and very skinny (for the Rochers de Naye train, taking sightseers to a nearby peak with views less exciting than those you've just enjoyed).

From here, it's an easy train trip to Lausanne, or a quick bus ride or about a one-mile lakefront hike to Château de Chillon (see the Lake Geneva and French Switzerland chapter).

Golden Pass Connections

From Luzern by Train to: Zürich (2/hr, 1 hr), **Zürich Airport** (2/hr, 1.25 hrs, most change in Zürich), **Bern** (2/hr, 1–1.5 hrs), **Lugano** (hourly, 2.5 hrs, half with change in Arth-Goldau), **Chur** (hourly, 2.25 hrs, change in Thalwil).

From Interlaken Ost (East) by Train to: Lauterbrunnen (2/hr, 20 min), **Spiez** (3/hr, 25 min), **Brienz** (1–2/hr, 20 min), **Bern** (2/hr, 55 min), **Zürich** and **Zürich Airport** (2–3/hr, 2–2.25 hrs, transfer in Bern).

From Montreux by Train to: Lausanne (4/hr, 25 min), **Bern** (2/hr, 1.5 hrs, transfer in Lausanne), **Geneva** (2/hr, 1–1.25 hr).

William Tell Express

The William Tell Express figures it deserves the most famous name in Switzerland. Tell exists only in legend, but his story—being forced to shoot an apple off his son's head because he refused to bow to the Habsburg hat—helped inspire the Swiss to rebel against their Habsburg rulers. The train route crosses the place where the first Swiss cantons pledged "all for one and one for all," the birthplace of the Confoederatio Helvetica in 1291. The trip is half by boat and half by train from Luzern to the Italian-speaking region of Ticino (the towns of Lugano and Locarno).

Don't go out of your way to do this trip. The boat ride is low-altitude and more pastoral than thrilling, and the train ride is more interesting as a lesson in Swiss engineering than impressive for its views. (Because the train cuts through the highest mountains inside the Gotthard tunnel, it only reaches 3,600 feet above sea level.)

But if you're connecting Luzern and Italian Switzerland anyway, this route is undeniably scenic. You can book the official "William Tell Express" trip, or simply buy regular tickets with none of the hoopla. I'd save money and gain flexibility by just riding the boat and train on regular departures and skip the much-promoted tourist package. Even if you don't buy the package, you can still ride the fancy panoramic train (without a seat reservation) at no extra charge.

Orientation to the William Tell Express

The Route
The William Tell Express begins with a slow boat trip along the length of Lake Luzern from the city of Luzern to Flüelen (2.75

hrs). Then a train cuts down into the Italian-speaking canton of Ticino (2 hrs). In the town of Bellinzona, you'll choose between two end points: Lugano or Locarno (I prefer Lugano).

The 2.75-hour boat trip from Luzern to Flüelen is lazy and very pretty. As the traditional steamer blows its old-time horn, you glide by idyllic lakeside resort towns and under mighty peaks. If you're in a hurry, you can get a flavor for the lake by doing a shorter round-trip cruise during your time in Luzern. Then take the train to Flüelen (1 hr from Luzern, as opposed to 2.75 hrs by boat); you'll see essentially the same scenery as the William Tell "Express" boat, but three times faster.

Whether you ride the boat or train from Luzern, in Flüelen you can join the William Tell Express panoramic train (departs Flüelen at 12:16 and 14:16). In Bellinzona, you can either transfer to a nonpanoramic train to Lugano or stay on the same train to Locarno.

Another option is to skip Flüelen entirely. Standard regional trains (without panoramic cars) make the Luzern–Lugano trip along the same route hourly in each direction (2.5 hrs total, www .rail.ch).

Cost and Schedule

The value of buying the official William Tell Express tourist trip is dubious (163 SF first class to Locarno, 166 SF first class to Lugano; no second-class option for official tourist trip). The only things that come "extra" with this pricey package are a mediocre lunch on the boat, a reserved seat on the panoramic train, a brochure about the route, and a souvenir Swiss Army–knife keychain. Travelers using a first-class Eurailpass or Swiss Pass pay a 39-SF reservation fee (86 SF with a second-class pass) to buy this official trip, but you're better off skipping the package altogether. Your railpass already covers the entire route, including the boat.

There are two official William Tell Express departures daily in each direction (running May–Oct only). Going north to south: The boat leaves Luzern at 9:12 and 11:12, docks in Flüelen where the panoramic train departs at 12:16 and 14:16, and arrives in Lugano at 14:27 and 16:27. Going south to north: The train departs Lugano at 9:30 and 11:30, meets the boat and leaves Flüelen at 12:00 and 14:00, and arrives in Luzern at 14:47 and 16:47. As always, be sure to confirm all times.

Information: The official William Tell Express departures are operated by the Lake Lucerne Navigation Company (tel. 041-367-6767, www.lakelucerne.ch). For more information, see www .wilhelmtellexpress.ch.

Helpful Hints

Boat Ride: If you're doing the full William Tell Express route, board the boat at pier 1 across from the Luzern train station. Present your ticket and pick up your package deal, including a lunch voucher and information flyers. There's no real baggage check on the boat; travelers just stack their backpacks and suitcases in a corner.

Lunch: The official William Tell Express boat trip comes with a forgettable lunch.

Train Trip: On the official William Tell Express train from Flüelen, you'll find first class and the panoramic car way out on the platform in sector C. Yellow slips mark which seats are reserved. If you have no reservation, take any seat without a yellow marker.

Self-Guided Tour

Here's what you'll see if you're doing the entire William Tell Express route. If you're taking only the train, skip to that section.

William Tell Boat Trip

The boat trip crisscrosses the **Vierwaldstättersee** (the "Lake of Four Forest Cantons"—or simply "Lake Luzern"). The trip is popular with the older generation of European tourists, who eat and drink their way through the lazy route. On a sunny day, you can sit on the deck and enjoy the mountain views. Survey the boat before you settle on a seat—consider sun, shade, and wind.

After two hours, you sail into the **canton of Uri,** and the landscape gets rougher, the slopes steeper, and the villages fewer and more rustic. This is William Tell country. The legendary Swiss national hero represents the essence of the country's spirit, still felt today: the desire for independence from foreign rule. William Tell has been a popular muse: Schiller wrote a play about him based on ancient Swiss chronicles, and Rossini set the legend to music in an 1829 opera.

Swiss patriots get excited as the boat approaches **Rütli.** The meadow above is the birthplace of the Swiss Confederation. In 1291, three representatives of the founding cantons met here and swore allegiance to each other, against their oppressive neighbors. More than 700 years later, Switzerland is still a confederation—but now its cantons number 26.

SCENIC RAIL JOURNEYS

Some hikers choose to disembark at Rütli and head for the mystical meadow marked by a big Swiss flag. Then they follow the **Weg der Schweiz** ("Path of Switzerland"), a trail leading around the lake. Along the way, they contemplate stone signs representing each of the 26 cantons in the order they joined the union. The canton markers are spaced according to each canton's population (the 20-mile-long trail is designed to have exactly 5 millimeters for each Swiss citizen).

Later, the boat stops at **Tellskapelle.** This 16th-century frescoed chapel marks another legendary spot: where William Tell jumped ship on the way to prison and swam to freedom.

The last stop is **Flüelen,** where the panoramic train awaits.

William Tell Train Trip

From Flüelen, the train climbs from 1,540 feet up to 3,600 feet, at the Gotthard tunnel—the primary north–south transportation route through the Alps. You enter a classic alpine world of snowcapped mountains towering above wild valleys, with narrow gorges carved by eons of angry white water. Wooden chalets, pine forests, and lush meadows dotted with munching cows complete this image of picture-perfect Central Switzerland.

The train tracks are protected from avalanches, landslides, and waterfalls by concrete galleries. Gazing out the window, you'll see some of the greatest accomplishments of Swiss road and railroad engineering. **Wassen,** marked by its striking chapel, is the climax for trainspotters—with more trains passing per minute than just about anywhere else. First, the chapel is on your right. Then the train loops around the tiny town, and the chapel is on your left. Your train disappears into a tunnel, and when you emerge, the same chapel is still there. The train actually spirals up the slopes. (The William Tell Express package comes with a schematic map that illustrates this.)

Göschenen (where you can transfer to Andermatt and on to the Glacier Express—see page 321) is the last stop before the 9.5-mile-long **Gotthard tunnel.** After 10 minutes of rocketing through darkness, you emerge in a whole different world—a different climate, canton (Ticino, rather than Uri), and language (Italian, rather than German). Since the 13th century—long before this tunnel was built—the Gotthard Pass has been *the* major trade route over this part of the Alps, connecting northern and southern Europe. The trade continues to rumble under rather than over the pass. These days, heavy truck traffic brings pollution and traffic jams—but little money—to Switzerland. But an ambitious new high-speed train tunnel, currently under construction, will allow shippers to transport merchandise by train and get trucks off the roads.

SCENIC RAIL JOURNEYS

Welcome to **Ticino,** Switzerland's botanical garden. While the weather around Lake Luzern is often iffy, Ticino feels Mediterranean—warm and southern—making it a favorite weekend destination for the Swiss. Rather than cuckoo-clock-like chalets, the houses are now plain, square, and made of stone. Instead of conifers, the forests are full of chestnut trees. You'll see vineyards, oleander, and even palm trees. And the upcoming train stops are announced in Italian now: *"Prossima fermata...."*

While life seemed almost too good in the pristine and touristic Lake Luzern region, here in the valley of **Leventina,** the economy is tougher. Unemployment rates are high, young folks have to commute into the cities farther south for a job, houses and roads aren't as well maintained, and window boxes no longer come with so many flowers.

As you approach **Biasca,** notice a modern square building with pebble walls on your left-hand side. This is the information center for the new 30-mile-long Gotthard Base Tunnel, which will be the longest train tunnel in the world (Tue–Sun 9:00–18:00, closed Mon; 12–40 SF guided tours of former work sites leave 4/day at 9:30, 13:30, 14:00, 15:30, call or book reservation on website; tel. 091-873-0550, www.infocentro.ch). You'll see industrial buildings and factories around Biasca.

If heading to Lugano, you may need to change trains in **Bellinzona.** (The official William Tell train continues to Locarno.) The train to Lugano passes the northern tip of Lake Maggiore and goes through a quiet, lush valley lined with picturesque villages and chestnut trees. Enjoy your time in Italian Switzerland!

William Tell Express Connections

From Luzern by Train to: Zürich (2/hr, 1 hr), **Zürich Airport** (2/hr, 1.25 hrs, most with change in Zürich), **Bern** (2/hr, 1–1.5 hrs), **Interlaken Ost** (hourly, 2 hrs), **Lausanne** (hourly, 2.25 hrs direct), **Appenzell** (2/hr, 2.75 hrs, change in Herisau or in Zürich and Gossau), **Chur** (hourly, 2.25 hrs, change in Thalwil).

From Lugano by Train to: Zürich (hourly, 2.75 hrs, half with change in Arth-Goldau), **Interlaken Ost** (hourly, 4.75 hrs, 1–2 changes), **Bern** (hourly, 3.75 hrs, transfer in Zürich, Olten, or Luzern). From Lugano, you can continue on to the **Bernina Express** (next).

Bernina Express

The Bernina Express is one of the most exciting train rides through the Swiss Alps, thanks to its diversity: starting with the sunny palm-tree ambience of Lugano, getting a taste of Italy along beautiful Lake Como, climbing up and over the twisting Bernina Pass, and seeing mountain towns like Pontresina before finishing up in eastern Switzerland. The little red train with panoramic cars spirals up to 7,380 feet, passing steep mountains and cliffs, glaciers, waterfalls, and a wild, rugged landscape.

Orientation to the Bernina Express

The Route

The Bernina Express combines a bus trip through Italy with a train ride up and into the mountains. The bus begins in Lugano, but soon crosses the border to run along the west side of Italy's Lake Como, eventually arriving at Tirano, where the route continues by train. From Tirano, the train crosses back into Switzerland and twists north up the steep mountainside, mastering a very steep grade on regular tracks (no cogwheels) en route to the most spectacular stretch: over the Bernina Pass. Then the train winds back down the other side, stops in mountain towns (such as Pontresina), and finally deposits you in your choice of towns: Chur, St. Moritz, or Davos.

The route can be reversed (Chur/St. Moritz/Davos to Tirano by train, then bus to Lugano). In fact, this way arguably provides an even better experience: Approaching Pontresina from the north is breathtaking, and it gets even better when the train gets to the Bernina Pass.

Planning Your Time: The trip is spectacular but long. It helps to break up the journey with an overnight or two in the Pontresina area (see the Pontresina, Samedan, and St. Moritz chapter). The Bernina Express is especially enjoyable in July and August, when you may be able to take an open-top yellow train car between Tirano and St. Moritz (depending on the weather).

If you have more time, consider taking a standard regional train along this route (rather than the official Bernina Express train with panoramic cars). That way, you can get off as you like for hiking and exploring (see "Local Train Alternative" under "Helpful Hints," later).

Cost and Schedule

A one-way trip on the Bernina Express from Lugano to Chur costs 80 SF second class, 118 SF first class. If you're only going as far as

Pontresina, it's cheaper (51 SF second class, 68 SF first class). The entire trip (including the bus) is covered by a Eurailpass or a Swiss Pass, though reservations cost extra.

If you do the official Bernina Express trip, **seat reservations** are required for both the bus and the panoramic train (9 SF for train, 12 SF for bus, buy easy-to-get reservation from driver as you board). Remember, you can do the same stretch on a regular regional train without reservations (optional seat reservation-5 SF; no such option for bus).

The bus leaves daily in summer (mid-May–mid-Oct) from outside Lugano's train station at 10:00 and heads for Tirano (facing the lake with the station at your back, walk about 100 yards to the left; bus stop has yellow sign for St. Moritz and Tirano).

At 12:55, you'll arrive in Tirano. From here, trains continue north over the mountains. All trains follow the same tracks as far as Pontresina, where they fan out to three different end points: to Chur (departs Tirano 14:04, arrives Chur 18:28), to St. Moritz (departs Tirano 14:49, arrives St. Moritz 17:11), or to Davos (departs Tirano 14:31, arrives Samedan 16:44, arrives Davos 18:16). The Davos-bound train, which runs in summer only, is the only direct panoramic train from Tirano to Samedan.

If you're doing it the other way around, here are some options: From Chur, the train leaves at 8:30 and arrives in Tirano at 12:35. From St. Moritz, the train departs at 9:41, arriving in Tirano at 11:57. From Davos, the train leaves at 8:40 and reaches Tirano at 12:20. The bus from Tirano leaves at 14:25 and arrives in Lugano at 17:30. Remember to confirm all times.

From Tirano, you can also break off the official Bernina Express route and head south to Varenna, a favorite stop on Lake Como. Direct Italian regional trains (about €4) take 1.5 hours, departing Tirano at 13:10, 15:10, 17:10, and 19:10.

In winter (mid-Oct–mid-May), the bus service stops, but the Bernina Express train still runs between Tirano and Chur, and Tirano and St. Moritz, but not Tirano and Davos. (Standard regional trains continue on all those routes.)

Information: The Bernina Express is operated by Rhaetian Railway (tel. 081-288-4340, www.berninaexpress.ch). You can buy an English guidebook about the Bernina Express on the train or at gift shops along the way (12 SF). A recorded English commentary plays on the train's loudspeaker. Lugano bus info: tel. 081-288-5454.

Helpful Hints

Bus Trip: The Lugano–Tirano leg of the Bernina trip (through Italy) is on a bus. Make yourself comfortable—the seats recline, and the footrests, armrests, and individual fans give you more comfort than on a standard PostBus. There are no WCs or food on the bus, so buy your snacks and drinks before boarding (a convenient spot is the Aperto shop at Lugano's train station, daily 6:00–22:00). The bus stops for a WC and snack break in Italy (Swiss francs accepted). Bags can be put under the bus. The bus trip is almost entirely through Italy.

Train Trip: Once you reach Tirano, you'll switch to a panoramic train. The train has five cars: one is first class only, with panoramic windows that don't open. The other four are regular cars (with nonpanoramic windows that open); two have first- and second-class seating, and two are second class only.

Topless Trains: If traveling in July or August, ask about sitting in the yellow "convertible" train car with flip seats and no roof (they can go on the Tirano–St. Moritz tracks because there are no long tunnels). The railway decides the day before—depending on the weather—whether to add these cars to the train (available in both first and second class).

Local Train Alternative: The train segment of the Bernina Express can be done on a standard regional train. These trains stop at all stations, allowing you to hop off and walk around in the beautiful scenery. You can get off at Poschiavo for a quick visit, or at the Bernina Pass for hiking, or at Diavolezza to do a cable-car trip. Alp Grüm and Ospizio Bernina are starting points for several great hikes. Take advantage of the frequent and easy train connections, and make as many short stops as time and interest allow.

Self-Guided Tour

Bernina Express Bus Trip

The bus trip is more scenic than relaxing. Lakes Lugano and Como are almost fjord-like, lined with little Italian getaways. For the best views, sit on the right-hand side (seat numbers don't seem to matter).

At first, the bus takes you around Lake Lugano on narrow, windy roads, frequently honking its horn to warn oncoming traffic at tight passages. Leaving Lugano, you'll pass the town of Gandria (fun to visit from Lugano by boat—see page 270). Shortly after Gandria, you cross the border into **Italy** (it's a nonevent—bus doesn't stop, no need to show passports). You may notice a change in architecture: Whereas the Swiss love meticulously manicured gardens and painstakingly renovated houses, the Italians take things a bit easier.

Once the bus leaves Lake Lugano, the road broadens and takes you through modern Italian villages before hitting picturesque **Lake Como** (Lago di Como). Above the town of Menaggio are your first views of the lake. The village across the lake on the right (by the funny hump of land) is the *real* Bellagio (not the Las Vegas casino). At the nearby village of Dongo, the Italian fascist dictator Mussolini was captured at the end of World War II. Tunnels occasionally disrupt your views, but you can catch glimpses of the lush lakefront. In Gravedona, the street gets narrow enough to make getting the bus through a tight squeeze. Posh private villas and gardens line the street; look for the 12th-century Romanesque Church of Santa Maria del Tiglio. From here, the trip takes you to the tiny harbor town of Domaso. This area is touristy, with plenty of campgrounds, hotels, and swimming pools.

Shortly before noon, the bus stops for 15 minutes in **Sorico,** at the northern tip of Lake Como. You'll have a chance to use the WC and buy a snack or drink at Bar Pace (Swiss francs accepted). Check out the big photograph behind the bar—George Clooney posing with the bar's proud owner on a 2002 visit. Clooney owns a grandiose villa on Lake Como.

The bus then crosses the **"Pian di Spagna"**—famous for a tense standoff between Spanish and Swiss troops during the religious wars of the Counter-Reformation. The trip continues up the fertile **Valtellina Valley,** where some of northern Italy's white wine is produced. The sunny slopes on the left side are reserved for vineyards, the right lower slopes are for woodland, and the bottom of the valley is occupied by apple plantations. For centuries (from 1512 until Napoleon in 1797) this region belonged to Switzerland's largest canton, Graubünden. This region is Italian today, but many Swiss still think of the local Veltlin wine as their own.

Tirano is our last stop in Italy. In the old town, the bus passes an impressive Renaissance church (Madonna di Tirano, on the left) before arriving at the train station at 12:55. You have time for lunch and some sightseeing before hopping on the Bernina Express train (departs at 14:04 to Chur, at 14:31 to Davos, and at 14:49 to St. Moritz). Or, to cram in more sightseeing, take an earlier departure on a regional train to gain time for a stopover in the fine town of Poschiavo (described next), and catch your Bernina Express train from there later (confirm times at the Tirano station information window).

If you're interested in the Poschiavo side-trip, see the next section. Otherwise, skip ahead to "Bernina Express Train Trip, Part One."

Poschiavo

From the Poschiavo train station, walk to the main street and turn left, following the signs to *Centro* and the TI. Cross the river over the pedestrian bridge and continue left, then right, then left, following the *Information* signs. The main square, **Piazza Comunale,** is lined with Neoclassical and Neo-Gothic buildings, including an impressive Catholic church (Chiesa di San Vittore Mauro). A church stood here as early as 703, but the building has been rebuilt and renovated several times: The bell tower dates from 1202, and the Baroque front door was carved in the 1700s. Don't miss the little yellow building just before the church, with the intricate wrought-iron grills. Have a peek inside, and don't be startled by the skulls lining the walls—you're standing in front of the local ossuary.

The **TI** is located in the old Town Hall, below the 12th-century church tower. Pick up a map and the English translation for a short orientation walk: Go from the main square a block north and find the **Church of St. Ignazio.** It's ironic that this Protestant church's namesake, St. Ignatius of Loyola, was the founder of the militant Jesuit order—whose main purpose was to fight "heretic" Protestants. Notice the inscription above the central pulpit, which is fervently Protestant: *Chiesa cristiana vangelica riformata da gli errori e superstizioni umane* ("Christian evangelical church, reformed from human errors and superstitions").

Then it's back to the station...you've got a train to catch.

Bernina Express Train Trip, Part One: From Tirano to Pontresina

From Tirano, the train crosses the center of town before climbing up to **Brusio.** Here the train takes the famous circular viaduct, the only one in the world—an ingenious construction allowing the train to reach higher altitudes without the help of a cogwheel mechanism. As the train twists up, you can see the front and back cars curving in front of and behind you, riding over the viaduct.

Lie back and enjoy the most scenic part of the trip. You'll pass dark old pine forests with needle-and-moss-covered boulders. Chestnut forests, tobacco plantations, and vineyards contribute to the lush tableau. Wildflowers along the track include bright-orange lilies and mountain azaleas. The train slaloms up the steep moun-

tain and offers more and more views of waterfalls, steep cliffs, and the Poschiavo valley and lake far below you.

Thirty minutes after leaving Poschiavo, and before you reach the Bernina Pass, you'll spot the first glacier, **Palü Gletscher** (behind the little lake of Palüsee on the left). It lies nestled between the peak Piz Varuna (11,330 feet) on the left and the eastern summit of Piz Palü on the right (12,790 feet).

The groaning of the train is a reminder that this is the only train crossing over the Alps without a tunnel. It goes right over the summit. Ospizio Bernina—at the **Bernina Pass**—marks the highest point of this trip (7,380 feet). You'll see the White Lake (Lago Bianco), whose color comes from the snowmelt, also called "glacier milk." A watershed sign (yellow, reading *Wasserscheide*) explains that this is a European continental divide: From here, rivers flow either north (toward the Inn, Danube, and finally to the Black Sea) or south (to the Adriatic Sea via the Adda and Po Rivers).

Behind the White Lake, you can see the glaciers of **Sassal Masone** and **Piz Cambrena**. This mountain pass not only separates European drainage basins, but also cultures. In winter, when the train line was more susceptible to bad-weather closures, the remote Italian-speaking valley of Poschiavo was often cut off from Switzerland and turned itself toward its southern neighbor, the valley of Veltlin (where you were just riding the bus).

The train crosses the barren landscape and descends into the **Engadine** valley. This part of Switzerland was discovered by tourists and convalescents at the end of the 19th century. Imagine the gorgeous skiing here in the winter, which still attracts the rich and famous. After the railroad opened this secluded valley to the world, the first hotels and sanatoriums were built (the air and sunshine supposedly helped fight various diseases). Poets found their muse in the wild, romantic landscape, while painters flocked in, attracted by the quality of the light. Keep an eye out for typical Engadine architecture—small windows set in thick walls, etched *sgraffito* decorations, and carved wooden doors (for more on this architecture, see page 291).

The **Montebello curve** offers you the best views over the Morteratsch glacier on the left, with the impressive peaks in the background. From left to right: the Bellavista Range (12,770 feet), Crest Agüzza (12,690 feet), and the highest peak in the canton, Mount Bernina (13,280 feet). Mount Bernina was first climbed in 1850 by a team led by rangers from the village of Schanf. Their gear consisted only of thick woolen pants, a shirt and jacket, hobnailed shoes, and a hat with a black veil to shade them from the strong sunshine.

As you continue, the tracks are lined by more and more larch trees. The milky-white waters from Lago Bianco and the Morteratsch glacier run wild in a broad riverbed alongside the tracks, as satisfied cows chew away on the meadows while water-

SCENIC RAIL JOURNEYS

falls tumble down the cliffs. From the Morteratsch station, there's a fine one-hour hike to the edge of the glacier, past posts tracking the glacier's recent retreat.

Next stop: **Pontresina.** This town is a good place to break the journey (see the Pontresina, Samedan, and St. Moritz chapter). Consider spending a night or two in Pontresina, exploring the quaint village of Samedan, visiting the glitzy resort of St. Moritz, and maybe doing some hiking before continuing on your way.

If you're going to **St. Moritz,** your train trip is nearly over (about 10 min after Pontresina). But on the way to **Chur** or **Davos,** there's more to see....

Bernina Express Train Trip, Part Two: From Pontresina to Chur

Although you're leaving the glaciers behind, your trip will still lead you through magnificent mountain scenery, with steep cliffs and deep gorges.

First, you'll slide through the broad and mellow valley around Samedan, following the shortest river in Switzerland, the Flazbach. On the right, look for the funicular heading up to **Muottas Muragl,** a viewpoint overlooking the valleys that come together in Samedan (for details, see page 286). Samedan is home to Europe's highest airport. It serves glider enthusiasts and the rich and famous who come to vacation in St. Moritz.

After Samedan, in **Bever,** the train leaves the valley and climbs to another spectacular leg of its journey. The section between Bever and Bergün boasts amazing engineering work. Technicians from all over the world come here to admire the diversity of spiral tunnels, looping viaducts, galleries, and bridges that span the Albula Gorge.

The train works its way up along a cheerfully splashing mountain creek, between the Arven pine and larch trees and some isolated farmhouses. The **Albula tunnel,** the highest subterranean alpine crossing in Europe, takes you up to 5,970 feet. This pass serves as another barrier between cultures and climate—the weather is often different on either side of the tunnel. Hikers can follow the tracks and read the information panels about the construction of the train line. The street along the tracks is closed in winter and considered a paradise for sledders. Every winter, 100,000 sled enthusiasts enjoy this closed, windy road, giving them the ride of their lives on a three-mile, downhill, car-free stretch.

From **Preda,** the train loops down through five spiral tunnels and two straight tunnels, crossing nine viaducts and going under two galleries—it's considered the most ingenious railway line ever built. It covers almost eight miles and descends more than 1,365 feet in altitude. The village of **Bergün** will be visible three separate times as you loop around the valley. Bergün greets you with a modern, public open-air swimming pool and an onion-shaped 17th-century "Roman tower." As the train continues winding down the pretty valley, you'll often be able to see other parts of the track below or next to you. Any track you see is one you've either already been on—or will soon be on....

At **Filisur,** the Bernina Express route splits again. Some trains head directly to Davos (no stops en route), while others continue to Chur. I'll continue to narrate the Chur route.

After Filisur, the Chur-bound train enters a tunnel, and an announcement reminds you to ready your camera and position yourself on the left side. Just after the tunnel, you'll cross the famous **Landwasser viaduct.** A masterpiece of engineering, its pillars were built without scaffolding. Iron towers, which formed the center of each pillar, were built first. With the help of cranes set up atop each pillar, materials were hoisted up and the brick was laid. The 425-foot-long viaduct curves elegantly in a radius of 330 feet. Below, the wild Albula River carves the dramatic gorge; above, your train's panoramic windows allow you to see the steep, rugged cliffs looming over the tracks (a particularly beautiful stretch is right after Solis). Notice how nicely the dark limestone masonry matches the surrounding landscape (it was quarried right here).

Thusis is the commercial hub of the broad and lush Domleschg valley. The trip takes you down along the Vorderrhein ("Front-Rhine") River. Notice the many fortresses, castles, towers, and ruins along the river, a reminder that taxes were levied on the traders traveling this major route between northern and southern Europe. One of Switzerland's most popular mineral waters originates in Rhäzüns. The 13th-century castle above the town now belongs to a local chemical company.

Reichenau marks the confluence of two arms of the Upper Rhine (the Vorderrhein and the Hinterrhein—"Back-Rhine"). This town became wealthy from the taxes it got from the passing merchants. The 17th-century Reichenau Castle on the Hinterrhein was once used as a school, but is now privately owned.

The train follows the Rhine at the foot of Calanda Mountain to our final stop, **Chur.** You can catch the Glacier Express (explained next) from Chur or from St. Moritz.

Bernina Express Connections

From Lugano by Train to: Luzern (hourly, 2.5 hrs, half with change in Arth-Goldau), **Zürich** (hourly, 2.75 hrs, half with change in Arth-Goldau), **Interlaken Ost** (hourly, 4.75 hrs, 1–2 changes), **Bern** (hourly, 3.75 hrs, transfer in Zürich, Olten, or Luzern).

From Pontresina by Train to: **St. Moritz** (hourly, 11 min), **Samedan** (hourly, 6 min; 2 buses/hr, 15 min), **Zürich** (hourly, 3.5 hrs, transfer in Samedan and Chur), **Tirano** (hourly, 2.25 hrs; up to 3 panoramic trains per day in summer).

From Chur by Train to: **Zürich** (2/hr, 1.25–1.5 hrs), **Luzern** (hourly, 2.25 hrs, transfer in Thalwil), **Appenzell** (hourly, 2–2.5 hrs, 1–3 changes). To reach destinations in western Switzerland—such as Bern, Interlaken, or Lake Geneva—you'll transfer in Zürich (see "Zürich Connections" on page 62).

Glacier Express

This most promoted of the Swiss scenic rail routes travels between Zermatt in the southwest of Switzerland and various resort towns in eastern Switzerland (St. Moritz, Chur, and Davos). If you stay on for the whole ride, you'll spend almost eight hours crossing 291 bridges, going through 91 tunnels, and reaching an altitude of 6,670 feet.

While it's an impressive and famous journey, the Glacier Express is not necessarily the be-all and end-all of Swiss rail trips. Much of the journey is down in valleys (as opposed to along the sides of cliffs), meaning that high-altitude views are a little lacking. But the stark landscape, carved by the glaciers that gave the train its name, is striking. The trip offers a dramatic way to connect eastern Switzerland with tucked-away-in-the-mountains Zermatt (see the Zermatt and the Matterhorn chapter).

Orientation to the Glacier Express

The Route

The Glacier Express is a misnomer—it's hardly an express. Not only does it take its time (traveling at about 20 mph to make the full trip in almost 8 hrs), but it also makes several stops along the way. The route cuts along the southern part of Switzerland, between St. Moritz/Chur/Davos (in the east) and Zermatt (in the west). You can ride in either direction.

Planning Your Time: The most distinctive stretch of the trip is the high-mountain pass between Disentis and Brig. If you don't want to commit to the whole eight hours, you can try to connect a trip with this segment only (about 3 hrs). Remember that you can join or leave the trip whenever you like (for example, Chur in the east and Brig in the west link conveniently into Swiss rail lines to other major destinations).

Cost and Schedule

You'll pay 133 SF for second class, or 221 SF for first class, between St. Moritz and Zermatt. The entire trip is covered by the Swiss Pass (except the reservation fee, described below). But a Eurailpass covers only part of the journey; two segments are privately run and not covered by Eurail (Disentis–Brig-46 SF second class; Brig–Zermatt-34 SF; plus a 10-SF fee if you buy these tickets on the train).

If you're riding the full length of the Glacier Express *sans* railpass, the cost is high enough to warrant a look at the Half-Fare Travel Card, which can quickly pay for itself (99 SF for 1 month, see page 357).

All Glacier Express trains have panoramic first- and second-class cars with air-conditioning. Some Glacier Express trains also have "premium" trains with headsets for commentary and the option of an in-seat meal. On these trains, the second-class panoramic seating gets extremely crowded in summer, so consider splurging on first class.

In addition to your train ticket or pass, you'll have to pay a **reservation fee** of 15 SF (same price for first or second class; 33 SF for "premium" trains; off-season 10 SF for regular Glacier Express, 13 SF for "premium" trains). If you're not starting or ending in St. Moritz, or if you're getting off along the way, you can choose cheaper standard regional trains. But if you want to take a direct train between St. Moritz and Zermatt, the pricier Glacier Express is your only option.

From mid-May through mid-October, four trains run daily in each direction. Going from east to west, the train begins either in St. Moritz (departs at 9:18, 9:19, and 10:04) or in Davos (departs at 9:50); all trains stop in Chur along the way (11:38, 11:39, 12:14, and 12:15). Going from west to east, the trains depart Zermatt at 9:00, 9:13, 10:00, and 10:13. Off-season, frequency drops to one per day in each direction (east to west: departs St. Moritz at 9:04; west to east: departs Zermatt at 10:00). Official Glacier Express trains often stop running in fall (mid-Oct–mid-Dec) to allow for maintenance, but regular regional train service continues.

The train takes almost six hours to connect Zermatt and Chur, or almost eight hours for Zermatt to St. Moritz or Davos. Confirm all times before your trip.

Information: The Glacier Express is operated jointly by the Matterhorn Gotthard Bahn (MGB), based in Brig (tel. 027-927-7777, www.glacierexpress.ch or www.mgbahn.ch), and the Rhätische Bahn (RhB), based in Chur (tel. 081-288-4340, www.rhb.ch). The headsets in the "premium" panoramic cars offer recorded narration; for more insight, pick up a guidebook before you board, or buy the 15-SF official guide by Merian on the train.

Helpful Hints

Picking the Best Seat: I find it more enjoyable to sit facing front. For most of the trip—including the most dramatic stretch, between Disentis and Brig—it's also slightly preferable, if you're coming from the east, to sit on the left-hand side of the train (generally seat numbers ending in 1, 2, 3, and 8), which is the right-hand side if you're coming from the west (same seat numbers). Note that if you start in Zermatt with any of the seat numbers I've mentioned, you might begin your trip facing backward; the car will soon change direction in Brig.

Luggage: You'll keep your luggage with you (they don't check it through)—just slip it between the backs of the seats.

No-Show Bridges: Most promotional materials show the Glacier Express train venturing across ancient aqueducts and old stone bridges. It makes for picturesque publicity. But realize that you don't see these bridges from the train itself...because you're on them.

Eating on the Glacier Express: The train has a fancy restaurant car that offers lunch, which is handy if you're in for the full eight hours. For 41 SF, you get a salad (summer) or soup (winter), a main dish, and a dessert; 28 SF buys you just the main dish (drinks cost extra). Their trademark gizmo: a tilted wine glass. Since lunch is generally served when the train is going up a steep incline (11:00–13:30), these gimmicky glasses always get a laugh. Reservations are required for lunch (request when booking your ticket).

To save a few francs, it's fine to bring your own **picnic,** and most cars have tables—perfect for a grocery-store feast.

Self-Guided Tour

The Glacier Express

All Glacier Express trains—whether they begin in St. Moritz or Davos—go through Chur. I'll describe the route starting at Chur and heading toward Zermatt. (For details on most of the trip from St. Moritz to Chur, see "Bernina Express Train Trip, Part Two: From Pontresina to Chur," earlier.)

Just outside of Chur (near where the St. Moritz train line hits the Chur line), you'll be following the **Vorderrhein Gorge,** nicknamed the "Swiss Grand Canyon." It was carved by the Rhine River (though way up here in the Alps, this "Baby Rhine" is a little tyke, and not navigable). After about nine miles, the train diverges from the Rhine and enters a pastoral region called Surselva, centered on the town Ilanz. This is Romansh country, where the fourth official language of Switzerland is kept alive—barely—in communities like this one. Romansh, like French and Italian, is a

Glacier Express Elevations

OBERALP PASS
6,670'

ZERMATT
5,263'

ANDERMATT
4,711'

DISENTIS
3,707'

BRIG
2,202'

REICHENAU
1,981'

CHUR
1,919'

ST.
MORITZ
5,824'

ELEVATION IN FEET

The train takes 7.5 hours to travel 180 miles (290 kilometers),
going through 91 tunnels and crossing 291 bridges.

Romance language—but it's more directly descended from Latin than most. From this valley (Reichenau, at roughly 2,000 feet above sea level, is the lowest altitude of the route), the big climb begins.

As you approach **Disentis,** the tracks begin to twist along the edge of a canyon—making the scenery more dramatic (a taste of what's to come). You'll pull into Disentis, with its big 17th-century Benedictine Monastery looming in your window. Your car will jiggle as the cogwheel engine is attached. This new engine has gears that can lower to latch onto the cogs of an extra rail with grippable teeth. At 10 percent incline (that's 100 meters of gain per kilometer, or about 500 feet per mile), conventional train wheels start to slip. The solution: a cogwheel (a.k.a. rack-and-pinion drive).

You'll work your way up the mountain alongside the Baby Rhine River. Just west of Sedrun is the staging ground for the excavation of the Gotthard Base Tunnel (which will run 30 miles under the mountain from Erstfeld to Bodio when it opens—*Gott* willing—in 2017). Just past Rueras, the track steepens and the train slows to allow its gears to latch into the cog rail. After

Tschamut, the last inhabited place before Oberalp Pass, you enter a long series of snow sheds—designed to protect the tracks (and trains) in case an avalanche strikes.

You'll emerge from the sheds at **Oberalp Pass,** the literal high point of this journey (6,670 feet), and glide along the Oberalp Lake. Notice the extensive network of avalanche fences high above you—a reminder of the many generations of Swiss farmers who have learned to live on the land. The reddish streaks you might see on the snow? Believe it or not, that's sand from the Sahara Desert—caught up in high-altitude winds and carried all the way to the Swiss Alps.

As you descend from the pass, you'll travel over, then through, the modern town of **Andermatt,** home to a Swiss Army base. Deep below you is the 9.5-mile-long Gotthard Tunnel, which takes trains unscenically from Goschenen to Airolo. In this desolate terrain, notice the huge boulders embedded in the ground, deposited there by glaciers.

Soon after, you'll go through the 9.5-mile-long Furka Basis Tunnel. While it might seem like a view-killer, realize that this tunnel—finished in 1982—makes it possible for the Glacier Express to continue running through the winter. Automobiles are allowed onto the train to ride smoothly and safely between Realp and Oberwald. This is especially handy in the winter, when the road is closed.

You'll emerge into the region of **Goms,** with more pretty villages. The village of Fiesch/Kühboden has a cable car up to Eggishorn, boasting views of all the Alps All-Stars: the Matterhorn, Mont Blanc, Eiger, Mönch, and Jungfrau.

Soon after, the train meets up with another one of Europe's great rivers, the **Rhône.** The "Baby" Rhône, just a bubbly little mountain stream here (originating from the once-mighty Rhône glacier nearby), flows all the way to Marseille, France, and into the Mediterranean.

Finally, you'll arrive at **Brig,** an ugly industrial town with good connections to other train lines (transfer here if you're not continuing on to Zermatt). From Brig it's 20 miles on to Zermatt and the Matterhorn, following the craggy Nikolaital Valley. Keep an eye out for vineyards—the highest in Europe. We're out of milk country and into wine country. At Stalden, a road leads up another valley to the resort of Saas-Fee. Shortly before the village of Randa, you pass a cone of rubble left by a huge avalanche that wiped out two miles of road and track here in 1991.

At **Täsch,** vast parking lots mark the end of the road for drivers. From here it's train only into the traffic-free terminus of this line, Zermatt. Think about how much the terrain has changed since you started the trip: from fertile farmlands, to tundra above the tree line, to this rough and rocky terrain.

As you continue along the valley lined with quarries, you'll begin to get your first glimpses of the unmistakable shape of the **Matterhorn**—a fitting exclamation point marking the end of this long journey. **Zermatt**—with its bunker-like, avalanche-proof train station—lies just around the bend.

Glacier Express Connections

From Chur by Train to: Zürich (2/hr, 1.25–1.5 hrs), **Luzern** (hourly, 2.25 hrs, transfer in Thalwil), **Appenzell** (hourly, 2–2.5 hrs, 1–3 changes, easiest via St. Gallen). To reach destinations in western Switzerland, such as Bern or Interlaken, you'll transfer in Zürich (see "Zürich Connections" on page 62).

From Zermatt: Zermatt is connected to the outside world by the 80-minute train ride to Brig. Brig is also a handy place to bail out of the Glacier Express route, if you're coming from the east and not going all the way to Zermatt. If you're coming from or going to Lausanne or Montreux, you'll save time changing trains in Visp, a town between Zermatt and Brig (Zermatt–Lausanne via Visp: hourly, 3 hrs).

From Brig by Train to: Bern (1–2/hr, 1 hr), **Lausanne** (1–2/hr, 1.75 hrs), **Interlaken Ost** (1–2/hr, 1.25 hrs, transfer in Spiez), **Luzern** (1–2/hr, 2.25–2.75 hrs, transfer in Bern or Olten), **Zürich** (1–2/hr, 2.25 hrs, some transfer in Bern).

Chur

The routes of the Glacier Express and the Bernina Express intersect in Chur—supposedly Switzerland's oldest and warmest town.

It's a handy transportation hub for these two scenic train lines and has a charming-enough old town. Overall, Chur (pronounced "khoor") is just a typical Swiss burg—fine for passing through, but not worth a detour. If you've got time to kill, you can wander up through the cobbled old town to two big churches (the Romanesque Cathedral and the Gothic Church of St. Martin), some remains of the medieval city wall, and the town museum (Rätisches Museum, 6 SF, no English descriptions). Follow the handy red signs pointing you to the attractions. Public WCs are next to the cathedral.

Orientation to Chur

Chur fans out over the foothills from the Rhine River. The train station is at the bottom (north end) of the town center.

Tourist Information: The TI, downstairs in the train station (next to the railway *Reisebüro*), offers a free town map marked with sights, hotels, and restaurants. If you're here for longer, you can also pick up their free *City Guide* brochure detailing museums and attractions, and the *Accommodations Guide* (Mon–Fri 7:30–20:00, Sat–Sun 8:00–18:00, tel. 081-252-1818, www.churtourismus.ch).

Arrival in Chur: Chur's brand-new train station sits atop a long underground concourse, where you'll find the TI, shops, the handy Bahnhofplatz parking garage, and other services. To get to the old town, follow *Stadtzentrum* signs up the escalator, then walk straight up Bahnhofstrasse. In two blocks, you'll reach the big roundabout at Postplatz. The old town is straight ahead.

Internet Access: Two different places in the **train station** have pay Internet terminals: in the railway's "Change" office downstairs (stand-up kiosk), and at a well-marked "Internet Corner" upstairs. In the town center, the **library** *(Kantonsbibliothek)* has free access, but it's limited to 15 minutes (Mon–Fri 9:00–17:30, Sat 9:00–16:00, closed Sun, Karlihofplatz, tel. 081-257-2828).

Sleeping in Chur

(1 SF = about $1, country code: 41)

Chur is about halfway between Appenzell and the Pontresina area, both of which are more appealing for an overnight stay. Sleep in Chur only if you must, in order to connect to one of the scenic rail lines. These moderately priced places are in the atmospheric old town, an easy 10- to 15-min walk from the train station.

Hotel Restaurant Rebleuten, in a 500-year-old building, overlooks a quiet little square a block off Kornplatz. The 13 small rooms are cozy and comfortable. The hotel is warmly run by the Stöhr family (Ss-70 SF, Sb-85 SF, Db-140 SF, Pfisterplatz 1, tel. 081-255-1144, fax 081-255-1145, www.rebleuten.ch, info @rebleuten.ch).

Hotel Freieck has a mod lobby and 39 rooms over a low-key café. Their cheaper standard rooms, with old-fashioned furniture, are plenty nice; you'll pay more for a modern "superior" room (Sb-90–130 SF, Db-150–220 SF, Tb-190–260 SF, prices depend on type of room and season—highest May–mid-Oct, elevator, pay Internet access, Reichsgasse 44, tel. 081-255-1515, fax 081-255-1516, www.freieck.ch, hotel@freieck.ch, Stockmann family).

Hotel Franziskaner is charming and well-located and rents reasonably priced rooms above a popular restaurant (S-60 SF,

D-120 SF, Db-150 SF, free Wi-Fi, Kupfergasse 18, tel. 081-252-1261, fax 081-252-1279, www.hotelfranziskaner.ch, info@hotel franziskaner.ch).

Chur Connections

Chur is a convenient spot to catch either the Glacier Express or the Bernina Express. It also offers speedy, frequent connections to Zürich, making it an ideal junction for spicing up your trip with a scenic train ride.

From Chur by Train to: Zürich (2/hr, 1.25–1.5 hrs), **Luzern** (hourly, 2.25 hrs, transfer in Thalwil), **Appenzell** (hourly, 2–2.5 hrs, 1–3 changes, easiest via St. Gallen). To reach destinations in western Switzerland—such as Bern, Interlaken, or Lake Geneva—you'll transfer in Zürich (see "Zürich Connections" on page 62).

SWITZERLAND IN WINTER

One of my favorite Swiss memories happened one winter night on the snowy slopes of the Berner Oberland. My friend Walter (who runs Hotel Mittaghorn in Gimmelwald) and I, warmed by hot chocolate laced with schnapps, decided to go sledding between mountain-high villages. We strapped flashlights to our heads, miner-style, and zoomed through the crisp, moonlit night.

That said, this is a summertime book. I've included plenty of tips on hiking, while mostly ignoring the winter-sports scene. But winter activities are an important part of the Swiss culture (and tourist industry).

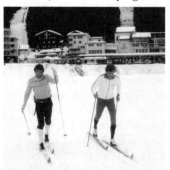

Just a century ago, clever entrepreneurs in the Swiss Alps realized that skiing (which began as a method of wintertime transportation in Scandinavia 4,000 years ago) could be a profitable extension of their resorts' spring and summer seasons. Telemark (cross-country) skiing came first, then alpine (downhill) skiing, and, more recently, snowboarding. Generations of Swiss skiers have honed their skills on these slopes. Big names include Erica Hess, Vreni Schneider, Maria Walliser, and Karl Molitor (whose family currently runs a ski rental shop in Wengen in the Berner Oberland).

You don't have to be a skier or snowboarder to enjoy Switzerland in the winter. Ski resorts offer plenty of other activities, including snowshoeing, sledding, ice skating...and shopping. Or just ride up a lift, rent a chair in the sun, and warm up with a glass of *Pflümli* (plum liqueur).

Top Winter Destinations

The winter-sports season begins in early December and runs through Easter. Peak time hits at Christmas and New Year's—during this period, hotel prices in resort towns surpass summer highs.

While Switzerland's resorts vary greatly, they share a rich ski culture, an astounding variety of terrain, relatively mild temperatures (compared to many American destinations), and a lively après-ski scene. For those who can afford them, the best winter activities are in the Berner Oberland (Mürren, Wengen, Grindelwald, and Gstaad); the southern canton of Valais (Zermatt, Saas-Fee, Crans-Montana, and Verbier); and the eastern canton of Graubünden (St. Moritz, Davos, Klosters, and Arosa).

The **Berner Oberland** offers the ultimate diversity of terrain and character, as well as great sledding and stellar views (see the Gimmelwald and the Berner Oberland chapter). The cliff-hanging town of Mürren is relatively uncrowded and a good home base for expert skiers, with the 10,000-foot Schilthorn peak as the backbone of its ski area. Across the valley, Wengen offers skiing for all skill levels, fine accommodations, and shopping, with a complex lift system connecting it to Kleine Scheidegg, Männlichen, and Grindelwald. Grindelwald, a little closer to Interlaken, is a bit pricier, but has the world's longest sled run and easy access to more than 100 miles of downhill trails, including the area's best range of beginners' runs (www.grindelwald.com).

The canton of **Valais** ("valley"), known for its excellent wine-making along the banks of the Rhône, is also a popular skiing destination. Connected to Italy by several high-mountain passes, Valais is home to Switzerland's best-known sight: the Matterhorn (see the Zermatt and the Matterhorn chapter). The area around the Matterhorn, including the villages of Zermatt and Saas-Fee, enjoy a high elevation and good skiing.

The **Graubündner Alps** contain 14 different passes. St. Moritz, situated in the Upper Engadine valley, is so well-known that it's a registered trademark (see the Pontresina, Samedan, and St. Moritz chapter). This resort town offers designer boutiques, luxury accommodations, a natural mineral-spring spa...oh, and ski slopes, too. In addition to skiing, winter visitors to St. Moritz play polo and cricket on snow, go bobsledding on natural ice, or try skijoring—skiing while being pulled by riderless horses.

Skiing Tips

Expect to spend 50–70 SF a day on lift tickets. You may find

cheaper prices in the off-peak season (before mid-Dec and after Easter), if you buy a multiple-day pass, or if you have a Swiss Pass. Prices may also be lower for seniors, teenagers, and kids (exact age cut-offs vary). Most ski areas offer half-day afternoon passes.

Rental prices are a bit higher than what you'd find in the US. Depending on the fanciness of the gear, you'll pay 40–70 SF for skiing or snowboarding equipment. If you haven't packed ski wear, you'll pay about 40 SF to rent ski pants, a jacket, and gloves.

Many rental shops in Switzerland belong to the Intersport rental network (www.intersportrent.ch), which sets fairly high standards for its member shops. Places outside this network can be cheaper, but Intersport shops are generally a safe bet and offer a useful bonus: Many of them let you pick up rental gear at one ski area and drop it off at another in the region for no charge (an especially handy option in the Berner Oberland).

Always ask your hotelier if they've arranged any special rental deals through local shops. Rental prices don't vary much (since so many shops are part of the Intersport network), so choose a place that's close to your hotel or convenient for getting up the mountain.

Swiss ski resorts are deservedly popular, and slopes can get crowded. Peak crowd times are Christmas, New Year's, mid-February to mid-March (when European school holidays hit), and Easter. The Berner Oberland also fills up in mid-January for world-class racing. Start skiing as soon as slopes open—the hordes don't usually arrive until 10:00 or later. This is especially true in swankier resorts, where well-heeled tourists enjoy long nights and short ski days.

Resources: For in-depth information on the winter scene, see *Where to Ski and Snowboard Worldwide: The Reuters Guide, Leocha's Ski Snowboard Europe, The Great Skiing & Snowboarding Guide* (Cadogan Guides), and Lonely Planet's Switzerland guidebook.

Christmas Celebrations

Switzerland is an ideal place to celebrate the winter holidays. Imagine spending your days exploring Christmas markets in cozy Swiss cities, sipping hot mulled wine *(Glühwein)*, picking out your favorite handmade ornaments, then relaxing at night in a warm little chalet, making figure-eights with your cube of bread through a steaming pot of cheese fondue.

Swiss Christmas markets are a treat, whether in big cities (such as Bern, Zürich, and Basel) or smaller towns (Interlaken, Appenzell, Chur, and many others). While some of the bigger markets start at the beginning of December and run through Christmas Eve, smaller towns host markets for just one week or weekend. The Swiss Tourist Board's website lists details (www .myswitzerland.com/christmas).

You'll find all cities festively decorated, but Zürich's remarkable display of tasteful, twinkling lights is arguably Switzerland's best. This being the land of Calvin—the most austere of Protestant Reformers— most Christmas decorations are relatively understated here, but they're still charming.

In the village of Gimmelwald, residents in each home adorn a window for Advent. Just as children open a different little paper window each day on an Advent calendar, Gimmelwald residents reveal a new decorated house window on a different house each day. The debut of a new Advent window often comes with a party. Under a cold sky, with stars reflecting off the snow and the moon inside a halo, the village gathers. In a kind of roving block party, neighbors emerge to meet friends and enjoy grilled sausages, hot mulled wine, and folk music on the accordion. Men take sections of logs (the size of a four-foot chunk of telephone pole), cut the ends into a point, and plant them upright in the snow. Coated with tar, they're set ablaze—torches to light and warm the cozy yet frigid occasion. In the distance, under flickering torchlights, children ride old-time wooden sleds, going up and down, up and down.

For the Swiss, a communal pot of fondue is purely a winter specialty. Invitations to a cozy Swiss party include the word *FIGUGEGL* (fee-GOO-geck-ul), which stands for *Fondue isch guet und git e gueti Lune*—"Fondue is good and gives a good mood." According to tradition, if you drop your bread into the pot, you must kiss the person to your left.

Each Christmas season, usually on St. Nicholas Day (December 6), Swiss children receive a visit from Samichlaus— that's Swiss German for St. Nicholas. With his black-clad, soot-faced henchman, Schmutzli, by his side, Samichlaus goes door to door, visiting the town's children. He knocks on the door, and when the frightened but excited kids answer, Samichlaus consults his big book of sins—co-authored by village parents—and does some light-hearted moralizing. Schmutzli stands by as a menacing enforcer. (According to tradition, Schmutzli is supposed to carry a stick or a switch for beating bad children and a sack for carrying them away to be eaten, but this scare tactic to whip kids into behaving is rarely invoked anymore.) Then Samichlaus asks the kids to earn a little forgiveness by reciting a poem. After the poems and assurances of reform, Samichlaus allows them to reach deep into his bag for a smattering of tangerines, nuts, gingerbread, and other treats.

Cutting and decorating the Christmas tree—traditionally done on December 24—is a family affair. Real candles, kept upright by dangling ornamental counterbalances, are attached, then lit by the children. (Locals are bold with their candles; to me, it feels as if their pine houses, with open beams, are ready to go up in flames.) Presents are opened while the candles burn. The tree stays up after Christmas; candles are lit again on New Year's Eve for good luck. Some traditional rural Swiss churches also light candles on their trees for Christmas Eve services.

Other Festivities

Second only to Christmas is *Fasnacht,* the Germanic equivalent of Mardi Gras or Carnival. Traditionally celebrated in the days before or after Ash Wednesday (Feb 17 in 2010, March 9 in 2011), *Fasnacht* features a parade of locals in traditional masks and garish, larger-than-life costumes. Visitors also enjoy a variety of

quirky traditions, which vary from town to town (in Basel, for example, celebrations begin promptly at 4:00 in the morning, and feature roving fife-and-drum bands). This pre-Christian ceremony likely dates from a pagan tradition to frighten away evil winter spirits and welcome the renewal of springtime. The most famous *Fasnacht* celebrations in Switzerland occur in Basel (www.fasnacht.ch), Bern (www

.fasnacht.be), and Luzern (www.luzerner-fasnacht.ch). If you'll be in Switzerland at this time of year, it's worth the effort to catch one of these weird and wonderful celebrations.

SWITZERLAND: PAST AND PRESENT

Switzerland has a unique and impressive story—forging unity from diversity, and somehow remaining above the fray when Europe goes ballistic. Despite four languages, diverse geography, ill-defined borders, and many religious sects—and despite being surrounded by continental Europe's four big powers (France, Germany, Austria, and Italy)—the Swiss cantons banded together to form an independent federal system that still works today.

Even if you're not going to Switzerland for the history (who would?), you'll encounter it. You can play gladiator inside a fighting arena from Roman times, or tour medieval castles and battle-grounds, left over from when the Swiss wrestled their independence from foreign rulers. Stripped-down cathedrals attest to the religious violence of the Reformation that almost tore the country apart. You'll ride the ingenious cogwheel trains and cliff-climbing funiculars of Switzerland's progressive 18th and 19th centuries, when the country was at the forefront of the emerging Industrial Age. The specters of Nazi Germany and the Soviet Union arise in underground fortresses and bomb shelters now open to the public. And finally, you'll see the Switzerland of today—gleaming cities, state-of-the-art transportation, and happy citizens. I love to go a-wandering along the history path, so strap on your rucksack, and let's go.

Early History: Celts and Romans (c. 500 B.C.–A.D. 500)

Switzerland's star attraction—the Alps—were born 500 million years ago, when the ocean floor was rocked by earthquakes that folded the earth upward, creating a long range of mountains (for all the details, see the sidebar on page 38). This landscape shaped the history and character of the Swiss people. It kept early populations physically isolated, leading to still-present cultural divisions, and fostering an ethos of independence. Switzerland's location at the heart of Western Europe forced it to be international in outlook, yet the impregnable mountains allowed it to remain apart and neutral.

The first Swiss (c. 500 B.C.) were a Celtic tribe called the Helvetii. Their memory survives today in the country's official name, Confoederatio Helvetica. "Helvetia," the female symbol of Switzerland, appears dressed in robes and armed with a spear and shield, on coins, stamps, and statues.

In 58 B.C., the Helvetii were defeated by Julius Caesar, the Roman general and future ruler. The Romans established a capital at Avenches (where evocative ruins remain—see the end of the Bern and Murten chapter), built the cities of Zürich, Geneva, Basel, and Lausanne, and assimilated the Helvetii into their Europe-wide empire. Roman culture thrived in Switzerland for almost 500 years.

As Rome fell (c. A.D. 400), Germanic tribes swarmed in. In the north, the Alemanni snuffed out Roman culture in north-central Switzerland and established their Germanic language. In the west, the Burgundians adopted the Latin language, which eventually evolved into French. But these tribes never penetrated the nooks and crannies of the most remote mountain areas, and in these regions, particularly in the southeast, people still converse in Romansh, a language that's changed little from the colloquial Latin spoken by Roman-era occupiers. South of the Alps, Swiss Latin speakers gradually switched to modern-day Italian. These linguistic/cultural divides remain today.

The Middle Ages: The Holy Roman Empire (c. 500–1291)

Like most of Europe during the dark medieval centuries, Switzerland was poor, feudal, and swept by barbarian invasions. The mostly pagan Swiss were slowly converted to Christianity by traveling Irish monks, including St. Gallus (seventh century), who gave his name to the canton of St. Gallen. Swiss lands became part of Charlemagne's empire (c. 800) and its successor to the east—the Germanic kings of the Holy Roman Empire.

Around the turn of the first millennium, Switzerland began to prosper. Cities such as Bern and Luzern were founded, welcoming skilled craftsmen and traders. High in the Alps, clever engineers built bridges and catwalks to open a vital north–south highway through the St. Gotthard Pass (see page 311). This trade route proved so prosperous that the Holy Roman Emperor ensured access to it by granting the Swiss a measure of independence *(Reichsfreiheit)*. Switzerland got a taste of freedom, and when the Habsburg emperor tried to bring the country under tighter control, the Swiss had had enough.

The Old Confederacy (1291–1500)

On August 1, 1291 (celebrated today as the country's national day), Swiss citizens gathered together and swore an oath. "We will be a single nation of brothers..." they asserted, and rose up against Habsburg rule. The three cantons of Uri, Schwyz, and Unterwalden united, proclaiming independence and democratic institutions. In a legend of the time, the Swiss William Tell refused to bow to the Habsburg hat, a symbol of their power. As punishment, he was forced to shoot an apple off his own son's head. His son lived to see another haircut, and Tell led the rebellion.

The Swiss had to battle the powerful Habsburg family for two full centuries to completely drive them out. In the west, the Swiss battled Burgundy, trouncing them at the pivotal Battle of Murten. One by one, other cantons and cities (Luzern, Zürich, Bern) joined the confederacy, as these Swiss areas won more and more concessions from neighboring rulers.

During these centuries of warfare, the Swiss earned a reputation as Europe's fiercest warriors. Swiss mercenaries became a lucrative export, hired by foreign kings to fight their wars and protect their palaces (including the Swiss Guards, who still protect the Vatican today).

By 1499, Switzerland had won independence from Habsburgs and Burgundians—in fact, if not yet in name.

Reformation and Enlightenment (c. 1500–1700)

The Protestant Reformation split Switzerland in two. In Zürich, Ulrich Zwingli preached Protestantism (see sidebar on page 48), John Calvin brought his French flock to Geneva, and the Dutch humanist Desiderius Erasmus taught at Basel. While the cities went Protestant, the more rural cantons stayed true to the Catholic faith, plunging the country into religious warfare (1529–1531). Angry rioters stormed Catholic cathedrals, stripping them of their "graven images," and leaving them with the austere interiors travelers see today (including Zürich's Grossmünster, Bern's Münster, and Lausanne's cathedral).

While Europe suffered through a century of religious wars, Switzerland's struggles were relatively short-lived. Swiss mercenaries fought other countries' wars...and Switzerland grew rich.

When peace came to Europe with the Treaty of Westphalia (1648), the agreement also officially recognized Switzerland as a fully independent nation.

1700s and 1800s

Through the Age of Enlightenment, Switzerland had bucked the European trend toward absolute monarchs. As the country steadily advanced economically and technologically, it moved in a firmly democratic direction.

On August 10, 1792, a revolutionary mob in Paris stormed the palace, arrested the King of France, and slaughtered the king's body-guards—800 Swiss mercenaries died. This pivotal event in European history is memorialized in Luzern's Lion Monument to fallen Swiss Guards (described in the Luzern and Central Switzerland chapter).

Riding the wave of the French Revolution, Napoleon Bonaparte occupied Switzerland (1798) and tried (unsuccessfully) to establish a strong central government. With Napoleon's defeat (and the Congress of Vienna, 1815), the European powers restored Switzerland's freedom. They also set it on its future political course—neutrality in all conflicts.

In 1848, amid a Europe-wide wave of liberal reforms, Switzerland's tradition of democracy was finally set down in a constitution. The new Confederation was modeled after America's form of government, but with an even stronger "federalist" (i.e., decentralized) emphasis. The country's national capital was established in the low-key town of Bern.

As a neutral country, Switzerland built a reputation as a leader in international relations. The world's diplomats descended on

Geneva (1863–1864), producing two landmark institutions: the International Red Cross (still run from Geneva), and the Geneva Conventions of conduct during war (which were updated significantly in 1949). When the modern Olympic Games were founded in 1894, Lausanne became the movement's world headquarters (with an Olympic Museum, described in the Lake Geneva and French Switzerland chapter).

It was also around this time that the country began to welcome hordes of tourists, beginning with French, English, and German aristocrats on the "Grand Tour," who passed through Switzerland on their way to Italy. Next came the British mountaineers, whose reverence for the Alps was part of the Romanticist outlook on nature—for the first time, Europeans looked at mountains as objects of beauty and inspiration, rather than as frustrating obstacles. Visitors marveled at the mountain scenery and the "sublime" rush it gave them. In this heyday of European travel, Switzerland virtually invented mass tourism as we know it—pioneering ways of mark-

ing its mountains, offering the first organized vacations, investing in a well-oiled infrastructure, and establishing a reputation for efficiency, cleanliness, quality, and ease (even inventing English-language names for places whose local names were considered too intimidating for foreign visitors). Switzerland's system of high-altitude trains, funiculars, and mountain lifts was built to carry 19th-century tourists to previously unheard-of heights. Today's visitors stay in the same resort towns (Interlaken, Zermatt, Luzern, St. Moritz), ride the same kind of lifts, and see echoes of themselves in the stylized travel advertisements from that Romantic age.

20th Century: World Wars

Switzerland entered the 20th century on the cutting edge of progress. Its trains and communications systems were top-notch. The

artist Paul Klee (1879–1940), with his playful, eccentric style, would contribute to the Modernist movement (see his works at the Rosengart Collection in Luzern, and at the Paul Klee Center in Bern). Carl Jung (1875–1961) pioneered the blossoming field of psychoanalysis. And in the quiet city of Bern, an anonymous patent clerk was rewriting

humankind's understanding of how the universe worked—Albert Einstein (1879–1955, see page 106).

In World War I (1914–1918), Switzerland declared itself neutral and escaped the devastation that hit the rest of Europe. After the War, Geneva served as the seat of the League of Nations, a short-lived forerunner to the United Nations.

When World War II broke out (1939–1945), Swiss neutrality was not taken for granted. As Nazi Germany and fascist Italy flanked the country, 850,000 Swiss men grabbed their rifles and mobilized to protect the borders. Switzerland avoided invasion by military readiness and by trading with the Nazis—some would say "appeasing" the Nazis (see below). Switzerland sheltered refugees and acted as a mediator between the Allies and the Axis.

After the war, Switzerland's policy of neutrality led the country to refuse membership in various international alliances and organizations, including the United Nations, NATO, and the European Union.

Switzerland Today

Switzerland maintains a delicate balance between its traditional, neutral past and the high-tech, global future.

As it has been for 700 years, the government is a federalist democracy that allows each canton maximum autonomy. On the national level, the bicameral parliament is strong, the executive branch is handled by committee, and the president is a figurehead. The federal government handles foreign affairs, national defense, currency, and the federal courts—and leaves most everything else to the 26 cantons. The man-on-the-street can always make his voice heard thanks to frequent referenda, wherein citizens gather enough signatures to require a public vote on an issue. This form of government is often called "direct democracy," because of the power it invests in the individual. Compared to most modern democracies, Swiss citizens have a direct say in many political matters and leave fewer decisions to elected representatives.

Four political parties (Liberal, Conservative, Social Democrat, People's Party) rule in an ever-changing array of coalitions, as they have since World War II. No single point of view dominates, and collaboration is essential. There's also a universal understanding that, whatever your politics, the good of Switzerland comes first.

The Swiss economy has been sluggish since the downturn of 2008. Still, Zürich remains a global center of banking and finance. Stability is enhanced by strong social security and a collaborative approach to settling labor disputes between unions and employers.

In foreign affairs, Switzerland remains neutral...but ever-vigilant. Every able-bodied man serves in the army and stays in the reserves. Each house has a gun and a fully stocked bomb shelter. (Swiss vacuum-packed emergency army bread, which lasts two years, is also said to function as a weapon.) Switzerland bristles with

600,000 rifles in homes and 12,000 heavy guns in place. Airstrips are hidden inside mountains, accessed by camouflaged doors. With the push of a button, all road, rail, and bridge entries to Swiss territory can be destroyed, sealing off the country from the outside world. Sentiments are changing, though, and Switzerland has come close to voting away its entire military. Today, you can visit once-hidden military installations, now open to the public as museums (for example, Fortress Fürigen, described in the Luzern and Central Switzerland chapter).

Swiss neutrality is not so simple in our increasingly inter-connected global economy. For example, Switzerland is home to the European community's high-tech particle accelerator labora-tory, called CERN (also the place where the World Wide Web was created). Of the country's hot-button topics, the question of whether to join the European Union has been at the forefront, dominating political discussion for the last decade. In 2002, the Swiss made a big step away from total neutrality when vot-ers approved a referendum to join the United Nations. In 2008, Switzerland joined the Schengen Agreement, opening its borders to its neighboring countries and most of the EU. Is EU mem-bership next? Referendum after referendum shows the Swiss still evenly divided on the issue, as they weigh the huge potential gains with significant potential costs.

While it's nice to think of Swiss neutrality as born of paci-fism, many realists argue that it's more about money: Switzerland's neutrality policy is key to one of its main sources of income. Many Swiss banks allow foreigners to deposit money there with few questions asked. Critics charge that these secret bank accounts harbor the dirty money of mobsters, terrorists, dictators, guide-book authors, tax evaders, and sleazy businessmen. In 2009, Switzerland's biggest bank (UBS) responded to pressure from the US, agreeing to release names of formerly secret US clients accused of tax evasion.

Switzerland also has a reputation as a safe haven from prosecu-tion, harboring a long list of foreigners (from alleged Communist Charlie Chaplin to Ugandan dictator Idi Amin). In 2009, that reputation took a hit when Swiss authorities arrested a fugitive from US justice, film director Roman Polanski.

Switzerland is rethinking its policy of neutrality in light of World War II. Critics have charged that, though neutral in the War, Switzerland helped the Nazi war effort by trading with them. (It's an open secret that a significant number of German-speaking Swiss weren't all that opposed to the Nazi regime.) They exchanged Swiss francs (the only currency accepted throughout Europe) for Nazi gold—knowing full well that the gold had been stolen from other nations and Holocaust victims. In the 1990s, Swiss banks were sued to account for the ill-gotten bullion in their vaults. A 2002 commission formed by the Swiss government agreed that Switzerland could have done more to resist the Nazis and to help Jewish refugees...but restitution has been slow in coming.

Another big issue in Switzerland is how to deal with the rising tide of immigrants. The country's high standard of living makes it an appealing place to live, and Switzerland has more foreign-born citizens than most countries (about 23 percent, compared with 13 percent in the US). But many of those immigrants are wealthy Europeans enjoying the country's easy tax laws. It's the less-desirable immigrants who have drawn fire—those who arrive with little wealth and then feed off the generous social services.

Opinions on this and many other issues are generally divided along geographic/linguistic lines. City dwellers and French- and Italian-speakers tend to favor immigrants' rights, EU membership, and other progressive issues, while rural German-speakers are more likely to be conservative. In 2009, when Switzerland voted to ban the construction of new minarets—sparking controversy across Europe—only four cantons opposed the initiative, all of them in French-speaking areas.

With 2,500 years of history, Switzerland has seen many shifts—from Celts to Romans to Habsburgs, from wars to neutrality to technological progress. But what's striking is how little Switzerland has changed. The Alps are still there, and they're still big and rugged. The government, after 700 years in existence, remains a model of democracy and international cooperation. Switzerland is

fully modern, but you'll also encounter quaint pockets of the past. Take time to see Swiss history alive today—from the cow parades of Appenzell to the Roman ruins in Avenches, and from the turrets of Château de Chillon to the farmers of Gimmelwald, who still make hay while the sun shines.

Notable Swiss People

William Tell (c. 1280–1354)

On Nov. 18, 1307, a Swiss peasant aimed his crossbow at an apple resting on his son's head and shot it cleanly. He was forced to take this dangerous target practice after refusing a bailiff's order to show obedience to the Habsburg emperor. In revenge, this same archer later ambushed and killed the bailiff—launching a revolt for Swiss independence. William (Wilhelm) Tell may be Switzerland's George Washington, but historians say the famous hero is total fiction—a similar Danish legend even predates the Swiss one. Don't "tell" the Swiss—up to 60 percent still believe there was a real William Tell.

Huldrych Zwingli (1484–1531)

The son of a farmer, Huldrych Zwingli started out as a Catholic true believer, but, under the influence of Renaissance humanists,

turned into a religious revolutionary. Known as the "third man of the Protestant Reformation" (the other two were Martin Luther and John Calvin), he used his position as the top pastor in Zürich to challenge Rome, insisting that Christians study the Bible to guide their beliefs. Many Protestant faiths, including the United Church of Christ and the Presbyterian Church, trace their theology back to Zwingli.

Jean-Jacques Rousseau (1712–1778)

One of the most influential writers of the 18th century, Jean-Jacques Rousseau ran away from his humble Geneva home for France when he was 16, but he always considered himself Swiss, not French. His writings celebrated nature and human passion (over cold reason), unleashing forces that would result in the French Revolution, Romantic literature, and even a return to breastfeeding. A bestselling novelist (publishers could not print his books fast enough, so they rented them out by the day), his descriptions of the Swiss countryside helped start the 19th-century craze for visiting the Alps.

Madame Tussaud (1761–1850)

An entertainment empire began when Swiss-born Anna Maria Grosholtz moved to Paris and learned how to sculpt wax. It was an auspicious time and place—she was able to create figures of Voltaire, Jean-Jacques Rousseau, and Benjamin Franklin. Later, during the French Revolution, she made death masks from decapitated heads. After marrying François Tussaud (becoming "Madame Tussaud"), she moved to London and eventually opened a museum of wax figures, which still shows some of her original work.

Henri Dunant (1828–1910)

In 1859, Geneva businessman Henri Dunant witnessed one of the bloodiest battles of the 19th century—the Battle of Solferino in northern Italy, where about 40,000 soldiers were killed or wounded. He wrote a book that not only described the carnage, but proposed a neutral organization that would care for those wounded in wartime. His leadership led to the founding of the International Red Cross and the Geneva Conventions, which put humanitarian limits on the waging of war. He won the first Nobel Peace Prize in 1901.

Carl Jung (1875–1961)

After Freud, Carl Jung had the greatest impact on modern psychology; there probably wouldn't be a New Age movement or the Myers-Briggs personality test without him. The Zürich psychologist popularized such terms as "introvert/extrovert," "personality complex," and "collective unconscious." He once said that the Swiss are a "primitive" people (their love of cows reminded him of African animalism), and that under their legendary efficiency is a deeply buried "earth mysticism."

Hermann Hesse (1877–1962)

A favorite author of the 1960s counterculture due to his themes of self-discovery and enlightenment, German-born Hesse became a Swiss citizen in 1923. Always publicity-shy, upon winning the Nobel Prize for Literature in 1946 he wrote to a friend, "To hell with this damn business." His best-known works include *Steppenwolf*, *Siddhartha*, and *The Glass Bead Game* (a.k.a. *Magister Ludi*).

Paul Klee (1879–1940)

Paul Klee's mastery of color and tone created highly individual art that critics have described as "musical" and "childlike." Born and raised in Bern, Klee became a teacher at the famous Bauhaus school in Weimar, Germany, but when Hitler came to power in 1933, he was fired. He returned to Switzerland as the Nazis stripped his paintings from museums and classified it as "degenerate." You can decide for yourself when you see his work at museums in Bern and Luzern.

Le Corbusier (1887–1965)

"The house is a machine for living in." With this and other edicts, Swiss-born architect Le Corbusier changed the shape of 20th-century cities. His plan for Paris' Marais district was emblematic—rows of identical towers set between freeways replacing public squares and winding streets. The Parisians turned him down, but many office and housing projects in Europe and America followed his precepts. Charles-Edouard Jeanneret-Gris (his real name) was one of the most influential architects of his time, but today many regard his International Style as sterile and socially destructive.

Jean Piaget (1896–1980)

According to *Time* magazine, Geneva psychologist Jean Piaget was "the first to take children's thinking seriously." Until his ground-breaking work, parents and teachers regarded children as empty vessels into which they poured knowledge. While studying his own three children, Piaget deduced that children are constantly testing their own theories of how the world works, asserting that "children have real understanding only of that which they invent themselves."

Elisabeth Kübler-Ross (1926–2004)

She grew up in a strict, Protestant family, but Elisabeth Kübler-Ross defied tradition and got her M.D. in 1957. A year later, she left Zürich for the US, where she was appalled by the way doctors and hospitals treated the dying. The five stages of grief she first explained in *On Death and Dying*—denial, anger, bargaining, depression, and acceptance—have become a modern touchstone, often applied to any catastrophic personal loss.

Ursula Andress (1936–)

When the bikini-clad Andress walked out of the ocean in the first James Bond movie, *Dr. No,* the indelible image of the "Bond heroine" was born. Tough, smart, and outrageously beautiful, Andress was a great match for Sean Connery's 007, even though the producers dubbed her voice because of her Swiss-German accent. Though many of her subsequent films were subpar, the list of her leading men is not: Laurence Olivier, Frank Sinatra, Marcello Mastroianni, Peter Sellers, and even Elvis Presley.

Roger Federer (1981–)

By the time he was 28, Roger Federer had already won five US Opens, three Australian Opens, one French Open, and six Wimbledons—a record 15 Grand Slam titles and more than $50 million in prize money. Born and raised near Basel, Federer ranks with Tiger Woods and Michael Jordan as a worldwide sports icon; he's regarded by many as the greatest tennis player of all time.

APPENDIX

Contents

Tourist Information

Tourist Offices

The Swiss national tourist office in the US is a wealth of information. Before your trip, get the comprehensive "Welcome to Switzerland" brochure and request any specifics you want (such as regional and city maps, festival schedules, and hiking information). Call 877-794-8037 or visit www.myswitzerland.com (info .usa@myswitzerland.com).

In Switzerland, your best first stop in every town is generally the tourist information office—abbreviated **TI** in this book. Throughout Switzerland, you'll find TIs are usually well-organized and always have an English-speaking staff. Most TIs are run by the government, which means their information isn't colored by a drive for profit.

A TI is a great place to get a city map, advice on public transportation (including bus and train schedules), walking-tour information, tips on special events, and recommendations for nightlife. Many TIs have information on the entire country, or at least the region, so try to pick up maps for destinations you'll be visiting later in your trip. If you're arriving in town after the TI closes, call ahead or pick up a map in a neighboring town.

Although TIs offer room-finding services, they're a good deal only if you're in search of summer and weekend deals on business hotels. The TIs can help you with small pensions and private homes, but you'll save both yourself and your host money by going direct with the listings in this book.

Communicating

Hurdling the Language Barrier

Switzerland has four official languages: German, French, Italian, and Romansh (an obscure Romantic tongue). Most of the destinations in this book are in the German-speaking territory. No matter where you are, most young or well-educated people—especially those in larger towns and the tourist trade—speak at least some English. Still, you'll get more smiles by using the local pleasantries. See the German, French, and Italian Survival Phrases at the end of the appendix.

In German-speaking Switzerland, locals speak sing-songy *Schwyzertütsch* (Swiss German) around the house, but in schools and at work, they speak and write in the same standard German used in Germany and Austria (called "High" German, or *Hochdeutsch*—though many Swiss prefer to call it *Schriftdeutsch*, or "Written German"). The standard greeting is a hearty *Grüezi* (GRIT-see). "Thank you" is derived from French, but pronounced a little differently: *Merci* (MUHR-see). They also sometimes use the more German-like *Dankche* (DAHN-kheh with a very gutteral "kh"). The exact pronunciation (and even spelling) of Swiss German words varies substantially by region.

English—like Dutch, Danish, Swedish, and Norwegian—is a Germanic language, making German easier on most American ears than Romance languages (such as Italian and French). German is a phonetic language—its pronunciation rules are set in stone, and there are no silent letters.

These tips will help you pronounce German words: The letter *w* is always pronounced as "v" (e.g., the word for "wonderful" is *wunderbar*, pronounced VOON-dehr-bar). The vowel combinations *ie* and *ei* are pronounced like the name of the second letter—so *ie* sounds like the letter *e* (as in *hier* and *Bier*, the German words for "here" and "beer"), while *ei* sounds like the letter *i* (as in *nein* and *Stein,* the German words for "no" and "stone"). The vowel combination *au* is pronounced "ow" (as in *Frau*). The vowel combinations *eu* and *äu* are pronounced "oy" (as in *neu, Deutsch,* and *Bräu,* the words for "new," "German," and "brew"). To pronounce *ö* and *ü,* purse your lips when you say the vowel; the other vowel with an umlaut, *ä,* is pronounced the same as *e* in "men." (In written German, these can be depicted without an umlaut as the vowel followed by an *e: oe, ue,* and *ae,* respectively.) Written German always capitalizes all nouns.

Give it your best shot. The locals will appreciate your efforts.

Telephones

Smart travelers use the telephone to reserve or reconfirm rooms, get tourist information, reserve restaurants, confirm tour times, or phone home. Generally the easiest, cheapest way to call home is to use an international phone card purchased in Switzerland. This section covers dialing instructions, phone cards, and types of phones. If you need more in-depth information than we provide below, see www.ricksteves.com/phoning.

How to Dial

Calling from the US to Switzerland, or vice versa, is simple—once you break the code. The European calling chart in this chapter will walk you through it.

Dialing Domestically in Switzerland

Switzerland has a direct-dial phone system (no area codes). To call anywhere within Switzerland, just dial the number. For example, the number for a Gimmelwald hotel I recommend is 033-855-1658. To call it from Zürich's train station, just dial 033-855-1658. If you call it from Gimmelwald's cable-car station, it's the same: 033-855-1658. All Swiss phone numbers are 10 digits, including the initial zero.

Dialing Internationally to or from Switzerland

If you want to make an international call, follow these three steps:

1. Dial the international access code (00 if you're calling from Europe, 011 from the US or Canada).

2. Dial the country code of the country you're calling (see European Calling Chart in this chapter).

3. Dial the entire phone number, keeping in mind that calling many countries requires dropping the initial zero of the area code or local number (the European Calling Chart lists specifics per country).

European Calling Chart

Just smile and dial, using this key:
AC = Area Code, LN = Local Number.

European Country	Calling long distance within ...	Calling from the US or Canada to ...	Calling from a European country to ...
Austria	AC + LN	011 + 43 + AC (without the initial zero) + LN	00 + 43 + AC (without the initial zero) + LN
Belgium	LN	011 + 32 + LN (without initial zero)	00 + 32 + LN (without initial zero)
Bosnia-Herzegovina	AC + LN	011 + 387 + AC (without initial zero) + LN	00 + 387 + AC (without initial zero) + LN
Britain	AC + LN	011 + 44 + AC (without initial zero) + LN	00 + 44 + AC (without initial zero) + LN
Croatia	AC + LN	011 + 385 + AC (without initial zero) + LN	00 + 385 + AC (without initial zero) + LN
Czech Republic	LN	011 + 420 + LN	00 + 420 + LN
Denmark	LN	011 + 45 + LN	00 + 45 + LN
Estonia	LN	011 + 372 + LN	00 + 372 + LN
Finland	AC + LN	011 + 358 + AC (without initial zero) + LN	999 (or other 900 number) + 358 + AC (without initial zero) + LN
France	LN	011 + 33 + LN (without initial zero)	00 + 33 + LN (without initial zero)
Germany	AC + LN	011 + 49 + AC (without initial zero) + LN	00 + 49 + AC (without initial zero) + LN
Gibraltar	LN	011 + 350 + LN	00 + 350 + LN
Greece	LN	011 + 30 + LN	00 + 30 + LN
Hungary	06 + AC + LN	011 + 36 + AC + LN	00 + 36 + AC + LN
Ireland	AC + LN	011 + 353 + AC (without initial zero) + LN	00 + 353 + AC (without initial zero) + LN

European Country	Calling long distance within ...	Calling from the US or Canada to ...	Calling from a European country to ...
Italy	LN	011 + 39 + LN	00 + 39 + LN
Montenegro	AC + LN	011 + 382 + AC (without initial zero) + LN	00 + 382 + AC (without initial zero) + LN
Morocco	LN	011 + 212 + LN (without initial zero)	00 + 212 + LN (without initial zero)
Netherlands	AC + LN	011 + 31 + AC (without initial zero) + LN	00 + 31 + AC (without initial zero) + LN
Norway	LN	011 + 47 + LN	00 + 47 + LN
Poland	LN	011 + 48 + LN (without initial zero)	00 + 48 + LN (without initial zero)
Portugal	LN	011 + 351 + LN	00 + 351 + LN
Slovakia	AC + LN	011 + 421 + AC (without initial zero) + LN	00 + 421 + AC (without initial zero) + LN
Slovenia	AC + LN	011 + 386 + AC (without initial zero) + LN	00 + 386 + AC (without initial zero) + LN
Spain	LN	011 + 34 + LN	00 + 34 + LN
Sweden	AC + LN	011 + 46 + AC (without initial zero) + LN	00 + 46 + AC (without initial zero) + LN
Switzerland	LN	011 + 41 + LN (without initial zero)	00 + 41 + LN (without initial zero)
Turkey	AC (if there's no initial zero, add one) + LN	011 + 90 + AC (without initial zero) + LN	00 + 90 + AC (without initial zero) + LN

- The instructions above apply whether you're calling a land line or mobile phone.
- The international access codes (the first numbers you dial when making an international call) are 011 if you're calling from the US or Canada, or 00 if you're calling from virtually anywhere in Europe (except Finland, where it's 999 or another 900 number, depending on the phone service you're using).
- To call the US or Canada from Europe, dial 00, then 1 (the country code for the US and Canada), then the area code and number. In short, 00 + 1 + AC + LN = Hi, Mom!

Calling from the US to Switzerland: To call from the US to the recommended Gimmelwald hotel, dial 011 (the US international access code), 41 (Switzerland's country code), then 33-855-1658 (the hotel's number without its initial 0).

Calling from Switzerland to the US: To call from Gimmelwald to my office in Edmonds, Washington, I dial 00 (Europe's international access code), 1 (the US country code), 425 (Edmonds' area code), and 771-8303.

Note: You might see a + in front of a European number. When dialing the number, replace the + with the international access code of the country you're calling from (00 from Europe, 011 from the US or Canada).

Phone Cards

You'll find two types of prepaid phone cards in Switzerland: insertable (best for local calls, but work only in public pay phones) and international (best for calling home). If you have a live card at the end of your trip, give it to another traveler to use up.

Insertable Phone Cards: An insertable, prepaid "Taxcard" allows you to dial from any public pay phone, as most Swiss phone booths no longer accept coins. Simply take the phone off the hook, insert the card, wait for a dial tone, and dial away. The price of the call is automatically deducted while you talk, and at the end of the call, the phone will helpfully beep to remind you to remove your card and will show the card balance.

These cards are sold at post offices and many newsstand kiosks and gas stations in 5-SF, 10-SF, and 20-SF denominations (because cards work only in Switzerland—and are occasionally duds—avoid the pricier ones).

International Phone Cards: These are the cheapest way to make international calls from Europe—with the best cards, it costs literally pennies a minute, and they can be used from any type of phone (but if calling from a hotel, make sure you won't be charged for a toll-free call). These cards also work for local calls, but aren't likely to beat the local rates you'll get at a pay phone.

The cards are sold all over; look for them at many post offices, newsstands, mini-marts, and exchange bureaus. Ask the clerk which of the various brands has the best rates for calls to America. Some cards are rechargeable (you can call up the number on the card, give your credit-card number, and buy more time). Some shops also sell cardless codes, printed right on the receipt.

To use the card, scratch to reveal your code (or locate the code on your receipt), then dial the free access number. Following the recorded instructions, enter your code, then dial the number you're calling. Usually the prompts are in fairly concise English, but if not, experiment: Dial your code, followed by the pound sign (#), then the number, then pound again, and so on, until it works. Sometimes the star (*) key is used instead of the pound sign.

Remember that you don't need the actual card to use a card account, so it's sharable. You can write down the access number and code in your notebook and share it with friends.

US Calling Cards: These cards, such as the ones offered by AT&T, Verizon, or Sprint, are the worst option. You'll nearly always save a lot of money by using a locally purchased international phone card instead.

Public Phones and Hotel-Room Phones

Swisscom **public pay phones** are easy to find, especially at train stations and post offices. Most take only insertable phone cards, though a few take coins as well. Local calls cost 0.50 SF for the first minute, then 0.04–0.08 SF/min after (calls are cheapest outside business hours; calling mobile phones is pricier). International calls are more expensive (about 0.35 SF/min), so if you'll be calling home a lot, an international phone card can save you money.

Calling from your **hotel-room phone** can be cheap for local calls (ask for the rates at the front desk first), but are usually a rip-off for long-distance calls, unless you use an international phone card. A few hotels have cheap direct-dial rates for North America—but again, always check rates at the front desk before calling. Incoming calls are free, making this a cheap way for friends and family to stay in touch (provided they have a good long-distance plan for calls to Europe—and a list of your hotels' phone numbers). In-room phones are rare in guest houses and private homes.

Mobile Phones

Many travelers enjoy the convenience of traveling with a mobile phone.

Using Your Mobile Phone: Your US mobile phone works in Europe (if it's GSM-enabled, tri-band or quad-band) and on a calling plan that includes international calls. For example, with a T-Mobile phone, you'll pay $1 per minute to make or receive a call, and about $0.35 apiece for text messages.

You can save money if your phone is electronically "unlocked"—then you can simply buy a **SIM card** (a fingernail-sized chip that stores the phone's information) in Europe. SIM cards, which give you a European phone number, are sold at mobile-phone stores and some newsstand kiosks for about $5–10. When you buy the card, you'll also get some prepaid calling time (25 SF gives you about 75 minutes). Simply insert the SIM card in your phone (usually in a slot behind the battery), and it'll work like a European mobile phone. When buying a SIM card, always ask about fees for domestic and international calls, roaming charges, and how to check your credit balance and buy more time.

Many **smartphones,** such as the iPhone or BlackBerry, work in Europe—but beware of sky-high fees, especially for data downloading (checking email, browsing the Internet, watching videos, and so on). Ask your provider in advance how to avoid unwittingly "roaming" your way to a huge bill. Some applications allow for cheap or free smartphone calls over a Wi-Fi connection (described under "Calling over the Internet," below).

Using a European Mobile Phone: Local mobile-phone shops all over Europe sell basic phones for around $30–50 (which often includes a bit of calling credit as well). You'll also need to buy a SIM card (explained above) and prepaid credit for making calls. If you remain in the phone's home country, domestic calls are reasonable, and incoming calls are free. You'll pay more if you're "roaming" in another country. If your phone is "unlocked," you can swap out its SIM card for a new one when you travel to other countries.

Calling over the Internet

Some things that seem too good to be true...actually are true. If you're traveling with a laptop, you can make calls using VoIP (Voice over Internet Protocol). With VoIP, two computers act as the phones, and the Internet-based calls are free (or you can pay a few cents to call from your computer to a telephone). The major providers are Skype (www.skype.com) and Google Talk (www.google.com/talk).

Useful Phone Numbers

Emergencies: Dial 112.

Directory Assistance: Dial 111 for domestic numbers, dial 191 for international numbers.

Train Info: 0900-300-300 (1.20 SF/min).

US Embassy, in Bern: Jubilaeumsstrasse 93, Mon–Fri 9:00–11:30, closed Sat–Sun, tel. 031-357-7234, http://bern.usembassy.gov.

Travel Advisories

US Department of State: tel. 202/647-5225, www.travel.state.gov
Canadian Department of Foreign Affairs: Canadian tel. 800-267-6788, www.dfait-maeci.gc.ca

US Centers for Disease Control and Prevention: tel. 800-CDC-INFO (800-232-4636), www.cdc.gov/travel

Email and Mail

The Internet can be an invaluable tool for planning your trip (researching and booking hotels, checking bus and train schedules, and so on). It's also useful to get online periodically while you travel—to reconfirm your trip plans, check the weather, catch up on email, blog or post photos from your trip, or call folks back home (explained earlier, in "Calling over the Internet").

Some hotels offer a computer in the lobby with Internet access for guests. Smaller places may sometimes let you sit at their desk for a few minutes just to check your email, if you ask politely. If you're traveling with a laptop, see if your hotel has Wi-Fi (wireless Internet access) or a port in your room where you can plug in a cable to get online. Most hotels offer Wi-Fi for free; others charge by the minute.

If your hotel doesn't have access, ask your hotelier to direct you to the nearest place to get online. Most of the towns where I've listed accommodations also have Internet cafés. Many libraries offer free access, but they also tend to have limited opening hours, restrict your online time to 30 minutes, and may require reservations.

Mail

Even when post offices are closed, you're never too far from a yellow mailbox with an automated stamp dispenser (most train stations have one). Type in the value of stamp you want (postcard or letter to the US: 1.40 SF economy, 1.80 SF express), insert coins, and press the pound key. These machines don't give change, so if you have any amount left in the machine, print out a stamp for that amount and use it toward your next postcard.

While you can arrange for mail delivery to your hotel (allow 10 days for a letter to arrive), phoning and emailing are so easy that I've dispensed with mail stops altogether.

Transportation

By Car or Train?

Because Switzerland's train network is excellent, I recommend using public transportation here. Only a few areas—like the Appenzell region and the French Swiss countryside—are better by car. Cars are an expensive headache in the bigger cities.

Trains

Trains are generally slick, speedy, and punctual, with synchronized connections. They're also clean, roomy, and, in Switzerland, entirely non-smoking. Virtually all Swiss stations have luggage lockers. Few places in Switzerland are

Public Transportation

Legend:
- Rail
- Mountain Rail
- Boat
- Bus

Note: Not all transportation routes shown.

50 Kilometers
50 Miles

out of reach of the train system, though some frustrating schedules make the more out-of-the-way recommendations (such as Taveyanne in the French Swiss countryside) not worth the time and trouble for the less determined.

Swiss trains and stations are marked "SBB CFF FFS." All those letters mean the same thing ("Swiss Federal Railways"), in three different languages: German, French, and Italian.

Schedules

Switzerland has a train info number you can dial from anywhere in the country: toll tel. 0900-300-300 (1.20 SF/min). For Swiss timetables, visit Germany's excellent all-Europe timetable, http://bahn.hafas.de/bin/query.exe/en, or the Swiss site, www.rail.ch. At most train stations, attendants and/or machines will print out a step-by-step itinerary for you, free of charge. Major stations also have handy travel offices offering general help.

Tickets

If you're traveling without a railpass, get train tickets at the station—either at the ticket windows, or at the easy-to-use machines. Though you may see some people buying their tickets from conductors on the train (for an additional 5 SF), don't assume you can do so on all trains. If the side of the train displays a yellow-eye logo, you need to get a ticket before boarding or risk being fined 80 SF.

Swiss Railpasses

Because of high ticket prices, railpasses are a good deal in Switzerland, even for a three-day trip. But for such a little country, Switzerland has a dizzying array of train passes and deals. I've listed the most popular ones here. For the latest prices, see www.ricksteves.com/rail.

The **Swiss Pass** is the basic version, covering all trains, boats, and buses, plus admission to most Swiss museums (see page 358), and offering a half-price discount on most high-mountain trains and lifts. It comes in both consecutive-day and flexipass versions. Both versions completely cover the cost of any transportation for a specified number of days (but do not cover seat or overnight-train reservations).

If you're traveling with at least one other person, get the "Saver" version of the pass, which is 15 percent cheaper than individual passes. Second class (available to any age) is 33 percent cheaper than first class.

The **Half-Fare Travel Card** gives you a 50 percent discount on all national and private trains, postal buses, lifts, and steamers (99 SF for one month, sold only in Switzerland). This can save you

Comparing Swiss Pass Coverage

All passes that include Switzerland cover national network trains, boat trips on Swiss lakes, and many sightseeing and private rail discounts.

Here are the key routes where coverage varies:

Route or Bonus	Eurail/ Select or Two-Country Passes	Swiss Card or Transfer Ticket	Swiss Pass or Flexipass
Swiss Family Card (kids travel free)	No	Applies	Applies
Postal buses	No	Covered	Covered
Urban transport in 35 cities ($2/trip)	No	No	Covered
Swiss museum admissions	No	No	Covered
Brig-Disentis section of the Glacier Express scenic route ($45 2nd class, reservation extra)	No	Only if it's fastest, most direct route (from south border to south destination)	Covered
Brig-Zermatt private train to see the Matterhorn ($35 2nd class)	No	Only if Zermatt is final destination	Covered
Jungfrau Region Railways (e.g., from Interlaken: $7 to Lauterbrunnen, $10 to Grindelwald, $13 to Wengen; $180 round-trip to Jungfraujoch)	25% discount above Interlaken	50% discount with Swiss Card; Jungfraujoch not covered on in- and outbound round-trip	50% discount above Mürren, Grindelwald, or Wengen, except only 25% off Kl. Scheidegg-Jungfraujoch
Many high mountain lifts (e.g., Stechelberg-Schilthorn $90 round-trip/$70 off-peak)	No	50% discount with Card, not with Transfer Ticket	50% discount
Half-fare option: 50% transport discount between fully covered flexi travel days	No	50% discount with Card, not with Transfer Ticket	50% discount with flexipass
Passholder rate on international night trains	Applies	No	Applies
7 p.m. rule for night trains	Applies	No	No

All "covered" services start use of a travel day on a flexipass, but discounts do not.

money if your Swiss travel adds up to more than $200 in point-to-point tickets. The **Swiss Card** is a variation on this, sold only in the US and at a few border stations. It includes the same 50 percent discount and adds two train rides: one ride from any point of entry (such as the German border or Zürich's airport) to any other point in Switzerland and one back from that point to any border ($250 first class, $179 second class).

Regional passes cover all trains, buses, and boats in a particular area, such as the Berner Oberland (Berner Oberland Pass, see page 132), Zermatt area (see page 198), or Central Switzerland, around Luzern (Tell-Pass, see page 86). Buy these (in Switzerland,

Lift Lingo

The Swiss have come up with a variety of ways to conquer peaks and reach the best viewpoints and trailheads with minimum sweat. Known generically as "lifts," each of these contraptions has its own name and definition. Use the right terms, and impress your new Swiss friends.

Cogwheel Train: A train that climbs a steep incline using a gear system, which engages "teeth" in the middle of the tracks to provide traction. Also known as "rack-and-pinion train" or "rack railway." In German, it's a *Zahnradbahn* (*train à cremaillère* in French and *ferrovia a cremagliera* in Italian).

Funicular: A car that is pulled by a cable along tracks up a particularly steep incline, often counterbalanced by a similar car going in the opposite direction (meaning you'll pass the other car exactly halfway through the ride). Funiculars, like cogwheel trains, are in contact with the ground at all times. In German, it's a *Standseilbahn* (*funiculaire* in French and *funicolare* in Italian).

Cable Car: A large passenger car, suspended in the air by a cable, which travels between stations without touching the ground. A cable car holds a large number of people (sometimes dozens at a time), who generally ride standing up. When a cable car reaches a station, it comes to a full stop to allow passengers to get on and off. In German, it's a *Seilbahn* (*téléphérique* in French and *funivia* in Italian).

Gondola: Also suspended in the air by a cable, but smaller than a cable car—generally holding fewer than 10 people, who are usually seated. Gondolas move continuously, meaning that passengers have to hop into and out of the moving cars at stations. Also, while cable-car lines usually have two big cars—one going in each direction—gondolas generally have many smaller cars strung along the same cable. In German, it's a *Gondel* (*télécabine* in French and *telecabine* in Italian).

Confusingly, the "car" compartment of a cable car is sometimes referred to as a "gondola."

not the US) only if you're very focused on a single region, but note that there's usually no need to have both a regional pass and an all-Switzerland pass (or Eurailpass).

Other deals include the **Swiss Family Card,** allowing children under 16 to travel free with their parents (20 SF per child at Swiss stations, or free with Swiss train passes when requested with purchase in the US).

Railpasses

Prices listed are for 2010 and are subject to change. For the latest prices, details, and train schedules (and easy online ordering), see my comprehensive *Guide to Eurail Passes* at www.ricksteves.com/rail.

"Saver" prices are per person for two or more people traveling together. "Youth" means under age 26.

SWISS PASS AND SWISS FLEXIPASS

	Individual 1st Class	Individual 2nd Class	Saver 1st Class	Saver 2nd Class	Youth 1st Class	Youth 2nd Class
4 consecutive days	$399	$266	$340	$226	$299	$200
8 consecutive days	576	384	490	328	432	290
15 consecutive days	697	465	593	395	523	350
22 consecutive days	805	536	685	475	604	403
1 month	885	590	753	503	664	443
3 days in 1 month flexi	383	255	326	217	N/A	N/A
4 days in 1 month flexi	463	309	395	263	N/A	N/A
5 days in 1 month flexi	536	358	457	305	N/A	N/A
6 days in 1 month flexi	609	407	519	347	N/A	N/A

Covers all trains, boats, buses, and most museums plus 50 percent off high mountain rides, and—if you have a flexipass—50 percent off any ride taken between your counted "flexi" days. Kids under 16 free with parent, otherwise half of full fare.

SWITZERLAND–AUSTRIA PASS

	Individual 1st Class	Saver 1st Class	Youth 2nd Class
4 days in 2 months	$415	$353	$291
Extra rail days (max 6)	47	39	32

The fare for children 4–11 is half the adult individual fare or Saver fare. Kids under age 4 travel free.

GERMANY–SWITZERLAND PASS

	Individual 1st Class	Saver 1st Class	Youth 2nd Class
5 days in 2 months	$467	$398	$329
6 days in 2 months	515	438	362
8 days in 2 months	609	520	428
10 days in 2 months	704	602	495

The fare for children 4–11 is half the adult individual fare or Saver fare. Kids under age 4 travel free.

Map key:

Approximate point-to-point one-way second-class rail fares in US dollars. First class costs 50 percent more. Add up fares for your itinerary to see whether a railpass will save you money.

FRANCE–SWITZERLAND PASS

	Individual 1st Class	Saver 1st Class	Youth 2nd Class
4 days in 2 months	$437	$371	$309
Extra rail days (max 6)	47-50	40-43	32-36

Covers many Swiss boats as well as trains. The fare for children 4–11 is half the adult individual fare or Saver fare. Kids under age 4 travel free.

SWISS TRANSFER & SWISS CARD

The **Swiss Transfer Ticket** gives you one train ride in from any Swiss airport or border station to any point in Switzerland, then one trip out to any airport or border for $196 in first class or $130 in second class. Each direction must be completed in a day by the fastest, most direct route and both trips must occur within a month. Sold only outside Switzerland.

The **Swiss Card** includes one roundtrip within a month as above, plus 50% discounts between those two trips on all Swiss railways, lake steamers, postal buses, and high mountain lifts for $261 in first class or $187 in second class. Also available at a few Swiss airports and border stations.

Eurailpasses

If you're also traveling to other countries, consider a Eurail Selectpass, which gives you up to 15 travel days (within a 2-month period) in three, four, or five adjacent countries: Choose among Switzerland, Germany, Austria, France, Italy, and most other European countries (allow about $400 for 5 days in 3 countries, and up to about $950 for 15 days in 5 countries). A 21-country Eurail Global pass is cost-effective only if you're doing a whirlwind trip of Europe (allow roughly $875 for 3 weeks). These rates are per person for two or more adults traveling together; solo travelers age 26 or older will pay about 15 percent more (unlike with the Swiss Pass, if you're over 26, you have to buy a first-class pass).

If you're combining your trip to Switzerland with travel in France, Germany, or Austria, you may want to consider a **two-country pass**.

Railpass Bonuses and Discounts

If you buy a railpass, know what extras are included—for example, boat cruises on the big Swiss lakes are covered by most railpasses. In addition, Swiss railpasses can get you free entry to many museums and discounts on many mountain lifts. Always ask. Note that while Eurailpasses include some deals in Switzerland beyond simple trains (such as on some mountain lifts), the discounts and coverage of these passes generally aren't as extensive as the Switzerland-only passes (for example, lifts in Zermatt are discounted and postal buses nationwide are free with a Swiss Pass, but both are full price with a Eurailpass).

If your railpass is a flexipass (it covers a certain number of days in a given span, rather than consecutive days), it's worth knowing when, and when not, to use up your flexi-days. Trips that are merely discounted, rather than free with the pass—most notably many mountain lifts—don't use up a day of your pass. Any time you use the pass for a free trip, however, it counts as using a flexi-day. This can be fine and cost-effective if you're already using the pass to cover other transportation that day. But if you've got no other use for your pass that day than your "free" trip (such as a short boat or train ride), it can make sense to pay out of pocket for it rather than use up a valuable day of your flexipass.

If you have a Swiss flexipass (rather than a Eurailpass), note that when you're *not* using a travel day, your pass gets you a 50 percent discount on all rides taken before the use of your last travel day. Unlike flexipasses for most other countries, a Swiss flexipass expires once you've used up all your travel days—even if that's well before the end of the one-month time frame noted on your pass. It can be smart to use your first travel day near the beginning of your trip, and your last travel day near (or at) the end of your trip; then you can use your flexipass throughout your entire trip for transportation discounts on the days you're not using travel days. It's confusing, but once you figure out the system, you can make it work to your advantage.

Train Notes

Scenic Rail Journeys: In addition to being convenient for transportation, many of Switzerland's trains are also breathtakingly scenic. Several trips are particularly beautiful and billed as special "theme" routes for tourists. For many visitors, these are a Swiss highlight, and I've devoted an entire chapter to them (see page 299).

Private Lines: Switzerland has some privately owned train lines. For instance, a large segment of the Glacier Express scenic journey is private. Private lines are usually covered by Swiss railpasses, but not covered by Eurailpasses (though Eurailpasses can get you discounts on certain trips). If your railpass doesn't cover an entire journey, pay for the "uncovered" portion at the station before you board the train.

Check Your Bags: If you're town- or mountain-hopping through Switzerland by train, you can lighten your load by sending your baggage ahead (drop it off at the station, pay 10 SF with ticket or railpass, maximum 55 pounds). Your bag will show up within 24 hours of your arrival (usually faster) and will be held for two days (after that, you're charged a few francs a day). For twice the price, you can have same-day service to certain stations (in by 9:00, delivered by 18:00 or so).

Bike 'n' Rail: Hundreds of local train stations rent bikes for 33 SF a day and sometimes have easy "pick up here and drop off there" plans (40 SF/day; see www.switzerlandmobility.ch). For mixing train and bike travel, ask at stations for information booklets or see www.rent-a-bike.ch.

Renting a Car

To rent a car in Switzerland, you must be at least 20 years old with a valid license (age requirements vary by rental company). Drivers under the age of 25 may incur a young-driver surcharge.

For driving in Switzerland, your US driver's license is all you need. If you're also planning to drive in Austria or Italy, you're officially required to get an International Driving Permit ($15 through your local AAA, plus two passport photos, www.aaa.com).

Research car rentals before you go. It's cheapest to arrange most car rentals from the US. Call several companies and look online to compare rates, or arrange a rental through your hometown travel agent. Two reputable companies among many are Auto Europe (www.autoeurope.com) and Europe by Car (www.ebc travel.com). For the best rental deal, rent by the week with unlimited mileage (but for long trips, consider leasing—see below). To save money on gas, ask for a diesel car.

Expect to pay about $500 per person (based on 2 people sharing the car) for a small economy car for two weeks with unlimited mileage, including gas, parking, and insurance.

I normally rent the smallest, least-expensive model (e.g., a Ford Fiesta) with a stick shift. For a bigger, roomier, more powerful but inexpensive car, move up to a Ford Focus or VW Polo. Minibuses are a great budget way to go for five to nine people.

Almost all rentals are manual by default, so if you need an automatic, you must request one in advance; beware that these cars are usually larger models (not as maneuverable on narrow, winding roads). An automatic transmission adds about 50 percent to the car-rental cost over a manual transmission.

Compare pick-up costs (downtown can be cheaper than the airport) and explore drop-off options. Returning a car at a big-city train station can be tricky; get precise details on the car drop-off location and hours.

When picking up the car, check it thoroughly and make sure any damage is noted on your rental agreement. Find out how your car's lights, turn signals, wipers, and gas cap function. When you return the car, make sure the agent verifies its condition with you.

If you drop your car off early or keep it longer, you'll be credited or charged at a fair, prorated price. Always keep your receipts in case any questions arise about your billing.

Car Insurance Options

Accidents can happen anywhere, but when you're on vacation, the

Driving: Distance & Time

25 Kilometers
25 Miles

To Colmar
To Freiburg
GERMANY
To Füssen

45m·.75h
45m·.75h

Basel
95m
1.5h

Zürich

Appenzell

140m·2.75h
90m·2.25h

55m·1h

60m·1h

60m·1.25h
50m·1h

115m·2.5h

LIECHT.
To Innsbruck

FRANCE

120m·2h

60m·1h

75m·1.5h

35m·.75h

80m·2h

AUSTRIA

To Beaune

Murten

20m·.5h

Bern

70m·1h

Luzern

85m·1.5h

75m·1.25h

Chur

100m
2.75h

40m·1h

60m·1h

35m·.75h

45m·1h

Inter-laken

Pontresina

To Bolzano

Lausanne

135m·2.75h

15m·.5h

55m·1h

70m·3h

130m·2.75h

130m·4.75h

50m·1.75h

80m
3h

Montreux

35m·.75h

90m·1.5h

10m·.25h

Lauter-brunnen

105m
1.75h

85m·3h

30m
1.25h

Geneva

85m·2h

95m·3h

75m·2.25h

Tirano

50m·1h

Täsch

Zermatt

Lugano

120m·3.5h

20m·.5h

85m·1.75h

Chamonix

Note: Drivers must park in Täsch to get to Zermatt

50m·1h

Como

100m·2h

To Lyon

95m·1.5h

FRANCE

ITALY

Milan

m=miles
h=hours

Note: Your times may vary based on traffic, cows, construction, and road conditions

last thing you need is stress over car insurance. Limit your financial risk by choosing one of these three options: Buy Collision Damage Waiver (CDW) coverage from the car-rental company, get coverage through your credit card (free, but more complicated), or buy coverage through Travel Guard.

While each rental company has its own variation, the basic **CDW** costs $15–25 a day (figure roughly 25 percent extra) and reduces your liability, but does not eliminate it. When you pick up the car, you'll be offered the chance to "buy down" the basic deductible to zero (for an additional $10–30/day; this is often called "super CDW").

If you opt for **credit-card coverage,** there's a catch. You'll technically have to decline all coverage offered by the car-rental company, which means they can place a hold on your card (which can be up to the full value of the car). In case of damage, it can be time-consuming to resolve the charges with your credit-card company. Before you decide on this option, quiz your credit-card company about how it works and ask them to explain the worst-case scenario.

Finally, you can buy CDW insurance from **Travel Guard** ($9/day plus a one-time $3 service fee covers you for up to $35,000, $250 deductible, tel. 800-826-4919, www.travelguard.com). It's valid everywhere in Europe except the Republic of Ireland, and some Italian car-rental companies refuse to honor it. Residents of

APPENDIX

Washington state aren't eligible for this coverage.

For more fine print about car-rental insurance, see www.rick steves.com/cdw.

Leasing

For trips of two and a half weeks or more, leasing (which automatically includes zero-deductible collision and theft insurance) is the best way to go. By technically buying and then selling back the car, you save lots of money on tax and insurance. Leasing provides you a new car with unlimited mileage and a 24-hour emergency assistance program. You can lease for as little as 17 days to as long as six months. Car leases must be arranged from the US. One of many reliable companies offering affordable lease packages is Europe by Car (US tel. 800-223-1516, www.ebctravel.com).

Driving

You can get anywhere quickly on Switzerland's fine road system, the world's most expensive per mile to build. Drivers pay a one-time, 40-SF fee for a permit to use Swiss autobahns—check to see if your rental car already has one (if not, buy it at the border, gas station, or car rental agency). Anyone caught driving on a Swiss autobahn without this tax sticker is likely to be stopped and fined.

Use your headlights day and night like the Swiss do; the Swiss government strongly recommends doing so (but stops short of requiring it). Seat belts, however, are required, and two beers under those belts are enough to land you in jail. Children under 12 (yes, 12) need to ride in a child-safety seat.

Fuel: Gas is expensive—often around $8 per gallon. US credit and debit cards won't work at pay-at-the-pump stations, but are generally accepted (with a PIN code) at staffed stations. Diesel rental cars are common; make sure you know what type of gas your car takes before you fill up.

Signage: Know the universal road signs (shown in this chapter and explained in charts in most road atlases and at service stations). *Dreieck* (literally, "three corners") means a Y in the road;

 AND LEARN THESE ROAD SIGNS

Speed Limit (km/hr)

Yield

No Passing

End of No Passing Zone

One Way

Intersection

Main Road

Freeway

Danger

No Entry

No Entry for cars

All Vehicles Prohibited

Parking

No Parking

Customs

Peace

APPENDIX

Autobahnkreuz is an intersection (*carrefour* in French). Exits are spaced about 20 miles apart and often have a gas station (*bleifrei/sans plomb* are German/French for "unleaded"), a restaurant, a mini-mart, and sometimes a tourist information desk. Exits and intersections refer to the next major city or the nearest small town. Look at your map and anticipate which town names to watch out for. Know what you're looking for—miss it, and you're long autobahn-gone. When navigating, you'll see *nord, süd, ost, west,* or *mitte* (*nord, sud, est, oest,* or *centre* in French).

To get to the center of a city, follow signs for *Zentrum* or *Stadtmitte* (or *centre-ville* in French). Ring roads go around a city.

Parking: You can pick up the "cardboard clock" (*Parkscheibe,* available free at gas stations, police stations, and *Tabak* shops) and display your arrival time on the clock and put it on the dashboard, so parking attendants can see you've been there less than the posted maximum stay.

Cheap Flights

While trains are usually the best way to connect places that are close together, if your trip extends beyond Switzerland, you may save time and money by flying.

Well-known cheapo airlines in Europe include easyJet (www.easeyjet.com), RyanAir (www.ryanair.com), and BMI Baby (www.bmibaby.com). Those based in Switzerland are Flybaboo (www.flybaboo.com) and Helvetic (www.helvetic.com).

A visit to www.skyscanner.net sorts the numerous options offered by the many discount airlines, enabling you to see the best schedules for your trip and come up with the best deal. Other good search engines include www.mobissimo.com and www.wegolo.com.

Be aware of the potential drawbacks of flying on the cheap: nonrefundable and nonchangeable tickets, minimal customer assistance, the typical use of airports far outside town, and pricey baggage fees. If you're traveling with lots of luggage, a cheap flight can quickly become a bad deal, due to per-piece baggage fees. To avoid unpleasant surprises, read the small print—especially baggage policies—before you book.

Resources

Resources from Rick Steves

Rick Steves' Switzerland is one of more than 30 titles in a series of **books** on European travel, which includes country guidebooks; city and regional guidebooks; and my budget-travel skills handbook, *Rick Steves' Europe Through the Back Door.* My phrase books—for German, French, Italian, Spanish, and Portuguese—

APPENDIX

are practical and budget-oriented. My other books are *Europe 101* (a crash course on art and history, newly expanded and in full color), *Travel as a Political Act* (a travelogue sprinkled with advice for bringing home a global perspective), *European Christmas* (on traditional and modern-day celebrations), and *Postcards from Europe* (a fun memoir of my travels over 25 years). For a list of my books, see the inside of the last page of this book.

My **TV series,** *Rick Steves' Europe,* covers European destinations in 70 shows, including three episodes that explore the Swiss Alps. My weekly public radio show, *Travel with Rick Steves,* features interviews with travel experts from around the world. All the TV scripts and radio shows (which are easy and free to download to an iPod or other MP3 player) are at www.ricksteves.com.

If your travels take you beyond Switzerland to Italy, France, or Great Britain, take advantage of my free self-guided **audio tours** of the major sights in Venice, Florence, Rome, Paris, and London. Simply download them from www.ricksteves.com or iTunes (search for "Rick Steves' tours" in the iTunes Store), then transfer them to your MP3 player.

Maps

The black-and-white maps in this book are concise and simple. My staff, who are well-traveled in Switzerland, have created these maps to help you locate recommended places and get to local TIs, where you can pick up a more in-depth map of the city or region (usually free).

Better maps are sold at newsstands and bookstores in Europe, which have a good selection, especially in touristy areas. Take a look before you buy to be sure the map has the level of detail you want. For drivers, I recommend a 1:400,000-scale map of the whole country, or even larger-scale maps of particular regions. Train travelers can usually manage fine with the freebies they get with their railpass and from the local tourist offices.

Other Guidebooks

If you're like most travelers, this book is all you need. But if you'll be traveling beyond my recommended destinations, $30 for extra

Begin Your Trip at www.ricksteves.com

At our travel website, you'll find a wealth of free information on European destinations, including fresh monthly news and helpful tips from thousands of fellow travelers. You'll also find my latest guidebook updates (www.ricksteves.com/update) and my travel blog.

Our **online Travel Store** offers travel bags and accessories specially designed by Rick Steves to help you travel smarter and lighter. These include our popular carry-on bags (roll-aboard and rucksack versions), money belts, totes, toiletries kits, adapters, other accessories, and a wide selection of guidebooks, planning maps, and DVDs.

Choosing the right **railpass** for your trip—amidst hundreds of options—can drive you nutty. We'll help you choose the best pass for your needs, plus give you a bunch of free extras.

Rick Steves' Europe Through the Back Door travel company offers **tours** with more than two dozen itineraries and 300 departures reaching the best destinations in this book... and beyond. We offer a 14-day Best of Germany, Austria, and Switzerland tour that visits the Berner Oberland. We also have two different Best of Europe tours, both of which make a stop in the Berner Oberland. You'll enjoy great guides, a fun bunch of travel partners (with small groups of generally around 28), and plenty of room to spread out in a big, comfy bus. You'll find European adventures to fit every vacation length. For all the details, and to get our Tour Catalog and a free Rick Steves Tour Experience DVD (filmed on location during an actual tour), visit www.ricksteves.com or call the Tour Department at 425/608-4217.

maps and books is money well spent. For several people traveling by car, the extra weight and expense of a few books are negligible.

The following books are worthwhile, though not updated annually; check the publication date before you buy.

Lonely Planet's guide to Switzerland is thorough, well-researched, and packed with good maps and hotel recommendations for low- to moderate-budget travelers. The similar *Rough Guide to Switzerland* is written by insightful British researchers.

If you'll be spending a lot of time on the train, consider *Switzerland Without a Car* (Bradt), which provides helpful descriptions of what you'll see out the window. Students, backpackers, and nightlife-seekers should consider the highly opinionated *Let's Go: Austria and Switzerland* (by Harvard students, has the best hostel listings).

Dorling Kindersley publishes snazzy Eyewitness Guides, including one on Switzerland. Though pretty to look at, these books weigh a ton and are skimpy on actual content.

The popular, skinny *Michelin Green Guide: Switzerland* is excellent, especially if you're driving. Michelin Guides are known for their city and sightseeing maps, dry but concise and helpful information on all major sights, and good cultural and historical background. English editions are sold in Europe at gas stations and tourist shops.

Recommended Books and Movies

To get in the mood for your trip, consider these books and films, which take place partly or entirely in Switzerland.

Nonfiction

For a look at how this diverse nation holds itself together, try *Why Switzerland?* (Steinberg), which explains how a country with four official languages can still have a common culture. *La Place de la Concorde Suisse* (McPhee) follows a mountain unit of the Swiss Army on patrol, exploring how mandatory military service (for men) keeps Switzerland from breaking apart (despite its French title, it's written in English).

Mark Twain's *A Tramp Abroad* is a humorous account of Twain's 1878 "walking tour" through the Alps. For more about mountains, try *The White Spider* (Harrer), which chronicles the first successful ascent of the Eiger's north face; *The Climb Up to Hell* (Olsen) about an ill-fated 1957 Eiger climb; and Jon Krakauer's collection of mountaineering essays, *Eiger Dreams*.

Fiction

The most famous novel about Switzerland (and the source of many Swiss clichés) is the children's classic *Heidi* (Spyri). A refreshing

370 Rick Steves' Switzerland

antidote is Max Frisch's 20th-century riddle *I'm Not Stiller*.

Nobel Prize–winning author Thomas Mann was German, but his masterpiece, *The Magic Mountain*, takes place in a sanatorium high in the Swiss Alps, where troubled patients are trying to recover from tuberculosis as World War I is about to start. Another Nobel laureate—Ernest Hemingway—set the climax of his anti-war epic *A Farewell to Arms* on Lake Maggiore and in Lausanne.

In *Hotel du Lac* (Brookner), the heroine is sent by her friends to a Swiss hotel to recover from a misguided love affair, but her stay turns out to be much more than a simple rest cure. Another Swiss inn is the setting for John le Carré's thriller *The Night Manager*, where a fussy hotel worker is recruited by British intelligence to bring down a millionaire gunrunner.

While several novels and movies recount the story of William Tell, the most enduring version of the legend is by German poet/philosopher/playwright Friedrich Schiller, whose now-classic play broadened the tale into a rallying cry against tyranny.

Films

Hollywood has largely typecast Switzerland as little more than a range of high mountains. (One exception is 2002's *The Bourne Identity*, which set key scenes in urban Zürich...but filmed them mostly in Prague.) Clint Eastwood directed and starred in *The Eiger Sanction* (1975), a spy thriller partially shot in Kleine Scheidegg. The James Bond film *On Her Majesty's Secret Service* (1969) includes stunning action sequences on the slopes of the Schilthorn, in the Piz Gloria revolving restaurant, and down a bobsled run (see page 174). *Five Days One Summer* (1982) is a Sean Connery flick with some breathtaking climbing sequences sandwiched between soap-opera scenes about an incestuous love triangle. For a more wholesome tale, try *Third Man on the Mountain* (1959), a Disney film about a young man in a 1860s Swiss village who longs to climb the Citadel (a.k.a. the Matterhorn).

For Switzerland beyond the mountains, try some foreign-language films. Krzysztof Kieslowski's *Red* (1994), the last part of his *Three Colors* trilogy, is set in Geneva. Alain Tanner is Switzerland's most acclaimed director, and his 1975 French-language film, *Jonah Who Will Be 25 in the Year 2000*, takes a Big-Chill look at former student activists living in Geneva. Xavier Koller's Oscar-winning *Journey of Hope* (1990) follows three members of a Kurdish family in search of a better life in Switzerland.

The Swissmakers (1978), a multilingual comedy about foreigners trying to get Swiss citizenship, is the most popular Swiss movie ever made (but may still be hard to find in the States). Or, if you're in the mood for something completely different, many of India's "Bollywood" movies use Swiss scenery. The romance *Dilwale*

Dulhania Le Jayenge (literally *The Brave Heart Will Take the Bride*, 1995), which ran for a record 11 years in Indian movie theaters, was shot in Swiss locations with its actors speaking a mixture of Hindi and English.

Holidays and Festivals

This is a partial list of holidays and festivals. For more information, contact the Swiss national tourist office (US tel. 877-794-8037, www.myswitzerland.com, info.usa@myswitzerland.com). Not all holidays are celebrated in every canton (particularly religious ones). If you find yourself in a town closed down for an unexpected holiday, consider going on to your next stop (call ahead), where everything may well be in full swing.

Jan 1	New Year's Day
Jan 2	Berchtoldstag (St. Berchtold Day), Harder Potschete (parade), Interlaken
Jan 6	Epiphany (closings)
Mid-Jan	Lauberhorn ski race, Wengen; Inferno ski race, Mürren (www.inferno -muerren.ch)
Feb	Fasnacht (Carnival), especially celebrated in Luzern, Zürich, and Bern
March 19	Josefstag (St. Joseph's Day)
March–May	International Jazz Festival (www .jazzfestivalbern.ch), Bern
Late March	International Easter Music Festival (1 week, www.lucernefestival.ch), Luzern
Good Friday	April 2 in 2010, April 3 in 2011
Easter Monday	April 5 in 2010, April 6 in 2011
Third Monday in April	Sechseläuten (Spring Festival, 2 days, www.sechselaeuten.ch), Zürich
Last Sun in April	Open-Air Parliament (public selection of delegates), Appenzell
May 1	Labor Day
Ascension	Christi Himmelfahrt (May 13 in 2010, June 2 in 2011)
Whitmonday	Pfingstmontag (May 24 in 2010, June 13 in 2011)
Corpus Christi	Fronleichnam (June 3 in 2010, June 23 in 2011)
Early June	Berner Tanztage (dance festival, www .tanztage.ch), Bern

Mid-June–Early July	Zürich Festival (3 weeks, www.zuercher-festspiele.ch)
Late June–early Sept	William Tell Performance (open-air theater, www.tellspiele.ch), Interlaken
Early July	Estival Jazz (free open-air festival, www.estivaljazz.ch), Lugano
Early July	City Festival (www.festivalcite.ch), Lausanne
Mid-July	Montreux International Jazz Festival (2 weeks, www.montreuxjazz.com)
Mid-July	Gurten Open-Air Rock Festival (4 days, www.gurtenfestival.ch), Bern
Aug 1	Swiss National Day (parades and fireworks)
Early Aug	Street Parade (city-wide rave, 1 day, www.streetparade.ch), Zürich
Aug 15	Assumption of Mary (Maria Himmelfahrt)
Mid-Aug–Mid-Sept	Luzern Festival in Summer (4 weeks, classical, www.lucernefestival.ch)
Oct	Festa d'Autunno (food and wine festival, 3 days), Lugano
Nov 1	All Saints' Day
Mid-Nov	Luzern Festival at the Piano (1 week, www.lucernefestival.ch)
Late Nov	Traditional Onion Market Fair (1 day), Bern
Dec	Christmas fairs
Dec 6	St. Nicholas Day
Dec 8	Immaculate Conception
Dec 25	Christmas
Dec 26	St. Stephen's Day

Conversions and Climate

Numbers and Stumblers

APPENDIX

- Europeans write a few of their numbers differently than we do. 1 = 1, 4 = 4, 7 = 7.
- In Europe, dates appear as day/month/year, so Christmas is 25/12/2011.
- Commas are decimal points and decimals commas. A dollar and a half is 1,50, and there are 5.280 feet in a mile.
- When counting with fingers, start with your thumb. If you hold up your first finger to request one item, you'll probably get two.

- What Americans call the second floor of a building is the first floor in Europe.
- On escalators and moving sidewalks, Europeans keep the left "lane" open for passing. Keep to the right.

Metric Conversions (approximate)

A kilogram is 2.2 pounds, and 1 liter is about a quart, or almost 4 to a gallon. A kilometer is six-tenths of a mile. I figure kilometers to miles by cutting them in half and adding back 10 percent of the original (120 km: 60 + 12 = 72 miles, 300 km: 150 + 30 = 180 miles).

1 foot = 0.3 meter	1 square yard = 0.8 square meter
1 yard = 0.9 meter	1 square mile = 2.6 square kilometers
1 mile = 1.6 kilometers	1 ounce = 28 grams
1 centimeter = 0.4 inch	1 quart = 0.95 liter
1 meter = 39.4 inches	1 kilogram = 2.2 pounds
1 kilometer = 0.62 mile	32°F = 0°C

Clothing Sizes

When shopping for clothing, use these US-to-European comparisons as general guidelines (but note that no conversion is perfect).

- Women's dresses and blouses: Add 30 (US size 10 = European size 40)
- Men's suits and jackets: Add 10 (US size 40 regular = European size 50)
- Men's shirts: Multiply by 2 and add about 8 (US size 15 collar = European size 38)
- Women's shoes: Add about 30 (US size 8 = European size 38½)
- Men's shoes: Add 32–34 (US size 9 = European size 41; US size 11 = European size 45)

Climate

The first line is the average daily high temperature; the second line, the average daily low; the third line, the average number of days without rain. For more detailed weather statistics for destinations in this book (as well as the rest of the world), check www.worldclimate.com.

	J	F	M	A	M	J	J	A	S	O	N	D
Bern												
	38°	42°	51°	59°	66°	73°	77°	76°	69°	58°	47°	40°
	29°	30°	36°	42°	49°	55°	58°	58°	53°	44°	37°	31°
	20	19	22	21	20	19	22	20	20	21	19	21

Temperature Conversion:
Fahrenheit and Celsius

Europe takes its temperature using the Celsius scale, while we opt for Fahrenheit. For a rough conversion from Celsius to Fahrenheit, double the number and add 30. For weather, remember that 28°C is 82°F—perfect. For health, 37°C is just right.

APPENDIX

Essential Packing Checklist

Whether you're traveling for five days or five weeks, here's what you'll need to bring. Remember to pack light to enjoy the sweet freedom of true mobility. Happy travels!

- ❏ 5 shirts
- ❏ 1 sweater or lightweight fleece jacket
- ❏ 2 pairs pants
- ❏ 1 pair shorts
- ❏ 1 swimsuit (women only—men can use shorts)
- ❏ 5 pairs underwear and socks
- ❏ 1 pair shoes
- ❏ 1 rainproof jacket
- ❏ Tie or scarf
- ❏ Money belt
- ❏ Money—your mix of:
  - ❏ Debit card for ATM withdrawals
  - ❏ Credit card
  - ❏ Hard cash in US dollars ($20 bills)
- ❏ Documents (and back-up photocopies)
- ❏ Passport
- ❏ Printout of airline e-ticket
- ❏ Driver's license
- ❏ Student ID and hostel card
- ❏ Railpass/car rental voucher
- ❏ Insurance details
- ❏ Daypack
- ❏ Sealable plastic baggies
- ❏ Camera and related gear
- ❏ Empty water bottle
- ❏ Wristwatch and alarm clock
- ❏ Earplugs
- ❏ First-aid kit
- ❏ Medicine (labeled)
- ❏ Extra glasses/contacts and prescriptions
- ❏ Sunscreen and sunglasses
- ❏ Toiletries kit
- ❏ Soap
- ❏ Laundry soap
- ❏ Clothesline
- ❏ Small towel
- ❏ Sewing kit
- ❏ Travel information
- ❏ Necessary map(s)
- ❏ Address list (email and mailing addresses)
- ❏ Postcards and photos from home
- ❏ Notepad and pen
- ❏ Journal

If you plan to carry on your luggage, note that all liquids must be in three-ounce or smaller containers and fit within a single quart-size baggie. For details, see www.tsa.gov/travelers.

Hotel Reservation

To: _____   _____
              hotel   *email or fax*

From: _____   _____
                name   *email or fax*

Today's date: _____ / _____ / _____
                    day   *month*   *year*

Dear Hotel _____ ,
Please make this reservation for me:

Name: _____

Total # of people: _____   # of rooms: _____   # of nights: _____

Arriving: _____ / _____ / _____   My time of arrival (24-hr clock): _____
                day *month* *year*   (I will telephone if I will be late)

Departing: ____ / ____ / ____
                day   *month*   *year*

Room(s): Single ____   Double ____   Twin ____   Triple ____   Quad ____

With: Toilet ____   Shower ____   Bath ____   Sink only ____

Special needs: View ____   Quiet ____   Cheapest ____   Ground Floor ____

Please email or fax confirmation of my reservation, along with the type of room reserved and the price. Please also inform me of your cancellation policy. After I hear from you, I will quickly send my credit-card information as a deposit to hold the room. Thank you.

_____
Name

_____
Address

_____
City   *State*   *Zip Code*   *Country*

APPENDIX

Before hoteliers can make your reservation, they want to know the information listed above. You can use this form as the basis for your email, or you can photocopy this page, fill in the information, and send it as a fax (also available online at www.ricksteves.com/reservation).

German Survival Phrases for Switzerland

When using the phonetics, pronounce Ī as the long I sound in "light."

Hello.	**Grüetzi.**	**grit**-see
Do you speak English?	**Sprechen Sie Englisch?**	**shprehkh**-ehn zee **ehng**-lish
Yes. / No.	**Ja. / Nein.**	yah / nīn
I (don't) understand.	**Ich verstehe (nicht).**	ikh fehr-**shtay**-heh (nikht)
Please.	**Bitte.**	**bit**-teh
Thank you.	**Merci.**	**mur**-see
I'm sorry.	**Es tut mir leid.**	ehs toot meer līt
Excuse me.	**Entschuldigung.**	ehnt-**shool**-dig-oong
(No) problem.	**(Kein) Problem.**	(kīn) proh-**blaym**
(Very) good.	**(Sehr) gut.**	(zehr) goot
Goodbye.	**Ciao.**	chow
one / two	**eins / zwei**	īns / tsvī
three / four	**drei / vier**	drī / feer
five / six	**fünf / sechs**	finf / zehkhs
seven / eight	**sieben / acht**	**zee**-behn / ahkht
nine / ten	**neun / zehn**	noyn / tsayn
How much is it?	**Wieviel kostet das?**	**vee**-feel **kohs**-teht dahs
Write it?	**Schreiben?**	**shrī**-behn
Is it free?	**Ist es umsonst?**	ist ehs oom-**zohnst**
Included?	**Inklusive?**	in-kloo-**zee**-veh
Where can I buy / find...?	**Wo kann ich kaufen / finden...?**	voh kahn ikh **kow**-fehn / **fin**-dehn
I'd like /	**Ich hätte gern /**	ikh **heh**-teh gehrn /
We'd like...	**Wir hätten gern...**	veer **heh**-tehn gehrn
...a room.	**...ein Zimmer.**	īn **tsim**-mer
...a ticket to ___.	**...eine Fahrkarte nach ___.**	ī-neh **far**-kar-teh nahkh
Is it possible?	**Ist es möglich?**	ist ehs **mur**-glikh
Where is...?	**Wo ist...?**	voh ist
...the train station	**...der Bahnhof**	dehr **bahn**-hohf
...the bus station	**...der Busbahnhof**	dehr **boos**-bahn-hohf
...tourist information office	**...das Touristen- informationsbüro**	dahs too-**ris**-tehn- in-for-maht-see-**ohns-bew**-roh
...toilet	**...die Toilette**	dee toh-**leh**-teh
men	**Herren**	**hehr**-rehn
women	**Damen**	**dah**-mehn
left / right	**links / rechts**	links / **rehkhts**
straight	**geradeaus**	geh-**rah**-deh-**ows**
When is this open / closed?	**Um wieviel Uhr ist hier geöffnet / geschlossen?**	oom **vee**-feel oor ist heer geh-**urf**-neht / geh-**shloh**-sehn
At what time?	**Um wieviel Uhr?**	oom **vee**-feel oor
Just a moment.	**Moment.**	moh-**mehnt**
now / soon / later	**jetzt / bald / später**	yehtst / bahld / **shpay**-ter
today / tomorrow	**heute / morgen**	**hoy**-teh / **mor**-gehn

In the Restaurant

I'd like / We'd like...	Ich hätte gern / Wir hätten gern...	ikh **heh**-teh gehrn / veer **heh**-tehn gehrn
...a reservation for...	...eine Reservierung für...	ī-neh reh-zer-**feer**-oong fewr
...a table for one / two.	...einen Tisch für ein / zwei.	ī-nehn tish fewr īn / tsvī
Non-smoking.	Nichtraucher.	**nikht**-rowkh-er
Is this seat free?	Ist hier frei?	ist heer frī
Menu (in English), please.	Speisekarte (in Englisch), bitte.	**shpī**-zeh-kar-teh (in **ehng**-lish) **bit**-teh
service (not) included	Trinkgeld (nicht) inklusive	**trink**-gehlt (nikht) in-kloo-**zee**-veh
cover charge	Eintritt	**īn**-trit
to go	zum Mitnehmen	tsoom **mit**-nay-mehn
with / without	mit / ohne	mit / **oh**-neh
and / or	und / oder	oont / **oh**-der
menu (of the day)	(Tages-) Karte	(**tah**-gehs-) kar-teh
set meal for tourists	Touristenmenü	too-**ris**-tehn-meh-**new**
specialty of the house	Spezialität des Hauses	shpayt-see-ah-lee-**tayt** dehs **how**-zehs
daily special	Tageshit	**tah**-gehs-hit
appetizers	Vorspeise	**for**-shpī-zeh
bread	Brot	broht
cheese	Käse	**kay**-zeh
sandwich	Sandwich	**zahnd**-vich
soup	Suppe	**zup**-peh
salad	Salat	zah-**laht**
meat	Fleisch	flīsh
poultry	Geflügel	geh-**flew**-gehl
fish	Fisch	fish
seafood	Meeresfrüchte	**meh**-rehs-**frewkh**-teh
fruit	Obst	ohpst
vegetables	Gemüse	geh-**mew**-zeh
dessert	Nachspeise	**nahkh**-shpī-zeh
mineral water	Mineralwasser	min-eh-**rahl**-vah-ser
tap water	Leitungswasser	**lī**-toongs-vah-ser
milk	Milch	milkh
(orange) juice	(Orangen-) Saft	(oh-**rahn**-zhehn-) zahft
coffee	Kaffee	kah-**fay**
tea	Tee	tay
wine	Wein	vīn
red / white	rot / weiß	roht / vīs
glass / bottle	Glas / Flasche	glahs / **flah**-sheh
beer	Bier	beer
Cheers!	Prost!	prohst
More. / Another.	Mehr. / Noch ein.	mehr / nohkh īn
The same.	Das gleiche.	dahs **glīkh**-eh
Bill, please.	Rechnung, bitte.	**rehkh**-noong **bit**-teh
tip	Trinkgeld	**trink**-gehlt
Delicious!	Lecker!	**lehk**-er

For more user-friendly German phrases, check out *Rick Steves' German Phrase Book and Dictionary* or *Rick Steves' French, Italian & German Phrase Book.*

French Survival Phrases

When using the phonetics, try to nasalize the n̲ sound.

Good day.	**Bonjour.**	bohn̲-zhoor
Mrs. / Mr.	**Madame / Monsieur**	mah-dahm / muhs-yur
Do you speak English?	**Parlez-vous anglais?**	par-lay-voo ahn̲-glay
Yes. / No.	**Oui. / Non.**	wee / nohn̲
I understand.	**Je comprends.**	zhuh kohn̲-prahn̲
I don't understand.	**Je ne comprends pas.**	zhuh nuh kohn̲-prahn̲ pah
Please.	**S'il vous plaît.**	see voo play
Thank you.	**Merci.**	mehr-see
I'm sorry.	**Désolé.**	day-zoh-lay
Excuse me.	**Pardon.**	par-dohn̲
(No) problem.	**(Pas de) problème.**	(pah duh) proh-blehm
It's good.	**C'est bon.**	say bohn̲
Goodbye.	**Au revoir.**	oh vwahr
one / two	**un / deux**	uhn̲ / duh
three / four	**trois / quatre**	twah / kah-truh
five / six	**cinq / six**	san̲k / sees
seven / eight	**sept / huit**	seht / weet
nine / ten	**neuf / dix**	nuhf / dees
How much is it?	**Combien?**	kohn̲-bee-an̲
Write it?	**Ecrivez?**	ay-kree-vay
Is it free?	**C'est gratuit?**	say grah-twee
Included?	**Inclus?**	an̲-klew
Where can I buy / find...?	**Où puis-je acheter / trouver...?**	oo pwee-zhuh ah-shuh-tay / troo-vay
I'd like / We'd like...	**Je voudrais / Nous voudrions...**	zhuh voo-dray / noo voo-dree-ohn̲
...a room.	**...une chambre.**	ewn shahn̲-bruh
...a ticket to ___.	**...un billet pour ___.**	uhn̲ bee-yay poor
Is it possible?	**C'est possible?**	say poh-see-bluh
Where is...?	**Où est...?**	oo ay
...the train station	**...la gare**	lah gar
...the bus station	**...la gare routière**	lah gar root-yehr
...tourist information	**...l'office du tourisme**	loh-fees dew too-reez-muh
Where are the toilets?	**Où sont les toilettes?**	oo sohn̲ lay twah-leht
men	**hommes**	ohm
women	**dames**	dahm
left / right	**à gauche / à droite**	ah gohsh / ah dwaht
straight	**tout droit**	too dwah
When does this open / close?	**Ça ouvre / ferme à quelle heure?**	sah oo-vruh / fehrm ah kehl ur
At what time?	**À quelle heure?**	ah kehl ur
Just a moment.	**Un moment.**	uhn̲ moh-mahn̲
now / soon / later	**maintenant / bientôt / plus tard**	man̲-tuh-nahn̲ / bee-an̲-toh / plew tar
today / tomorrow	**aujourd'hui / demain**	oh-zhoor-dwee / duh-man̲

APPENDIX

In the Restaurant

I'd like / We'd like...	**Je voudrais / Nous voudrions...**	zhuh voo-dray / noo voo-dree-oh<u>n</u>
...to reserve...	**...réserver...**	ray-zehr-vay
...a table for one / two.	**...une table pour un / deux.**	ewn tah-bluh poor uh<u>n</u> / duh
Non-smoking.	**Non fumeur.**	noh<u>n</u> few-mur
Is this seat free?	**C'est libre?**	say lee-bruh
The menu (in English), please.	**La carte (en anglais), s'il vous plaît.**	lah kart (ah<u>n</u> ah<u>n</u>-glay) see voo play
service (not) included	**service (non) compris**	sehr-vees (noh<u>n</u>) koh<u>n</u>-pree
to go	**à emporter**	ah ah<u>n</u>-por-tay
with / without	**avec / sans**	ah-vehk / sah<u>n</u>
and / or	**et / ou**	ay / oo
special of the day	**plat du jour**	plah dew zhoor
specialty of the house	**spécialité de la maison**	spay-see-ah-lee-tay duh lah may-zoh<u>n</u>
appetizers	**hors-d'oeuvre**	or-duh-vruh
first course (soup, salad)	**entrée**	ah<u>n</u>-tray
main course (meat, fish)	**plat principal**	plah pra<u>n</u>-see-pahl
bread	**pain**	pa<u>n</u>
cheese	**fromage**	froh-mahzh
sandwich	**sandwich**	sah<u>n</u>d-weech
soup	**soupe**	soop
salad	**salade**	sah-lahd
meat	**viande**	vee-ah<u>n</u>d
chicken	**poulet**	poo-lay
fish	**poisson**	pwah-soh<u>n</u>
seafood	**fruits de mer**	frwee duh mehr
fruit	**fruit**	frwee
vegetables	**légumes**	lay-gewm
dessert	**dessert**	duh-sehr
mineral water	**eau minérale**	oh mee-nay-rahl
tap water	**l'eau du robinet**	loh dew roh-bee-nay
milk	**lait**	lay
(orange) juice	**jus (d'orange)**	zhew (doh-rah<u>n</u>zh)
coffee	**café**	kah-fay
tea	**thé**	tay
wine	**vin**	va<u>n</u>
red / white	**rouge / blanc**	roozh / blah<u>n</u>
glass / bottle	**verre / bouteille**	vehr / boo-teh-ee
beer	**bière**	bee-ehr
Cheers!	**Santé!**	sah<u>n</u>-tay
More. / Another.	**Plus. / Un autre.**	plew / uh<u>n</u> oh-truh
The same.	**La même chose.**	lah mehm shohz
The bill, please.	**L'addition, s'il vous plaît.**	lah-dee-see-oh<u>n</u> see voo play
tip	**pourboire**	poor-bwar
Delicious!	**Délicieux!**	day-lee-see-uh

For more user-friendly French phrases, check out *Rick Steves' French Phrase Book and Dictionary* or *Rick Steves' French, Italian & German Phrase Book.*

Italian Survival Phrases

Good day.	**Buon giorno.**	bwohn JOR-noh
Do you speak English?	**Parla inglese?**	PAR-lah een-GLAY-zay
Yes. / No.	**Sì. / No.**	see / noh
I (don't) understand.	**(Non) capisco.**	(nohn) kah-PEES-koh
Please.	**Per favore.**	pehr fah-VOH-ray
Thank you.	**Grazie.**	GRAHT-seeay
You're welcome.	**Prego.**	PRAY-go
I'm sorry.	**Mi dispiace.**	mee dee-speeAH-chay
Excuse me.	**Mi scusi.**	mee SKOO-zee
(No) problem.	**(Non) c'è un problema.**	(nohn) cheh oon proh-BLAY-mah
Good.	**Va bene.**	vah BEHN-ay
Goodbye.	**Arrivederci.**	ah-ree-vay-DEHR-chee
one / two	**uno / due**	OO-noh / DOO-ay
three / four	**tre / quattro**	tray / KWAH-troh
five / six	**cinque / sei**	CHEENG-kway / SEHee
seven / eight	**sette / otto**	SEHT-tay / OT-toh
nine / ten	**nove / dieci**	NOV-ay / deeAY-chee
How much is it?	**Quanto costa?**	KWAHN-toh KOS-tah
Write it?	**Me lo scrive?**	may loh SKREE-vay
Is it free?	**È gratis?**	eh GRAH-tees
Is it included?	**È incluso?**	eh een-KLOO-zoh
Where can I buy / find...?	**Dove posso comprare / trovare...?**	DOH-vay POS-soh kohm-PRAH-ray / troh-VAH-ray
I'd like / We'd like...	**Vorrei / Vorremmo...**	vor-REHee / vor-RAY-moh
...a room.	**...una camera.**	OO-nah KAH-meh-rah
...a ticket to ___.	**...un biglietto per ___.**	oon beel-YEHT-toh pehr
Is it possible?	**È possibile?**	eh poh-SEE-bee-lay
Where is...?	**Dov'è...?**	DOH-veh
...the train station	**...la stazione**	lah staht-seeOH-nay
...the bus station	**...la stazione degli autobus**	lah staht-seeOH-nay DAYL-yee OW-toh-boos
...tourist information	**...informazioni per turisti**	een-for-maht-seeOH-nee pehr too-REE-stee
...the toilet	**...la toilette**	lah twah-LEHT-tay
men	**uomini, signori**	WOH-mee-nee, seen-YOH-ree
women	**donne, signore**	DON-nay, seen-YOH-ray
left / right	**sinistra / destra**	see-NEE-strah / DEHS-trah
straight	**sempre diritto**	SEHM-pray dee-REE-toh
When do you open / close?	**A che ora aprite / chiudete?**	ah kay OH-rah ah-PREE-tay / keeoo-DAY-tay
At what time?	**A che ora?**	ah kay OH-rah
Just a moment.	**Un momento.**	oon moh-MAYN-toh
now / soon / later	**adesso / presto / tardi**	ah-DEHS-soh / PREHS-toh / TAR-dee
today / tomorrow	**oggi / domani**	OH-jee / doh-MAH-nee

In the Restaurant

I'd like...	Vorrei...	vor-REHee
We'd like...	Vorremmo...	vor-RAY-moh
...to reserve...	...prenotare...	pray-noh-TAH-ray
...a table for one / two.	...un tavolo per uno / due.	oon TAH-voh-loh pehr OO-noh / DOO-ay
Non-smoking.	Non fumare.	nohn foo-MAH-ray
Is this seat free?	È libero questo posto?	eh LEE-bay-roh KWEHS-toh POH-stoh
The menu (in English), please.	Il menù (in inglese), per favore.	eel may-NOO (een een-GLAY-zay) pehr fah-VOH-ray
service (not) included	servizio (non) incluso	sehr-VEET-seeoh (nohn) een-KLOO-zoh
cover charge	pane e coperto	PAH-nay ay koh-PEHR-toh
to go	da portar via	dah POR-tar VEE-ah
with / without	con / senza	kohn / SEHN-sah
and / or	e / o	ay / oh
menu (of the day)	menù (del giorno)	may-NOO (dayl JOR-noh)
specialty of the house	specialità della casa	spay-chah-lee-TAH DEHL-lah KAH-zah
first course (pasta, soup)	primo piatto	PREE-moh peeAH-toh
main course (meat, fish)	secondo piatto	say-KOHN-doh peeAH-toh
side dishes	contorni	kohn-TOR-nee
bread	pane	PAH-nay
cheese	formaggio	for-MAH-joh
sandwich	panino	pah-NEE-noh
soup	minestra, zuppa	mee-NEHS-trah, TSOO-pah
salad	insalata	een-sah-LAH-tah
meat	carne	KAR-nay
chicken	pollo	POH-loh
fish	pesce	PEH-shay
seafood	frutti di mare	FROO-tee dee MAH-ray
fruit / vegetables	frutta / legumi	FROO-tah / lay-GOO-mee
dessert	dolci	DOHL-chee
tap water	acqua del rubinetto	AH-kwah dayl roo-bee-NAY-toh
mineral water	acqua minerale	AH-kwah mee-nay-RAH-lay
milk	latte	LAH-tay
(orange) juice	succo (d'arancia)	SOO-koh (dah-RAHN-chah)
coffee / tea	caffè / tè	kah-FEH / teh
wine	vino	VEE-noh
red / white	rosso / bianco	ROH-soh / beeAHN-koh
glass / bottle	bicchiere / bottiglia	bee-keeAY-ray / boh-TEEL-yah
beer	birra	BEE-rah
Cheers!	Cin cin!	cheen cheen
More. / Another.	Ancora un po.' / Un altro.	ahn-KOH-rah oon poh / oon AHL-troh
The same.	Lo stesso.	loh STEHS-soh
The bill, please.	Il conto, per favore.	eel KOHN-toh pehr fah-VOH-ray
tip	mancia	MAHN-chah
Delicious!	Delizioso!	day-leet-seeOH-zoh

For more user-friendly Italian phrases, check out *Rick Steves' Italian Phrase Book & Dictionary* or *Rick Steves' French, Italian, and German Phrase Book.*

INDEX

Swiss cuisine, 27–29; tipping, 17.
See also specific destinations
Ebenalp: 221–224
Eiger: 134
Einstein Museum (Bern): 111
Einstein, Albert: 106–107
Electricity: 12–13
Email: 354–355
Emergencies: 12
Engadine: architecture, 291;
Bernina Express, 318; general
information, 277–278; transpor-
tation, 278–279
Engadiner Museum (St. Moritz):
296
Entertainment: costs, 6. *See also
specific destinations*
EU status: 341
Eurailpass: 300–301, 361–362
Euros: 16
Exchange rates: 14

F
Fasnacht: 333–334
Federer, Roger: 345
Festivals and holidays: 7, 371–372;
Christmas, 331–333; *Fasnacht,*
333–334
Filisur: 320
Films: 370–371
Findelnbach (Zermat): 196
First (Grindelwald): 134
Flights: 366. *See also* Airfare;
Airlines; Airports
Flüelen: 308, 309
Fluhalp (Zermatt): 196
Fortress Fürigen Museum of War
History: 92, 94
Fraumünster (Zürich): 50–51;
Chagall windows, 52–53
French: restaurant phrases, 380;
survival phrases, 379
French Revolution: 338
French Swiss countryside: 8; Bulle,
256–257; Cailler Chocolate
Factory, 257; Gruyères, 253–258;
maps, 252; transportation,
251–252
Fromageries: 254–256
Funiculars: 359;
Allmendhubelbahn, 169; Alp

Languard, 285; Lugano vicinity,
269–270; Rothorn, 201
Furi (Zermatt): 196

G
Gardens: Giardino Belvedere
(Lugano), 268–269; Oberhofen
Castle (Interlaken), 144; Ricola
Herb Garden, 200–201
German: restaurant phrases, 378;
survival phrases, 377
Giardino Belvedere (Lugano):
268–269
Gimmelwald: eating, 164;
general information, 8, 131,
134, 155–157; hiking, 177–183;
maps, 156, 178–179; nightlife,
162; self-guided walk, 157–161;
sleeping, 162–164
Glacier des Diablerets: 259–260
Glacier Express: 321–326
Glacier Garden (Luzern): 79–80
Glacier Palace (Zermatt): 196, 200
Goat parade (Zermatt): 196–197
Golden Pass train route: 303–308
Gondolas: 359; Klein Matterhorn,
199; Rothorn, 201
Gorner Glacier: 196
Gornergrat: 196, 202–203
Götthard tunnel: 311
Gourmetweg (Zermatt): 196
Graubünden: 282
Graubündener Alps: 330
Grindelwald: 134
Grossmünster (Zürich): 50
Grütschalp (Lauterbrunnen): 134
Gruyères: 253–258; eating, 258;
sleeping, 257–258
Gstaad: 306
Guidebooks: 366–367, 369

H
H.R. Giger Museum (Gruyères):
254
Half-Fare Travel Card: 357–358
Helvetii: 33, 44, 119, 336
Hesse, Hermann: 344
Hiking: Allmendhubel
(Mürren), 183–184; Appenzell,
214–215; Berner Oberland,
177–187; Bernina Express

MAP INDEX

Rick Steves
EUROPEAN TOURS

ADRIATIC • ATHENS & THE HEART OF GREECE • BARCELONA & MADRID • BELGIUM & HOLLAND • BERLIN, VIENNA & PRAGUE BEST OF EUROPE • BEST OF ITALY BEST OF TURKEY • BULGARIA • EASTERN EUROPE • ENGLAND • FAMILY EUROPE GERMANY, AUSTRIA & SWITZERLAND HEART OF ITALY • IRELAND • ISTANBUL LONDON • PARIS • PARIS & HEART OF FRANCE • PARIS & SOUTH OF FRANCE PORTUGAL • PRAGUE & BUDAPEST • ROME SAN SEBASTIAN & BASQUE COUNTRY SCANDINAVIA • SCOTLAND • SICILY SOUTH ITALY • SPAIN & MOROCCO ST. PETERSBURG, TALLINN & HELSINKI VENICE, FLORENCE & ROME • VILLAGE FRANCE • VILLAGE ITALY • VILLAGE TURKEY

VISIT **TOURS.RICKSTEVES.COM**

Great guides, small groups, no grumps

Free information and great gear

▸ Plan Your Trip

Browse thousands of articles and a wealth of money-saving tips for planning your dream trip. You'll find up-to-date information on Europe's best destinations, packing smart, getting around, finding rooms, staying healthy, avoiding scams and more.

▸ Eurail Passes

Find out, step-by-step, if a rail pass makes sense for your trip—and how to avoid buying more than you need. Get a bunch of free extras!

▸ Graffiti Wall & Travelers' Helpline

Learn, ask, share—our online community of savvy travelers is a great resource for first-time travelers to Europe, as well as seasoned pros.

Rick Steves' Europe Through the Back Door, Inc.

urn your travel dreams into affordable reality

Free Audio Tours & Travel Newsletter

Get your nose out of this guide-book and focus on what you'll be seeing with Rick's free audio tours of the greatest sights in Paris, Rome, Florence and Venice.

Subscribe to our free *Travel News* e-newsletter, and get monthly articles from Rick on what's happening in Europe.

▶ Great Gear from Rick's Travel Store

Pack light and right—on a budget—with Rick's custom-designed carry-on bags, roll-aboards, day packs, travel accessories, guidebooks, journals, maps and DVDs of his TV shows.

130 Fourth Avenue North, PO Box 2009 • Edmonds, WA 98020 USA
Phone: (425) 771-8303 • Fax: (425) 771-0833 • www.ricksteves.com

Rick Steves®

www.ricksteves.com

TRAVEL SKILLS
Europe Through the Back Door

EUROPE GUIDES
Best of Europe
Eastern Europe
Europe 101
European Christmas
Postcards from Europe

COUNTRY GUIDES
Croatia & Slovenia
England
France
Germany
Great Britain
Ireland
Italy
Portugal
Scandinavia
Spain
Switzerland

CITY & REGIONAL GUIDES
Amsterdam, Bruges & Brussels
Athens & The Peloponnese
Budapest
Florence & Tuscany
Istanbul
London
Paris
Prague & The Czech Republic
Provence & The French Riviera
Rome
Venice
Vienna, Salzburg & Tirol

PHRASE BOOKS & DICTIONARIES
French
French, Italian & German
German
Italian
Portuguese
Spanish

RICK STEVES' EUROPE DVDs
Austria & The Alps
Eastern Europe
England
Europe
France & Benelux
Germany & Scandinavia
Greece, Turkey, Israel & Egypt
Ireland & Scotland
Italy's Cities
Italy's Countryside
Rick Steves' European Christmas
Spain & Portugal
Travel Skills & "The Making Of"

PLANNING MAPS
Britain, Ireland & London
Europe
France & Paris
Germany, Austria & Switzerland
Ireland
Italy
Spain & Portugal

JOURNALS
Rick Steves' Pocket Travel Journal
Rick Steves' Travel Journal

RICK STEVES APPS FOR THE iPHONE OR iPOD TOUCH

With these apps you can:

► Spin the compass icon to switch views between sights, hotels, and restaurant selections—and get details on cost, hours, address, and phone number.

► Tap any point on the screen to read Rick's detailed information, including history and suggested viewpoints.

► Get a deeper view into Rick's tours with audio and video segments.

Go to iTunes to download the following apps:

Rick Steves' Louvre Tour

Rick Steves' Historic Paris Walk

Rick Steves' Orsay Museum Tour

Rick Steves' Versailles

Rick Steves' Ancient Rome Tour

Rick Steves' St. Peter's Basilica Tour

Once downloaded, these apps are completely self-contained on your iPhone or iPod Touch, so you will not incur pricey roaming charges during use overseas.

Rick Steves books and DVDs are available at bookstores and through online booksellers.

Rick Steves guidebooks are published by Avalon Travel, a member of the Perseus Books Group.

Rick Steves apps are produced by Übermind, a boutique Seattle-based software consultancy firm.

Credits

To help update this book, Rick relied on...

Researchers
Cathy McDonald

Cathy, a guidebook editor for Rick Steves, brings a former geologist's perspective on Switzerland's mountain landscapes. She lives in Seattle, where she has written about the Pacific Northwest for more than 15 years as a freelance travel writer for *The Seattle Times*.

Cameron Hewitt

Cameron writes and edits guidebooks for Rick Steves, specializing in Eastern Europe. For this book, Cameron circled the colorful fringe of Switzerland, from French-speaking Lake Geneva, to Germanic Appenzell, to the Romansh resorts of the Upper Engadine, to *molto Italiano* Lugano. When he's not traveling, Cameron lives in Seattle with his wife Shawna.

Contributor
Gene Openshaw

Gene is the co-author of seven Rick Steves books. For this book, he wrote material on art, history, and contemporary culture. When he's not traveling, Gene enjoys composing music, recovering from his 1973 trip to Europe with Rick, and living everyday life with his daughter.

Images

Location	Photographer
Front color matter: Gimmelwald	Dominic Bonuccelli
Front color matter: Lauterbrunnen Valley	David C. Hoerlein
Introduction: Above Grindelwald	Rick Steves
Zürich: View of Zürich from Limmat River	Cameron Hewitt
Luzern and Central Switzerland: Chapel Bridge	Cameron Hewitt
Bern and Murten: Bern Overview	Rick Steves
Gimmelwald and the Berner Oberland: Gimmelwald	Dominic Bonuccelli
Zermatt and the Matterhorn: The Matterhorn	Susana Minich
Appenzell: Appenzell	Cameron Hewitt
Lake Geneva and French Switzerland: Château Chillon	Cameron Hewitt
Lugano: Lake Lugano	Cameron Hewitt
Pontresina, Samedan, and St. Moritz: Samedan	Cameron Hewitt
Scenic Rail Journeys: Bernina Express	Rick Steves
Switzerland in Winter: Mürren	Cameron Hewitt
Switzerland Past and Present: Gimmelwald	Dominic Bonuccelli

Rick Steves' Guidebook Series

Country Guides

Rick Steves' Best of Europe
Rick Steves' Croatia & Slovenia
Rick Steves' Eastern Europe
Rick Steves' England
Rick Steves' France
Rick Steves' Germany
Rick Steves' Great Britain
Rick Steves' Ireland
Rick Steves' Italy
Rick Steves' Portugal
Rick Steves' Scandinavia
Rick Steves' Spain
Rick Steves' Switzerland

City and Regional Guides

Rick Steves' Amsterdam, Bruges & Brussels
Rick Steves' Athens & the Peloponnese
Rick Steves' Budapest
Rick Steves' Florence & Tuscany
Rick Steves' Istanbul
Rick Steves' London
Rick Steves' Paris
Rick Steves' Prague & the Czech Republic
Rick Steves' Provence & the French Riviera
Rick Steves' Rome
Rick Steves' Venice
Rick Steves' Vienna, Salzburg & Tirol

Rick Steves' Phrase Books

French
French/Italian/German
German
Italian
Portuguese
Spanish

Other Books

Rick Steves' Europe 101: History and Art for the Traveler
Rick Steves' Europe Through the Back Door
Rick Steves' European Christmas
Rick Steves' Postcards from Europe
Rick Steves' Travel as a Political Act

Avalon Travel
1700 Fourth Street
Berkeley, CA 94710, USA

Text © 2010, 2009, 2008, 2007, 2006, 2005, 2004, 2003, 2002 by Rick Steves. All rights reserved.
Maps © 2010, 2009, 2008, 2007 by Europe Through the Back Door. All rights reserved.
Photos are used by permission and are the property of the original copyright owners.

Printed in the United States of America by Worzalla
First printing March 2010
ISBN 978-1-59880-125-5
ISSN 1552-1818

For the latest on Rick's lectures, guidebooks, tours, public radio show, and public television series, contact Europe Through the Back Door, Box 2009, Edmonds, WA 98020, tel. 425/771-8303, fax 425/771-0833, www.ricksteves.com, rick@ricksteves.com.

Europe Through the Back Door Reviewing Editors: Cameron Hewitt, Gretchen Strauch, Risa Laib
ETBD Editors: Tom Griffin, Cathy Lu, Jennifer Madison Davis
Avalon Travel Senior Editor & Series Manager: Madhu Prasher
Avalon Travel Project Editor: Kelly Lydick
Copy Editor: Jennifer Malnick
Proofreader: Patrick Collins
Indexer: Carl Wikander
Research Assistance: Cathy McDonald, Cameron Hewitt
Production & Typesetting: McGuire Barber Design
Cover Design: Kimberly Glyder Design
Graphic Content Director: Laura VanDeventer
Maps & Graphics: David C. Hoerlein, Lauren Mills, Laura VanDeventer, Brice Ticen, Barb Geisler, Mike Morgenfeld, Chris Marciewicz, Lohnes and Wright, Albert Angulo, Hank Evans, Tim Knights
Photography: Cameron Hewitt, David C. Hoerlein, Rick Steves, Susana Minich, Dominic Bonuccelli, Julie Coen, Cathy McDonald, Bruce Hale
Front cover photo: Château de Chillon, Montreux © David C. Hoerlein
Front matter color photos: p. i, Gimmelwald © Dominic Bonuccelli; p. iv, Lauterbrunnen Valley © David C. Hoerlein

Distributed to the book trade by Publishers Group West, Berkeley, California

Although the author and publisher have made every effort to provide accurate, up-to-date information, they accept no responsibility for loss, injury, cold fondue, or inconvenience sustained by any person using this book.